Culture in Australia
Policies, Publics and Programs

Culture in Australia offers an incisive and up-to-date examination of the forces that are reshaping Australian cultural priorities, policies and practices at the start of the twenty-first century. Drawing on the work of some of Australia's leading cultural analysts, its concerns range broadly across the cultural sector encompassing art and heritage institutions, publishing, broadcasting, sport, tourism, museums, the music industry, film and youth cultures. These are placed in the context of the major national and international forces that are redrawing the cultural landscape in contemporary Australia. Engagingly and accessibly written, *Culture in Australia* offers a challenging introduction to current debates and dialogues focused on the need to imagine new cultural futures for an increasingly diverse and mobile people.

Tony Bennett is Professor of Sociology at the Open University and was previously Professor of Cultural Studies and Director of the Australian Key Centre for Cultural and Media Policy at Griffith University, Brisbane. His previous books include (with Michael Emmison and John Frow) *Accounting for Tastes: Australian Everyday Cultures* (Cambridge University Press, 1999); *Culture: A Reformer's Science* (1998); *The Birth of the Museum: History, Theory, Politics* (1995); and *Outside Literature* (1991). He has published extensively in various journals including *Critical Inquiry*, *Economy and Society*, *Cultural Studies*, and *New Formations*.

David Carter is Director of the Australian Studies Centre at the University of Queensland and President of the International Australian Studies Association. His publications include *A Career in Writing: Judah Waten and the Cultural Politics of a Literary Career* (1997), *Outside the Book: Contemporary Essays on Literary Periodicals* (1991) and (with Wayne Hudson) *The Republicanism Debate* (1993).

Culture in Australia

Policies, Publics and Programs

Edited by

Tony Bennett
Open University

David Carter
University of Queensland

CAMBRIDGE
UNIVERSITY PRESS

PUBLISHED BY THE PRESS SYNDICATE OF THE UNIVERSITY OF CAMBRIDGE
The Pitt Building, Trumpington Street, Cambridge, United Kingdom

CAMBRIDGE UNIVERSITY PRESS
The Edinburgh Building, Cambridge CB2 2RU, UK
40 West 20th Street, New York, NY 10011–4211, USA
10 Stamford Road, Oakleigh, VIC 3166, Australia
Ruiz de Alarcón 13, 28014 Madrid, Spain
Dock House, The Waterfront, Cape Town 8001, South Africa

http://www.cambridge.org

First published 2001

Printed in Australia by Ligare Pty Ltd

Typeface (New Aster) 10/13.5 pt. *System* QuarkXPress® [MT]

A catalogue record for this book is available from the British Library

National Library of Australia Cataloguing in Publication data
Culture in Australia: politics, publics and programs.
Includes index.
ISBN 0 521 80290 3.
ISBN 0 521 00403 9 (pbk.).
1. Australia – Intellectual life. 2. Australia –
Civilization – 1990– . 3. Australia – Cultural policy. I.
Bennett, Tony, 1947 – . II. Carter, David John, 1954 – .
306.0994

ISBN 0 521 80290 3 hardback
ISBN 0 521 00403 9 paperback

Contents

Acknowledgements

The editors wish to thank, first, the staff of the Australian Key Centre for Cultural and Media Policy for their support in helping to organise the Reshaping Australian Cultural Institutions workshop from which this book is derived. Special thanks here go to Karen Perkins, Bev Jeppesen and Glenda Donovan at Griffith University.

The success of the workshop was also due to the invaluable work of Mary Hapel of the Research School of Social Sciences at the Australian National University. We are also grateful to Professors Geoffrey Brennan and Frank Castles of the Research School of Social Sciences and joint coordinators of the Reshaping Australian Institutions program for supporting the project from the outset. We are especially grateful to all those who participated in the workshop in person or through written contributions but who are not represented in this book: Ann Curthoys, Bill Green, Sneja Gunew, Ghassan Hage, Barry Hindess, Lesley Johnson, Alison Lee, Ian McCalman, Julie Marcus and Jill Matthews.

Phillipa McGuinness of Cambridge University Press was an early enthusiast for the project and her support was later continued by Peter Debus.

We would also like to thank Molly Freeman of the Sociology Discipline and Sophie Taysom of the Pavis Centre for Social and Cultural Research, The Open University, and Janice Mitchell, School of Film, Media and Cultural Studies, Griffith University, for their help in finalising the typescript. The School of Humanities, Griffith University, has supplied generous institutional support.

Contributors

Tony Bennett is Professor of Sociology at the Open University, having previously served as Professor of Cultural Studies at Griffith University where he was also the Director of the Australian Key Centre for Cultural and Media Policy. His recent publications include *The Birth of the Museum* (1995), *Culture: A Reformer's Science* (1998) and (with Michael Emmison and John Frow) *Accounting for Tastes: Australian Everyday Cultures* (1999). He is a Fellow of the Australian Academy of the Humanities.

David Carter is an Associate Professor in the School of English, Media Studies and Art History at the University of Queensland where he is also Director of the Australian Studies Centre. He previously taught Australian studies, literature and cultural studies in the School of Humanities at Griffith University. His publications include *A Career in Writing: Judah Waten and the Cultural Politics of a Literary Career* (1997) which was awarded the Walter McCrae Russell prize for literary scholarship, and (with Wayne Hudson) *The Republicanism Debate* (1993).

Jennifer Craik is Associate Professor in the School of Film, Media and Cultural Studies, and a researcher in the Australian Key Centre for Cultural and Media Policy at Griffith University. Her publications include *The Face of Fashion: Cultural Studies in Fashion* (1994), *Resorting to Tourism: Cultural Policies for Tourism Development in Australia* (1990) and *Public Voices, Private Interests: Australia's Media Policy* (1995, co-edited with J.J. Bailey and A. Moran).

Michael Emmison is Associate Professor in the School of Social Sciences at the University of Queensland. He is co-editor of *Class Analysis in Contemporary Australia* (1991), and the co-author of *Accounting for Tastes: Australian Everyday Cultures* (1999) and of *Researching the Visual* (2000).

Kay Ferres is a Senior Lecturer in the School of Humanities at Griffith University. Her teaching and research interests are located in the fields of gender studies, literature and history. These interests converge in two current projects: an account of the way civics and citizenship education has been articulated to the project of revitalising civil society and a biographical study of Rosa Campbell Praed. Her publications include *An Articulate Country: Reinventing Australian Citizenship* (2001; with Denise Meredyth), *Deciphering Culture: Ordinary Curiosities and Subjective Narratives* (2000; with Jane Crisp and Gillian Swanson), *Christopher Isherwood: A World in Evening* (1994) and the edited anthology, *A Time to Write* (1993).

John Frow is Regius Professor of Rhetoric and English Literature at the University of Edinburgh, and previously served as the Darnell Professor of English at the University of Queensland. His most recent books are *Time and Commodity Culture* (1997) and (with Tony Bennett and Michael Emmison) *Accounting for Tastes: Australian Everyday Cultures* (1999). He is a Fellow of the Australian Academy of the Humanities.

Gay Hawkins is a Senior Lecturer in the School of Media and Communications at the University of New South Wales in Sydney. In 1993 she published *From Nimbin to Mardi Gras: Constructing Community Arts*, an analysis of the impacts of the invocation of 'community' in arts policy. More recently she has been working on the relation between quality and difference in public service broadcasting and on theories of value. Publications on these issues include her essay 'Public service broadcasting in Australia: value and difference' in A. Calabrese and J. Burgelman (eds) *Communication, Citizenship & Social Policy* (1999).

Chris Healy is a Senior Lecturer in Cultural Studies at the University of Melbourne. He is the editor of *The Lifeblood of Footscray* (1986) and co-editor of *Beasts of Suburbia* (1994). His book, *From the Ruins of Colonialism: History as Social Memory* (1997) was shortlisted for the 1998 Gleebooks Prize in the NSW Premier's Literary Awards.

James Jupp is Director of the Centre for Immigration and Multicultural Studies at the Australian National University. He was general editor of the encyclopedia *The Australian People* (1988) and is preparing a second edition for the centenary of federation. Dr Jupp has published extensively on immigration and multiculturalism. His latest book, *Immigration,* was published in 1998.

Geoffrey Lawrence is Foundation Professor of Sociology and Director of the Institute for Sustainable Regional Development at Central Queensland University, Australia. Apart from having a strong interest in sports sociology, he has conducted Australian-based studies into aspects of rural social disadvantage, agro-biotechnologies and structural change in farming. With Jim McKay, Toby Miller and David Rowe, he is the author of *Globalization and Sport: Playing the World* (2001). Forthcoming books include *A Future for Regional Australia: Escaping Global Misfortune* (Cambridge University Press, 2001) and *Environment, Society and Natural Resource Management* (Edward Elgar, 2001).

Catharine Lumby is Associate Professor of Media and Communications Studies at the University of Sydney. She is a senior writer and columnist for the *Bulletin* magazine and the author of two books, *Bad Girls: The Media, Sex and Feminism in the 90s* (1997) and *Gotcha: Life In A Tabloid World* (1999).

Jim McKay is an Associate Professor in the Department of Anthropology and Sociology at the University of Queensland, where he teaches courses on gender and popular culture. He is the editor of the *International Review for the Sociology of Sport*. His most recent books are *No Pain, No Gain? Sport and Australian Culture* (1991); *Managing Gender: Affirmative Action and Organizational Power in Australian, Canadian and New Zealand Sport* (1997); with Michael Messner and Donald Sabo, *Men, Masculinities and Sport* (2000); and with Geoffrey Lawrence, Toby Miller and David Rowe, *Globalization and Sport: Playing the World* (2001).

Toby Miller is Professor of Cultural Studies and Cultural Policy Studies at New York University. He is the editor of *Social Text* and *Television and New Media*, co-editor of the Cultural Politics and Sport and Culture book series for the University of Minnesota Press, and co-editor on the Web of Blackwell's *Cultural Theory Resource Centre*. His books include *The Well-Tempered Self: Citizenship, Culture, and the Postmodern Subject* (1993); *Contemporary Australian Television* (1994, with S. Cunningham); *The Avengers* (1997); *Technologies of Truth: Cultural Citizenship and the Popular Media* (1998); *Popular Culture and Everyday Life* (1998, with A. McHoul); *SportCult* (1999, edited with R. Martin); *A Companion to Film Theory* (1999) and *Film and Theory: An Anthology* (2000, both co-edited with R. Stam); and the co-authored *Globalisation and Sport: Playing the World* (2001).

Helen Molnar is currently working as a media consultant after serving as Associate Professor in Media Studies at RMIT. She has worked extensively with Aboriginal and Torres Strait Islanders and Pacific Islanders in developing media policies for indigenous peoples. She has also published extensively in this area and is presently the communications specialist in the Australian National Commission for UNESCO.

Tom O'Regan is Professor in the School of Film, Media and Cultural Studies at Griffith University where he is also the Director of the Australian Key Centre for Cultural and Media Policy. He is the founding editor of *Continuum: The Australian Journal of Media and Culture*. His main publications include *Australian Television Culture* (1993) and *Australian National Cinema* (1996).

David Rowe is Associate Professor in Media and Cultural Studies and Director of the Cultural Industries and Practices Research Centre at the University of Newcastle. Among his publications are three books edited with Geoffrey Lawrence, the most recent of which is *Tourism, Leisure, Sport: Critical Perspectives* (1998). His sole-authored books are *Popular Cultures: Rock Music, Sport and the Politics of Pleasure* (1995) and *Sport, Culture and the Media: The Unruly*

Trinity (1999). His most recent book is the co-authored *Globalization and Sport: Playing the World* (2001). In addition to his academic writing, he is a frequent commentator on social and cultural matters in the print and electronic media.

Tim Rowse (FAHA) is currently a Senior Fellow in History, Research School of Social Sciences, ANU, and has recently finished a biography of H.C. Coombs. His books include *Australian Liberalism and National Character* (1978), *Arguing the Arts* (1985), *Remote Possibilities: The Aboriginal Domain and the Administrative Imagination* (1992) and *After Mabo: Interpreting Indigenous Traditions* (1993).

Terry Smith (FAHA, CIHA) is Power Professor of Contemporary Art and Director of the Power Institute, Foundation for Art and Visual Culture at the University of Sydney. He is author of *Making the Modern: Industry, Art and Design in America* (1993), and editor of *Ideas of the University* (1996), *In Visible Touch: Modernism and Masculinity* (1997) and *First Peoples, Second Chance: The Humanities and Aboriginal Australia* (1999). He has published extensively in the fields of Australian art history, contemporary Aboriginal art, and critical theory.

Nicholas Thomas is Professor of Anthropology at Goldsmiths College, University of London, having served previously as Professor and Director of the ARC Special Centre for Cross-Cultural Research at the Australian National University. His publications include *Entangled Objects: Exchange, Material Culture and Colonialism in the Pacific* (1991), *Colonialism's Culture: Anthropology, Travel and Government* (1994) and *Possessions: Indigenous Art/Colonial Culture* (1999). He is a Fellow of the Australian Academy of the Humanities.

Robin Trotter is a Research Fellow with the Australian Key Centre for Cultural and Media Policy. Her research interests include museums, cultural tourism, and cultural development (with a special interest in regional and rural communities). She also maintains an ongoing interest in cultural policy matters, especially heritage and cultural development. She has published in *Media Information Australia*, *Queensland Review* and the *Journal of Australian Studies*, is the principal author of *Museums and Citizenship: A Resource Book* (1996) and contributes regularly to *The Year's Work in Critical and Cultural Theory*.

Graeme Turner (FAHA) is Professor of Cultural Studies and Director of the Centre for Critical and Cultural Studies at the University of Queensland. His major publications include *National Fictions: Literature, Film and the Construction of Australian Narrative* (1986), *British Cultural Studies: An Introduction* (1990), *Making it National: Nationalism and Australian Popular Culture* (1994) and, with Frances Bonner and David Marshall, *Fame Games: The Production of Celebrity in the Australian Media* (2000).

Acronyms

ABA	Australian Broadcasting Authority
ABC	Australian Broadcasting Corporation (formerly Commission)
ABS	Australian Bureau of Statistics
ACA	Australian Consumers' Association
ACCC	Australian Competition and Consumer Commission
AFC	Australian Film Commission
AFTRS	Australian Film, Television and Radio School
AGCIT	Australian Government Committee of Inquiry into Tourism
AGPS	Australian Government Printing Service
AIATSIS	Australian Institute for Aboriginal and Torres Strait Islander Studies
AIR	Association of Independent Record Labels
AIS	Australian Institute of Sport
ALA	Aboriginal Languages Association
ALP	Australian Labor Party
AMPAL	Australian Music Publishers' Association Limited
AMRA	Australian Music Retailers' Association
ANTA	Australian National Travel Association
ANU	Australian National University
ANZAC	Australian and New Zealand Army Corps
ARIA	Australian Record Industry Association
ASAL	Association for the Study of Australian Literature
ASC	Australian Sports Commission
ATC	Australian Tourist Commission
ATIA	Australian Tourism Industry Association
ATN	Australian Tourism Net
ATO	Australian Taxation Office
ATSIC	Aboriginal and Torres Strait Islander Commission
BBC	British Broadcasting Corporation

BRACS	Broadcasting for Remote Aborigines Community Scheme
BIE	Bureau of Industry Economics
BTR	Bureau of Tourism Research
BRS	BRACS Revitalisation Scheme
CBC	Canadian Broadcasting Commission
CCCWG	Canadian Content and Culture Working Group
CER	Closer Economic Relations Treaty
CIRCIT	Centre for International Research on Communication and Information Technologies
CLF	Commonwealth Literary Fund
DAA	Department of Aboriginal Affairs
DCA	Department of Communications and the Arts
DCITA	Department of Communications, Information Technology and the Arts
DETYA	Department of Education, Training and Youth Affairs
DISR	Department of Industry, Science and Resources
DT	Department of Tourism
ECCs	Ethnic Communities' Councils
EEO	Equal Employment Opportunity
FECCA	Federation of Ethnic Communities' Councils of Australia
FFC	Film Finance Corporation
GAL	Global Arts Link
GAT	General Agreement on Trade in Services
GATT	General Agreement on Tariffs and Trade
GIL	Global Info. Link
HREOC	Human Rights and Equal Opportunity Commission
HKF	Harris, Kerr, Forster and Co.
HLGAVP	High Level Group on Audiovisual Policy
HoCSCCMS	House of Commons Select Committee on Culture, Media and Sport
IAC	Industries Assistance Commission
ICA	Indigenous Communications Australia
IMF	International Managers Forum (Australia)
LGAQ	Local Government Association of Queensland
NAVA	National Association for the Visual Arts
NESB	Non-English-Speaking Background
NIBS	National Indigenous Broadcasting Service
NIMAA	National Indigenous Media Association of Australia
NIRS	National Indigenous Radio Service
NGO	Non-Governmental Organisation
NMAC	National Multicultural Advisory Council
NSOs	Amateur Sporting Organisations
OMA	Office of Multicultural Affairs

ONT	Office of National Tourism
PC	Productivity Commission
PKF	Pannell, Kerr, Forster and Co.
PRIZM	Potential Rating Index for Zip Markets
PSA	Prices Surveillance Authority
PSB	Public Service Broadcasting
RAA	Regional Arts Australia
RADF	Regional Arts Development Fund
RTIF	Regional Telecommunications Infrastructure Fund
SBS	Special Broadcasting Service
SCT	(House of Representatives) Select Committee on Tourism (subsequently Australian Standing Committee on Tourism)
TAPE	The Aboriginal Program Exchange
TCA	Tourism Council of Australia
TRIPS	Trade Related Aspects of Intellectual Property
TTF	Tourism Task Force
UNESCO	United Nations Educational, Scientific and Cultural Organisation
WAAMA	Western Australian Aboriginal Media Association

Introduction

Over the course of the 1990s, culture in Australia regularly appeared as front-page news. There was a series of high-profile debates on major policy questions and ongoing controversies surrounding issues of public concern in the media. Arguments over the introduction and regulation of pay-TV and, more recently, digital television; reports and then legislation on the parallel importing of music CDs and the similar issue of foreign-published books, which remains unresolved; the politically volatile question of media ownership, raised in turn by politicians and proprietors; the Mansfield Report into the Australian Broadcasting Corporation (1996) and the ever-present threat of budget cuts, commercialisation or political interference which that organisation faces; the restructuring and policy reorientation of peak bodies such as the Australia Council, the National Gallery, the Australian Opera; the Nugent Report into Australia's Major Performing Arts Organisations (1999); debates over the Americanisation of Australian cinema, which were revived by the opening of the new Fox Studios in Sydney; attacks on arts funding which were linked, by conservative politicians, to attacks on multiculturalism and Aboriginal funding; and the prolonged 'cash for comment' episode in which leading talkback radio personalities were revealed to have accepted money and other gifts from private businesses in return for favourable commentary – these are just a few of the issues which brought culture out from the weekend supplements and into the daily headlines.

Many of the particular issues which emerged in this period provided the occasion for debates over wider questions which are also the recurring themes in *Culture in Australia* – the threats (or promises) of increasing commercialisation, globalisation and digitisation. Each term contains, and so to some extent conceals, a wide array of diverse economic, institutional, technological and cultural tendencies which, as the essays in this volume show, must be critically examined and disaggregated rather than lumped together into simple negative or celebratory generalisations. Many public commentators see commercialisation increasing in every sphere of culture, from sport to public art galleries to public television; many see governments as less and less committed to regulation or public subsidy, and more and more to market forces or 'consumer choice'. Increasing commercialisation is often linked to the economic and political force

1

of 'globalisation', which has been a persistent debating point for those concerned to defend a national culture or national cultural industries, for those demanding more regulation from government and, simultaneously, for those demanding less regulation. Digitisation, through the convergence of different media technologies, promises to redefine the boundaries between the different media industries, to break down national economic barriers, and thereby to make unprecedented demands on government policy making. In each area there are new challenges to established ideas of national culture, the role of the state in protecting or promoting culture, and the values and rights linked to citizenship, cultural expression and cultural participation.

Over the last two decades what we understand by 'culture' – in government, in the universities, in the cultural organisations and industries themselves – has changed in very significant ways. It is now commonly argued by arts organisations that culture is not merely an elite or marginal activity but 'necessary and integral to the vitality and diversity of contemporary Australian society' (Stevenson 2000, pp. 1–2). Governments have acknowledged the force of such arguments by committing themselves to major policy statements in the area and to public subsidy of a range of cultural organisations and cultural forms. By the same token culture is now recognised to be 'big business', a major sector of the Australian economy in terms of employment and gross domestic product. Cultural organisations making their case to governments can no longer rely, and probably no longer wish to rely, simply on arguments for the virtue of culture 'in itself'. As Stevenson suggests, 'as an industry sector, the arts are required to generate economic and symbolic wealth and contribute generally to national prosperity' (2). Cultural tourism is increasingly supported as a promotional strategy – in some cases a survival strategy – on national, regional and local levels. Cultural diplomacy has been embraced by Austrade, the federal government's international trade promotion body. Arts bodies such as the Australia Council talk not just in terms of artistic excellence or individual creativity but also in the language of professional development and industry expertise.

In short, policy-makers, producers, practitioners and analysts have become accustomed to understanding culture in terms of the *cultural industries*. This once-negative term, introduced to indicate the mass-produced and therefore inferior nature of 'mass culture', is now used positively as a way of acknowledging that culture is not simply a matter of individual creation and private consumption but the product of complex institutions, sophisticated technologies and specific economic relations. Culture is no longer understood merely as a private good but as something of national economic and social significance, a public good.

In the same process, culture has come to be seen increasingly as a major focus of *policy*. The intervention – and investment – of local, state and federal governments in culture has increased dramatically since the early 1980s despite 'economic rationalism' and chronic funding shortages in particular cultural spheres. If governments have, in some instances, been less inclined towards direct public subsidy, other forms of investment, for example in new cultural centres, new festivals and awards or heritage sites, have become a significant and commonplace part of a government's portfolio. Two understandings of culture which recur in the policy environment, culture as a set of economically-significant industries and culture as a national, public good, have been both complementary and contradictory at different times and for different cultural domains.

Over the longer term, the story of culture becoming an object of policy concern has been one of expansion, of government extending the reach of policy into new areas of culture whether by way of regulation or subsidy. Museums, art galleries, radio, cinema, television and rock music, as well as opera and classical music, newspaper and book publishing, the internet, advertising, sport and tourism – all are now routinely taken to be within the sphere of a government's concern. In the commercial sphere, the federal government has continued to regulate in areas such as media ownership, censorship and import restrictions. Although, in some of these areas, the tendency at present is towards deregulation, this will most likely emerge as a restructuring of government cultural policy rather than its demise.

There have also been major shifts in the terms and conceptual frameworks through which culture has been studied in the universities. The end of the 1990s saw the completion of the process whereby cultural studies moved from a marginal into a significant, if not central, place within universities, often displacing or settling in alongside more traditional disciplines such as English or communications. These relationships have often been hostile, as cultural studies was seen to be the vehicle whereby strange new theories and topics were introduced into the humanities curriculum. Although unease about cultural studies has not entirely disappeared, it is now commonplace to find studies of television, popular music, advertising or museums, not just in cultural studies departments but also, say, in literature or history departments. Cultural studies has successfully extended the kinds of texts which are seen to be culturally significant beyond the traditional literary or historical genres to include popular culture forms and practices; this has, in turn, helped to alter the ways in which literature and history themselves are studied. Cultural studies – at least in some of its current manifestations – has also moved beyond its own earlier critical concern with reading cultural texts in 'ideological' terms (in order to discern those forms and practices which affirmed or, alternatively, resisted dominant ideologies). It has shifted towards more empirically based, but no less theoretically informed, interests in cultural institutions, cultural industries, audiences (or cultural publics) and cultural policy. *Australian* cultural studies has been at the cutting edge internationally of the emergence of the study of cultural policy or culture and governmentality (Bennett 1998; Cunningham 1992; Cunningham and Turner 1997). Many of the authors represented in this book have been at the forefront of these developments, and the essays collected here reflect, and reflect upon, these new concerns for the study of culture and cultural institutions.

The kinds of changes in the public presence of culture which we have just outlined are the result of shifts not only in the understanding of what we mean by culture but also in the actual structures and 'situation' of culture in Australia. As suggested, the contexts within which culture is produced, circulated and received are undergoing significant change as a consequence of the increasing globalisation of cultural flows, changing conceptions of the appropriate role of governments in the cultural sphere, and the strong tendency to make the arts and cultural sectors behave like private markets. Another factor, in part a consequence of the globalisation and expanding commodification of culture, has been the way that the boundaries between 'high' and 'low' cultures have been significantly blurred – a process that began to accelerate in the 1960s but more especially in the 1980s and 1990s. The point is not that cultural markets and value-systems are no longer structured through this division, or that traditional high cultural forms no longer carry prestige. Rather there has been a series of 'cross-overs' between the different domains in terms of markets, technologies, institutions and values. As John Frow has argued, high culture is now 'fully absorbed within commodity productions ... Within the overall cultural market high culture forms a "niche" market – but this is also true of many, increasingly differentiated, low cultural products' (Frow 1995, p. 23). The nexus between culture and class – while still important – has to some extent been dissolved by the broad reach of popular culture forms such as pop music or television. Rather than designating clear differences between different cultural forms, then, 'the terms "high" and "low" represent a division that is operative within all cultural domains' (25). Contemporary 'high art' creative practice is typically marked by a combination of genres or styles, and by transgressive sorties into low culture forms, while cinema, television and rock music have been seen as providing 'flagship' cultural achievements for the nation (as in the closing ceremony of the 2000 Sydney Olympics). Elite and publicly subsidised forms such as ballet and dance have become the vehicle for social critique, especially in relation to issues of race and national identity.

The blurring of high and low cultures has been a general phenomenon, but it has had specific local effects in Australia which has witnessed something of a renaissance in both high culture and popular cultures since the 1970s, in cinema, television and popular music as much as in literature, the visual arts, dance and design. Moreover, the dynamics at work at both ends of the 'cultural scale' are closely interrelated; indeed it would be possible to argue that it has been the force of new developments in popular culture which has largely driven the changes in the traditional high culture domains. The centrality and pervasiveness of the media – both the 'old' and the 'new' media forms – in shaping and reshaping the broader field of culture in Australia inevitably becomes a major issue in many of the essays which follow.

The recent changes in Australian culture have also been at the level of the cultural institutions. Since the mid-1980s, in literature and the visual arts, in the film, television and music industries, and in the performing arts, a mature, sophisticated cultural system has come into being defined by the presence of established and (within limits) diverse local production and distribution industries, a differentiated (though relatively small) local market, an established (though never secure) regime of government regulation and intervention, and a professional (if not always user-friendly) infrastructure of agents, critics, administrators and media. Of course, this will not always translate into enthusiastic markets, quality product, or continuous careers and institutions. Australian culture remains structurally weak in its relation to overseas, especially American, cultures. Nonetheless, there is now a substantial 'ecology' of Australian film, television, music, literature, dance and so forth – cultures which, however fragile, now have their own local dynamics, their own diversity and density, their own 'self-sustainability'.

In all of these fields, and despite the threats associated with words such as 'globalisation' or 'Americanisation', cultural institutions and cultural practices in Australia have developed a new relationship to international cultures, in ways that suggest that the international need not always be understood as the opposite of the local or the national. Because of the new 'density' of Australian culture described above, overseas culture is no longer something that Australian creators or audiences feel they need to import or 'catch up with' in order to remedy an essential lack in the local culture. Australian culture is itself an international culture (just as Australia is, in many fields, a culture exporting nation). The international, as it were, is now here as well as there, inside as well as out. There is a sense in which Australia can now be seen as *exemplary* rather than merely supplementary, as in the old colonial metaphors; exemplary, that is, of a postcolonial, multicultural or postmodern nation. Although much of the optimism associated with the Keating years has dissipated since 1996, this new vision remains as something that Australian artists, writers, producers, performers, critics and historians can make known to us.

However, despite the positives for Australian culture and cultural institutions in this situation, a great deal of public discourse about culture in Australia over the last decade has been characterised by stories of decline. The launch of the Keating Labor Government's *Creative Nation* policy in October 1994 represented, for many, a high point in public recognition of the value of the 'creative industries'. It drew together a range of diverse, and potentially contradictory, ways of defining and positively valuing cultural activities: a sense of culture that was broader than the 'arts' alone; an industry/economic argument for culture's significance to the nation; an argument based on national identity defined in terms of creativity and national independence; a cultural export/cultural diplomacy argument; and a vision that linked culture and national identity to the new electronic multimedia technologies. The Coalition Government elected in

1996 has generally been seen as less committed to a national cultural policy and to the support of public cultural institutions such as the ABC or the Australia Council, both of which have suffered budget cuts. More generally, the pressures of commercialisation and globalisation are perceived to have redoubled their force with the combined effects of deregulatory policies, 'borderless' telecommunications and media technologies, and multinational economics (corporate takeovers and foreign ownership threaten local cultural industries just as much as other industries). Another area of concern has been with audiences, reflecting changes in the make-up of the varied publics for different kinds of culture in Australia. There has, for example, been uncertainty about the constitution of a 'national audience' – whether such a thing still exists and, if it does, what its relation is to ethnic minority or Indigenous audiences; there is an ongoing tension, for the makers and marketers of culture, between mass and increasingly differentiated publics; and there are competing claims in the policy area as concerns with 'access and equity' or 'diversity' are balanced against the criterion of 'excellence'.

The essays presented in this book address the cultural, institutional and industry changes, the policy debates, and the tensions, threats and controversies outlined above as these have emerged in specific cultural domains or industries and in the discourses surrounding them. While taking full cognisance of the vulnerabilities and structural weaknesses of the Australian cultural industries, the individual essays generally take a more cautious, even cautiously optimistic, view than that expressed in the crisis-filled stories of cultural decline. By breaking down a simple, general narrative of Australian culture into its smaller component parts, into its institutional, industrial, generic or policy dimensions, the stories and analyses that emerge present a more complex, nuanced and dynamic picture. Each essay highlights particular issues or themes which have emerged as critical in the area of culture being examined, issues selected in order to show the contemporary dynamics and historical pressures shaping its institutions and practices – for example, international production in the cinema, the parallel importing issue in the music industry, or commercialism in public broadcasting.

The book has its origin in a workshop organised by the editors on behalf of the Australian Key Centre for Cultural and Media Policy as a part of the Reshaping Australian Institutions program of the Research School of Social Sciences at the Australian National University. The focus of the workshop, as of the present volume, was on Australian cultural institutions, the changing pressures and possibilities that are reconfiguring their practices, and how these practices are perceived and evaluated. It is important that we not only understand cultural institutions and practices but also understand how they have been understood – by practitioners, publics and policy makers. Our concern, directly and indirectly, has also been to review the 'state of the discipline' and to question the adequacy of popular and academic understandings of contemporary Australian culture; this focus remains a guiding principle in the present selection of essays.

The essays collected here represent a selection of the papers presented at the workshop plus a number of others commissioned subsequently in order to address both a range and balance of issues and cultural domains. *Culture in Australia* does not aim to be exhaustive in its 'coverage' of culture in Australia. Our aim, rather, is to highlight the changing circumstances of Australian culture and of the cultural industries in Australia – and the changing ways in which these have been understood – by focusing on key areas where significant shifts and challenges have occurred: cinema, popular music, visual art, tourism and leisure, literature, public broadcasting, youth cultures, sport, multiculturalism, heritage, museums, Indigenous media and regional cultures. In addition there are essays which take a broader or longer historical view of, for example, issues concerning the emergence of public cultural subsidy in Australia (Tim Rowse on the evolution of H.C. Coombs' policy thinking), academic interventions in cultural debate (Graeme Turner on the changing meanings of the 'popular' in cultural studies), and the unequal distribution of cultural tastes and access (in the analysis of class and culture by Tony Bennett, Michael Emmison and John Frow).

Culture in Australia is organised into three parts corresponding to the three key terms of the book's subtitle – policies, publics and programs. Part 1, Policy and Industry Contexts, covers four key areas of contemporary Australian culture which have been particularly open, or vulnerable, to internationalisation and globalisation: cinema, popular music, the visual arts and tourism. In each area, there have been major shifts in the institutional or industry context over the last decade such that policy, although crucial in shaping each field, has in some ways been struggling to keep up. The tensions which are traced in these chapters, between globalisation and national or local cultures, between market forces and public subsidy or protection, and between national and Indigenous or post-colonial discourses, describe the themes for many of the essays in the following two sections. They also describe the themes that emerge in Tim Rowse's historical account of H.C. Coombs' attempts not only to formulate but to institutionalise a national cultural policy. In an historically significant manner, Indigenous cultures became inevitable and problematic for a line of cultural thinking that began very differently, with notions of a common national culture in which Aboriginal cultures were scarcely an issue.

Part 2, Australian Culture and its Publics, interrogates the ways in which culture, although often conceived as a 'whole way of life' or a national charac-teristic, is unevenly and unequally distributed across increasingly differentiated publics in Australia. The essays reveal both gains and losses as cultural institu-tions shift in order to accommodate changing publics – to broaden audiences or to 'niche market' more effectively or, quite often, to attempt to do both at once. The high/low culture distinction has shifted ground but is still pervasive in organising culture – in distinguishing, for example, between different television genres and audiences, and in distributing cultural competencies or participation in, say, sport, music or reading. Class, age and gender continue to play decisive roles in organising different patterns of access to cultural resources and in organising both media representations and policy responses – for example, in the area of youth cultures. Essays in this section also consider how notions of the public or the popular have been deployed in cultural criticism, for example in understanding literature's social and institutional significance or in the complex shifts in how cultural studies has defined the 'popular' in 'popular culture' and used it as a critical concept.

Part 3, Programs of Cultural Diversity, focuses on the intersection between Australian cultural policies and the emphasis, both from within communities and from government, on cultural diversity. Policies and institutions governing multicultural, ethnic minority or Indigenous cultures were placed under increasing pressure in the second half of the 1990s by very public attacks on 'special interest' funding from the One Nation Party, certain Coalition politicians and some prominent journalists, and by the general tendency towards private market rationales. Policies and programs formed around notions such as multiculturalism, heritage and Indigeneity have all been reconfigured but remain unsettled, contentious areas of policy formation. Indigenous issues, above all, are central – both inevitable and unsettling – to any stories of national culture. At the same time, regional cultures have emerged as an element of cultural diversity in Australia. The promotion, perhaps even the invention, of local cultural characteristics and traditions has been embraced as a means of sustaining distinctive cultures (and economies). The threat, again, has most often been seen to come from globalisation, although, as Robin Trotter shows, some regional cultural organisations have turned globalisation to their own advantage.

This final emphasis on a dynamic relation between the opportunities and threats, the structural weaknesses and the strengths which characterise the institutions of culture in Australia is a recurrent and connecting theme in the essays comprising *Culture in Australia*. They all argue for readjustments to common ways of understanding culture in Australia. Their analyses resist both a triumphant nationalist or globalising rhetoric. Equally they resist the overgeneralised stories of doom and gloom that see Australian culture disappearing under the combined pressures of commercialisation, privatisation, internationalisation and Americanisation. Each suggests the multi-dimensional aspects of culture, and of different cultures, in Australia, demonstrating how textual, institutional, technological, economic and policy aspects all bear on the production, circulation and evaluation of cultural products and practices.

References

Bennett, Tony (1998) *Culture: A Reformer's Science*, Sydney: Allen & Unwin.
Cunningham, Stuart (1992) *Framing Culture: Culture and Policy in Australia*, Sydney: Allen & Unwin.

Cunningham, Stuart and Graeme Turner (1997) *The Media in Australia: Industries, Texts, Audiences*, 2nd edition, Sydney: Allen & Unwin.

Frow, John (1995) *Cultural Studies and Cultural Values*, Oxford: Clarendon.

Stevenson, Deborah (2000) *Art and Organisation: Making Australian Cultural Policy*, St Lucia: University of Queensland Press.

Part 1
Policy and Industry Contexts

Introduction

Since World War II and especially since the late 1960s in Australia there has been a quite remarkable development of both cultural industries and cultural policy. In cinema, broadcasting, music, literature and the visual arts the complex structures of a mature cultural system with institutional continuity and diversity – an infrastructure of producers, workers, artists, agents, publicists, markets, critics, fans and so forth – came into being relatively suddenly in the sixties and seventies. A number of these developments were 'policy-led', most spectacularly in the case of the Australian cinema revival which was dependent upon federal government assistance through the Australian Film Development Commission and then the Australian Film Commission, more quietly through assistance to Australian writers through the Australia Council's Literature Board. In other areas, such as the visual arts, the developments were primarily 'market-led' – in this case through the burgeoning of private dealer galleries – although a shift towards more contemporary Australian art in the buying policies of major government institutions was also critical.

Except for the government's commitment to the ABC, federal cultural policy before the war was largely a matter of regulation, for example through the control of broadcast licences in radio or censorship regimes. During the war, a gradual shift in emphasis emerged through discussions within government and among intellectuals of proposals for a national cultural council. As Tim Rowse indicates in Chapter 5, much of the energy in this discussion was devoted to proposals for a national theatre. The war had been interpreted not merely as a military challenge but as a challenge to Australia's culture or 'civilisation'

(Palmer 1942; Penton 1943). What had white Australia achieved, after all, to justify its continued existence? What had it contributed to the store of civilisation? Had it proved itself a nation? There was a sense that the national cohesion which the war had produced needed to be maintained, and that this would be achieved in and through cultural forms, or, more mundanely perhaps, that a smooth return to the post-war world required a culture-rich society to sustain its citizens. Post-war reconstruction, therefore, also meant the (re)construction of a national culture, although the significance attributed to the term 'national', as Rowse also shows, varied widely.

Both 'industry' and 'culture' arguments were present in these early debates of the 1940s and 1950s, and by and large they could work together towards the same ends. Industry arguments emphasised the need for employment and professional careers for artists and arts workers, and for Australia to have its own production capabilities. Culture arguments emphasised the need for a national culture and the role of culture in producing national community, identity and well-being. For some the emphasis was on bringing cultural excellence to local audiences (and practitioners), educating them up to modern and sophisticated standards, while for others the point was to promote the national culture itself. Television gave both sides of the argument a new urgency in the 1960s. The dominance of imported programming exposed the lack of a local production industry and the apparent vulnerability of Australian cultural expression – and Australian audiences – to foreign influences. The Vincent Report (1963) revealed the dominance of imported programming on Australian television particularly in the area of drama and the need for regulation to support a local production industry to meet local content quotas (Flew 1995, pp. 77–9; Jacka 1997, pp. 76–9). Although the report was shelved, and its recommendations opposed by the commercial broadcasters, it played a crucial role in the lobbying processes both inside and outside government for large-scale public subsidies.

The late 1960s and early 1970s represent a major turning point. By the middle of the 1970s, national cultural policy was manifested in a range of institutions such as the Australia Council, the Australian Film Commission and the Australian Broadcasting Tribunal, and in a mixed regime of regulation and subsidy. The 'flagship' institutions of policy making and implementation were defined by their association with public subsidy rather than with regulation alone; with a range of civic and democratic objectives as well as those of artistic excellence; and with the promotion not just of culture but of a national culture. In a conceptual and political shift that was in many ways unprecedented (and which has been largely unremarked) the national culture itself could now be identified with 'excellence' rather than with 'community' alone.

Tim Rowse (1985) has characterised federal cultural policy in three distinct phases which he terms voluntary entrepreneurship, statutory patronage and decentralised patronage. The first phase covers the period from the establishment of the ABC in 1932 through to the late 1960s–early 1970s period described above. Its characteristic institution was the Elizabethan Theatre Trust (1954) which, as Rowse describes it in Chapter 5, depended upon the mobilisation of old and new elites committed to a 'voluntary cultural mission' to bring the virtues of cultural excellence to those perceived as 'starved' of it. The Trust helped establish the Australian Opera (1956), the Australian Ballet (1961) and the National Institute of Dramatic Arts (1959) (Stevenson 2000, pp. 19–21). The second phase, of statuary patronage, is that set in place in the late 1960s–early 1970s and characterised by large-scale, publicly funded national institutions with an explicit policy charter (Stevenson 2000, pp. 22–3, 43–63). The third phase, decentralised patronage, identifies the emergence of a new discourse around cultural funding – a shift from notions of bringing high cultural value to the public and towards 'the idea that there are identifiable communities whose social or cultural interests must be served by the work of artists or arts companies who receive certain forms of federal financial support' (Stevenson 2000, p. 23 citing Rowse 1985, pp. 25–6). The notion of the national community (and that of the 'arts community') was 'supplemented' by the notion of different communities whose interests should be served. Hence the establishment of Community and Aboriginal Boards within the Australia Council.

Although the tensions between industry or commercial arguments, on the one hand, and cultural or community arguments, on the other, often generated competing claims on government, the public subsidy regime was a more or less settled arrangement throughout the 1980s and into the 1990s. A mixed system had evolved based around local content requirements for television and radio, financing support for film, a strong commitment to the national broadcasters (the ABC and SBS), 'protection' for the performing arts, literature and the visual arts, and expanding programs to support popular music and emerging multi-media and new technology forms. There were controversies about funding levels and bias and about shifts in policy emphasis, but the policy frameworks and mechanisms grounded in the major arts and cultural institutions remained relatively stable and evolving.

At the end of the 1990s, however, there was much less certainty and stability around understandings of cultural policy and the commitment or capacity of the national government to support and shape a favourable cultural environment. As Tom O'Regan argues in Chapter 1, by the end of the decade the acclaimed benefits of 'internationalism' to Australian culture industries – in this case, the cinema – could easily look more like the threat of 'globalisation'. These responses were heightened by increasing signs of a government wanting to make the arts and cultural sector subject to market principles and to withdraw from, or at least significantly restructure the nature of support for, cultural practice and the culture industries. What had appeared, in the 1994 *Creative Nation* cultural policy statement, to be an historically momentous convergence between officially sanctioned national policy and critical national discourses to do with multiculturalism, the republic, Indigenous issues and Asia, for example, was rudely disrupted by the election of the Howard Liberal-National Party Coalition and of Pauline Hanson at the 1996 federal election. Although the Hawke and Keating Labor Governments had been financial deregulators they had not been driven to large-scale cultural deregulation or withdrawal of public support through direct budget cuts. Those once critical of the narrowness and elitism of certain of the major cultural agencies now often find themselves defending these institutions against further political intervention, budget cuts or policy downgrading.

What has globalisation meant for the culture industries in Australia? As the chapters in this section reveal, there can be no simple answer to this question. Instead we need to consider a series of effects which will be registered differently across the different domains of culture. Globalisation has not been simply an economic development involving more and more integrated transnational markets and more and more integrated multinational corporations controlling those markets. It has also meant increasing international access for and integration of Australian cultural industries and markets, manifested by, for example, the rise of co-productions in cinema and television or, rather differently, the mix of European-Australian, immigrant, Indigenous and Pacific influences in the visual arts described by Terry Smith in Chapter 3. Globalisation is also a technological development, a series of causes and effects involving the convergence of media and broadcast technologies. These developments challenge the economic bases of the culture industries in Australia – not just because independent Australian companies might be swallowed up by multinationals but because the very nature of production and its control and 'release' are altered. This in turn challenges regulation and subsidy regimes strongly grounded in notions of a centralised national agency. The challenges are suggested by O'Regan in relation to cinema and television but they can be generalised more broadly for the other domains of media and cultural policy: 'television was becoming less a national and more an international medium. In their turn digital television, multi-channel marketplaces and varieties of platform for the delivery of audio-visual content promised to change decisively the economics of local production and regulatory structures'. Australian cultural industries and their products – and even the individual personnel within them – are often no longer 'Australian' in any straightforward sense. Companies are linked to or owned by multinationals; they produce for export as well as for local consumption; content, technologies, rights and personnel are highly transferable; products are co-funded, co-produced, co-marketed; audiences show strongly marked local, national *and* 'foreign' preferences.

These are precisely the issues addressed in the opening two chapters of *Culture in Australia*, Tom O'Regan's analysis of industry and policy structures in relation to the cinema in Australia and David Rowe's in relation to popular music. These two domains of culture share a number of aspects – the significance of technology to their production and reproduction; hence their proximity to emerging convergence technologies; their distribution right across the range of 'high' and 'popular' cultures; the structural weakness of their Australian industries in relation to the multinationals (Hollywood/'The Big Six'); and the integration of their Australian products and personnel into international markets. In many ways they can be taken as paradigmatic of contemporary culture (such that more traditional domains such as literature/print culture are becoming increasingly like cinema and popular music in their structures rather than the reverse). Indeed as Rowe suggests, citing Lash and Urry (1994), the contemporary culture industries have emerged, not as idiosyncratic elements among the modern forms of production, but as 'the very model for contemporary economic exchange and organisational form'.

O'Regan examines the shifting industry and policy responses to two crucial shaping discourses for filmmaking and film policy: internationalism and national cultural diversity. The 1990s were marked by more intensive patterns of international financing, co-production, off-shore production in Australia, and shifts in technology and story telling consequent upon this internationalism. These developments could be taken as evidence of the increasing maturity and robustness of the local film and television industries. O'Regan discusses Alex Proyas' *Dark City* (1998) as a positive example of emerging tendencies towards 'the increasing non-coincidence of filmmaking in Australia and Australian film'. By way of contrast, Ana Kokkinos' *Head On* (also 1998) is taken as a positive example of a continuing strand of Australian filmmaking which is about reconfiguring national identities through cultural diversity. By the end of the decade, internationalism (and culturally diverse nationalism) looked less promising. The major film agencies were reporting the decline of local production, investment in local product, and local audiences for Australian films. Local creators had not greatly benefited from the international proliferation of demand or production opportunities. At the same time, government thinking seemed to be moving further away from protection towards market principles. Industry and culture arguments increasingly diverged, the former promoting international co-production, the latter, domestic production. Film appeared to be in danger of being overrun by the imperatives of the 'new economy'. Policy responses have been characterised above all by their irresolution and conservatism.

David Rowe uses the debate over parallel importing of recorded music as a case study which reveals the contours, structures and faultlines of the Australian music industry. Familiar arguments opposing nationalist and internationalist positions were reworked over the course of this debate by the pressures of a globalised industry, producing some odd alignments (Peter Garrett, Pauline Hanson, the 'Big Six' companies and the Australian Record Industry Association on one side; the Howard Government, the Australian Consumers' Association and some independent record companies on the other). Copyright issues emerge as central to the debate about globalisation, casting doubt, as Rowe suggests, over 'total-ising accounts' which underestimate the continued force of rights regimes still grounded in national or regional agreements. In ways that parallel O'Regan's argument, Rowe points to the constraints on 'good policy making' which the parallel importation debate revealed, not least the obscuring of other, arguably more significant issues such as the internet selling and downloading of music.

Terry Smith's history of the institutional structures governing the visual arts – a history of increasing institutionalisation, internationalisation and industrial-isation – also comes to focus on the policy challenges presented by the present dynamics in the system. Indeed, Smith sees these dynamics as leading to new patterns beyond those previously 'settled' around the visual arts, a 'dispersive deinstitutionalisation' and increasing competition within and fragmentation of the arts as culture industry. Although the culture industry discourse has emphasised the large numbers of Australians involved in productive activities associated with the visual arts and the significant economic contribution of the sector, although the institutions are now many and varied (the art market, educational, governmental), the benefits have not necessarily accrued to the artists themselves. Smith draws particular attention to the striking initiative of the Canadian government in introducing 'Status of the Artist' legislation as a possible model for Australian policy making.

Jennifer Craik's examination of tourism in Chapter 4 reveals another complex field caught between industry policy and cultural policy in a manner likely to produce contradictions as readily as it does productive synergies. Through the emerging discourses of 'cultural tourism', the tourist industry has been signifi-cantly integrated into cultural policy at local, regional, state and national levels. Tourist rhetoric and imagery continues to be a powerful, if not usually very subtle, mode of projecting images of the nation for both domestic and inter-national consumption. Indeed it has emerged as one of the most powerful ways of 'nationing' a diverse array of sites, events, 'experiences' and even people. The most important and most problematical of recent developments, as Craik shows, has been the area of Indigenous cultural tourism. This has the potential to become a significant industry for Indigenous communities themselves, but it is almost inevitable that Indigenous priorities will, sooner or later, come into conflict with the demands and expectations of tourists, the broader industry and national tourism objectives.

The final chapter in Part 1 is Tim Rowse's study of H.C. Coombs' thinking on the issues of national culture and national cultural policy from the 1940s through to the 1970s. This time-span covers the crucial period of the develop-ment of federal cultural policy in Australia as described above and Coombs was the key player in each of the stages Rowse describes. This chapter provides a fine-grained analysis of the early phases of the development of cultural policy and its major institutions, elaborating on the general points Rowse made in his 1985 book *Arguing the Arts*. Most significant for its bearing on the present structures of cultural policy is the 'self-complicating' development of Coombs' rhetoric, moving from a sense of national community and cultural improvement in which Indigenous culture played no role, to an optimistic, modernising notion of different cultural streams merging together, to a more difficult and confronting sense of cultural differences that cannot simply be reconciled. Cutting across this analysis is an argument towards understanding Coombs' thinking and its institutional outcomes in terms of class, specifically the rise of a new professional-managerial class.

The concerns raised in these five chapters – globalisation and internationalisation, the development and restructuring of cultural markets and institutions, the interchange between industry and cultural policy, the relations between Indigenous and national imperatives, and the role of class (and other categories of difference) in marking cultural distinctions – are taken up further in the context of other cultural domains in the chapters that follow in Parts 2 and 3.

References

Flew, Terry (1995) 'Images of nation: economic and cultural aspects of Australian content regulations for commercial television' in Jennifer Craik, Julie James Bailey and Albert Moran (eds) *Public Voices, Private Interests: Australia's Media Policy*, Sydney: Allen & Unwin, pp. 73–85.

Jacka, Elizabeth (1997) 'Film' in Stuart Cunningham and Graeme Turner (eds) *The Media in Australia: Industries, Texts, Audiences*, Sydney: Allen & Unwin, pp. 70–89.

Lash, Scott and John Urry (1994) *Economies of Signs and Space*, London: Sage.

Palmer, Vance (1942) 'Battle', *Meanjin* 8.

Penton, Brian (1943) *Advance Australia – Where?*, London: Cassell.

Rowse, Tim (1985) *Arguing the Arts: The Funding of the Arts in Australia*, Ringwood, Vic.: Penguin.

Stevenson, Deborah (2000) *Art and Organisation: Making Australian Cultural Policy*, St Lucia: University of Queensland Press.

Chapter 1

'Knowing the Processes But Not the Outcomes': Australian Cinema Faces the Millennium

Tom O'Regan

The certainties of the 1990s

> A film ... circulates in a sphere which can be described as transnational with none of the specificity so desired by nationalists. It does so because its mode of communication doesn't rely exclusively on the local or the national for success.
>
> (Burnett 1996, p. 258)

Adrian Martin aptly titled a 1994 essay 'Ghosts ... of a national cinema'. He asked 'where do we draw the borders around "Australia" – and do we need to?' The issue for Martin turned not only on the 'question of the inevitable, unstoppable increase in international co-production' but also on the 'question of self-defined cultural identity' which 'impacts on the films we make' (Martin 1994, p. 15). Critical and policy debate on Australian cinema over the 1990s was dominated by both questions, with debates over the directions, possibilities and limits of internationalism and over an Australian cultural identity which needed to be reconfigured in ways welcoming of cultural diversity. Central to both moves was an attempt to render positive the cultural exchange between national film industries and the personnel in them, and between Australian filmmakers and a culturally diverse citizenry. This was accompanied by considerable optimism at the start of the decade that internationalism and cultural diversity could be managed in ways that benefited filmmaking, film culture and the broader Australian culture and society.

Over the 1990s Australian filmmaking became much more internationally oriented as a matter of policy and necessity. With severe economic recession at the start of the 1990s, a commercial television system teetering on bankruptcy and the declining value of tax concessions impacting on private funding sources, greater international integration was seen as a necessity. But over the 1990s it acquired a life of its own. Policy makers saw the Australian cinema as more than just a national industry servicing a self-defining national culture. With directors and Australian-based productions telling stories set inside and outside Australia, the production industry was more internationally integrated than at any time in its recent past with the film industries of New Zealand (Jane Campion's *The Piano* 1993), North America (Bruce Beresford's *Black Robe* 1992 and Peter Weir's *Green Card* 1991), Europe (Wim Wender's 'ultimate road movie', *Until the End of the World* 1992) and to a lesser extent Asia (Clara Law's *Floating Life* 1996). Critics lauded *Romeo + Juliet* (1996) described by its director, Baz Luhrmann, as that 'Canadian/East Brunswick co-production [made] with a bit of American interference and money' (Bilcock and Savage 1998, p. 22). For its part, *Floating Life* raised the question of whether Australian cinema could not also be Hong Kong cinema, just as *The Piano* did with respect to New Zealand.

Producers sought international production finance and co-production partners. State governments and companies increasingly sought 'off-shore' film production most notably through the Warners Roadshow studio on the Gold Coast (e.g., *Fortress*, Steve Gordon 1993) and as of 1998 the Fox Studios in Sydney (e.g., *Matrix*, Andy and Larry Wachowski 1999). Also driving international integration was the emerging ensemble of local and international audiovisual services which favoured international connection. There was a renewed internationalisation of film production in North America, Europe and Japan. The emergence of more television, video and viable pay-TV operations stimulated interest in international connections at a development stage which worked to the benefit of both filmmakers and television drama producers alike. The gradual, though uneven, turnaround of cinema attendances after decades of decline in the major Western markets in Europe, Australasia and North America created favourable conditions for the big budget film and attracted American distributor interest in acquiring Australian and international rights to smaller Australian films such as Scott Hicks' *Shine* (1996).

Organisations like CiBy 2000 and Miramax helped maintain the self-evidently 'Australian film' with modest budgets and Australian casts, settings and crews by funding films such as *Muriel's Wedding* (P.J. Hogan 1994). For his part, Rolf de Heer put together with his European partners a remarkable cycle of films beginning with his jazz film *Dingo* (1992) moving through his odyssey story of a thirty-five-year-old child-man entering society in *Bad Boy Bubby* (1994), the essay film on belonging and environmental values, *Epsilon* (1995), his film about a seven-year-old who refuses to speak in *The Quiet Room* (1996) and finally his collaboration with Heather Rose on a love triangle involving a woman with cerebral palsy, her carer and the man they both pursue in *Dance Me to My Song* (1998).

An increasingly free-wheeling internationalism characterised the Australian filmmaking milieu as actors, directors, cinematographers, producers and art directors responded to domestic circumstance and the opportunities created by international production. John Seale won an Oscar for best cinematography in 1997 for *The English Patient* (Anthony Minghella, 1996). P.J. Hogan followed up *Muriel's Wedding* with *My Best Friend's Wedding* (1997); Jocelyn Moorhouse followed up *Proof* (1991) with *How to Make an American Quilt* (1995); and most impressively of all Baz Luhrmann followed up *Strictly Ballroom* (1992) with *Romeo + Juliet* (1996). Such internationalism even suggested a positive sense of expatriation where Australian contributions in cinematography, special FX, direction and acting were seen as delivering an Australian inflection to international practice as they put to work in another context the lessons, techniques and strategies that had previously been honed on Australian films. These several developments help underwrite an emerging fuzziness around what is and is not an Australian film. This kind of internationalism provides one way of thinking about Australian cinema in the 1990s and beyond: it accentuates the negotiation and renegotiation of the international boundaries of Australian film by producers, policy makers and critics.

At the same time, filmmakers, critics and policy makers alike purposefully enlarged the terms in which the local and the national were presented through notions of multiculturalism, cultural diversity and regional specificity. Some of these preoccupations, most particularly the public policy of multiculturalism, which provided an official civic definition of Australia after 1989, accentuated international connectedness and emphasised the mixed nationalities and ancestries of the Australian people. This provided a new justification and centrality for a filmmaking set outside the country, whether in Denis O'Rourke's *The Good Woman of Bangkok* (1992) or Pauline Chan's *Traps* (1994). (*Good Woman* was almost entirely set in Thailand with a Thai lead, *Traps* is set in 1950s Vietnam and made in Vietnam and Australia.) It also encouraged the recognition of the integrity of various diasporas within Australia from Michael Jenkins' *Heartbreak Kid* (1993) to Ana Kokkinos' *Only the Brave* (1994), just as it promoted a new local civic and popular multicultural identity for the Australian in titles such as *Strictly Ballroom* and John Ruane's *Death in Brunswick* (1992).

In *The Heartbreak Kid* the romance is entirely a Greek-Australian affair – signalling Greek Australia as a 'normal' part of Australia and as a diaspora; while in *Strictly Ballroom* the romance plot is between an ethnically unmarked 'Australian' man and a non-English speaking (NES) background woman. The latter film acquires a utopian dimension. With their respective fathers' and her grandma's blessing, the couple successfully challenge the conventions of Australian ballroom dancing. The emerging Australian in both films is inescapably hybrid: in *The Heartbreak Kid* Greek-Australian, in *Strictly Ballroom* part older Anglo-Australian and part Spanish-Australian. After a succession of films set outside the country and taking NES Australia as their focus, there seemed to be a preparedness on the part of Australians to confuse themselves with the world, emphasising what Ross Gibson (1992, p. 81) would call the 'international contamination' in our midst. Internationalism was both positively endorsed and promoted as manageable on national terms and to the local advantage of the minority group and the culture at large.

Cultural diversity was also registered and discussed in more local terms. There was the regional in the farming community of David Elfick's *No Worries* (1993) and the downwardly mobile Adelaide 'family' business in Ray Argall's *Return Home* (1990). Aboriginals' and Islanders' presence continued to be marked in a mini-cycle of films from James Ricketson's *Blackfellas* (1993) to Rachel Perkins' *Radiance* (1998). Various problematic subcultures such as the skinheads in Geoffrey Wright's *Romper Stomper* (1992) and the working-class boys in Rowan Woods' *The Boys* (1998) continued a tradition begun with *Wake in Fright* (Ted Kotcheff, 1971) and *Stone* (Sandy Harbutt, 1974). Sexual preference themes made a more sustained appearance with the gays of Geoff Burton and Kevin Dowling's *The Sum of Us* (1994), the lesbian couples in Ann Turner's *Dallas Doll* (1994) and Kokkinos' *Only the Brave,* and the transvestites and transsexuals of Stephan Elliott's *Adventures of Priscilla Queen of the Desert* (1994). The high-profile cycle of women-centred stories begun in the 1970s with titles such as *My Brilliant Career* (Gillian Armstrong, 1979) continued with Jane Campion's late 1989 success *Sweetie* followed up by titles like Gillian Armstrong's *Last Days of Chez Nous* (1992), Shirley Barrett's *Love Serenade* (1996) and Samantha Lang's *The Well* (1997). These several developments seemed to have ensconced diversity and difference at the heart of how we think about Australian cinema.

So ascendant did multiculturalism seem to be that critics proselytised for a 'post-national' culture which would displace a hegemonic Anglo-Celtic culture. Mark Roxburgh (1997, p. 6) celebrated Clara Law's *Floating Life* as displacing 'popular notions of Australian national identity' which are 'highly exclusive, and are the product of white, male hegemony', proffering instead a 'different version of our history, one which allows us to conceive, dialogically, heterogenous notions of Australian national identities' (6). For Roxburgh, Law had produced a film in which her Chinese-Australian characters have reached a 'third space' moving as they do 'beyond the contained grid of fixed identities' (Roxburgh citing Ang 1996, p. 45). In a similar fashion Felicity Collins (1999, p. 107) claims that there is something 'un-Australian' about the 'redemptive, apocalyptic and conciliatory endings' of both Margot Nash's *Vacant Possession* (1994) and Law's *Floating Life* which 'insist on bringing the past into the present, on connecting spirit and place, on opening up the local terrain to a different future'. They represent a welcome 'dislocation' of 'white masculinity'.

The rhetoric of cultural diversity led equally in the complementary direction of 'mainstreaming', well encapsulated by the title of a short film developed by the

Media, Arts and Entertainment Alliance in conjunction with the Office of Multi-cultural Affairs: *What about Ernie Dingo as Mr Darcy?* (1996). This short film was designed to encourage more extensive casting of people of diverse backgrounds in roles where ethnicity does not enter into the story to shape it. Opening up such mainstream roles to actors of diverse backgrounds is a determinedly 'melting pot' or, as I have described it elsewhere (O'Regan 1996, pp. 317–24), a 'new world' cinema and television strategy. It is based less on the maintenance of ancestral community identity and associated idealisms than on normalising statuses and creating synthetic composite identities including subcultures. The benefits of this mainstreaming to the film industry, as Anne Britton, Alliance Joint Federal Secretary contended, were several:

> We believe that actors, filmmakers and audiences will all benefit from 'non-traditional casting'. Actors will have enhanced employment opportunities; filmmakers will be able to take advantage of an expanded and more diverse casting pool; and audiences will see a more realistic portrayal of Australian society.
>
> (*The Alliance* 1996, p. 3)

If the fact that the argument still had to be made for casting against cultural stereotypes indicated that there was a long way to go, it also showed the extent of industry sensitivity to the issue. Britton went on to observe that Australian cinema and television compares unfavourably with other English-speaking countries when it comes to the casting of non-Anglo performers in mainstream roles.[1] On the same page *The Alliance* also reported that casting agents and producers were finding it difficult to locate Aboriginal and Torres Strait Island performers to match the work available to them.

Thus two related but different strategies for dealing with cultural diversity – multicultural and new world strategies – emerged in the 1990s. Some of the stakes in this difference are gestured to in my *Australian National Cinema*:

> Working within the domain of popular art, the new world identity provides relatively unselfconscious public identities that can be readily consented to. It suffers the same opprobrium as do all such popular identities: it is consumer and fashion driven, it is ephemeral, it is utopian, it is not serious, it is hegem-onic. By contrast, the multicultural society and multicultural cinema is a more critically acceptable identity. It is an official, critical intellectual and self-conscious creation. It can discount the authority, legitimacy and reach of the settler cultural and aesthetic tradition, which provide the basic grammar of Australian film and television production to imagine possibilities shaped by other less dominant interests. It sees itself as providing new vocabularies for film and television production and nationhood.
>
> (O'Regan 1996, p. 326)

Further encouraging this sense of a settled order was the relative stability of the institutions and funding arrangements, both through the Australian Film Commission (AFC) and the Australian Film Finance Corporation (FFC), and through the additional funding arrangements flowing from the *Creative Nation* (Department of Communications and the Arts 1994) national cultural policy statement – the Commercial Television Drama Fund and SBS Independent. These federal organisations helped stabilise and standardise the film milieu. While some of these programs, like the Commercial Television Drama Fund, have run their course, the Commonwealth's principal institutions – the AFC and FFC – survived intact the incoming Howard Liberal-National Coalition Government in 1996 and subsequent inquiries.

For its part *Creative Nation*, as the nation's first coordinated national cultural policy, ensconced under the one portfolio the carriage and content portfolios of communication and the arts.[2] This positioned 'culture' – or, rather, cultural production – in a pivotal position at the centre of governmental strategy. This stress upon content seemed to mark the Keating Labor Government's (1992–96) determination to configure carriage issues in ways that benefited positive content outcomes. Culture, it seemed, was being positioned as a matter for the whole of government. 'Content industries matter', wrote Cutler & Company (1994, p. 3) in their influential report *Commerce in Content*, because 'they are at the intersection of significant industry development, and of the quality of life of the Australian community as reflected in its self-expression of culture, identity and the building of "knowledge banks"'. At least in the first half of the 1990s there was a sense that the content industries could manage on their own terms the transition to screen in a digital age. With generous and multifaceted governmental assistance Australian creative producers could, it seemed, grow their place in new and existing platforms and find themselves at the forefront of the development of an Australian 'knowledge' and 'information-based' economy.

While the Warners Roadshow studio had progressively introduced off-shore production into the policy mix, it was initially quarantined to Queensland where it boosted employment and skills development and established a parallel industry partially disconnected from the national film and television milieu. In the first part of the 1990s these studios seemed to have added to capacity without affecting Australian filmmaking. The Fox studio marked both a further consolidation of studio infrastructure (this time in Sydney) and presented in its management practices the pleasing prospect of the studios sector being brought closer to the mainstream of Australian film and television.

Underwriting this stability of issues and concerns were the relatively settled production, transmission and reception components of the domestic market. There was a healthy exhibition sector as a burgeoning cinema-building program added cinema screens and led to increased attendances over the decade. At the same time an expanding and increasingly mature video rental industry functioned as a highly profitable second-run cinema. Production facilities evolved during this decade towards digital post-production and pre-production services (Aisbett and Jonker 1997). The slow take-up of pay-TV over the decade and the stalling of free-to-air television expansion – with the sixth channel in metropolitan markets initially designated as a community broadcasting channel and later caught up in a moratorium on new commercial television services – also ensured that traditional media continued to play a central role with new media taking a back seat.

Transitions: *Head On* and *Dark City*

By the end of the 1990s this settled picture was starting to fray. Two films released in 1998 – Ana Kokkinos' *Head On* and Alex Proyas' *Dark City* – help outline the significant continuities and new directions we can expect of Australian filmmaking over the coming decade. With its uncompromising focus on ethnicity and homosexuality – the film is about being Greek-Australian and being gay – *Head On* confirms existing trajectories of an urban and multicultural filmmaking. It also confirms the continuing importance of women in the Australian film industry and the value of the policy initiatives which have helped produce this outcome. Kokkinos joins an impressive line-up of Australian women directors including Gillian Armstrong, Jane Campion, Jocelyn Moorhouse, Samantha Lang and Shirley Barrett (Barber 1998, pp. 4–6; Taylor 1995).[3] For its part *Dark City* points towards new configurations based around studio and digital developments, the telling of 'universal stories' and the increasing non-coincidence of filmmaking in Australia and Australian films. It also represents the involvement of and film's connection with the computing and fledgling multimedia industries. Describing himself as a technician not an artist, Proyas is at home with the 'pointy heads' who have given Australia a 'reputation as a post-production powerhouse' providing hi-tech film services (Manktelow 1998, p. 42). Interestingly both films are made by Australians of Greek background – pointing to what Bill Mousoulis (1999) calls the 'more than fair' involvement of Greek-Australians in feature film and audiovisual production more generally.[4] Both are also art films attracting favourable critical comment as important trendsetting films.

   With its exploration of Melbourne's inner-city suburbs and multi-ethnic neighbourhoods, *Head On* easily fits the critical vocabulary we have developed for celebrating difference as central to an emerging national experience. Kokkinos is testing the boundaries of what it is to be Australian and of what it is possible to show (explicit gay sex). She claims her multicultural identity as a Greek-Australian as another Australian identity. But *Head On* was also released at a time when many of the 'cultural norms' which a post-national multicultural filmmaking took for granted were being contested both inside and outside government. The political disturbance of One Nation, vicious national debates about native title and the stolen generation, and the Prime Minister's repudiation of 'black armband' views of history, republicanism and political correctness all brought critical multiculturalists into sometimes open opposition with conservative politicians, including the Prime Minister.

A post-national critical vocabulary which was once central to government and stressed critical multicultural forms increasingly functioned to structure a quasi-oppositional, quasi-official filmmaking and critical milieu. (This recalled the earlier situation of the Creative Development Branch of the AFC in the late 1970s and early 1980s.) In this milieu *Head On* visibly affirmed dearly held cultural and ethical values and political orientations. It also provided a sense of continuity for a cultural elite at a time when national cultural definition had become a site of public rancour and division. *Head On* could, in this context, be presented as marking the true or real Australia in conversation with itself in an uncompromising, authentic and extraordinary story.

The significance of Alex Proyas' *Dark City* lies elsewhere. It was the first feature from Fox Studios (Barber and Sacchi 1998). It represents the heightened integration of the Australian industry with both the North American and now resurgent British cinema – an integration likely to profoundly affect the financing and investment patterns, symbolic content and corporate strategies of Australian cinema. But it is also the 'Australian film' of a director whose previous film – the Brandon Lee vehicle, *The Crow* (1994) – influenced subsequent international cinema. Proyas is one of only a handful of Australian film directors (George Miller, Gillian Armstrong and Jane Campion also come to mind) whose films have had and are capable of having this impact.

As Proyas' first feature since *The Crow*,[5] *Dark City* is a sci-fi film dealing with memory and parallel worlds in an ambience recalling the great German expressionist films of the 1920s such as Fritz Lang's *Metropolis* (1926). Its claim to significance lies not only in its treatment of the sci-fi genre and its astonishing art direction but also in its pioneering of a range of production and post-production practices later put to work on *The Matrix* (1999) to such good effect. On the assumption that today's special effects are tomorrow's ordinary filmmaking practice, the production strategies and technologies of this film are likely to change medium-budget filmmaking (Nicholls 1984, p. 12).

There is no evidence on-screen that *Dark City* could be set in Australia or that it is an Australian film. This is a filmmaking that happens to occur in Australia. But neither, despite the city in question being a 'noir American city', is it an 'American film'. It is a city of the imagination, not any particular city but 'all cities' (Ebert 1998). As such it provides one indication of a possible trend in Australian filmmaking as it embraces studio production – a plethora of stories that address their own artificial and fictive story spaces. Australian cinema is being loosened from a storytelling that needs, almost reflexively, to be 'true to the actual' (of a specifically Australian experience) and instead becomes one that is 'true to the probable' (of a broader [post-]modern imaginary). It also marks a decisive shift as filmmaking in Australia becomes less synonymous with an Australian filmmaking just as Australian locations become less synonymous with Australia, as Sydney becomes, in *Dark City* and the *The Matrix*, a 'generic city'. With *Dark City* Australian filmmaking is being reshaped, as digital production and post-production practices lead it away from its longstanding location base and towards studios and post-production models of filmmaking and television.

Writing in 1998, Toby Miller (p. 175) argued that:

> The Gold Coast Studio set up a third tier of Australian-based screen production in addition to notions of culturally valuable film culture and commercially driven film industrialism – a floating multinational space that some accuse of promoting 'cultural imperialism'. It makes money for investors and keeps already trained personnel in work, but textuality and industrial impact are other questions.

Miller went on to claim that such productions do not 'represent' Australia so much as 'investment patterns' (179). Certainly *Dark City* is part of an increasing corporate integration of the various audiovisual markets under the impact of globalisation. It is also part of a trend of increasing 'foreign production and international co-production' (AFC and FFC 1999, p. 6). This trend has increasingly attracted the attention of politicians who are drawn to the employment, economic multiplier effects and technological and technical capacity-development these productions represent.

But *Dark City* is more than the 'investment patterns' which have seen footloose international productions coming to Australia to tap domestic film industry capacity and creativity, take advantage of exchange rate differences between Australia and the USA, and meet the desire of senior creative personnel (like Baz Luhrmann, Gillian Armstrong and George Miller) to make films out of their native country. Films like *Dark City* call out for a more expansive interpretation that gives them serious recognition as both Australian films and as an Australian contribution to an English language culture shared in Australasia, USA, UK and beyond (see O'Regan and Venkatasawmy 1998).

The Australian in *Dark City* and *Babe* (Chris Noonan, 1995) is not so much an intrinsic identity as a way of composing culture: a take on Shakespeare as in Luhrmann's *Romeo + Juliet*, a reformulation of the sci-fi film as in *Dark City*. These films mark the extent to which Australian cinema is becoming increasingly integrated – albeit as a minor part of – into a broader Anglophone and world cinema. Sydney in turn is part of an emerging map of international production centres with significant filmmaking capacity and critical mass within the English language – a junior partner to London, Los Angeles and New York; and a kind of sister city to Vancouver and Toronto. *Dark City* confirms Robert Sklar's observation that Australian cinema is losing its 'clear delineation as a national cinema'; instead 'its achievements would be regarded as individual rather than national' (1993, p. 502). It also indicates that Australian cinema is in some respects no longer as separated from Hollywood, as the international integration implicit in both the Fox and the Warners Roadshow studios affects the heartland of Australian production (see Langley and Colbert 1997). The boundary between the Australian self and the American other is becoming blurred, raising the question as to whether the category 'Australian film' is now the best category to capture filmmaking in Australia.

Head On and *Dark City* provide a way of answering the question of Australian filmmaking in the first decade of the new millennium. It is a scenario marked by both continuity and change. Proyas and Kokkinos are two of the many Australians of a NES background who have substantially shaped Australian film-making. They join, among others, Carl Schultz (*Careful He Might Hear You*, 1983), Igor Auzins (*We of the Never Never*, 1982), George Miller (*Mad Max*, 1979), Paul Cox (*Man of Flowers*, 1983), Yoram Gross (*Blinky Bill*, 1994), Nadia Tass (*Malcolm*, 1986) and Rolf de Heer (*Bad Boy Bubby*, 1994). Proyas, like the directors of these Australian film classics, was also not making ethnically marked films but rather taking up a 'new world' production strategy.

Kokkinos … background into a topic, conducting a … hose Tsiolkas' novel because it 'provided a … -Australian milieu in which she had grown … So we have a continuation of 'quality' film- … ocus, its 'multicultural', gender and sexual … psychological thriller which suggests an

… ain is nothing less than how we make … In *Head On* the experiment is plotting … ing templates for presenting Australian … : *City* it is visual manipulation software … part of popular art's many genres and … timedia development (advertising) and … *On*, a multicultural filmmaking agenda … resenting them; for *Dark City* a new … and with it a cinema which confuses … nity inherent in cinema to go out and … tage new worlds unseen before.[6]

…nium

… nd strategies which had begun the … ier. There was still the continuing … ange between national film indus- … alian filmmakers and a culturally diverse citizenry. But there was a corresponding attention to the negatives of this international cultural exchange for Australian filmmaking, and a rancorous public debate over Australia's cultural diversity with the rise and fall of Pauline Hanson's One Nation Party and a bitter political debate about multiculturalism and native title.

If there was considerable optimism at the start of the decade that internationalism and cultural diversity could be managed in ways that benefited filmmaking, film culture and the broader Australian society, by the end of the decade there was considerably less optimism that this was possible. The tide of change brought about by industry developments of digitisation, convergence and global integration increasingly threatened the local filmmaking ecology while emerging governmental priorities for the new information and knowledge-based economy threatened to sideline cultural production.

The immediate but insufficient cause for these uncertainties was the election in 1996 of the John Howard-led Liberal and National Party Coalition Government. This change of federal government brought a new set of policy actors close to government and with it new priorities. The policy priority of the Howard Government's first term was principally to wind back both the size and the expectations held of government. (The 1996 National Commission of Audit in Commonwealth Finances recommended that the Howard government wind back the size of the federal government by 10–20 per cent over three years.) With all other sectoral-specific considerations being subordinated to this goal, the Howard Government's first term was experienced as a 'policy free zone' as new policy development was mostly on hold and initiatives were either wound up or continued at static or lower funding levels. The ABC faced substantial budget cuts in the mid-1990s (this was an ABC which had become increasingly important to the drama and documentary sectors over the early 1990s), successful programs such as the Commercial Television Production Fund were wound up and funding declined in real terms for the film funding agencies – the AFC and FFC.

While the Howard Government reaffirmed its support for both the AFC and FFC, there were increasing concerns about levels of funding and a perceived lack of policy leadership. The policy environment was becoming increasingly uncertain with the Productivity Commission (PC 1999a, 2000), an important barometer for long-term policy development, questioning the very foundations of broadcasting regulation. The Commission particularly attacked the policy of *quid pro quo*s underwriting Australian content regulations which had shaped broadcasting regulation and film policy development alike over the 1980s and 1990s (PC 2000, p. 254).

There was substantial agreement as to the major problem facing the film industry and film policy makers – that of making the transition to a more fragmented, diverse and internationally integrated audiovisual system. But there was little agreement on how to maximise the opportunities and minimise the threat these new configurations posed to the local film industry and local content creators more generally.

Interrogating internationalism

The reality of internationalisation replaced the favourable projections of internationalism of the early to mid-1990s. By late 1999 the AFC and FFC were reporting to the federal government that:

> While foreign production and international co-production has risen, Australian production has remained static over the last four years, with a recent downturn in television drama production.
>
> (AFC and FFC 1999, p. 6)

There was, in their estimation, a crisis in domestic production. The filmmaking that happened to be done in Australia was, it seemed, eclipsing Australian film and television series production.

It was not hard to find culprits for this paradox of crisis amidst plenty. A mature US audiovisual marketplace was producing, through its highly developed and mature pay-TV sector, a surfeit of product aimed at the very market niches previously occupied by 'quirky' and 'eccentric' Australian films. Australian films were now competing in the same part of the market as higher budgeted US films. The rise in cinema attendances and cinema rebuilding through the multiplex (which might have been expected to benefit Australian filmmakers) had the reverse effect. Multiplexes advantaged Hollywood blockbuster movies at the expense of smaller Australian movies (Reid 1999). Local share of the Australian box-office declined: the 1999 share of 3 per cent contrasted with the average 1990s share of 6 per cent which was in turn lower than the average share of the 1980s of 12 per cent (AFC 1998, p. 150).

For their part, the maturing multi-channel television markets in Europe were substituting their own local programs for Australian imports, severely diminishing the international market for Australian series and serials. ABC-TV's hit series *SeaChange* (1999–), the highest rating program on ABC-TV, was nearly wound up because of the inability of its producers to secure international sales. For its part a comparatively underdeveloped Australian pay-TV industry was neither of the size nor the capacity to provide Australian content providers with a ready alternative source of production and financing at the higher end of production. (There was some hope for improvement here however as pay-TV interests did help the ABC launch a second series of *SeaChange*!)

Meanwhile the free-to-air television networks – Seven, Nine and Ten – continued to support local production but at levels of investment well below those obtaining in the 1980s. The television networks stabilised, and in some cases reduced, their licence fees for drama and documentary programming with the consequence that as budgets rose, the production industry was getting less from the networks. Indeed the networks increasingly looked to lower budgeted Australian productions to fill quota rather than expanding their commissioning of television drama. At the same time the costs of their international programming increased. Furthermore, there was research indicating that youth were more engaged and interested in American drama series and cinema than in the Australian equivalents. This posed serious long-term problems for a successful local television drama production presence on television schedules (see Bennett, Emmison and Frow 1999, pp. 201–25).

With the Fox and Warners Roadshow studios equipping Australian-based production (at both the high-end feature level and the lower-end television series production) with state-of-the-art digital production facilities, and with the favourable exchange rate between the US and the Australian dollar, the making of films and television series such as *Beastmaster* (1999–) in Australia became more attractive. While never approaching the Canadian level of foreign film production, Australian studios, locations and facilities were nonetheless able to attract a steady stream of 'runaway productions' (productions developed for US release but filmed in another country) and international co-productions (Monitor Company 1999). Over the decade the interest in co-productions with Australian partners also shifted from movies to television series – partly reflecting the more integrated circumstances of global television drama production. With the co-production arrangements having been developed to facilitate movies rather than television series and tele-movies investment, industry concerns were raised about the consequences for domestic television drama series of long-running series like *Beastmaster* being produced under co-production arrangements (AFC and FFC 1999, p. 25). Although it was difficult to specify a relation between increasing international activity and declining local activity in the context of stagnant domestic production, film production interests and critics increasingly made such connections.

Internationalism looked threatening from another direction after the 1998 High Court decision on New Zealand content counting as Australian content on Australian television screens (Kaufman 1998, pp. 3–4). Domestic content regulations, it seemed, could no longer be taken for granted. This decision was the culmination of a series of court cases brought on by New Zealand producers using the Closer Economic Relations (CER) trade treaty to challenge the exclusionary nature of the Australian Broadcasting Authority's Australian content regulations (see Given 1997; Lealand 1997; Leiboff 2000). While the court decision generated considerable disquiet from Australian film and television production interests, who forecast the 'dumping' of New Zealand programming on Australian network television to make up 'cheap' content points, the immediate result of the expanded regulations was neither an increase in New Zealand production nor any evidence of dumping. What the court cases did do, however, was set the Australian and New Zealand film and television industries against each other. It also set the Australian industry against sections of its own Liberal-National Party Coalition Government which was, at times, openly sympathetic to the New Zealand case.

But the most significant disquiet centred on the High Court's decision to subordinate culture and cultural regulation to the disciplines of economic regulation represented by the international trade and investment treaties system (Leiboff 2000; Britton 1997). As Nick Herd, Executive Director of the Screen Producers Association of Australia, posed the issue:

> Fundamental is the ability of Australia to determine how it creates its own cultural identity on television. This has been government policy since television began and is the basis of Australian content regulation ... Removing a requirement for Australian culture on Australian television screens opens the way for increased foreign programming on Australian television services.
>
> (Herd 1998, p. 24)

The New Zealanders in this play were dangerous for the precedent they were setting, a legal precedent which might be later taken up by the Americans seeking to expand their own access to Australian markets (see Britton 1997).

Further compounding this sense that the ground rules of the industry were changing were the increasing linkages between Australian and international production companies. Through alliances and takeovers, prominent local producers such as Artists Services, Yoram Gross Productions and Grundy became integrated into the global operations of Granada, EM-TV and Pearson's respectively. The local production industry, which had been almost exclusively a locally controlled sector, became increasingly divided between those who were attached to major international production companies and those who were not. Indeed the unattached local production companies felt under increasing threat and in some cases called for special consideration (including priority access to funds) *vis-à-vis* their international counterparts.

This trend on the part of the local production industry was simply part of a larger trend for Australian media and telecommunications to become decidedly more international in ownership and control. The second telecommunications carrier, Optus, is now part of the larger Cable and Wireless telecommunications group, the Ten Network has as a substantial shareholder Canwest, and Rupert Murdoch's News Corporation is involved in both Australian pay-TV and, of course, Fox Studios. These international involvements inevitably raised the issue of Australia becoming a secondary, subsidiary market for larger international players with unknown consequences for local content creators.

Film and television globalisation was also integrating film personnel more quickly and more extensively into the international industry. The industry became increasingly locked into first-time director-writer auteurs. The first feature films of successful directors became a means for them to quickly develop international careers at the expense of staying to develop the local industry. (But some, like Bill Bennett, came back to Australia burnt by their international experiences.) This was in stark contrast to earlier periods when both Bruce Beresford and Peter Weir, for example, made a succession of Australian films in the 1970s and early 1980s before embarking on their distinguished international careers.

But perhaps the most critical factor in film and TV globalisation was the prospect of significant long-term changes brought about by expanding audio-visual services with unpredictable consequences for ownership, control and programming. Several developments were pressing in: the long-awaited take-off of pay-TV in its various forms, the advent of digital television, the development of new satellite and internet-based TV services and the explosion of transactional services. These seemed not only to be segmenting but also destabilising the previously ordered sequences of domestic release and consumption. Many of these new services were based on several models: a user-pays, a hybrid of user-pays and advertiser support and a hybrid of service types as in datacasting (which links television, the internet and the telephone). As such they represented the emergence of television as a private good alongside its already existing aspect as a free-to-air public good where normal commercial transactions – parallel to buying a cinema ticket or a book – had not been applicable. Previously television had relied on the advertising support of both the private and public sectors (in the case of the commercial TV networks and SBS), or consolidated tax revenues (for the ABC and SBS).

With pay-TV and emerging pay-per-view TV, television was becoming less a national and more an international medium. In their turn digital television, multi-channel marketplaces and varieties of platform for the delivery of audio-visual content promised to change decisively the economics of local production and challenge the adequacy of existing support and regulatory structures. The problem facing cultural policy and the domestic production industry alike was well encapsulated by the European Union's High Level Group on Audiovisual Policy:

> At the heart of the matter is the question of whether the predicted explosion in demand for audiovisual material will be met by European productions or by imports. The European audiovisual market is already fragmented, due to linguistic and cultural diversity. The danger is that the channel proliferation brought about by digital technology will lead to further market fragmentation, making it even more difficult for European producers to compete with American imports.
>
> (High Level Group on Audiovisual Policy 1998, p. 6)

This question, with its very real consideration that local content creators might not be able to take advantage of an explosion of demand, increasingly haunted film policy makers and filmmakers in Australia. While all could identify the problem as one of maximising the opportunities and minimising the threats to local industries and local content creators of a more diverse, fragmented and expanding audiovisual industry, there were no clear ideas either nationally or internationally about the best instruments for delivering a workable solution. All that seemed certain was that the old instruments, like domestic content regulations, might no longer work. With more audiovisual services seeming to compromise the capacity of content regulation to function in a fragmented marketplace, internationalisation looked to be threatening, not supportive of, a local filmmaking ecology.

Cultural development versus industry development

The coincidence of purpose and focus among filmmakers, critics, policy makers and politicians that marked the first part of the 1990s was fragmenting into two competing and increasingly irreconcilable policy priorities for government. The traditional priority of securing domestic production capacity was increasingly at odds with an industry development priority of expanding audiovisual services to facilitate Australia's transition to a 'new economy' nation. Industry development, represented by overseas production and co-productions, was counterposed to cultural development, represented by Australian production.

When representatives of the AFC and the FFC appeared before the Productivity Commission (PC) Inquiry into Broadcasting Regulation in late 1999, the PC not only challenged their submission but their industry prognosis (PC 1999b, pp. 984–1007). The PC consistently maintained that the opportunities for content creators in an emerging digital environment characterised by multi-channelling, a developing pay-TV industry, new developments such as datacasting, and the imminent development of alternative online-based platforms for the distribution of content including pay-per-view were such that the production industry should welcome regulatory and industrial change. They should not continue to line up behind the commercial networks in defending the broadcasting *quid pro quo* – which placed them very much at the mercy of the television networks as gate-keepers on the level and variety of program development.

Supporting an open television system characterised by multi-channelling, minimal technological barriers for the entry of new players, the existence of various delivery platforms and a pervasive move towards digitisation and expanded online services, the PC argued that the increase in the number of outlets would provide more scope for content creators and content providers. The PC also challenged the AFC and FFC over their critical comments on co-productions and runaway productions. Operating within an industry development paradigm which foregrounded employment, skills and professional development, capacity-building and foreign investment, the PC welcomed the integration and expansion of audiovisual services including co-productions and runaway productions. Within an industry development perspective the 'Australian film' and 'television program' became simply one of the instruments for industry development rather than an end in itself. What mattered to the PC was the exercising and development of skills and capacity, rather than on *which* productions these capacities and skills were exercised. The PC was operating within an emerging international policy paradigm which constructs the content industries as knowledge industries, and promotes creative industry development through training initiatives and a concern to expand the skills (technological and knowledge) base as a means to remain internationally competitive (CCCWG 1996; DCITA 2000; HLGAVP 1998; HoCSCCMS 1998).

By contrast, both film agencies and the production industry were operating within a cultural development paradigm emphasising a product orientation. They were concerned that industry development priorities could not easily deal with, let alone recognise, the significance to the Australian production industry of the emerging crisis in Australian-initiated production. They saw the local film as an end in itself without which the film industry could not adequately function. They saw the PC's recommendations for deregulation – such as relieving pay-TV of Australian content requirements and permitting the development of multi-channelling – as exacerbating this crisis through undermining the content standard. They were also concerned at the ways this would compromise the *quid pro quo*s at the heart of the Australian audiovisual sector whereby the networks met Australian content obligations and in return received 'protection' from competition. Within their cultural development paradigm the stress was placed on the need to develop a sustainable Australian culture which would allow Australians 'to dream our own dreams, to tell our own stories' and which would be distinct from though clearly connected with the broader international film milieu. Without substantive agreement on how to accomplish a reconciliation between cultural development and industry development, achieving a workable balance between them remains significant unfinished business.

Film and the new economy

A related policy problem zone was the relation between audiovisual services and a 'new economy' marked by digitisation, online services, and the convergence of telecommunications and broadcasting, information and entertainment. The Howard Government, as did its predecessor, talked up the new economy. It conducted reviews into convergence issues, promoted the transition to digitisation, datacasting and other new media, and set up the far-ranging Productivity Commission Broadcasting Inquiry. But as Julian Thomas observes, its policy development hardly matched its rhetoric.

The present Commonwealth government, like earlier governments, speaks endlessly of new media, but has no new media policy. The result is that the Australian economy is internationally identified as 'old economy', with potentially serious consequences for continuing growth. A digital broadcasting policy which rewards a comfortable group of incumbents, prohibits new competition and at the same time forbids a whole range of new services serves only to reinforce the image of a country returning to the protectionist, defensive ethos of an earlier era.

(Thomas 2000, p. 18)

As the 1990s drew to a close the mismatch between public rhetorics and policy actions widened. Thomas' trenchant criticism of the Howard Government's handling of media policy and the PC inquiry's recommendations turned on its digital television decisions over 1998–2000 which had ensconced in a new environment the existing television of privilege. The Howard Government had moved to replicate in the digital environment the existing make-up and character of television services. It continued moratoriums on the development of new commercial television services and prohibited multi-channelling by existing broadcasters. In return those broadcasters were given copious amounts of digital spectrum for both standard and high-definition delivery. It defined datacasting narrowly and worried at it being the vehicle for the provision of television by other means. It did its best to keep telecommunications and broadcasting in their separate regulatory boxes, confining online services to modem and telephone-line related delivery, eschewing the possibilities for the mass extension of internet and online services via the television set. Through these measures it continued to exercise significant control over ordinary transactions in the audio-visual sector.

This was surprising given that the Howard Government's public rhetoric was not that of a non-liberalising conservative government but that of a liberalising forward-looking government. Its 'new economy' strategy paid lip service to a more commercially situated audiovisual sector using varieties of channels and talking up the incentives for private investment in audiovisual production. It also discussed the need for a reshaping of the Australian film milieu such that alternative forms of entry could be provided outside of the more government-defined channels provided by the AFC and FFC. But it failed to meet early expectations that it would develop market-based production incentives to foster production across a variety of audiovisual formats with as far-reaching consequences for production as the 10BA production boom of the 1980s. The Gonski report's (1997, pp. 8–9) major recommendation for a Film Licensed Investment Company scheme as an 'alternative tax proposal' to 10BA and 10B tax incentives designed to 'increase the available investment base for film and television production' ran into early difficulties attracting investors. Likewise the new circumstance of a fragmented and dispersed audiovisual marketplace should have led to a diminishing role for film agencies in standardising a film milieu and capacity building, but this also did not happen.

But it seems inevitable that policy agendas that are at present mostly rhetoric will translate into action over the next decade. A primary concern of communications ministers across the industrialised countries of the late 1990s and beyond is to centralise telecommunications policy issues – information policy, convergence, the information superhighway, e-commerce. As Christina Spurgeon observed:

> the Australian strategy is now to add value to existing stocks of cultural, communications and other forms of national capital and to encourage private investment in infrastructure development on internationally competitive terms. In varying degrees, and in a variety of ways, national governments around the world are pursuing similar developmental paths in the hope that commodity-based economies might be transformed into information economies.
>
> (Spurgeon 1998, p. 26)

Where governments are more interested in developing an internationally competitive information infrastructure, governmental priorities are likely to shift towards the development of a healthy pay-TV sector and the successful uptake of digital television. In Australia, pay-TV and associated cabling is directly connected with telecommunications infrastructure development. Our cable and pay-TV operators are also our telephone companies. One of the consequences of this is that entertainment (pay-TV) and information (telephony, online services) are likely to be joined in pay-TV and through the cabling and telecommunications infrastructure.

While not previously associated with the film industry, the computing and information technology and the telecommunications sectors are now vitally concerned with influencing film and broadcasting policy issues. Prins Ralson, President of the Australian Computer Society (1998, p. 48), suggests that 'the development of our infant digital broadcasting industry is a crucial step for Australia as we seek to position ourselves as a key player in the Information Age'. Daniel Petre and David Harrington concur:

> Our delays in recognising the importance of major paradigm shifts in the media industry – such as colour and pay television – and our lack of preparedness to act upon those shifts has set back Australia's content production by decades, jeopardising our national identity in a global online world. In 1996 Australia is facing another major global media paradigm shift, one even more fundamental than colour or pay television. It involves the global production, dissemination, storage and analysis of digital information over online networks such as the Internet.
>
> (Petre and Harrington 1996, p. 9)

The audiovisual production sector now involves more than filmmakers and television stations: it involves the computing and telecommunications industry. The policy making club is being extended to include powerful new players whose interests are not those familiar to us from the last 30 years of subsidised film-making and the last 40 years of television content regulation. The Howard Government, like the film agencies and the screen producers, is finding it difficult to accommodate these new players and their demands. One likely consequence is that governments may be less interested in the arts than in what might be termed the 'creative industries' – those industries likely to grow out of the marriage of digital technology, design and the audiovisual.

For the better part of two decades influential Australian policy makers, critics, TV proprietors and lobbyists have feared a fragmented and diverse audiovisual media system characterised by abundance and openness. Each felt they had reason to fear it. The incumbents – the national broadcasters, particularly the ABC and the commercial stations and networks – saw new media as upsetting their customary 'ownership' of the television monitor, audiences and the broad-casting policy agenda. Each feared the erosion of their audience base and the pressures this would place upon themselves, their operations and even their very existence in the case of public service broadcasting. Australian content lobbyists worried over the fragmentation of audiovisual services and the pressure this would place upon Australian content provisions. With the progressive erosion of the free-to-air broadcast audience in a multi-channel environment they feared that commercial networks and stations would buck against Australian content provisions. They also confronted new media services for which content provisions were contentious.

In an audiovisual arena apparently dominated by commercial services, cultural critics and lobbyists feared both the loss of diversity and quality and the erosion of non-commercial services. Cultural critics also feared the disappearance of the 'electronic hearth' around which 'we would all gather' as segment-defined media usurped the position of society-forming media (see Turow 1997, p. 3). They feared for society itself as the polity seemed likely to descend into a rancorous disputation driven in part by the very logic of segmentation.

There was always an added national twist to this logic in Australia in that tele-vision's 'electronic hearth' was also a space for an Australian identity. With such a cacophony of voices available over cable, satellite, the internet and the free-to-air services, Australian voices could become progressively marginalised and in some cases disappear altogether. It seemed as if the Australian voice and identity was becoming doubly or trebly marginalised and relegated. As Phillip Adams argued in 1995, '[t]hese days the notions of national identity' on which a national cinema depended seem 'doomed' in the wake of 'global culture (still a euphem-ism for American culture)'.

With such bleak prospects for the future it is, perhaps, no wonder that procrastination has been the single most evident policy prescription for new media in Australia. By contrast, Eli Noam bluntly welcomes a media future based on a mix of different forms of television and distribution systems:

> Except for unusual events, the electronic hearth around which entire societies congregated nightly will be no more. But this communal experience of constant information sharing has been only an ephemeral episode in the history of mankind. It clashes with a more individualistic media past and a more information-rich future. It is a system based on scarcity of content production and scarcity of conduits. As these conditions change, the structure of television evolves ... and though the path will be full of new problems, in time we shall experience a television of openness, open to the access of new voices – commercial and nonprofit – open across frontiers, and open to viewer choices ... That is, video will become an everyday event, and devoid of its present special status as the national integrator that leads to anxieties over its control. And it will flourish without cultural high priests and public officials guarding its entrances, just as print communication does today.
>
> (Noam 1991, p. 344)

An unsettling multiculturalism

> The Asian currency crisis, the Wik ruling, the republic debate and the coming Olympics are all contributing to a growing complexity and disorder in the public political discourse on Australian ideologies of nationhood.
>
> (Thomas 1999, p. 202)

Controversies over Australia's cultural and political self-definitions in the late 1990s made it increasingly difficult to project an open-ended and optimistic multiculturalism. By the end of the decade there was nothing like the consensus cultural politics which had earlier made multiculturalism and an international, Asia-centred orientation a settled and relatively uncontentious politics. Government members who in Opposition had been critical of Labor's immigration, multiculturalism and Indigenous policy now found themselves running those policies in government. The strategies of multicultural and cultural diversity sponsored through the public purse came under public scrutiny.[7] At the same time, the Asian crisis of 1997–99 turned the much heralded Asian twenty-first century from Australia's opportunity to Australia's liability, putting pressure on 'our dollar', 'our economic growth', 'our immigration program' and further discrediting Labor's 'social engineering'.

Such civic rancour over multiculturalism, native title, the stolen generation, political correctness and One Nation inevitably repositioned understandings of cultural diversity. Cultural critics spoke of a new philistinism and racism as the commitment to multiculturalism seemed weakened (Stratton 1998; Hage 1998). Some, like the ethnic lobbies and Aborigines and Islanders, tried unsuccessfully to shame the government. The Keating period was looked back on with nostalgia by intellectuals.[8] Indeed when the Howard government finally moved to re-endorse multiculturalism as a policy of state in 1999 (National Multicultural Advisory Council 1999, pp. 1–4), its emphases had shifted. It was no longer promoted as delivering a cultural assertiveness to newly empowered groups as it was in the Keating years, rather the focus was on 'social harmony' – building bridges and developing solidarities among communities. Multiculturalism had become an intercommunal policy developed to build a tolerant and open society. Rights were, of course, still foregrounded, but so too were obligations and needs.

Multiculturalism is just one among a number of instruments for organising population cleavages into grids of gender, sexual orientation, English speaking and non-English speaking background, ethnicity, race, Aboriginality, the regions and disability for policy purposes. Increasingly, however, Australian governments are projecting populations for policy programs through understandings of social formations which connect demographics to geography. Geo-demographic techniques are being used to pinpoint disadvantaged districts within cities and regional areas to provide services to the district defined now as a community. In as much as people of different ethnic backgrounds are aggregated together into these socio-economically defined communities, this can be understood as a limited return to social class ways of comprehending populations and their interests. Certainly it is recognising disadvantage differently than say recognising income disparity between Vietnamese or Greek–Australians and the Australian-born. In this governments are catching up with the more fine-grained analysis of populations emerging out of marketing. Here 'the new portraits of society that advertisers and media personnel invoke involve the blending of income, generation, marital status, and gender into a soup of geographical and psychological profiles they call "lifestyles"' (Turow 1997, p. 3). Governments are increasingly recognising these 'lifestyles' so as to better target and deliver services to geo-demographically dispersed populations. Their political campaigning already works with these instruments, which permit political campaigns to address a culturally diverse public. To what extent will geo-demographic 'cleavages' supplement and in some cases supplant existing and more settled cultural cleavages of gender, ethnicity and race? Will they also become instruments for identity-formation? What will their consequences be for filmmaking and criticisms alike?

Conclusion

To be able to identify the processes is one thing, to know the outcomes or indeed the appropriate policy settings is another. Some things will remain the same.

A critical vocabulary which was once central to government and which stresses post-national, critical multicultural forms will continue to structure a quasi-oppositional, quasi-official filmmaking and critical milieu. But equally filmmaking and film policy development are in significant transition. Internationalisation, convergence and digitisation are transforming how politicians, policy makers, filmmakers and commentators understand filmmaking and film policy. Perhaps the rhetorical emphases of the present are the necessary prelude to a round of policy development more attuned and more responsive to these new circumstances. (If it is not, then what we have are reports like that of the Productivity Commission and the Convergence Review which are disconnected from actual policy development.) One thing is certain: we can no longer quarantine the filmmaking milieu from either the other parts of the communications industry or the other parts of government.

Most fundamentally, in a slow accretive way, the place, character and shape of Australian production, local content on television and its regulation, and public assessment of the audiovisual sector's performance will change to suit an increasingly fragmented, diverse and abundant audiovisual sector. Multiple changes in production, distribution and reception will make their imprint on both Australian filmmaking and policy development over the decade.

So too there should be changes to the contemporary lack of enthusiasm for *structurally* integrating the already close trans-Tasman connections. The enormous changes in New Zealand broadcasting from the late 1980s (see Lealand 2000) have created significant and ungrasped opportunities for integrated Australasian policy and industry development. International trends in Europe are towards the *regional* alignment of film and television policies. This includes reciprocation in content regimes and has the activist goal of taking advantage of Europe-wide synergies. With Europe taking cooperation among neighbours to new levels, Australasian film and broadcasting policy needs to work at realising greater structural integration so that producers, distributors and exhibitors can take advantage of an integrated market of 21 million. It has the framework of co-productions and an already substantial cultural exchange and cross-Tasman trade to build on. Such policy development also makes historical sense in terms of the ANZAC tradition; cultural sense as the peoples of Australia and New Zealand 'are perhaps as close as the peoples of any two countries can be' (cited in Given 1997, p. 38); multicultural sense as the diverse people of New Zealand make up a substantial component of Australia's immigrant population; and regional sense in terms of the consolidation and extension of longstanding regional arrangements.

The rancour and division are here to stay. If anything they represent Australia's emergence as a society, rather than a people. Our very multicultural character when coupled with our even more significant 'lifestyle' diversity perhaps demands that it should be so. Of the 40 or so lifestyle clusters identified in the PRIZM – Potential Rating Index for Zip Markets – analysis in the US, there is one that sticks in my mind. It is called 'shotguns and pickup trucks'. It is characterised by 'small rural towns with more mobile homes than the norm, more large families with school-age children, and more blue-collar workers with only a high school education' (Turow 1997, p. 47). When I read this I can't help thinking of Gympie (not far from where I was born) and the rise and fall of One Nation.

Notes

1 A survey undertaken by the Screen Actors Guild of America showed that 20 per cent of roles go to so-called 'minority' performers in TV dramas (*The Alliance* 1996, p. 3).
2 While the incoming Howard government explicitly distanced itself from *Creative Nation*, it nonetheless kept intact many of its programs and priorities.
3 Kokkinos cites her involvement as beginning in 1990 when she 'entered a program organised by Women in Film and Television' (Barber 1998, p. 5).
4 As Mousoulis (1999) describes it: 'In the past 20 years, 4% of all features made in this country were directed by Greeks. If we look at the figures for the past 5 years, however, this figure jumps to 7%. The Greek NESB (non-English speaking background) population is around 3%, so one would have to say that the representation is more than fair.'
5 Proyas' previous Australian-based feature was *Spirits of the Air, Gremlins of the Clouds* (1989).
6 *Dark City*, however, was not the success expected. Its successor, *The Matrix*, achieved that blockbuster status. For its part, *Head On*, with a more limited opening and carefully organised release, achieved a modest success.
7 Multicultural and cultural diversity strategies were contested through books and magazine articles which provided the rancorous reaction to what were now termed 'black armband' views of history and society: see the regular columns by Michael Duffy in the *Australian* and Peter Walsh in the *Australian Financial Review* over 1997–98 and also Paul Sheehan's bestselling book, *Among the Barbarians* (1998).
8 For example a normally circumspect Tony Bennett (1998, p. 232) couldn't resist this footnote in his new book: 'The suit should surely now be an object for sartorial longing in Australia where its urbanising and modernising associations have been underscored in the transition from Keating's finely cut Italian tailoring to John Howard's cavalry-twill racism.'

Guide to further reading

The literature in this area can be broadly divided into (1) film policy and industry analysis related works and (2) screen commentary seeking to establish broader trends in Australian filmmaking to better explain the films produced and their context of production. The policy-focused literature is sometimes also available on the internet – relevant sites for policy documents and reports are listed below. For discussion of contemporary trends in Australian cinema exhibition see Scott McQuire's *Maximum Vision: Large-Format and Special Venue Cinema* (Sydney and Brisbane: AFC and Australian Key Centre for Cultural and Media Policy (CMP), 2000) and Reid, with Berman and Curtis (1999). Reid has also documented the outlook of the film production industry in the early 1990s with *From Longshots to Favourites* (Sydney, AFC, 1993) and again at the end of the 1990s with *More Long Shots: Australian Cinema Successes in the 90s* (Sydney and Brisbane: AFC and CMP, 2000). Covering policy issues in the late 1990s is the AFC and FFC's *Report on the Film and Television Production Industry* (1999) and Gonski's *Review* (1997). A valuable overview and source of film industry data and analysis is the AFC series *Get the Picture* (1998). Marcia Langton's *'Well I heard it on the radio and I saw it on the television …'* (Sydney: AFC, 1993) is still the best discussion of film policy issues relating to Aborigines and Torres Strait Islanders. For a discussion of the impact of digitisation on Australian production see Aisbett and Jonker (1997) and Scott McQuire, *Crossing the Digital Threshold* (Brisbane and Sydney: AFC and CMP, 1998). For a discussion of the Australian audiovisual industry in the context of broadcasting regulation see the Productivity Commission's *Broadcasting* (2000); and in relation to convergence see DCITA (1999 and 2000). The trade journal *Encore* and the Australian and New Zealand film and TV industry newsletter *filmnet* (www.filmnet.org.au) provide regular news and overviews of industry activity and policy; for its part *Cinema Papers* (1974–2001) served as the journal of record with its interviews of creative personnel and reviews of contemporary film.

Critical commentary on contemporary film and broadcasting industry policy can be found most centrally in *Media International Australia*; commentary on the relation between films and their production contexts is regularly developed in *Metro*; cultural studies treatments of film-related issues can be found in the screen-cultural studies journal *Continuum* and occasionally in *UTS Review*. Deb Verhoeven's edited collection *Twin Peaks: Australian and New Zealand Feature Films* (Melbourne: Damned Publishing, 1999) and O'Regan (1996) place film within a policy and industry context. Albert Moran's edited *Film Policy: International, National and Regional Perspectives* (London: Routledge, 1996) does the same for film policy's international contexts. Policy issues are also discussed in the context of filmmaking careers in Raffaele Caputo and Geoff Burton's *Second Take: Australian Filmmaker's Talk* (Sydney: Allen & Unwin, 1999) and Virginia Wexman's edited *Jane Campion Interviews* (Jackson: University Press of Mississippi, 1999). Stuart Cunningham and Elizabeth Jacka's *Australian Television and International Mediascapes* (Cambridge: Cambridge University Press, 1996) surveys the place of Australian television on international television horizons and discusses its consequences for local production. For an earlier discussion of issues related to cultural policy and content regulation see Cunningham, *Framing Culture: Criticism and Policy in Australia* (Sydney: Allen & Unwin, 1992).

🖱 Websites

www.afc.gov.au
  Australian Film Commission
www.ffc.gov.au
  Film Finance Corporation
www.dcita.gov.au
  Department of Communications, Information Technology and the Arts
www.pc.gov.au
  Productivity Commission
www.aba.gov.au
  Australian Broadcasting Authority
www.filmnet.org.au
  filmnet, the Australian and New Zealand film and TV industry newsletter.
www.sensesofcinema.com   www.latrobe.edu.au/www/screeningthepast
  On-line journals, *Senses of Cinema* and *Screening the Past*, which provide critical
  discussion of cinema, including Australian cinema, and of film and broadcasting
  history.

References

Adams, Phillip (1995) 'Introduction' in James Sabine (ed.) *A Century of Australian Cinema*,
  Port Melbourne: Reed Books, pp.vii–xi.
Aisbett, Kate, and E. Jonker (1997) *Talking Digital: Impact of Digital Technology on Film
  and Television Creative Teams*, Sydney: AFTRS Research Department.
Alliance, The (1996) 'Quest for hidden indigenous talent' and 'Colour blind casting – what
  about Ernie Dingo as Mr Darcy?', *The Alliance* July, p. 3.
Ang, Ien (1996) 'The Asian woman in Australian multiculturalism', *Feminist Review* 52
  (Spring), pp. 36–49.
Australian Film Commission (1998) *Get the Picture: Essential Data on Australian Film,
  Television, Video and New Media*, Sydney: Australian Film Commission.
Australian Film Commission and Film Finance Corporation (1999) *Report on the Film and
  Television Production Industry*, prepared in response to a request by the Minister for
  the Arts and the Centenary of Federation, the Hon. Peter McGauran MP, Sydney,
  5 November 1999.
Barber, Lynden (1998) 'Reel women', *Weekend Australian* April 4–6, Review pp. 25–6.
Barber, Lynden and Marco Sacchi (1998) 'Shadow player', *Weekend Australian* 16–17
  May, Magazine pp. 32–4.
Bennett, Tony (1998) *Culture: A Reformer's Science*, Sydney: Allen & Unwin.
Bennett, Tony, Michael Emmison and John Frow (1999) *Accounting for Tastes: Australian
  Everyday Cultures*, Cambridge: Cambridge University Press.
Bilcock, Jill and Roger Savage (1998) 'AFI Conversations on Film: Jill Bilcock and Roger
  Savage on the making of Baz Luhrmann's *Romeo and Juliet*', *Metro* 113/114, pp. 20–4.
Britton, Anne (1997) 'True Blue takes on Blue Sky', *Media International Australia* 83,
  February, pp. 40–5.
Burnett, Ron (1996) 'The national question in Quebec and its impact on Canadian

cultural policy' in Albert Moran (ed.) *Film Policy: International, National and Regional Perspectives*, London: Routledge, pp. 249–61.

Canadian Content and Culture Working Group (1996) *Ensuring a Strong Canadian Presence on the Information Highway*, Report to Advisory Council on the Information Highway.

Collins, Felicity (1999) 'Bringing the ancestors home: dislocating white masculinity in *Floating Life, Radiance* and *Vacant Possession*' in Deb Verhoeven (ed.) *Twin Peeks: Australian & New Zealand Feature Films*, Melbourne: Damned Publishing, pp. 107–18.

Cutler & Company (1994) *Commerce in Content: Building Australia's International Future in Interactive Mutlimedia Markets*, A Report for the Department of Industry Science and Technology, CSIRO, and the Broadband Services Expert Group, Canberra, September.

Department of Communication and the Arts (1994) *Creative Nation: Commonwealth Cultural Policy*, Canberra: Commonwealth of Australia.

Department of Communications, Information Technology and the Arts (1999) *Convergence Review: Issues Paper*, Canberra: DCITA.

— (2000) *Convergence Report*, Canberra: DCITA.

Ebert, Roger (1998) '*Babe: Pig in the City*', *Chicago Sun-Times* 25 November.

Gibson, Ross (1992) *South of the West: Postcolonialism and the Narrative Construction of Australia*, Bloomington and Indianapolis: Indiana University Press.

Given, Jock (1997) 'Judiciary 1, Executive 0', *Media International Australia* 83, pp. 38–40.

Gonski, David (1997) *Review of Commonwealth Assistance to the Film Industry*, Canberra: DCA.

Hage, Ghassan (1998) *White Nation: Fantasies of White Supremacy in a Multicultural Society*, Sydney: Pluto Press.

Herd, Nick (1998) 'Superficial view of TV', *Australian Financial Review* 13 May, Letters, p. 24.

High Level Group on Audiovisual Policy (1998) *The Digital Age: European Audiovisual Policy*, Brussels: European Commission.

House of Commons Select Committee on Culture, Media and Sport (1998) *Fourth Report: The Multimedia Revolution* (HC 520–21).

Kaufman, Tina (1998) 'High Court decision opens door to NZ television programs', *Metro* 115, pp. 3–4.

Langley, Kim and Mary Colbert (1997) 'Hollywood Down Under', *Vogue Australia* 10 October, pp. 56–68.

Lealand, Geoff (1997) 'A fair suck of the sav: Project Blue Sky and the New Zealand case', *Media International Australia* 83, February, pp. 46–50.

— (2000) 'Regulation – what regulation? Cultural diversity and local content in New Zealand television', *Media International Australia* 95, May, pp. 77–89.

Lieboff, Marett (2000) 'The reconfiguration of culture post-Project Blue Sky: culture as a service in broadcasting law'. *Media International Australia* 95, May, pp. 63–76.

Manktelow, Nicole (1998) 'Special FX steal the show', *Australian* 31 March 1998, p. 42.

Martin, Adrian (1994) 'Ghosts ... of a national cinema', *Cinema Papers* April, pp. 14–15.

Miller, Toby (1998) *Technologies of Truth: Cultural Citizenship and the Popular Media*, Minneapolis: University of Minnesota Press.

Monitor Company (1999) *US Runaway Film and Television Production Study Report*, Los Angeles: Directors Guild of America and Screen Actors Guild.

Moran, Albert (1998) *Copycat TV: Globalisation, Program Formats and Cultural Identity,* Luton: University of Luton Press.

Mousoulis, Bill (1999) 'Is your film language Greek? Some thoughts on Greek-Australian film-makers', *Senses of Cinema* 1, December www.sensesofcinema.com/contents/00/1/greek.html

National Commission of Audit into Commonwealth Finances (1996) *Report of the National Audit Commission,* Canberra: AGPS.

National Multicultural Advisory Council (1999) *Australian Multiculturalism for a New Century: Towards Inclusiveness,* Canberra: Ausinfo.

Nicholls, P. (1984) *Fantastic Cinema: An Illustrated Survey,* London: Ebury Press.

Noam, Eli (1991) *Television in Europe,* New York: Oxford University Press.

O'Regan, Tom (1996) *Australian National Cinema,* London and New York: Routledge.

O'Regan, Tom and Rama Venkatasawmy (1998) 'Only one day at the beach', *Metro* 117, pp. 16–28.

Petre, Daniel and David Harrington (1996) *The Clever Country?: Australia's Digital Future,* Sydney: Lansdowne Publishing.

Productivity Commission (1999a) *Broadcasting,* Draft Report, Canberra: Ausinfo.

— (1999b) *Transcript of Proceedings at Sydney on Monday, 6 December 1999,* Melbourne: Productivity Commission.

— (2000) *Broadcasting,* Report no. 11, Canberra: Ausinfo.

Ralson, Prins (1998) 'Consumer misses out again', *Australian* 7 April, p. 48.

Reid, Mary Anne with assistance from Diana Berman and Rosemary Curtis (1999) *Distributing Australian Films: A Survey of Current Market Conditions and Distributors' Perceptions,* Sydney: Marketing Branch of the Australian Film Commission.

Roxburgh, Mark (1997) 'Clara Law's *Floating Life* and Australian identity', *Metro* 110, pp. 3–6.

Sheehan, Paul (1998) *Among the Barbarians,* Sydney: Random House.

Sklar, Robert (1993) *Film: An International History of the Medium,* London: Thames & Hudson.

Spurgeon, Christina (1998) 'National culture, communications and the information economy', *Media International Australia* 87, May, pp. 23–34.

Stratton, Jon (1998) *Race Daze: Australia In Identity Crisis,* Sydney: Pluto Press.

Taylor, Ella (1995) 'Creating havoc in Hollywood', *New Woman* July, pp. 78–83.

Thomas, Julian (2000) 'It's later than you think: the Productivity Commission's Broadcasting Inquiry and beyond', *Media International Australia* 95, May, pp. 9–18.

Thomas, Mandy (1999) *Dreams in the Shadows: Vietnamese-Australian Lives in Transition,* Sydney: Allen & Unwin.

Turow, Joseph (1997) *Breaking up America: Advertisers and the New Media World,* Chicago: University of Chicago Press.

Wark, McKenzie (1992) 'Speaking trajectories: Meaghan Morris, antipodean theory and Australian cultural studies', *Cultural Studies* 6, 3, pp. 433–48.

Chapter 2

Globalisation, Regionalisation and Australianisation in Music: Lessons from the Parallel Importing Debate

David Rowe

Introduction: Oz music and the big six

Australia, formed as a white settler nation in the Asian-Pacific region at the turn of the twentieth century, has never been afforded the degree of cultural insularity that its geographical isolation from the centres of Western corporate cultural capitalism would suggest. First, imperial Britain and, later, the aggressively entrepreneurial dream factories of the USA, have had a deep influence on Australian cultural values and institutions. It is not surprising, then, that in the field of music, as in film, literature, multi-media and other areas of cultural production, a forceful culturally nationalist current runs through institutional and public discourse (Breen 1993; Hayward 1992; Walker 1996). It is critical of the way in which a strong, often dominant non-Australian organisational hegemony in areas like production, distribution and ownership of intellectual property constitutes continuing cultural imperialism or neo-colonisation. The result is seen to be the retardation of the development of the Australian cultural industries and of a strong, confident and non-derivative national culture (Turner 1994). This position is opposed by arguments that local culture is conservative and staid without outside influence and that local audiences should be allowed to choose their cultural fare without the patrician imposition of edifying texts (Docker 1991). Furthermore, it is asserted that the wealth of contemporary nations is dependent on the free circulation of financial and cultural capital, so that medium-sized, export-oriented economies like Australia need foreign investment and can ill afford to be seen as inward-looking and protectionist (Rowe 1998).

These current debates – which are by no means unprecedented – are taking place against a backdrop of global change which, according to Lash and Urry (1994, p. 123), has seen the cultural industries emerge not as an idiosyncratic reflection of major trends in production, but as the very model for contemporary economic exchange and organisational form, where the 'irreducible core is the exchange of finance by a given culture firm for a bundle of intellectual property rights'. They further point out that 'there is no economic sector for which rights are more important than the music industry' (135). The music industry around the world has witnessed, among other developments, the realignment and reshaping of multinational music corporations and of independent music companies (Negus 1992); the intensified globalisation of popular and other forms of music (Robinson, Buck and Cuthbert 1991); convergence with other cultural forms such as sport (Rowe 1995); the emergence of the 'contra imperial flow' of so-called 'world music' (Mitchell 1996); and the development of new digital media technologies which problematise musical authorship and its associated moral and economic rights (Jones 1992), with one technological apparatus in particular, the internet, now threatening to disrupt the current global order of musical production, distribution and exchange. Of particular importance for this chapter are the challenges posed to the territorial regulation of copyright represented by trade liberalisation (Stewart, Tawfik and Irish 1994). The cultural and economic value of music making within individual countries and its international exchange guarantees that the various rights associated with it will be vigorously contested.

In the case of the Australian music industry, between 85 and 90 per cent of the trade in recorded music is currently controlled by the subsidiaries of five multinational corporations whose head offices are located elsewhere: Germany's Bertelsmann Music Group (BMG), Britain's Thorn EMI (EMI), Holland's N.V. Philips (Polygram), Japan's CBS (Sony), and the USA's Time-Warner (WEA), with the sixth controlled by an Australian-born US national whose parent company is based in the United States – Rupert Murdoch's News Corporation (Festival Records). It might be expected, then, that the 'battle lines' over foreign-owned oligopolies and industry reform would be clearly drawn. The fractious debate over changes to Australian copyright legislation over the last decade or so has shown, however, that the pattern of alliances and antagonisms is surprisingly complex and contradictory. For example, those opposed to the relaxation of music import restrictions in Australia have included the avowedly radical rock star Peter Garrett of Midnight Oil; the patently reactionary One Nation Party's Pauline Hanson; 'disgraced' Senator Mal Colston; the largest Australian independent record company, Shock Records; the Australian Record Industry Association (ARIA); all 'Big Six' record companies; the Australian

Labor Party since May 1995, in government and in opposition; and the United States Government. Those in favour of change have included the Liberal-National Coalition Government (in power since March 1996); the former Australian Labor Party Government between 1992 and April 1995; the Australian Consumers' Association (ACA); the Australian Competition and Consumer Commission (ACCC); and some independent record companies, retailers and music lawyers.

The main bone of contention has been the practice of parallel importing, which has been described by one opponent as the 'disemboweling [sic] of the music industry' (Tripp 1997a). In brief, parallel importing legally permits licence holders in one country to exercise their intellectual property rights by selling their cultural goods in another. In the case of recorded music, this means that compact discs and other traded musical products can be sold directly into the Australian market in competition with the local licence holders. For those opposed to this practice, the outcome is inevitably the swamping of the local music industry by cheap and/or 'pirated' (that is, illegally produced) imports leading to the decline and even destruction of the local music scene. For those in favour, it means ending the exploitation of music consumers by preventing restrictive trade practices that advantage local licence holders (who are mostly the subsidiaries of foreign-owned multinational corporations) by sustaining artificially high prices. While the battle lines over the practice of parallel importing are well drawn, the arguments, politics and motives apparent in each opposing camp are rather less clear cut.

This chapter takes the long running and perplexing issue of parallel importation in the Australian music territory as a useful point of entry for the analysis of the influence of globalism, regionalism and nationalism in the Australian music 'scene'. In so doing it will examine the tensions and contradictions between the ideas of free cultural trade, territorial copyright protection, regional governance and national cultural sovereignty. The positions of the United States, the world's largest exporter of non-material goods, and the European Union, home of half of the 'Big Six', are instructive in this regard, as are those adopted by musicians, distributors and retailers in Australia. The place of Asia, as a component of some conceptions of regionalism, is considered specifically in relation to the argument that parallel importing from that region will facilitate piracy and undermine investment, profits and royalties in the Australian music industry. Such debates and developments, it is concluded, are responses to the shifting balance of forces at global, regional, national and local levels that are significantly reshaping the Australian music industry. They also reveal, following such works as Paul Hirst's and Grahame Thompson's *Globalization in Question* (1996), the impediments to the free circulation of culture imposed by, among others, those Western economic powers that are the most vocal advocates of global free trade. Before turning in detail to the parallel importing debate, I will first appraise the industry that has produced it.

The shape of the Australian music industry

The Australian music industry, like other cultural industries, is a loose aggregation of structures, practices, personnel and texts. It consists of what we might call 'core' and 'ancillary' operations, the former consisting of specialist organisations responsible for the recording, manufacture, distribution, marketing, promotion, publication, performance and retail of music of various genres, sub-genres and marketing categories (classical, jazz, and so on). This organisational core interacts in a variety of ways with ancillary media (radio, magazines, newspapers, television and Internet) and with other organisations contributing to the process of music production and circulation in various ways (such as the provision of legal, managerial, accounting, design and catering services). The emphasis in this chapter is on popular music, the biggest selling marketing category, with 'Pop and rock account[ing] for close to ninety per cent of the Australian music market' (Capling 1996a, p. 22). The size of the labour force in this industry, like almost everything else in relation to it, is disputed. According to the *Financial Times* (1995, p. 2) the industry employs 60,000 Australians; for Tripp (1997b) it is 55,000. According, however, to Senator Richard Alston, the Coalition Minister for Communications, Information Technology and the Arts (citing statistics from the Australian Bureau of Statistics [ABS] and the Australian Music Retailers' Association [AMRA]), 'only about 5,200 people are directly employed in the industry', so making 'ridiculous' ARIA's claims that '50,000 jobs will disappear if … consumers are allowed to buy cheap CDs' (Alston 1997a, p. 15).

While there is doubt concerning the extent to which music is the exclusive, principal or partial source of income for various Australian workers, and the total value of the music market is also disputed according to definitions of music-related activity, recorded music industry 'unit' sales (CDs, cassettes, etc.) for the quarter year December 1996 to March 1997 were 15.8 million (HMV/University of Westminster 1997), a level which places the Australian industry in the top ten of the world's music markets. It is also a highly profitable one – the ABS estimates the rate of return on investment at 16 per cent, about five times the average for all industries in Australia. The Australian music industry has also, in international terms, experienced something of a 'long boom'. As one report put it, 'In contradiction to the situation generally describing the music industry at the moment, Australian music has been developing at a staggering rate … Figures from the Australian Record Industry Association show that business was up in 1996 by a record 15 per cent' (HMV/University of Westminster 1997). In fact, Australian industry sales were over four times greater in 1996 than in 1982, stabilising subsequently after a modest decline (Breen 1999, p. 81).

Yet the degree of foreign domination means that a very substantial proportion of this profit – $166 million in royalties in 1994–95 according to Senator Alston (1997a, p. 15) – is repatriated to other countries (mostly the USA and the UK), as is to be expected given the power of the multinational major record companies. Approximately 95 per cent of recorded music sold in Australia is manufactured in the country but, according to the ACA (1997), 'around 90 per cent of the industry's profitable repertoire is product licensed from overseas'. The local industry has a reputation for conservatism and caution in signing and promoting local artists and acts (Walker 1984). Australian record companies do export musical 'product', and much is made of the export success – since the early 1980s through to the present day – of Australian-originated acts (with some contributions from *expatriate* New Zealanders) including (in roughly chronological order) AC/DC, Midnight Oil, Men at Work, Nick Cave, INXS, Kylie Minogue, Crowded House (and Split Enz before it), Merrill Bainbridge, Peter Andre, Tina Arena, silverchair, Savage Garden and Natalie Imbruglia. Many of these artists are based overseas, however, and most are signed to multinational majors and their subsidiaries rather than to Australian independent companies. Furthermore, according to many music critics, such success comes 'despite, not because of' the support of 'local record companies' (Elder 1997, p. 10), with one opening an article with the provocative paragraph:

> If there were any morality in the Australian record industry there would have been big sackings on Tuesday. The overwhelming success of Savage Garden at the ARIA awards (an unprecedented 10 gongs) has demonstrated, once again, that the people who run the sad little colonial outpost that is our record industry are so out of touch with popular taste, so hidebound by their own narrow view of hipness, and so besotted with their ability to sell us already proven overseas product, that they can't recognise a successful local act when it comes banging on their door.
>
> (Elder 1997, p. 10)

In detailing how the group received risible interest from the local industry and was initially recorded by one of the less prominent Australian record companies (Roadshow Records), Elder notes that although the Sony company acquired the rights to the band's recordings in the USA and the rest of the world after a 'bidding war', Sony's Australian subsidiary did not hold them because it had determined that the group, which had sold over four million CDs and singles in a short time, 'just weren't good enough' (10). While it must be noted that such 'non-discovery' stories (like the one concerning the English record company executive who 'passed up' on The Beatles) are legion in the international music industry, and that there is no necessary connection between sales and cultural 'value', the institution of music in Australia is regularly criticised on the grounds that its domination by multinational corporations stunts the growth of local musical talent (see, for example, Harris 1992).

Unsurprisingly, then, in net terms importation of licensed musical material into Australia greatly outweighs its export to other markets. In late 1997, for example, an update on the Australian music market stated that:

> The industry needs to develop more domestic talent with worldwide crossover potential. Currently the market is composed of about 83.4% international repertoire, 4.75% classical and 11.9% domestic. To make the situation clearer, in 1996 only four of the year-end top 50 singles originated from Australia or New Zealand.
>
> (HMV/University of Westminster 1997)

Alongside complaints about the 'foreign monopoly' in the Australian music industry is the claim – made most systematically by the ACCC (formerly the Prices Surveillance Authority [PSA]) and forcibly by its head, Professor Alan Fels – that the concentrated market power flowing from restrictive trade practices is abused by inflating and sustaining the price of compact discs and of other recorded music products. The suggestion that music consumers are being 'ripped off' by rapacious overseas corporations prompted, as noted earlier, calls to permit parallel importation. This prospect dominated policy debate in the Australian music industry for most of the 1990s, with the impact of its introduction only now being felt in the early years of the new century. The long, heated policy debate over parallel importing now requires some ventilation.

Tracing the parallel importation debate

The music industry is not the only Australian cultural institution that has experienced a furore over a proposed relaxation of import provisions. John Curtain (1993, p. 241), for example, has described the 'acrimonious debate [which] erupted' in book publishing in the late 1980s and early 1990s over reforms to the Copyright Act 1968. In the case of books, Peter Garrett's part as the prominent artist opposed to change was played by the Booker Prize-winning Australian author Peter Carey, and that of Sony Music and EMI by HarperCollins and Reed. Indeed, it was widely believed that loosening the 'former rigid importation provisions in respect of books' would 'act as a precursor of a more flexible approach in respect of the parallel importation of sound recordings and computer soft-ware' (Turner 1992, pp. 184–5). The twists and turns in policy formation and implementation in both cultural industries have been many. In the case of book publishing, new arrangements were finally introduced whereby direct importation was permitted if local rights holders did not exercise those rights within a 'reasonable period' (in practice between 30 and 90 days). In the case of music, uncertainty remained for a lengthy period despite the 1990 PSA recommendation to permit parallel importation of sound recordings and the 1992 (Labor) Cabinet decision to introduce it from 1 July 1994. There followed the delay and subsequent abandonment of its introduction by that same government in April 1995 in return for formal price monitoring and a promise (not honoured to date) of investment by the major record companies of $270 million in developing the local industry. There followed the new 1996 Howard administration's decision to pursue deregulation; the subsequent Inter Departmental Committee Inquiry into CD Prices in February 1997; and the announcement in October 1997 that the federal government would, indeed, introduce legislation to permit parallel importation alongside more stringent penalties for piracy.

In the lead-up to a federal election in October 1998 and in the context of various degrees of 'horse trading' in the Senate (where the government did not have an absolute majority and where the Greens, the Australian Democrats and the Australian Labor Party opposed the proposed changes), parallel importing remained the key political issue in the music industry. The Shadow Minister for Industrial Relations, Finance and the Arts declared that parallel importing had the 'capacity to do significant damage' to the Australian music industry, while 'the economic case that there will be a consumer benefit is collapsing' (McMullan 1998, p. 10). When in May 1998 'in an inner-city rock venue' the Australian Labor Party announced its contemporary music policy (ALP 1998) – 'a document affirming Labor's opposition to Coalition plans to lift restrictions on parallel importation of CDs' – 'it won more cheers than many of the bands who normally occupy the stage'. This incurred a familiar retort from Senator Alston that the policy was 'a betrayal of consumers' (Jinman 1998, p. 4). Matters were finally settled at half past midnight on Sunday 12 July 1998 when the legislation passed into law during an extraordinary weekend session of Senate, after Senator Mal Colston, who had signalled his intention to oppose the change, unexpectedly absented himself from the chamber.

In analysing the debate that has unfolded in newspapers, on the internet, in parliament and in other sites, various themes (often of a binary nature) consistently emerged in the rhetorics of the participants. These include:

local employment v. foreign exploitation
lower prices v. foreign monopoly
producer v. consumer rights
the state as regulator v. the state as tax collector
orderly markets v. free trade
national control v. regional illegality.

As will become apparent, rhetorical positions did not fall neatly into these thematic structures, with opposing parties often mobilising the same elements of critique but with differential policy prescriptions and outcomes. This discursive confusion indicates the extent to which contending interests in a cultural institution dominated by overseas-based corporate entities, but supported (at least publicly) by subordinate local entities, produce somewhat unlikely alliances that obstruct the full completion of the 'project' of globalisation.

Those opposed to parallel importation predicted a number of adverse economic consequences flowing from its introduction, such as the 'dumping' of overseas product on the Australian market; the migration of capital and labour; the non-payment of royalties to Australian copyright holders; and wholesale retrenchments in the music industry. For example, Jeremy Fabinyi, Chief Executive of the Australian Music Publishers Association Limited (AMPAL), stated that the Copyright Amendment Bill introduced to the lower house 'encourages record companies to save a dollar or two in composer payments by sourcing their stock from South East Asia' (AMPAL 1997). Such arguments paint a picture of the Australian music scene as a healthy local industry with limited international input whereas, as we have seen, the 'sourcing' of overseas repertoire is much the more common practice. Paradoxically, therefore, the prominent Australian independent (that is, not corporately owned) Shock Records, self described in a press release as the 'country's largest fully owned independent record company', opposed parallel importation by linking the company's economic viability not to local production but to the importation of overseas music:

> It's ironic that in attacking a monopoly of the market by multinational companies, the government will end up harming local owned and operated businesses the most. Shock employs over 100 staff and distributes music by over 200 Australian artists. The Australian Music Industry Directory lists around 200 other Australian independent labels. The main way in which Shock Records is able to fund our investment in local talent is by acquiring Australian copyrights for releases by international artists from overseas independent labels. Without legislative protection for these copyrights there is now [sic] way we could continue to invest in Australian talent and employ as many staff as we currently do.
>
> (Shock 1997a)

The monopoly power of the majors is acknowledged here and, it is suggested, can only be countered by 'niche market' imports cross-subsidising local production. While this may be an important 'survival strategy', it can hardly be judged to be a sound basis for the development of 'local talent' which, according to the music lawyer Phil Dwyer (quoted in Button 1997, p. 6), is not subsidised by the majors but by 'the dole'.

Because of the clear market dominance of the multinational majors in Australia and its lack of consonance with the idea of a vibrant 'Oz music', those defending the status quo also commonly attacked their allies in the parallel importation debate. Shock Records was critical of the majors' 'bloated executive infrastructure with foreign sedans or limos, upper six figure wages & inflated expense accounts. We don't hold sales or marketing conferences at trendy holiday resorts' (Shock 1997b). Similarly, Peter Farnan, a guitarist with rock group Boom Crash Opera opposed to parallel importation, described the major record companies as 'bastards' who 'jerk us [musicians] around all the time' (quoted in Button 1997, p 6.). It is precisely this unflattering image of a 'system that allows foreign multinationals to make massive profits at the expense of the Australian consumer' (Alston 1997b), and of those same companies exploiting rather than developing Australia's musical resources (in the same way, for example, as the mining industry has been accused of the insensitive and parasitical exploitation of Australia's natural resources), that has had to be countered by anti-parallel importation interests by invoking cultural nationalist sentiments. So, while the 'Big Six' opposed parallel importation primarily on the grounds that profit can be maintained at higher levels in an oligopolistic rather than an open market, their allies in the independent sector (who are in most other instances their competitors and critics) felt compelled, somewhat uneasily, to rehearse anti-corporate rhetoric without being overly condemnatory of the Australian music industry. At the same time, they defended the economic arrangement maintaining the majors' dominance on the basis that the independents acquiring the local copyright to music produced overseas also derived some benefit from proscribing parallel importation. The cultural nationalist element of this argument is that it allows the employment of Australians (a function also discharged by the 'Big Six') and that the profits from selling and/or distributing non-Australian music can be diverted to support local music production. In this way, the interests of the 'bloated executive infrastructure' and the smaller enterprises dedicated to 'investment in local talent' are discursively reconciled.

In opposition to this coalition of disparate productive forces, the assertion of Australian consumer rights over and against those of a foreign-dominated local industry has been made constantly in the parallel importing debate as a counter to the nationalist arguments of producers. The ACA, in its submission to the Inter Departmental Committee Inquiry into CD Prices, stated that 'in effect the Copyright Act's importation provisions serve as a de facto trade barrier and confer monopolistic powers on the Australian-based (yet overseas-owned) holders of exclusive licences' (1997). The ACCC's comparative data on compact disc prices have been used and disputed by all parties, although the general acknowledgement of the abuse of market power has provoked attempts to uncouple 'an intellectual property issue' from 'a pricing issue' (Shock 1997a; see also Gudinski 1997). This perspective seeks, rather implausibly, to separate the question of ownership of intellectual property from the ability to capitalise on it under particular market conditions. For example, Tripp (1997b), an opponent of parallel importation as noted earlier, has lamented 'the idiotic and unilateral raising of prices by Warner Music Australia' made possible, it would seem, by the oligopolistic nature of the Australian music market.

The suggestion that the market, if left to its own devices, would correct pricing distortions through price 'stratification' by single companies and undercutting by low-overhead independents is, however, somewhat improbable given the concentration of market power already described. As has often been pointed out (for example, by the ACA), the record companies did not pass on to consumers the full benefits of a 1985 sales tax cut of 12.5 per cent by the Labor Government. At this point the state is implicated in industry concerns in a different way, influencing the pricing structure by taxation rather than by import (de)regulation, and giving rise to calls to abolish sales tax for recorded music altogether. Characteristically, the level of taxation in the Australian music business is disputed, being 22 per cent or 11 per cent depending on whether wholesale or retail price is the measuring point. The impact of the introduction of a 10 per cent Goods and Services Tax (GST) in July 2000 in place of sales tax has been similarly contested, with some claims that prices would increase rather than fall (Fenton-Jones 1999, p. 39; Shedden 1998). Under circumstances where competing interest groups spin off wildly diverging versions of institutional 'truth', the state is called upon by some parties to be activist in terms of banning parallel importation, regulating the growing internet music trade and providing industry support (such as export assistance through Austrade), but to be inactive in imposing taxation or intervening in the music market. The state has also been called on to be particularly vigilant in repelling threats from outside national borders, notably from import 'dumping' from the West and piracy from Asia, but to be non-interventionist in regard to foreign ownership and media content regulation.

The metaphor of the flood was consistently in evidence during the debate. For example, Shock Records stated that 'if the government removes import restrictions we will face a retail market flooded with cheap, dumped import CDs' (1997a). The concept of the 'flood' was conceptually linked with another water-based metaphor – that of 'piracy' (unlicensed production and sale) practised in the south-east Asian region. *Financial Times' Music and Copyright* described 'fears of a rise in counterfeit and pirate product if imports from Asia were permitted' (1995, p. 2), and the xenophobic Member for Oxley, Pauline Hanson (1997), linked the proposal to 'the darkness of the shadow of our old enemy, the United Nations and its Lima declaration'. The potential for the South-east Asian region to be a source of imported musical material (as opposed to an export market for Australian music) was repeatedly portrayed in a negative light. For example, Phil Tripp, in an open letter to Senator Alston, wrote:

> I'm not being alarmist about piracy either, but having had an office in China-town and having been involved in the music merchandise (t-shirt) industry as well, I am too aware of the opportunity that exists for massive importation of recordings from either pirate sources or countries which have virtually non-existent copyright laws. But the most ominous news comes from a friend and impeccable source in Hong Kong where 30 CD plants have sprung up in the last two years and also Macau which had no CD plants last year and now has 10 – operated predominantly by the Triads.
>
> (Tripp 1997b)

The region here takes on a somewhat sinister profile on account of laxity in the defence of intellectual property. Yet, in one intriguing twist, the same Phil Tripp, in a press release announcing his resignation from the Austrade Advisory Committee over the parallel importing issue, suggests that 'Malaysia, Singapore and other nearby Asian countries are a much more attractive option for our artists and companies to move to due to their business development and trade initiatives to attract entrepreneurs in addition to cheaper resources for recording, manufacturing and trade initiatives for exporting' (Tripp 1997a). Here, the Asian region is represented through the now somewhat dented concept of the 'tiger economies', rather than as the location of mass piracy (not to mention much stricter regulation in the areas of censorship, political expression and recreational drug use). Such inconsistencies aside, it is rare in the debate for the South-east Asian region to be presented as anything other than a source of pirated material under conditions where:

> Pirate sales in Australia were worth about 5% of the market in 1996 according to the Australian Record Industry Association, which wants to bring the percentage even lower, possibly reaching between 2% and 3%, in order to make the country one of the few pirate-free regions of the world. ARIA managing director Emmanuel Candi supports the view that parallel imports would mean a 30% increase in piracy levels and an annual loss in trade of an estimated $150–200m.
>
> (HMV/University of Westminster 1997)

While this projection of the rise, value and impact of piracy through parallel importation may have been exaggerated for strategic purposes, it is apparent that the favouring of trade regulation by ARIA, AMRA and other industry organisations requires that developing nations remain subordinate while the power of the already installed 'Triad' (that is, European, Japanese and North American companies, rather than the Chinese gangs mentioned above) is to be further entrenched. This is one of the besetting ironies of the currently dominant globalisation practices that produced what can only be described as the parallel importing *fiasco*.

After the parallel importation ball

Much of this chapter was researched and written during the full fury of the parallel importation debate in the Australian music industry as it moved, at least in its current incarnation, to its final act – the passage of the Copyright Amendment Bill (No. 2) on an invigoratingly chilly Canberra night in July. For a period of some eighteen months after the legislation was passed I monitored the debate and the discernible impacts of a change that was claimed, on one side, to herald substantial benefits in terms of consumer rights and, on the other, to cause major, even fatal damage to the music industry in Australia. The debate was dominated by the specific concerns of particularly voluble elements in the Australian music industry, while, for its long duration, other features of the cultural insitution of music were almost obliterated from public discourse. From the tenor of the debate we might expect that the introduction of legal parallel importation would have had thoroughgoing cultural ramifications.

Within three days of the passage of the legislation it was reported that Shock Records would 'dump half of its local artists' and the 'marketing and promotion of new talent would also be slashed', while Sony Music described the change as a 'moral and commercial disgrace' (Jinman, Dixon and Clennell 1998, p. 5). ARIA foreshadowed 'a political campaign in the lead-up to the federal election and has not ruled out legal action to claim compensation for lost income' (Lagan 1998, p. 1). As has already been noted, the political campaign did take place but the Coalition was returned. The only immediately ensuing legal action involved proceedings brought in April 1999 by the ACCC against ARIA, Sony Music, Warner Music and Universal Music, Music Industry Piracy Investigation Pty Ltd and various industry executives, alleging 'unlawful action to prevent or discourage Australian businesses from selling imported CDs to the detriment of competition and consumers'. This action followed 'complaints from CD retailers, who said they had been threatened with the withdrawal of significant trading benefits if they stocked parallel imports', and allegations that Polygram, Sony and Warner had 'colluded with Asian record companies to try to prevent Asian wholesalers from supplying CDs to Australian businesses' (Reece and Dodson 1999, p. 3).

The effect on CD prices, sales and piracy was, entirely predictably, vigorously debated as the new importation and distribution system was installed. The US-based International Intellectual Property Alliance stated that piracy had increased in Australia with 'no noticeable' cost benefits to consumers – claims described by Senator Alston as 'hogwash' and challenged by the ACA, whose feedback indicated price falls from around '$30 to $20' (Pearson 1999, p. 14). It became clear that price 'stratification' was occurring, with supermarket chains like Woolworths and several music retailers (including Australia's largest, Sanity Records) selling high volume imported CD titles at heavily discounted prices ($20 and below), while less popular and many back catalogue CDs could be well below, slightly cheaper than or at the same level as their pre-parallel importation prices (Cummins 1999; Douez 1999). The lack of dramatic and consistent change, it was variously argued, was due to various contingencies – 'profiteering' by companies sourcing cheaper imports but charging high prices; the comparative weakness of the Australian dollar and of many Asian currencies; inelastic (that is, non-price sensitive) consumer demand and purchasing; retailer 'loyalty' to established record companies and local distributors; the introduction of 'bonus tracks' exclusive to local releases, and so on (Donovan 1999; Farrant 1999; and various unattributed private communications). There is but one certainty based on the experience detailed above – whatever happens, its causes, dimensions and even whether it happened at all will continue to be hotly disputed by the usual antagonists.

One notable consequence of a policy debate fixated on parallel importation has been the obscuration and displacement of other issues of deep significance for music copyright in particular and the cultural institution of Australian music in general. The growth in the selling and downloading of music on the internet – both legally and illegally – is also of considerable relevance in Australia. According to Richard Mallett, APRA's Director of Broadcast and Online Licensing, the MP3 format 'makes music piracy possible on an unprecedented scale' (2000, p. 5). The bypassing of the major record companies and of the traditional 'physical' retail sector is still in its infancy: according to the *Sydney Morning Herald* (1999, p. 43): 'In August the best-known digital music site, MP3.com, sold 15,600 CDs on behalf of 26,700 artists … That's about half a CD per artist'. Nonetheless, the long and ultimately unsuccessful battle over parallel importing seems to have exhausted the participants and left something of a void in terms of policy activism (save for an Application to the Copyright Tribunal over the distribution of Mechanical Royalties). As Shane Homan (1999, p. 107) has noted, the progressive digitalisation of cultural production is making issues surrounding 'parallel distribution technologies' of greater significance than the 'parallel importation' of physical properties, so that 'the inspection of suspected pirate CDs at airports and docks will seem rather quaint as the industry attempts to monitor the transition to a post-industrial, multi-media landscape' (see also Thomas 1998). Significantly, in early 2000 disputes between record companies and retailers broke out over exclusive catalogue deals for internet sales and distribution. At the same time, several multinational companies initiated (ultimately successful) legal action in the USA against Napster for facilitating the online 'swapping' of copyright music files. In April 2001 they announced their intention to launch their own 'fee paying' service.

The illicit domestic 'burning' and downloading of copyright musical material using computing technologies – the contemporary equivalent of the analogue 'home taping' that caused similar controversies in the music industry of the 1970s and 1980s (Rowe 1995) – looms as a major cultural policy issue. However, the hyperbolic doom-saying of many music industry pressure groups over parallel importation – for example, 'Government sounds the death knell for Oz music' (AMPAL 1997) – may well have eroded its public credibility and policy influence. The Australian Labor Party, having promised to repeal the new law when returned to power, remained in opposition after over a decade of 'shameful failure' (Breen 1999, p. 2) to reform the industry when in government. According to a 1997 ABS 'Business of Music' study, in an industry composed principally of 153 music companies the most recent collective operating profit of the seven largest companies (including the independent Shock) was $41.2 million – almost three-quarters of the industry total (Breen 1999, pp. 198–9). The same report found that only around 10 per cent of local releases by the multinational record company subsidiaries were by Australian artists – almost half the proportion of the small label independent sector. This high level of mostly foreign industrial concentration hardly provided the political foundation for a viable twenty-first century music cultural policy for the ALP, not least because it had spent much of the previous two decades energetically championing the 'benefits' of financial deregulation, trade liberalisation and economic globalisation (Rowe 1998).

The announcement in January 2000 of the attempted merger of two of the multinational majors, Warner Music and EMI, dramatically demonstrates the speed and scale of global changes, especially those stimulated by the prospect of more extensive online sales and copying. But it also reveals the obstacles to such moves, with the merger aborted in October 2000 to appease regulatory authorities in paving the way for the complete merger in early 2001 of America Online (AOL) and Time Warner (with AOL's link with Bertelsmann, Europe's biggest media company, also sacrificed). Many commentators have noted a pattern of big, multi-function cultural corporations getting even bigger:

> Rapid consolidation in the global music industry has left control of publishing and recording in fewer hands than ever before. There are now only four major labels: Time Warner-EMI, Sony, BMG and Universal. Smaller concerns are either being swallowed up or are scrabbling to survive.
>
> (Cassy 2000, p. 24)

This increased vertical and horizontal integration (that is, exercising greater ownership and control over the entire production and consumption process across a wider range of products) of multinational music corporations extravagantly capital-enriched by the (now somewhat diminished) boom in 'hi tech' and traditional media stocks has profound implications for an Australian music scene where the majors already dominate.

Yet the 'scorched earth' nature of the parallel importing debate in Australia virtually occluded the consideration of the full range of pressing issues such as the 1999 review of the Commercial Radio Codes of Practice (and the determination of Australian content quotas, especially for 'new' music), cultural development and public subvention (or subsidy), training, education and career development, as well as the aforementioned new technologies and delivery systems. The federal government's $10 million Australian contemporary music development package, announced in 1998 and implemented late the following year, did attempt partially to fill the policy vacuum and to placate the government's music industry critics. This initiative included a series of Australia Council administered programs such as the International Managers Forum (Australia) (IMF), designed to 'develop effective marketing and business skills for managers'; support for the Association of Independent Record Labels (AIR), the Pacific Circle Music Expo 2000 and Musica Viva; as well as underwriting the Contemporary Music Touring Program (McGauran 1999). The benefits of such programs, which are in the main variations of earlier ones under previous governments, are unlikely to be major, given their financial modesty and ad hoc nature, although they have been highly effective in the serial production of new acronyms. The preoccupation with exclusive copyright protection (presented as a last ditch defence of Australian music culture) has only confirmed the afore-mentioned position articulated by Lash and Urry (1994) that contemporary economies of signs and space – and, we might add, cultural institutions – are profoundly shaped by contestation over intellectual property rights, whose loud assertion was the main 'Australian sound' of the 1990s.

Conclusion: globalisation and the reshaping of an Australian cultural institution

This brief analysis of the Australian music industry and its most vexatious policy issue of the last decade has not sought to be a comprehensive 'take' on the entire cultural institution. Through this specific analysis we have glimpsed various institutional features, especially the economic dominance by foreign-owned multinational corporations, the uneasy alliance between these and locally based companies, the cultural predominance of overseas repertoire, and the suspicion of regional involvement in the production of Australian music and related cultural products. This appraisal has also thrown light on more general ques-tions of global, regional and national cultural relations, and the calculations of nation states concerning their governance (Capling 1994; Zacker with Sutton 1996). It has indicated the need for due scepticism of some of the more totalis-ing accounts of globalisation (such as that by Ohmae 1990) by examining the effective defence of exclusive copyright in key territories by multinational corpo-rations based in particular nations and regions (rather than by 'rootless', truly transnational corporations which, as Hirst and Thompson [1996, p. 195] argue, are rare birds indeed). The United States and the European Union, in particular, have shown that in the supposedly deregulatory era of the post-Uruguay round of the General Agreement on Tariffs and Trade (GATT) and the ensuing Trade Related Aspects of Intellectual Property (TRIPS) agreement, national trade laws and bilateral and multilateral agreements retard rather than expedite full economic and cultural globalisation (Capling 1996b). Boldest of all has been the USA, whose Trade Representative, Charlene Barshefsky, threatened to impose 'Section 301' trade sanctions against Australia if it introduced parallel importa-tion for music and other intellectual property in which the USA has a major stake (Dwyer 1997). Such anti-deregulatory manifestations, as Hirst and Thompson note, are present at various organisational levels:

> the majority of companies, large and small, that are active in international markets have a strong interest in the continued public governance, national and international, of the world economy. Internationally they seek a measure of

security and stability in financial markets, a secure framework of free trade, and the protection of commercial rights. Nationally they seek to profit from the distinct advantages conferred by the cultural and institutional frameworks of the successful industrial states. If companies have such interests then it is highly unlikely that an ungoverned global economy composed of unregulated markets will come into existence.

(Hirst and Thompson 1996, pp. 188–9)

As we have seen, the 'political' rationale for cultural trade regulation is often the defence of local industry and of national culture. In the Australian music industry, the former is demonstrably overseas dominated and the latter is of at least doubtful health given the levels of ownership and control over musical production exercised by economic organisations based in other nations. Rothnie (1993, p. 561), after an extensive review of the subject, describes 'the problem posed by parallel imports' as 'intractable' because '[s]hort-term interest clashes with perceived long-term interest' over questions of pricing and production. This intractability (or at least multi-dimensionality) produced in our Australian music case study some awkward political practice and constantly thwarted the development of appropriate cultural policy.

'Progressive' practitioners of parliamentary and cultural politics have mostly found themselves in the Australian instance defending and justifying a status quo that their political philosophies would logically lead them to oppose. As a result, the reshaping of the industrial infrastructure of the Australian cultural institution of music has in recent times depended on the outcome of a struggle between a conservative federal government running a consumer rights, anti-foreign monopoly line and an unlikely coalition of overseas multinational corporations, authoritarian populist and 'leftish' politicians, and various local music producers. Such a phenomenon may not be historically unusual in institutional terms, but is hardly conducive to the making of 'good' cultural policy. This necessarily contested concept involves policy formation that is logical, consistent, viable, equitable, based on the best available empirical evidence, and in the wider public interest (qualities, it should be noted, that are by no means readily apparent in the organisation of Australian art and culture – see Stevenson 2000). Indeed, 'off the record' e-mail and telephone interviews with some of the prominent figures in the debate (who for ethical reasons cannot be identified) produced admissions that strategic exaggerations had been made concerning the impact of parallel importing on employment, profitability, piracy and levels of local investment. One, in a telephone interview, even noted that, far from reductions in local production, 'if anything the opposite has happened. Probably because it's harder to make a dollar on the overseas artists, companies are looking to home-grown product'. The last ditch attempt to repel parallel importation has meant, as noted above, that with this single 'blockbuster' issue resolved (few believe that the ALP, when in power, will ever be willing or able to repeal the amendments) and in the absence of the promised catastrophe, there is a lamentable lack of institutional preparedness to devise and execute comprehensive and timely cultural policy.

Finally, to what extent has this been a peculiarly Australian story, fashioned by the unique circumstances prevailing in a former British colony in the Asian-Pacific region? Julian Thomas (1998, p. 1) notes that 'the particular outrage created over CD imports is characteristic of a small Anglophone country which consumes a great deal more intellectual property than it produces, and which has a long history of protectionist industry policy'. If Australia's experience is similar to countries like Canada in this respect, there are also parallels with many other nations, including France, China and, ironically in this instance, Britain, where there is frequent debate about the erosion of 'national culture' by foreign (especially American) cultural content and corporations (see, for example, Goodwin 1998). As political economists of the media (such as Golding and Murdock 2000) have often pointed out, high levels of concentration of ownership and control are by no means uncommon in the cultural industries.

What we have seen here is that the 'project' of globalisation is by no means completed, not least because some of the most aggressive proponents of globalisation are also the most tenacious defenders of exclusive, territorial intellectual property rights. Paradoxically, many Australian cultural nationalists found common cause with their usual political opponents because of their mutual, immediate interest in copyright. At the same time, the idea of a 'sovereign cultural nation', if it ever was a reality, is an illusion in the age of transnational (especially digital) communication. No twenty-first century cultural policy can be created that is not already hemmed in by international obligations and established, structural industry interests. Such contradictions and complexities have created the strange anomaly that is the cultural institution of Australian music.

Note

I would like to thank Richard Lever, Kerry Beaumont and Georgia Paton of the Cultural Industries and Practices Research Centre, University of Newcastle, for ferreting out some highly instructive material on the parallel importing debate. My gratitude also to those individuals and representatives of organisations who gave 'off the record' responses to questions (presented by Georgia Paton) about the impact of the introduction of parallel importation in Australia.

📖 Guide to further reading

The literature in this area can be broadly divided into works concerned principally with the Australian context and those that are international in nature (some of which cover Australia). The Australia-focused literature is not large and may be difficult to access. The main books that concentrate on Australia and the south-east Pacific region are Philip Hayward (1992); Tony Mitchell (1996); Clinton Walker (1984 and 1996); three works (the first two edited) by Marcus Breen, *Missing in Action: Australian Popular Music in Perspective*, Volume I (Melbourne: Verbal Graphics, 1987), *Our Place, Our Music* (Canberra: Aboriginal Studies Press, 1989) and Breen (1999); and Gerry Bloustien's edited *Musical Visions* (Kent Town: Wakefield Press, 1999). *Perfect Beat: The Journal of Research into Contemporary Music and Popular Culture* is a useful Australian-based resource.

Of the international literature, the following works are useful and relevant: Deanna Campbell Robinson, Elizabeth B. Buck and Marlene Cuthbert, *Music at the Margins: Popular Music and Global Cultural Diversity* (Newbury Park, CA: Sage, 1991); Tony Bennett, Simon Frith, Lawrence Grossberg, John Shepherd and Graeme Turner (eds) *Rock and Popular Music: Politics, Policies, Institutions* (London: Routledge, 1996); Rowe (1995); Thomas Swiss, John Sloop and Andrew Herman (eds) *Mapping the Beat: Popular Music and Contemporary Theory* (Oxford: Blackwell, 1997) and Keith Negus, *Music Genres and Corporate Cultures* (London: Routledge, 1999). The established journal in the area is *Popular Music*.

⌨ Website

www.immedia.com.au
   Immedia! The best of the local music websites.

References

Alston, Richard (1997a) 'Scare campaign running out of ammunition', *Age* 17 October, p. 15.

Australian Labor Party (1998) *Contemporary Music Policy: Building Careers in Music*, Canberra: ALP.

— (1997b) 'Party of betrayers betrays consumers – again', DCA Press Release, 16 October.

Australian Consumers' Association (1997) 'Submission to the Inter Departmental Committee Inquiry into CD Prices', February.

Australian Music Publishers Associated Limited (1997) 'Government sounds death knell for Oz music', AMPAL Press Release, 24 November.

Breen, Marcus (1993) 'Making music local' in Tony Bennett, Simon Frith, Lawrence Grossberg, John Shepherd and Graeme Turner (eds), *Rock and Popular Music: Politics, Policies, Institutions*, London: Routledge, pp. 66–82.

— (1999) *Rock Dogs: Politics and the Australian Music Industry*, Sydney: Pluto Press.

Button, James (1997) 'Musical Shares', *Age* 25 October, p. 6.

Capling, Ann (1994) 'Bargaining for competitive advantage: government and the changing relationship between the state and multinational enterprises in Australia', *Journal of Industry Studies* 1, 2, pp. 1–22.

— (1996a) 'Gimme shelter!', *Arena Magazine* 21, pp. 21–3.

— (1996b) 'The conundrum of intellectual property rights: domestic interests, international commitments and the Australian music industry', *Australian Journal of Political Science* 31, 3, pp. 301–20.

Cassy, John (2000) 'Now there are four, as MP3 threatens the record labels', *Guardian* 25 January, p. 24.

Cummins, Kath (1999) 'Sanity records may prevail in showdown over CD retail prices', *Australian Financial Review* 8 January, p. 6.

Curtain, John (1993) 'Distance makes the market fonder: the development of book publishing in Australia', *Media, Culture & Society* 15, 2, pp. 233–44.

Docker, John (1991) 'Popular culture versus the state: an argument against the Australian content regulations for television'. *Media Information Australia* 59, February, pp. 7–26.

Donovan, Patrick (1999) 'CD prices: dollar blamed', *Age* 30 November, p. 4.

Douez, Sophie (1999) 'Going for a song', *Sun Herald Sunday Life!* 25 April, p. 16.

Dwyer, Michael (1997) 'US warns of trade war over CD, book imports', *Australian Financial Review* 7 February, p. 1.

Elder, Bruce (1997) 'Fresh from the garden', *Sydney Morning Herald* 27 September, p. 10.

Farrant, Darrin (1999) 'CD prices – facing the music', *Age* 10 October, p. 7.

Fenton-Jones, Mark (1999) 'Don't expect CD, video prices to fall', *Australian Financial Review* 17 December, p. 39.

Financial Times Music and Copyright (1995) 'Australia to retain protection against parallel imports', 26 April, 64, p. 2.

Golding, Peter and Graham Murdock (2000) 'Culture, communications and political economy' in James Curran and Michael Gurevitch (eds) *Mass Media and Society*, London: Edward Arnold (third edition), pp. 15–32.

Goodwin, Peter (1998) *Television under the Tories: Broadcasting Policy 1979–1997*, London: British Film Institute.

Gudinski, Michael (1997) 'On music, money and the mushroom effect', *Age* 17 October.

Hanson, Pauline (1997) 'Music industry: free trade', Speech in the Commonwealth House of Representatives, 1 October.

Harris, Michael (1992) 'In search of the lost chord: the politics of reform in the music industry'. *Policy* 8, 1, pp. 53–5.

Hayward, Philip (1992) 'Introduction – charting Australia: music, history and identity', in Philip Hayward (ed.) *From Pop to Punk to Postmodernism: Popular Music and Australian Culture from the 1960s to the 1990s*, Sydney: Allen & Unwin, pp. 1–8.

Hirst, Paul and Grahame Thompson (1996) *Globalization in Question*, Cambridge: Polity.

HMV Music/University of Westminster (1997) *The Australian Music Market*, Music Business Research Site, University of Westminster, December. www.wmin.ac. uk/media/music/welcome.html

Homan, Shane (1999) 'Australian music and the parallel importation debate', *Media International Australia* 91, pp. 97–109.

Jinman, Richard (1998) 'Labor hooks musos on imports line', *Sydney Morning Herald* 25 May, p. 4.

Jinman, Richard, Robyn Dixon and Andrew Clennell (1998) 'Record label to drop local acts', *Sydney Morning Herald* 14 July, p. 5.

Jones, Steve (1992) *Rock Formation: Music, Technology and Mass Communication*, Newbury Park, CA: Sage.

Lagan, Bernard (1998) 'Row as door opens to cheap foreign CDs', *Sydney Morning Herald* 13 July, p. 1.

Lash, Scott and John Urry (1994) *Economies of Signs and Space*, London: Sage.

McGauran, Peter (1999) 'Contemporary music boost', DCA Press Release, 7 December.

McMullan, Bob (1998) 'Not just consumers … citizens', *Media & Culture Review* 1, p. 10.

Mallett, Richard (2000) Letter to *Sydney Morning Herald: The Guide* 27 March–2 April, p. 5.

Mitchell, Tony (1996) *Popular Music and Local Identity: Rock, Pop and Rap in Europe and Oceania*, London: Leicester University Press.

Negus, Keith (1992) *Producing Pop: Culture and Conflict in the Popular Music Industry*, London: Edward Arnold.

Ohmae, Kenichi (1990) *The Borderless World*, London: Collins.

Pearson, Brendan (1999) 'US spots piracy in Australia', *Australian Financial Review* 19 February, p. 14.

Reece, Nicholas and Louise Dodson (1999) 'Legal action hits music firms', *Australian Financial Review* 4 September, p. 3.

Robinson, D.C., E.B. Buck and M. Cuthbert (1991) *Music at the Margins: Popular Music and Global Cultural Diversity*, Newbury Park, CA: Sage.

Rothnie, Warwick A. (1993) *Parallel Imports*, London: Sweet & Maxwell.

Rowe, David (1995) *Popular Cultures: Rock Music, Sport and the Politics of Pleasure*, London: Sage.

— (1998) '"My fellow Australians": culture, economics and the nation state', *Australian Studies* 13, 1, pp. 68–90.

Shedden, Iain (1998) 'CD industry in a spin', *Australian Online* 14 August.

Shock Records (1997a) 'Parallel imports will strike Australian music hardest of all', Press Release.

— (1997b) 'Shock to music industry – "Deliver low CD prices to consumers, or else!"', Press Release, 12 June.

Stevenson, Deborah (2000) *Art and Organisation: Making Australian Cultural Policy*, St Lucia: University of Queensland Press.

Stewart, George R., Myra J. Tawfik and Maureen Irish (eds) (1994) *International Trade and Intellectual Property: The Search for a Balanced System*, Boulder, CO: Westview Press.

Sydney Morning Herald (1999) 'Online musicians strike a sour note', 6 December, p. 43.

Thomas, Julian (1998) 'CDs and the politics of intellectual property', *Media & Culture Review* 1, pp. 1–2.

Tripp, Phil (1997a) 'Music industry expert quits Austrade Advisory Committee', Press Release, 11 November.

— (1997b) 'Open letter to Senator Richard Alston', *Loose Cannon!* 39.

Turner, Clive (1992) 'Copyright and parallel importation: the Australian experience and initiatives', *Intellectual Property Journal* 71, pp. 149–86.

Turner, Graeme (1994) *Making It National: Nationalism and Australian Popular Culture*, Sydney: Allen & Unwin.

Walker, Clinton (ed.) (1984) *The Next Thing: Contemporary Australian Rock*, Kenthurst, NSW: Kangaroo Press.

— (1996) *Stranded: The Secret History of Australian Independent Music, 1977–1991*, Sydney: Pan Macmillan.

Zacker, Mark W. with Brent A. Sutton (1996) *Governing Global Networks: International Regimes for Transportation and Communications*, Cambridge: Cambridge University Press.

Chapter 3

The Visual Arts: Imploding Infrastructure, Shifting Frames, Uncertain Futures

Terry Smith

'Institutions' and 'art' – can two less fitting bedfellows be imagined? Did not modernity require of art the constant generation of an open-ended, anti-academic originality? Does not postmodernity expect its art to be elusive, contingent, scarcely distinguishable from the imagery of spectacle, or, if different, sharply marginal or ironically evasive? Yet institutionalisation of a far-reaching kind accompanied Australian visual artists' movement through anti-modernism and into postmodernism during the 1970s, as did two other great forces: internationalisation and industrialisation. These formations frame most of what goes on in the visual arts in Australia today. Their unfolding and inter-action will shape its future. A key element of my argument will be that, despite their relative recentness and their tendency to hegemony, the impacts of these forces on visual arts practice is profound. The conditions in which visual artists, nowadays, must pursue their creative effort present less a carefully composed, well-balanced yet flexible picture resulting from prescient policy making than a fragile edifice in constant danger of implosive unravelling as the forces consti-tuting its frame shift suddenly and uncontrollably, or push it, relentlessly, off register. This is a direct result of the society-wide redirection toward economic rationalist value structures within the ruins of welfare economy and in the face of sporadic resurgences of occasional, localised welfare provision. Overall, this hard picture suggests that a new kind of post-institutional setting is an urgent requirement to sustain cultural practices at levels approaching the critical mass which they achieved in the 1980s. The alternative is appalling: behind a facade of brave new free market rhetoric, the realities of creative practice will slide back into the wash of amateurism – broken, to be sure, by occasional, exceptional achievement – which typified Australian visual art during the 1950s and early 1960s.

In 1996 the Bankstown, Sydney, branch of the Australian Taxation Office (ATO) decided to crack down on a number of people who, the officers suspected, were actually hobbyists yet were falsely claiming rebates on various material costs by pretending to be professionals. Applying the ATO criteria to measure 'serious business intent' (the only form of being, apart from wage-earning, recognised by the Office), the officers noted that these people had been 'trading for two years in succession without showing a profit' – indeed, were continually showing losses. On interviewing the artists among this group, the officers found that they were graduates of major art schools, were members of professional organisations, made strenuous and sometimes successful efforts to exhibit their work, and defined themselves by their vocation as artists despite being obliged to take all sorts of jobs to make ends meet and buy materials. In particular, they saw themselves as contemporary artists, creators of post-conceptual paintings, installations, performances and the like. They were unwilling, however, to change their product to meet the broad market demand for art, which was, the ATO officers pointed out, overwhelmingly disposed towards portraits and landscape paintings of the Australian bush. The rebates were withheld.

This incident marks out a borderline between cultural practice and the imperatives of the broader social structure, especially as these are defined institutionally. It is one of many such official brick walls into which artists run, on a daily basis. It stands in contrast to the continuing evidence – set out below – that Australians as individuals value the visual as well as the other arts deeply enough to participate in them in large numbers and to reward creative individuals and organisations, sometimes in material ways but mostly with the warmth of their interest. While it can be said that this generous impulse dominated public polity during the 1980s and early 1990s, and was given form by the committed efforts of many arts administrative system builders, it ceased to do so quite soon after the assumption of government by the Liberal Party in March 1996.

Looked at more broadly, the processes which are the central concern of this book – globalisation and regionalisation, a changing policy environment leading to a declining culture of public subsidy, new information technologies and the changing cultural composition of Australian society – have already had significant, but unequal, impact on most aspects of visual art production and dissemination in Australia during the past decade. In my view, these impacts will grow in significance, but differ in relative emphasis, over the next two decades. In the immediate future, their overall, combined impact will, I believe, amount to:

1 a shift from the intensive institutionalisation of the conditions, and, some argue, the nature of visual arts practice – that is, the multifaceted, subtle and widespread provision of generative infrastructural support for artists during

the past 30 years, the history of which will be detailed in this chapter – toward a dispersive deinstitutionalisation, and

2   a tipping of the balance of the processes which have industrialised the visual arts as part of a larger, emergent culture industry away from tendencies to coherence and normalisation, toward competition and fragmentation.

While the overall framework of interplay between evolving traditions and emergent institutionalising, internationalising and industrialising forces is true of art practice in other countries with settler colonial histories, there are some major factors that make the Australian experience unique. The drives to discover an imagery of identity and difference, to understand the world newly and truly, to create beautiful, engaging and original art – these goals impel artists working from within inherited European-Australian traditions, from immigrant experience, and from within the Contemporary Aboriginal Art movement, but do so differently in each case. Adding to these three civilisational 'waves' (to echo a Nugget Coombs analogy cited by Tim Rowse in this volume) is the increasingly relevant growth of craft-oriented visual art from the Pacific region. These four tendencies are distinctively aggregated in Australian culture, each of them dealing differently with both global forces and local demands.

Nor do these cultural formations remain separate, parallel, occasionally coincident in their trajectories: on the contrary, it is my belief that the visual art of the near future will be led by the remarkable emergence of unique kinds of 'between-cultures' communication. Often hybrid in form and independently critical in character, this tendency is taking on a distinctive character in our region, and is part of lateral, or postcolonial, globalisation. It has implications for cultural communication beyond the visual arts; indeed, it may well be the pattern of the future everywhere.

The institutionalisation of the visual arts: an historical sketch

There are, broadly speaking, three well-established sectors of visual arts practice, each with an economy and subculture of its own, and each with different relationships to the others. These are professional practice, amateur activity, and Aboriginal art. Aboriginal art is the most recent, and its institutionalisation is, at first glance, the most transparent. As it is thoroughly discussed in a number of excellent texts and reports, I will not detail its development here (see Edwards 1979, Sutton 1988, Isaacs 1984 and 1989, Altman 1989, Smith 1991a, Caruana 1993, Morphy 1999, Janke 1999). Rather, I will cite comparative figures and practices where appropriate to the broader picture.

During the early years of settlement, and for most of the nineteenth century, colonists drew few practical distinctions between professional and amateur art, despite inheriting hierarchies of aesthetic valuing which were tied more strongly to both media and genre *per se* than they were to performance within either media or genre. An 'historical' – that is, classical, biblical or imperial – subject in oils flaunted it at the top of a ladder set in place by the art academies of Europe, while its lower rungs were occupied by illustrations in newspapers and private sketches by ladies. Art clubs and societies arose early, some becoming part of mechanics institutes, as in the case of the Van Diemen's Land Mechanics School of Art, established in 1826. State galleries were founded in Melbourne, then Sydney, in the 1860s and 1870s (both claiming the title 'national') as centres of instruction in the arts and elevation of taste. Small circles of patrons emerged, some art collections were formed, some prizes and scholarships were awarded, and a few artists founded their own schools. Professional artists' associations were promoted by Tom Roberts and his fellow artists in the 1880s: the distinction was between them and 'gentlemen amateurs'. Australian art, then, was a public exercise in self-conscious construction: of a profession, of self, of nation (Smith 1996b).

These institutionalising forces continued through the first half of the twentieth century. The new Commonwealth Government supported the visual arts through the Arts Advisory Board (for a few years known as the Commonwealth Arts Advisory Board) from 1911 to 1972. In 1973 this function was subsumed into the new Australia Council for the Arts. For 60 years the Arts Advisory Board provided some support to artists and advised the government on acquisitions for Commonwealth properties and other art related issues, such as the need to establish a national gallery in Canberra. But these organisations were less powerful than individuals such as Julian Ashton and Sydney Ure Smith, tastemakers who were active institution-builders across the entire range of the visual arts. If we listed Ure Smith's interests at a typical moment in the 1930s, we would find him producing and exhibiting his etchings, active in the leading advertising firm Smith & Julius, publishing the journals *Art in Australia* and the *Australian National Journal*, both of which he founded, performing many roles as President of the NSW Society of Artists (1921–47) and as a trustee of the Art Gallery of New South Wales for decades, writing art criticism and broadcasting about art on the radio, organising exhibitions of Australian art abroad (famous examples being London 1923, the USA 1941), and publishing the series of books, *Present Day Art in Australia* (Underhill 1991).

Government patronage was intermittent between the wars, and focused on sustaining the major state galleries and the teaching of art in secondary schools. There was no parallel to the support of artists provided by the Federal Arts Project programs in the USA, nor much recognition of the powerful role which the visual arts, especially photography and film, could play in conveying social policy – a polite way of describing their impact in Germany, for example.

A shift in official perceptions of the value of the visual arts occurred in Britain, Canada and here during World War II. It is arguable that organisations such as the Society for Encouragement of Music and the Arts laid the groundwork for the slowly building post-war perception that the arts required wide-scale, lateral, that is, infrastructural, support as well as that given to single-site institutions such as the state galleries. State-based arts councils took up this role but were never adequately funded. Artists active in the crafts formed their own networks based around exchanges between workshops. Craft associations were established in each state (beginning with New South Wales in 1964). This quickly led to the emergence of the Crafts Council of Australia in 1971 which went on to have a great impact by providing advice, grants, a resource centre, magazines, films of master craftsmen and women at work, education programs, general marketing and advocacy (Cochrane 1992). Indeed, self-sustaining infrastructure bridging a variety of production and a multiplicity of markets was most thoroughly and successfully instigated in the crafts, a legacy which continues to this day.

I take it that institutionalisation is measurably present in a field of human activity when that field demonstrates the capacity to generate specific institutions across the whole range of its possible productivity, to encompass the decline and disappearance of institutions and to be able to create new, more appropriate ones. If this is so, then the visual arts institutionalised much more slowly than music and the performing arts. The 'voluntary entrepreneurs' who ran the Elizabethan Theatre Trust (established 1954) managed to create in short order such enduring institutions as the Australian Opera (1956), the National Institute of Dramatic Arts (1959) and the Australian Ballet (1961). Dominance of the cultural field by the 'flagship' companies persists to this day. In March 2000, the federal government announced its support for the key recommendations of the Nugent Inquiry into Music and the Performing Arts, agreeing to fund the major companies in these fields at expanded levels, while diminishing funding for smaller local, regional companies and leaving unchanged or reduced its funding for the other arts.[1]

To picture the evolution of infrastructure in the visual arts, let me list some important events.[2] I concentrate primarily on the national picture, with some reference to state initiatives, which were strong during the period, especially in Victoria throughout and in Queensland in the past decade. Recent research and publication is beginning to pay due attention to the national, state and local dimensions of governmental patronage (for example, Guldberg 2000; Stevenson 2000).

1960s

The first independent commercial art gallery devoted to contemporary Australian art opened in 1956, after which the number rapidly expanded during the following decade, especially in the capital cities. Except for a temporary setback to the economy in the early 1970s due to the oil crisis, growth continued until the 1980s, after which the sector remains static. By then, the market for contemporary art had come to match in size and variety that in London, for example. Popular art is sold on a large scale in a number of smaller galleries in country centres and suburbs. Some artists, such as Ken Done, have created distinctive brand identities for art, craft, clothing and other commodities that form the core of successful commercial enterprises. Corporate art collections, such as that of the Reserve Bank of Australia and of private companies such as ICI, BHP and Elders, were established. These continue to be founded, and to evolve. A number of new prizes aimed at contemporary artists were offered, for example the Helena Rubenstein Prize. Famous competitions, such as the Archibald Prize for Portraiture, founded in 1919, continued but were later regarded as *passé*. Amateur artists dominated the prizes at agricultural fairs and those offered by local councils.

Led by the example of the Dunstan Government in South Australia, state arts ministries and agencies were set up. Federal patronage culminated in the establishment of the Australian Council for the Arts in 1968. The key conceptual presumption behind this kind of support is well articulated by Tim Rowse's discussion in Chapter 5 of the individual who did most to secure it, Dr Nugget Coombs: culture was seen as 'a socially elevated form of leisure provided by an economically inefficient industry requiring political protection'. While it is questionable whether the term 'industry' makes much sense before the 1980s, except as an ironic analogy or as an aspiration on the part of some participants, the high cultural value highlighted here is accurate for more than half of the impulse. The other was social elevation itself, a Victorian value of raising the level of taste of the people. Government agencies have had an enormous influence on the development of the arts infrastructure, and the promotion of art. Particular agencies evolved to service international, national, municipal, capital city and regional needs.

Visual art courses grew rapidly in popularity in secondary schools during the 1960s and 1970s, as did adult and further education in the field. Tertiary art schools increased substantially in number, along with departments of art history and theory in universities. Audiences for the visual arts were being trained in great numbers. While the first courses in art history were offered at the University of Melbourne from 1947, a wave of new departments was created in the late 1960s. For example, the Power Institute began teaching at the University of Sydney in 1968, as well as exhibiting contemporary art and touring international critics and scholars in line with the bequest of expatriate artist J.J.W. Power to 'bring the latest ideas and theories concerning contemporary art to the people of Australia'. A plethora of art critical writing appeared in capital city newspapers, especially in the early 1970s, and was followed by the growth of art magazines and journals in the mid and later 1970s, most edited and written by young university and art school graduates.

Following the new building for the National Gallery of Victoria in 1968, state galleries expanded their outreach and increased their purchasing of both international and local contemporary art. This grew rapidly during the 1970s, as did the audience for this art, stimulated through regular exhibitions as well as the staging of large-scale contemporary art shows such as the Sydney Biennale (from 1973, first at the Sydney Opera House, subsequently at the Art Gallery of New South Wales and other venues).

1970s

A new era of contemporary Aboriginal art was inaugurated at Papunya in the Western Desert in 1971. Interest in this work slowly spread from tourist outlets in Alice Springs through expanded anthropological collections in museums, notably the South Australian Museum, travelling exhibitions in university galleries, then the gradual growth of private collections, interest by non-indigenous artists, and the creation of the first arts centres in remote communities such as Ramingining in central Arnhem Land.

In 1973 the Australian Council for the Arts became the Australia Council, which was incorporated as an independent statutory authority in 1975. Its aim was 'to foster the development of the arts in Australia'. Its more specific priorities were organised around the twin poles of sustaining excellence in arts practice and enabling ever-widening access to this excellence (Australia Council 1980). It became the single most significant institutional player in the arts during the following twenty years. At times, it was also the most powerful agency within specific art forms. The present discussion makes it clear that no other single institution had as much, and as wide-scale, infrastructural impact in the 1970s and 1980s. At the state level, a number of regional galleries were founded and placed on a professional footing, particularly in Victoria, New South Wales and Queensland. In certain state capitals there was strong patronage of arts institutions, notably by the Wran Government in Sydney.

Artists formed into action groups to campaign for representation of Australian and especially women artists in international survey exhibitions such as the Sydney Biennale. This quickly led to broader campaigns for professional conditions, and, during the 1980s, to the formation of the Artworkers Union and similar bodies such as the Queensland Artworkers Alliance, and to the establishment of the National Association for the Visual Arts (NAVA) and the Arts Law Centre. Even more broadly, certain artists sought a greater presence for the arts as part of working-class culture, a push which itself became institutionalised as the Art and Working Life Program of the Australia Council. Further fruit of action by artists was the emergence of artist-run spaces.

The nascent National Gallery of Australia became a vast Australian art purchasing operation, especially following the Fraser Government's reaction against the purchasing of international art, particularly Jackson Pollock's *Blue Poles*, during the brief Whitlam era. Tax concessions for the donation of tangible works to public galleries were introduced in the late 1970s.

1980s

The widespread art world recognition of contemporary Aboriginal art was signalled by the inclusion of Central Desert work in the Perspecta exhibition of 1981, and the purchasing of current Aboriginal art by the newly opened National Gallery of Australia and the National Gallery of Victoria. There was a measurable increase in the commissioning of public art, mainly in local government precincts but also in new building developments, notably the new Parliament House, Canberra. The establishment of Artbank in 1980 created a government-sponsored rental collection of contemporary art for offices and businesses. Visual artists participated in significant ways in the lead-up to and the celebration of the Bicentenary in 1988.

A new spate of art prizes was offered, notably from private sources such as the Moët and Chandon Fellowship and the Doug Moran Portrait Prize. Aboriginal artists began to win open competitions, and were also offered the National Aboriginal Art Award. Tax concessions for donations to non-profit arts organisations, such as the artist-run galleries and the contemporary art spaces, were introduced. Echoing practices in the United States and Europe, the Australian Contemporary Art Fair in Melbourne became, in 1988, the first commercial market place for visual arts in which many major commercial galleries participated.

1990s

By 1990 the notion of a 'cultural industry', initially conceived as an advocacy tool to show that the arts contributed in economic terms, had gathered enough strength to influence some aspects of policy. The Labor Government's *Creative Nation* (1994) was the first comprehensive cultural policy statement issued in this country by a sitting government. Previous statements had tended to emerge as part of pre-election policy. While continuing to emphasise the centrality of the major music and performing arts companies, *Creative Nation* recognised the importance of the new multimedia and digital arts.

Vi\$copy, a copyright collecting society for visual authors, began operations in 1995 with establishment funding of $1 million for four years. Although visual authors had been legally entitled to receive copyright payments since the late 1960s, there was a low public awareness of the legal obligation to seek artists' permission to reproduce work, and few were paid the royalty due.

The Australian Commission for the Future report, *A Framework for Improving Viability in Selected Sectors of the Cultural Industry* (1992), identified weaknesses in the money chain for the visual arts, particularly marketing and distribution, and business planning skills. As a result, in 1993 the Federal Government allocated $10.5 million, over four years, to the Cultural Industry

Development Program, which was managed by the Department of Communications and the Arts. Although no new funds were committed after the four years ended in 1997, the concept of culture meeting industry continued to be expressed in Departmental thinking. This was reflected in the slogan 'One Stop Shop' for an internet site (Arts Info: www.artsinfo.net.au) designed to provide information on all forms of arts support available in Australia, launched in August 1997.

Commercial galleries began to develop export markets; this initiative was then supported by the Visual Arts Export Strategy of the Australia Council and the Elite Touring Program, established in 1993 by the Department of Foreign Affairs and Trade, which assisted galleries to take works to the international trade fairs. The strategy did not survive budget cuts by the Coalition Government.

By the end of the 1990s the notion had taken hold that each of the arts was an industry sector and that together – along with some other closely-related industries, such as film and aspects of television and radio – they amounted to a 'cultural industry'. In contrast to the shock waves within arts communities which greeted the Industries Assistance Commission report into the performing arts chaired by Richard Boyer in 1976, and which led to its effective rejection, a sense of being, at least in some contexts, a worker within an industry began to be a self-perception on the part of some artists. It came more quickly to arts administrators, curators and others than to artists. Initially, perhaps, it seemed an analogy to other sectors of the economy which were, clearly, industries. Yet it is also, obviously, a self-perception which is economic in character: it accepts, however reluctantly, that the economic is the primary definer of public sector activity. It may have been a realism with regard to the impact of economic rationalism during those times. There is, here, a clear parallel to the shifts in self-perception which occurred within universities during the same period. It raises the question of whether value can be effectively defined in terms which are not reducible to the economic. A related question is whether cultural production can be regarded as industrial work and still be, in essence, creative. In the context of patronage, another way of putting these questions is to ask: is open-ended, non-interventionist, long-term and sustainable institutional support for creative practice still possible?

Some figures, some rhetoric

A sense of the scale of the cultural industry can be gained from the 1996 Census in which 255,098 people – or roughly one in 30 of all workers – declared themselves employed mainly in the cultural sector: 156,739 of them in cultural occupations and the remaining 98,359 in non-cultural jobs within the industry. Overall, this is a growth of 20 per cent in five years, compared to an average of 7.4 per cent for all industries. It is difficult to quantify visual artists in exact numbers, as professional craftspeople have been counted in some census years but not others. In 1996, however, among cultural workers 16,288 were visual artists including photographers; 23,913 were designers or illustrators; over 10,000 worked as directors in film, television, radio or the theatre; 762 were museum or gallery curators; and 879 were private art teachers. *Involvement* in the arts was measured in an ABS survey covering the twelve months ending March 1997. Of the 14,433,800 people aged fifteen and over, 4,735,300 undertook some cultural activity in the period, with 2,184,200 working in the area in some capacity, 877,000 of whom received some payment for their efforts. Involvement figures are much higher because they represent instances of activity, so one person may be counted a number of times. 497,203 were active in the visual arts; 371,900 in crafts; 240,000 in design; 38,000 in film production; 42,700 in cinema/video; 84,600 in radio; and 56,700 in television, while 144,800 were involved in organising art/craft shows, and 41,100 in arts organisations or agencies. In all, it adds up to a remarkable commitment to cultural activity by the people of Australia (Cultural Ministers Council, Statistics Working Group 1998a; ABS 1997a and 1997b).

As to the economic scale and significance of the cultural industries, *Creative Nation* was explicit:

> This cultural policy is also an economic policy. Culture creates wealth. Broadly defined our cultural industries generate 13 billion dollars a year ... Culture adds value, it makes an essential contribution to innovation, marketing and design. It is a badge of our industry. The level of creativity substantially determines our ability to adapt to new economic imperatives. It is a valuable export in itself and an essential accompaniment to the export of other commodities. It attracts tourists and students. It is essential to our economic success.
>
> (Commonwealth of Australia 1994b, p. 7)

While this is as eloquent a statement of the interplay between economic and cultural value as occurs in any official document, it is relevant to note the claims being made for tourism at the same time. John Morse, Director of the Australian Tourist Commission, said in 1997:

> By any measure, the growth in the tourism industry during the past decade has been remarkable. It is now the fastest growing significant industry in Australia, generating over $14.1 billion in export earnings and creating new jobs and opportunities in regions right across Australia.
>
> (cited in Stevenson 2000, p. 125)

The hyperbole certainly was flying in the mid-1990s. These sums represent about 1.6 per cent of the approximately $900 billion economy as a whole in 1993–94. Both industries received substantial governmental support to build infrastructure, innovate and expand markets locally and abroad. The convergence between these two booming sectors continues to be more and more marked, notably in the growth in sales of Aboriginal art to visitors and in the rapid expansion of interest and governmental investment in heritage, not only in primary tourist destinations but in localities 'right across Australia' (Bennett 1993, p. 88).

In money terms, governmental support for the arts at all levels has grown considerably from the surge in commitment in the late 1960s. It has, however, varied at each level. Figures from Guldberg and the Australian Bureau of Statistics show total cultural funding grew in dollar terms from $2,390.9 million in 1988–89 to $3,447.6 million in 1996–97. Of this total, federal funding rose from $1,198.3 million in 1988–89 to a peak of $1,395.6 million in 1995–96, after which the decline began. The Australia Council received $68.9 million in 1988–89, $74.4 million in 1995–96, after which the amount plateaus, losing real dollar value, and much of it becomes earmarked for distribution to major companies. State government cultural funding rose from $847 million in 1988–89 to $1,368.5 million in 1996–97 and continues to rise. Of this, state arts authorities disbursed $380.5 million at the earlier date, rising to $530 million by the later. Local government contributions to cultural growth were even more generous, from $345.6 million to $790.7 million, making this sector, proportionally, the most active in the field (ABS 1997a and 1997b; Guldberg 2000, appendix 4).

These amounts are considerable, and their disbursement has, in the overwhelming majority of cases, been effective in terms of the goals of the funding agencies, to say nothing of the evident vibrancy which animates all fields of the creative arts at the level of the work itself and its enthusiastic absorption by increasing audiences. But the governmental investment is, as well, extremely efficient in 'bangs for bucks' terms: a little over $3,000 million support to an industry generating $13 billion is a cheap investment. (Private patronage and corporate sponsorship, while growing, has insufficient profile as yet to effect this overall picture.) The inference is obvious: the crucial input is from the cultural producers and transformers themselves.

Australia's approximately 80,000 artists and related arts professionals constituted, in 1996, close to 2 per cent of the total workforce. There were surprisingly few cultural workers of ethnic background, over 60 per cent had tertiary qualifications, and as a proportion of the total workforce most tended to live in New South Wales and the Australian Capital Territory (Guldberg 2000, ch. 2). One per cent identified as Aboriginal or Torres Strait Islanders, predominantly painters and sculptors. This latter figure is less proportionally than the 360,000 to identify as Indigenous in the 1998 national census total population of 18 million, but closer to the 1996 proportion. In that year, 910 identified as full-time arts professionals, 380 as visual arts including crafts workers. The number of Indigenous people involved in the visual arts on a less than full-time basis is, however, usually estimated in much greater quantities: 8,000 in the Altman Report and as many as 10,000 in art world reporting and journalism (Altman 1989). In 1994 the Aboriginal and Torres Strait Islander Commission estimated the Indigenous arts and crafts market to be worth almost $200 million per year (ATSIC 1994, p. 24). Of this, $14.6 million was sales through recognised commercial galleries (ABS 1997c). Australia Council surveys of purchases of Indigenous art and artifacts/souvenirs by international visitors rose from $46 million in 1993 to $67 million in 1996 (Spring 1996 and Australia Council 1997b, cited in Janke 1999, p. 14).

How have artists fared on an individual basis during these 'boom' years? In sum, not so well. Real incomes declined in the years prior to 1996 (by 0.7 per cent annually compared to 0.4 per cent for the total workforce) and show no sign of increasing. While the median income for all arts professionals in 1996 was $26,900 (the average $30,885), this ranged from $33,000 median ($44,000 average) for TV, film, radio and stage directors to less than $10,000 for visual artists (Economic Strategies 2000, ch. 3; Throsby and Thompson 1994). Reports as to incomes to Aboriginal artists from sales of their art vary considerably, with estimates of average incomes of $1,000 per annum most common.

The present picture

An overview of the visual arts in Australia in the years around 2000 would highlight the following features. *Art practice* is shaped, in the broadest terms, by dichotomies such as high, official and experimental art compared to low, popular, commercialised art, the play between international and local concerns, the contrast between art committed to criticality in some sense and that which confirms taste and expectation, and the differences and exchanges between Aboriginal and non-Aboriginal orientations. Within these there are, of course, many further, often productive divisions: for example, between art made by Aborigines living in remote communities and that made by Aborigines living in the cities. The *art market* is now a highly professionalised, specialised sector, divided primarily along contemporary versus historical, Aboriginal and non-Aboriginal, primary and secondary (commercial galleries and auction houses) and professional artist versus amateur lines. The *educational infrastructure* supporting the visual arts is now quite vast; the visual arts are a strong presence at every level and in all types of educational institution. *Commercial culture* continues to be spectacularised, relying more and more on visual imagery to communicate, as does *information exchange*. By concentrating on seeding and sustaining those areas not considered vital to the interests of the art market or education, *governmental patronage* had succeeded in creating an art world which offers artists and those interested in interpreting or promoting the visual arts a wide range of opportunities to attempt a lifetime career. All of those involved in this 30-year effort have reason for justifiable pride.

But this mood must be momentary, because the other, most obvious thing about the current tendency of governmental patronage is that it has shifted decisively towards emphasising initiatives which will, the government hopes, lead to its own redundancy as a patron. This perspective is shared, in varying degrees, by all political parties. To the new right-wing minorities, it is simple and total: in view of the struggles of the 'battlers' and the disadvantaged, the arts should expect nothing, the privileged must be made to swim in the shark-infested waters of the market of life. This was explicitly stated by Pauline Hanson's One Nation party in the 1996 election, and was echoed by the Liberal Party's attack on arts 'elites' during the 1999 campaign period.

One way of measuring the significant shifts of recent decades is to assess the response of the Australia Council to them. In 1974, 50 per cent of Australia Council Visual Arts Grants went to individual artists. As other needs in the visual arts were identified and the arts industry evolved, the proportion of individual artist grants declined to around 20 per cent of grants by the mid 1980s, and has remained in that proportion of the Visual Arts/Crafts Board/Fund grants into the late 1990s. Other funding went to assist acquisitions by public galleries, exhibitions, education, access and promotion activities.

Much of the infrastructural development listed in the previous section was enabled by the quick and generous response on the part of the Australia Council to initiatives emergent from artists, critics, curators and, often, arts administrators themselves.

Starting with the Experimental Art Foundation in Adelaide in 1975, new exhibition spaces for contemporary art received continuing support. By the mid 1980s federal and state funding for contemporary art spaces had plateaued, a situation which continued into the late 1990s. This flattening off, then decline, in real support is general across the sector. The artist-in-residence scheme, placing artists in universities, was inaugurated in 1974 with the intention of creating work opportunities for artists. It spread to include schools, communities and workplaces. In these specific forms, the Council ceased funding most of the schemes during the 1980s, although some continue independently. Undoubtedly they have generated hundreds of jobs for artists, and the area of public art continues to flourish, mostly through local government projects, but also in private building development.

A successful type of infrastructural provision was the promotion of professional networks within the visual arts, for example, the Art Gallery Directors' Council, Art Museums Australia, the Association of Art & Design Schools, the Art Association of Australia, the Art and Working Life Program and many others. Some of these have ceased, having completed their work or through withdrawal of funding. Many continue in the same or different forms, or in association with contingent organisations. None are fully self-sustaining – all depend on winning grants, occasional philanthropy and untold quantities of in-kind work by unpaid members.

The internationalisation of Australian visual arts has been advanced by Council support of exhibitions (for example, in the Australian Pavilion at the

Venice Biennale), overseas studios (especially in Europe and the United States), educational exchanges and travel by artists. By the 1990s, as the Council fell into line with government policy to increase contact with Asia, residencies became available in various Asian countries. The Myer Foundation, with Mazda, established Asialink in the early 1990s. This mix may well be the proto-type for the future.

After the MacLeay Report to the House of Representatives Standing Commit-tee on Expenditure (1986), the Australia Council Act was amended to enable the government to give broad policy direction to the Australia Council, and the Council was restructured. The Visual Arts Board merged with the Crafts Board, but as far as visual arts policy was concerned there was minimal change. Crafts-people in later years argued they were gaining less support in this arrangement, as did visual artists. Nevertheless, it is arguable that the crafts, which had been developing their own industrial frameworks, niche markets and measured distribution systems for decades, were in less need of grant subsidisation than the other visual arts. This has proved to be the case *de facto*.

Promoters of smaller government might have been expected to mount the case that the massive investment in infrastructural support during the 1970s and 1980s has meant that self-sustenance of the kind demonstrated in the case of the crafts is now the rule throughout the visual and other arts, that success has reduced the need to maintain grants-type support, so that governments are justified in cutting these budgets. In the face, however, of the kinds of facts and figures set out in this paper, this line has not been pushed. Rather, reference is made to market forces, or silent assumptions made as to the supposedly 'natural' number and type of artists a small country like Australia might be expected to sustain.

One consistent theme harped upon by governments following the neo-liberal agenda is the necessity for the arts to earn more income, to become self-sufficient. This view has often drawn fierce opposition from those who argue that the production of art cannot fully adopt business characteristics. By the 1990s governments were giving priority to funding programs to improve business skills, and to bring small businesses together to market arts products (Australia Council 1997a). The Australia Council supported commercial galleries to expand markets overseas, establishing an Australian presence at the interna-tional art fairs. Other industry programs appear to have had little effect on the visual arts, although related design and craft areas, such as furniture design, benefited from these schemes.

The role of generating cultural policy for the federal government – along with the responsibility to support cultural projects of national and regional significance – was formally devolved to the Australia Foundation for Culture and the Humanities, located in Melbourne. After some initial attempts, the Founda-tion retreated from the policy role (in practice, impossible to concentrate in one agency anyway) then spent some years searching for relevance. After 1996, it turned more and more towards acting as a broker between cultural producers and businesses which, the federal government hopes, will pick up the slack left by its retreat from the field. In August 2000 this change was formalised when it was renamed the Australia Business Arts Foundation.

Another noticeable trend in arts policies is the move away from consideration of the needs of specific categories of art practice. For example, the Australia Council annual reports initially reported on grants to categories such as painting, sculpture and photography, but by the 1980s they moved to broader categories such as for artist-run spaces and individual artists' development. In the mid-1990s all Boards/Funds at the Council adopted uniform funding categories, regardless of the structure of an art form economy. Similarly, the Victorian Arts Ministry abandoned art form categories for generic policies.

During the 1990s there was a rapid turnover of policy approaches at all levels of government, reflecting the pressure of having to cope with shrinking funds for an expanding industry. State arts ministries increasingly diversified their approaches to arts funding, with the language of economic rationalism strongly emerging in many of their policies. For example, the West Australian Arts Ministry replaced the concept of subsidy to organisations with a funding category of 'investment'. Efforts to develop the arts as businesses are prominent in state policies. Australia Council arts boards became 'funds' in 1996. As indicated above, the actual dollar input has sharply declined at the federal level, increased somewhat at the state level, but grown most appreciably at the level of local government. A strong ethos of 'regionalism' emerged during this period (Macdonnell 1996; Smith 1999–2000).

The Maecenas-like support for arts infrastructure by Victorian Premier Jeff Kennett went against the widespread tendency on the part of government agencies towards withdrawal from their core responsibilities. It may well have contributed to the perception that led to his shock electoral defeat, largely in country electorates, in 1999. In the case of the leadership of the Australia Council (as distinct from the working body, whose efforts continue to be engaged and generative, if increasingly obliged – under reforms introduced by Hillary McPhee – to operate at arms length), this downward spiral collapsed into total retreat. When questioned on the ABC arts program *Express* (1 July 1998) about why she had not responded to One Nation's call for the total withdrawal of all arts funding, Australia Council chairperson Margaret Seares argued that the Council should not be seen as the only voice defending support for the arts or even debating policy in public. She views the Council as 'an arm of government', an advocate for the arts within government, but no longer as a leader or particularly a trendsetter in building culture in Australia. This is a sad, pale echo of the dreams which inspired the foundation of the Council.

In its most recent policy shift, the Council is seeking to reorient its activities towards broadening public interest in the arts, and towards persuading the creative transformers in the arts to do likewise. While the Council itself has had an advocacy section for some years, and while many arts organisations (the

Australian Chamber Orchestra, for example) are very successful self-promoters, a major effort will have to be made to overcome the perception that the arts are elitist. A report prepared by the advertising firm Saatchi & Saatchi, *Australians and the Arts: What Do the Arts Mean to Australians*, noted that 88 per cent of Australians placed a high or fairly high value on having some creative skill, 85 per cent found the skill of a great artist inspiring and 75 per cent felt that the arts helped them to define and express their cultural identity. Yet 74 per cent felt that they would like to understand the arts better, a quarter were disinclined towards the arts and half the population did not like mixing with those who go to art events, with 42 per cent agreeing that this was a 'class thing' (Saatchi & Saatchi 2000). While 65 per cent were positively involved in the arts, changing the views and the leisure habits of the remaining 35 per cent – and the practices of many cultural providers – is now seen as the priority for cultural policy. How successful this will be remains very much to be seen.

Taking all these changes together, the present picture is one in which governmental patronage is marked by plateaued if not declining funding, as well as staged withdrawal from strategic infrastructure creation, in favour of the operation of market forces, appeals to business and a celebration of minority populism. If governments persist along these lines, the striking achievements outlined in this chapter will become matters of historical memory and, quite probably, social amnesia.

The role of artists

Artists have significantly influenced the development of the visual arts industry, and continue to do so both as individuals and through various organisations such as the Artworkers' Union and the National Association for the Visual Arts. They have had considerable impact as participants on Australia Council boards and committees, especially in the 1970s and early 1980s when structures were being established. Contemporary artistic concerns with conceptualism, issue politics, feminism and the environment formed the content of many institutionalising agendas (see Smith 1991b and 1996a). Government agencies were able to work closely with the arts community in developing structures, particularly conditions which encouraged the creation of critical, innovative and experimental art in ways that would often be anathema to the commercial market, local cultures and official taste. The massive increase in the number of tertiary educated artists, the plateauing of arts funding budgets and, as the infrastructure grew, the increasing complexity of demands for arts funding – as well as the internal policy shifts outlined above – have resulted in a more distanced and bureaucratic approach from the government agencies. The arts community has learned that the trajectories of art practice and those of art institutions do not evolve in tandem. Of increasing relevance, too, were the reactionary attacks on arts funding itself – especially its direction towards experimental practice – from certain artists (notably the poet Les Murray and others who attacked its 'elitism') when the mood in the country turned sour in the mid-1990s.

The battles for fees, rights and industry conditions have resulted in higher expectations, particularly by younger artists. Among the areas of the arts industry as yet unprotected by law, on which artists and organisations continue to lobby, are the unauthorised reproduction of art, the lack of moral rights and the lack of resale royalties for artists. Interestingly, there was strong media coverage of these issues in the 1990s through reportage of the Indigenous visual arts. Contemporary Aboriginal Art, as an art movement and a market sector, has negotiated a particular hybrid of amateur and professional practices and values, redefining them *as they apply to itself* in the process. The extent to which this redefinition will impact on non-Aboriginal visual arts remains an open question.

In a much enlarged visual arts scene, the influence of artists on the evolution of the industry in the 1990s is not clear. The federal government remains the most important national support agency for the visual arts, in that, despite diminution, it still provides half of the funding – matching the combined spending of the state and territory arts ministries. However, the funding reaches only a small proportion of artists, and therefore the true direction of the national scene is probably quite anarchic. It clearly differs in the various states and localities, as state and local governments, as well as community groups, follow increasingly diverse and specific objectives.

The 1996 intervention by the Bankstown branch of the Australian Taxation Office triggered much activity. Lobbying by industry groups such as NAVA and representations from Arts Law led to a degree of flexibility on the part of the ATO (Pledge 1998). Nevertheless, the weight of the difference between the two worlds remains. In June 2000, during the final days before the implementation of the Ralph Report into the new business tax scheme, artists remained subject to being caught in a net intended for cheating hobby farmers, and having their modest requests for rebates on material outlays refused by a government which failed to acknowledge their special circumstances. A most strenuous lobbying effort, led by NAVA, persuaded Labor and Democrats senators to block the relevant legislation until the government – at the eleventh hour – accepted an exemption allowing professional artists earning $40,000 or less from non-art activities to write off their art costs such as paint, canvas and studio rent against income earned from secondary jobs.

After 30 years of progressive institutionalisation of the arts, although the scale of activity has grown massively, many of the structures developed have remained dependent on the public purse. With the exception of government-owned institutions such as the public galleries, many schemes can be seen as short term, although it appears in some areas, such as public art, that activity has continued and grown through various policy constructions. In the current climate, however, progressive development seems no longer certain. Variable, sporadic, uneven change is now the rule.

Although artists have mounted campaigns to improve working and industry conditions, and some have achieved a stable income by their middle years, the overall low levels of artists' incomes suggests an industry not yet fully established. The art workers who appear to have benefited from the growth of the visual arts, and who have regular incomes, are in the educational, curatorial and managerial areas. Certainly there is a marked lack of protection for artists from potentially exploitative situations, particularly those likely to occur in a context where an open market is strongly shaped by new technologies which themselves rely heavily on workers with the skills traditionally possessed in concentrated forms by visual artists.

The future

In May 1995 the Government of Canada finalised its proclamation of 'Status of the Artist' legislation. It contained three major components:

(i)   a statement of principles recognising the value of the artist to Canadian society (in parallel to fishermen and farmers);
(ii) the creation of a Council for the Status of the Artist with the task of continually providing advice to the minister responsible for culture on measures which would strengthen the socio-economic status of artists; and
(iii) the creation of the Canadian Artists and Producers Professional Relations Tribunal with three tasks: to define artistic sectors for collective bargaining; to determine the associations which are most representative of professional, self-employed artists and to certify these organisations; and to hear complaints of unfair labour practices and prescribe appropriate remedies.

Outstanding here is the conception of cultural relationships in flow, as changing so fast that they require expert bodies to provide redefinitions of them as they unfold. Limitations are that the structure should include all those who have what might be called 'transformative' effects on the arts within an industry, not just artists understood in the traditional sense. Critics, curators, gallerists, for example, would be included.

As we move into a time when agencies and institutions are being increasingly dismembered, when industries are being deregulated, when exchanges are increasing in speed and complexity, it seems to me that, in the arts, institutionalisation will occur in three forms: (i) through the formation of new, mobile, open, transient interest-communities (not discussed in this paper), (ii) through the adoption by large numbers of players in the industry (and by those in government and the private sector who interact with them) of a comprehensive set of equitable, sustainable, 'best practice' guidelines for all relationships and exchanges within the industry, and (iii) through legislative intervention into the mixed economy settings of the future.

Developing a set of guidelines in widespread and lengthy consultation with those involved is the goal of the Visual Arts Industry Guidelines project, funded by the Australian Research Council as a strategic partnership with key players in the visual arts industry, with support also from the Australia Council. It focuses on the relationships between practising visual artists and the rest of the industry, and on the complex interactions and mutual responsibilities of all sectors of this industry and the community. These include unresolved issues in taxation, insurance, superannuation, occupational health and safety, copyright, codes of practice, fee scales, moral rights and codes of ethics, along with lack of status and inadequate remuneration. It is the first attempt to address these issues in a comprehensive, comparative way. Outcomes may well be relevant across other arts practices. Models have been prepared covering relationships between artists and galleries, public art commissioning, residences and workshops, and competitions, awards and prizes. Others are in active preparation, covering topics listed above, along with papers which model money flows in the sector, criteria of professionalism, artworkers' rights and entitlements, the impact of new technologies, and the nature of unemployment. The primary goal of the project is to provide models for the comprehensive set of guidelines mentioned above (Jordan 2000).[3] These guidelines do not amount to an institutional solution, rather they are a matter of self-regulation and mutual accommodation.

Something like 'status of the artist' legislation, despite its degree of conceptual and practical problems, is, to me, the only valid kind of institutionalisation in the arts in the mixed economies in which we will increasingly live. But we should be under no illusions as to the ease with which something like this could occur in Australia, nor expect it to work like a magic wand (Cliche 1996). The Canadian legislation was inspired by a resolution concerning the status of the artist adopted by UNESCO at its conference in Belgrade in 1980. Canada is the only country to have reached the stage of enacting something into law.

The international environment, in these globalising times, can be harsh. While music and the performing arts – or, at least, the major companies – have recently received substantial federal government support, the sector as a whole remains subject to losing crucial cultural protections if, as the 1994 General Agreement on Trade in Services (GATS) provides, it becomes subject to the disciplines of free trade. In February 2000 a new round of negotiations were launched by the World Trade Organization. These will affect the various cultural sectors differently. Visual artists in Australia have long divided, and mixed, their local and international loyalties, more often than not in very productive ways. The art market is overwhelmingly interested in contemporary and historical Australian art. Therefore, few in the visual arts support parochialist bans on foreign actors, imported exhibitions and overseas films. Nevertheless, the new GATS round could make vulnerable to challenge, on the grounds of free trade, direct federal and state subsidies, taxation concessions and local content rules. The fundamental elements of the infrastructural provision outlined in this chapter could be shaken, the ideas for the future suggested here seriously derailed.

For a moment, in the later 1970s and early 1980s, Australia found a set of infrastructures – at least in the visual arts – which inspired the creativity at the core of its culture while maintaining in themselves the right mix of strength and flexibility to sustain them as live institutions. We need to find a different set of structures to work a mix appropriate to the moment in which we now find ourselves, one which is increasingly not of our own making.

Notes

1 The reference to 'voluntary entrepreneurs' is to the first of three stages of governmental funding prior to 1985 – the next two being 'statutory patronage' and 'decentralised patronage' – as characterised by Rowse (1985, ch. 1). Stevenson (2000, pp. 23–4) observes that the term 'decentralised' does not accurately describe the grant-giving of the Australia Council and the state granting bodies which was made more and more with service-to-community values in mind, and with greater use of peer assessment. This was an expanded form of statutory patronage. 'Decentralised' is, perhaps, more fitting as a polite term for the slow but steady withdrawal from sustaining support which has marked the last five years of federal patronage.

2 For much of the detail in the following I am indebted to Travers (1997), commissioned as preliminary research towards the project mentioned in note 3 below, and supported by a grant from the Research Institute for the Humanities and Social Sciences, University of Sydney. Other relevant texts include Battersby (1980), Rowse (1985), Throsby and Mills (1989), Macdonnell (1992), Commonwealth of Australia (1994a), Throsby, Mills and Thompson (1994).

3 The research team includes myself; Associate Professor Ron Callus, Director of the Australian Centre for Industrial Relations Research and Training at the University of Sydney; Ms Tamara Winikoff, Executive Director of the National Association of the Visual Arts; Mr Anthony Bond, General Manager, Curatorial Services, Art Gallery of New South Wales; David Throsby, Professor of Economics at Macquarie University; and Shane Simpson of Simpsons Solicitors. While this paper reflects some of the thinking emerging within the group, the opinions offered here are my own. The first product of the group's work was a draft Visual Arts Code of Practice, posted for comment in June 2000 on the NAVA website (www.culture.com.au/nava/). Research Officer Caroline Jordan has edited a series of ten articles on aspects of the research, to be published in instalments by the Australian journal *Art Monthly* from July 2000.

📖 Guide to further reading

Since the early 1970s the Australia Council has commissioned and published nearly 100 reports on arts organisations, artists' earnings, marketing, gallery attendance, attitudes to the arts and governmental patronage of the arts at all levels, including its own, as well as an equal number of specific studies of projects, programs and art activities. This amounts to a record of its own enterprise, and is a significant chronicle of infrastructural provision during the period. In recent years the Australian Bureau of Statistics (1997a–c) has taken a close interest in the cultural involvement of Australians, producing a number of key studies. It has also worked with the Statistics Working Group of the Cultural Ministers Council to produce a continuing series of compact pamphlets of key statistics, such as those on commercial art galleries, employment, cultural industries and attendance at cultural venues. Independent commentary on visual arts patronage and infrastructural provision is frequent in newspapers and in art journals such as *Art Monthly Australia* and *Artlink*. Sustained studies are rare. Rowse (1985) is the outstanding pathfinding work; it includes historical information along with critical analysis. It has been matched in terms of description and analysis by Stevenson (2000). Both these volumes cover the arts in general. There is no concentrated study of infrastructural provision for the visual arts. Smith (1984–85) is an early examination of the activity of the Visual Arts Board of the Australia Council to that time. The recent work of Guldberg (2000) concentrates strongly on statistics relating to visual artists and arts workers from a historical perspective. One of the outcomes of the Visual Arts Guidelines Research Project will be a book which surveys historical developments, critically examines current structures, proposes best practice models and sets out future policy directions for the visual arts in Australia. Of the websites listed below, those of DCITA and NAVA provide the most relevant information and the most useful links.

Websites

www.afch.org.au
   Australia Business Arts Foundation (formerly the Australia Foundation for Culture and the Humanities)
www.ozco.gov.au
   Australia Council
www.docita.gov.au
   Department of Communication, Information Technology and the Arts. DCITA's arts information network is at www.artsinfo.net.au; its cultural network portal is www.can.net.au
www.niaaa.co.au
   National Indigenous Arts Advocacy Association
www.culture.com.au/nava
   National Association for the Visual Arts
metapix.arts.usyd.edu.au/power/institute
   Power Institute, Foundation for Art and Visual Culture, University of Sydney

References

Aboriginal and Torres Strait Islander Commission (1994) 'Submission to the House of Representatives Standing Committee on Aboriginal and Torres Strait Islander Affairs, Enquiry into Aboriginal and Torres Strait Islander Culture and Heritage', Canberra, unpublished.

Altman, Jon (ed.) (1989) *The Aboriginal Arts and Crafts Industry, Report of the Review Committee*, Canberra: AGPS.

— (2000) 'The indigenous visual arts industry: issues and prospects for the next decade', *Artlink* 20, pp. 86–92.

Arts Training Australia (1995) *Mapping the Visual Arts and Crafts*, Sydney: Arts Training Australia.

Australian Bureau of Statistics (1997a) *Cultural Trends in Australia, A Historical Overview*, Canberra: DCA (4172.0).

— National Centre for Culture and Recreation Studies (1997b) *Artswork: A Report on Australians Working in the Arts*, Sydney: Australia Council.

— (1997c) *Commercial Art Galleries 1996–97*, Canberra: DCA.

Australia Council (1980) 'Statement of Purpose', Policy Statement, North Sydney: Australia Council.

— (1997a) *Marketing the Arts: A Study of Marketing and Audience Development by Australian Arts Organisations*, Sydney: Australia Council.

— (1997b) 'Submission to Our Culture: Our Future, October 1997' in Janke (ed.) (1999).

Battersby, Jean (1980) *Cultural Policy in Australia*, Paris: UNESCO.

Bennett, Tony (1993) 'The Shape of the Past' in Graeme Turner (ed.) *Nation, Culture, Text*, London: Routledge.

Caruana, Wally (1993) *Aboriginal Art*, London: Thames & Hudson.

Cliche, Danielle (1996) 'Status of the artist or of arts organizations? A brief discussion on the Canadian Status of the Artist Act', *Canadian Journal of Communications* 21: www.cjc-online.ca/

Cochrane, Grace (1992) *The Crafts Movement in Australia: A History*, Sydney: University of New South Wales Press.

Commonwealth of Australia (1994a) *Arts Policy in Australia. A History of Commonwealth Involvement in the Arts*, Canberra: Parliamentary Research Service.

— (1994b) *Creative Nation: Commonwealth Cultural Policy*, Canberra: DCA.

— (1999) *Cultural Tourism in Australia, Characteristics and Motivations*, Canberra: DCITA.

Cultural Ministers Council, *Statistics Working Group (1997) Commercial Art Galleries Australia 1996–97*, Canberra: ABS.

— (1998a) *Australia's Culture no. 7: Employment*, Canberra: DCA

— (1998b) *Australia's Culture no. 8: Cultural Industries*, Canberra: DCA.

— (2000) *Australia's Culture no. 9: Attendance at Selected Cultural Venues, April 1999*, Canberra: DCA.

Edwards, Robert (1979) *Australian Aboriginal Art*, Canberra: Australian Institute of Aboriginal Studies.

Guldberg, Hans Hoegh (2000) *The Arts Economy 1968–1998: Three Decades of Growth in Australia*, Sydney: Australia Council.

Isaacs, Jennifer (1984) *Arts of the Dreaming, Australia's Living Heritage*, Sydney: Lansdowne.

— (1989) *Australian Aboriginal Painting*, Sydney: Craftsman House.

Janke, Terri (ed.) (1999) *Our Culture: Our Future – A Report on Australian Indigenous Cultural and Intellectual Property Rights*, Sydney: Michael Frankel & Company for AIATSIS and ATSIC.

Jordan, Caroline (2000) 'A sustainable future for artists: an Australian dream or a real possibility?', *Art Monthly Australia* 130, pp. 29–32.

McCulloch, Allan (1994) *Encyclopedia of Australian Art*, Sydney: Allen & Unwin, 3rd edition, revised and updated by Susan McCulloch.

Macdonnell, Justin (1992) *Arts, Minister?: Government Policy and the Arts*, Sydney: Currency Press.

— (1996) 'A Review of Regional Arts Development in New South Wales', Sydney: NSW Ministry for the Arts, unpublished.

Morphy, Howard (1999) *Aboriginal Art*, London: Phaidon.

Pledge, Peter (1998) 'Visual artists claiming income tax business deductions', *Tax Matters for the Visual Arts*, Sydney: Arts Law Centre of Australia.

Rowse, Tim (1985) *Arguing the Arts: The Funding of the Arts in Australia*, Ringwood, Vic.: Penguin.

Saatchi & Saatchi (Paul Costantoura) (2000) *Australians and the Arts: What Do the Arts Mean to Australians*, Sydney: Australia Council.

Smith, Terry (1984–85) 'The Visual Arts Board: from a "Ministry of Mediocrity" to "Rational Reform"?', *Art Network* 14, pp. 22–7; 16, pp. 38–40; 17, pp. 40–2.

— (1991a) 'From the desert' in Bernard Smith with Terry Smith, *Australian Painting 1788–1990*, Melbourne: Oxford University Press.

— (1991b) 'Postmodern plurality 1980–1990' in Bernard Smith with Terry Smith, *Australian Painting 1788–1990*, Melbourne: Oxford University Press.

— (1996a) 'Generation X: The impacts of the 1980s' in Rex Butler (ed.) *What is Appropriation?* Sydney: Power Publications; Brisbane: Institute of Modern Art.

— (1996b) 'Australia, painting and graphic arts before 1900' and 'Australia, art education' in Jane Shoaf Turner (ed.) *Dictionary of Art*, London: Macmillan.

— (1999–2000) 'Between regionality and regionalism: middleground or limboland?', *Periphery* 40–41, pp. 3–8.

Spring, Jane (1996) *International Visitors and Aboriginal Arts 1996*, Sydney: Australia Council.

Stevenson, Deborah (2000) *Art and Organisation: Making Australian Cultural Policy*, St Lucia: University of Queensland Press.

Sutton, Peter (ed.) (1988) *Dreamings: The Art of Aboriginal Australia*, New York and Melbourne: Viking.

Throsby, David and Devon Mills (1989) *When Are You Going To Get A Real Job?: An Economic Study of Australian Artists*, North Sydney: Australia Council.

Throsby, David and Beverly Thompson (1994) *But What Do You Do For A Living? A New Economic Study of the Australian Artist*, Sydney: Australia Council.

Travers, Mary (1997) 'An outline of the evolution of the visual arts industry in Australia', Power Institute, University of Sydney, unpublished.

Underhill, Nancy (1991) *Making Modern Art: Sydney Ure Smith*, Melbourne: Oxford University Press.

Chapter 4

Tourism, Culture and National Identity

Jennifer Craik

Tourism: from industry policy to cultural policy

Since the 1980s, Australia has been in the grip of tourist fever. Tourism is regarded in the same way as the pot of gold at the end of the rainbow; once we've located the pot then undreamed of riches will follow. In the more sanguine language of industry policy, tourism is feted as a sunrise industry with the potential to replace declining industries and economic sectors as well as add value to other viable sectors. In addition to these prosaic economic calculations, tourism has increasingly been embraced as a component of cultural policy and as the definer or coordinating point of national identity and culture. Tourism thus performs a double duty as economic salvation and nationalist cultural iconography.

Perhaps because of the enthusiasm with which tourism is heralded, few commentators question this rosy picture. But does tourism have unlimited growth potential? What are the consequences of this massive growth of tourism? Why are governments so keen to endorse and support an industry that defines itself in the cowboy terminology of private industry and eschews the public sector? What are the likely implications and impacts of continued tourist growth on the Australian economy and culture? In particular, as Australian identity is increasingly defined in terms of Aboriginal culture and cultural diversity, how might the expansion of Indigenous cultural tourism impact not only on the Indigenous arena (economy, identity, social organisation) but on the need for the broader Australian community to redefine itself in relation to the global projection of an Aboriginal-centred sense of Australian identity?

Tourism is also often regarded as a symptom of modernity – that is, epitomising the search for places and experiences that are up-to-the-minute, stylish and oriented towards the future – and, for others, postmodernity – that is, fusing past, present and future in a liminal timelessness and spacelessness characterised by pastiche, simulacra and iconography (Rojek and Urry 1997). Yet travel for pleasure, discovery, education and adventure has a long history that the emphasis on modernity and postmodernity often ignores (Adler 1989; Casson 1974). Further, alongside its experiential and representational aspects, tourism must also be seen in relation to institutional and governmental arrangements and processes of nation building. Ways of representing, reflecting and promoting images of the nation and the character of its people have been central to the formation of modern citizenries, and consequently tourism and travel have benefited from limited investment by government, especially in supporting transport infrastructure, heritage sites and monuments. It is therefore important to understand how the role of government in tourist development has evolved in order to position it as a cultural institution, and in order to show how it has been shaped by economic, political and policy forces, on the one hand, and by ideological, symbolic and consumer preferences, on the other.

Tourism and industry policy

In Australia, travel was initially synonymous with settlement and hence government has always been obliged to pay some attention to this phenomenon. From the 1920s, Australian governments directly sponsored travel promotion, investment in transport infrastructure and the maintenance of attractions and places of interest. The travel industry also established an early presence in the form of the Australian National Travel Association (ANTA), which was set up in 1929. Intended as the peak industry body, it represented the interests of the travel and tourism sectors and responded to government policies and industry trends. This body has remained the primary lobby group, changing its name in 1985 to the Australian Tourism Industry Association (ATIA) to reflect the industry potential and government recognition of tourism as a growth industry. In 1995, it became the Tourism Council Australia (TCA) in order to present a less lobby-driven profile and reinvent itself as a sector specialist in partnership with government. The body represents 30,000 tourism industry operators and organisations and works in conjunction with state members and other industry bodies. Its fortunes, however, have been declining. In early 2001, the TCA was placed in receivership.

Since 1989, the premier representative position of the TCA has been challenged by the establishment of the Tourism Task Force (TTF). Consisting of 150 chief executives of major tourism operators, the TTF was established by John Brown who had been Minister for Sport, Recreation and Tourism in the Hawke Labor Government from 1983 to 1987. The Chief Executive of the TTF is

John Brown's son, Christopher. Brown formed the TTF in response to the perceived failure of the TCA to gain the ear of government and secure adequate industry assistance and considerations. The Browns maintain that a private organisation representing major tourism interests can be a more proactive industry lobbyist. The TTF, however, is widely perceived as 'a one man band' and its aggressive tactics criticised as counter-productive. Insofar as it has been a thorn in the side of governments, it has contributed to charges of 'clientelism' in tourism policy (see Craik 1992).

Tourism was a low priority for governments for many years (Craik 1991; Carroll 1991). The situation began to change after a report was commissioned by ANTA in conjunction with the federal and state governments in 1964. This was the first significant integrated study of tourism. The Harris, Kerr, Forster and Co. (HKF) report, *Australia's Travel and Tourist Industry 1965* (HKF 1966), predicted that Australia was 'on the threshold of a great opportunity' if it developed appropriate policies for tourism development. In essence, the report said that Australia had significant tourist potential pending major upgrading of infrastructure, attractions and services. This included a now familiar shopping list: adequate infrastructure; deregulation of transport, planning and employment conditions; development of attractions; and aggressive promotion (Craik 1991, pp. 222–4). It was not enough to have natural wonders, a sunny climate and the outback. It was necessary to address the needs and patterns of usage of tourists, rather than assume that they would fall into the 'making do' and 'take it or leave it' attitude of many Australian enterprises.

The report recommended industry assistance in the form of tax breaks and low interest loans as well as reiterating the need for direct government funding of tourism promotion. While many of the recommendations were not implemented, they have been largely reiterated in subsequent commissioned reports and inquiries and have set the long-term basis for tourism policy and the lobby agenda. In the short term, the government agreed to establish the Australian Tourist Commission (ATC) in 1967 as the generic national promotional body for Australian tourism.

In considering what unique attractions could be developed for inbound tourists, the report emphasised the potential of what is now called Indigenous cultural tourism. While prescient in this assessment, the concept at the time was at odds with official and mainstream ideas about Aboriginal culture. Yet industry lobbyists persevered and in 1969 commissioned another HKF report, this time on the tourist potential of Central Australia (HKF 1969). In evaluating tourism at Uluru and the Olgas, the report rightly focused attention on the centrality of Indigenous Australia to international tourist appeal. A third report was commissioned in 1971 to evaluate the tourist potential of the Great Barrier Reef, again comprehensively investigating the need to actively develop the area for tourism by innovative infrastructure development, interpretive centres, and the establishment of an overarching management authority to balance different uses with conservation and preservation. Central to this report was the recognition of the importance of the marine and coral biodiversity, amid Indigenous traditions and presence (Pannell, Kerr, Forster 1971; Craik 1991, pp. 144–6). All three reports remain comprehensive and forward-looking blueprints. Although none was implemented, they remain the benchmark for strategies for enhancing Australia's tourist potential.

These commissioned reports set the scene for greater government and public interest in tourism during the 1970s and 1980s. A number of factors gelled to prod governments to take another look at tourism and how it should be dealt with as an industry. Underpinning the strategy to gain a higher profile for tourism in governance was the redefinition of tourism as a sunrise industry, that is, as one that had the potential to replace other declining industries and as one with the added benefit of not being resource extractive, polluting or destructive. Tourism became seen as a thoroughly modern industry suiting the mobile habits of citizens, satisfying their quest for something new, and projecting the image of Australia as a 'now' place full of unique scenery, fauna and flora.

Tourism first appeared as a separate portfolio in the McMahon Coalition Government, with Peter Howson as minister from 1971–72. It was during the Whitlam Labor Government (1972–75) that tourism won a more senior position in government, with the establishment of the Department of Tourism and Recreation and Frank Stewart as minister. But after successive government reports and inquiries the early optimism faltered with the result that, under the Fraser Coalition Government (1975–83), funding to the ATC was cut and tourism reduced to a division within the Industry and Commerce department, with no minister. Despite this governmental loss of faith, inbound tourism grew steadily and then jumped dramatically from the late 1970s, with visitors exceeding one million in 1984, two million in 1988, three million in 1994, four million in 1999 and five million in 2001.

On these figures, tourism seemed set to deliver its potential. Several government inquiries and reports followed (Edelman and Grey 1974; SCT 1978; BIE 1979; AGCIT 1986; IAC 1989). These stressed that tourism should be regarded as a 'proper' industry – not just a marginal or fly-by-night service sector dominated by rogues and con men and shaped by short-term profit margins and electoral cycles, even though there was some evidence of this industry profile. The industry fought to gain concessions customary in other industries. The Hawke and Keating Labor governments gave tourism a strong if idiosyncratic profile under ministers John Brown (1983–87), Graham Richardson (1988–89), Ros Kelly (1990–93) and Michael Lee (1993–96). These ministers were popular with the media and public, although prone to controversy, and they each lobbied intensively for the industry.

While some concessions were granted, many industry observers continue to feel that tourism has not benefited from government largesse on anything like the same scale as the rural sector, mining industries or communications industries. This ambivalence was reflected in the framing of the national tourism strategy published in 1992 but implemented only in part (DT 1992). There is still considerable ambivalence about whether tourism is a real industry or not. This is matched on the industry's side by ambivalence about government: it is a fair weather industry, wanting no interference when times are good and immediately demanding compensation and special consideration when times are bad. But then, governments are notoriously fickle too. Once tourism became acknowledged as a key industry and economic sector, it lost some visibility within industry policy generally and therefore its 'special pleading' status.

Nonetheless, tourism fulfils both a 'boosterism' and bread-and-circuses role for governments when they want a 'feel good' effect generated by events such as the 1956 Melbourne Games, the 1982 Brisbane Commonwealth Games, the 1987 defence of the America's Cup in Fremantle, the 1988 World Expo in Brisbane and the 2000 Sydney Olympic Games. Despite supporting the 'froth and bubble' of tourism and especially special events that are tourism-related, governments distance themselves from tourism when they are preoccupied with more fundamental roles, such as welfare, defence or economic policy.

In sum, tourism may be regarded as a sunrise industry, but this has not always been to its advantage. In terms of industry policy, tourism has been treated as *consultative clientelism*, that is, governments have consulted when it suited them or pressure demanded (Craik 1992; Hall and Jenkins 1995, pp. 59–63). However, policies have been determined primarily by macro-economic parameters and the lobbying influence of certain big players within the tourism sector. These include airlines and other transport sectors and companies, state government tourism bodies, major accommodation chains, and vertically and horizontally integrated leisure and entertainment conglomerates. In this sense, tourism policy has been determined by the clout of a few significant figures and the serendipitous twists and turns of government policy. The fact that this has happened suggests that successive governments have not known how to treat tourism. It has not fitted comfortably into existing portfolios or policy processes and hence it has been something of a political football subject to push and pull factors and shaped by the loudest voices.

As we enter the new century, tourism policy suffers from no longer being the brash new kid on the block with the potential to bolster the fortunes of government. Despite all the hype – for example concerning the tourism potential of and spin-offs from the 2000 Sydney Olympics and the considerable growth in Indigenous cultural tourism – tourism has lost favour with Australian governments when compared with some other industries. Under the Howard Coalition Government, tourism was represented ineffectually by Minister John Moore (1996–98), then downgraded into a junior ministry and split across two larger portfolio areas. It was divided between Industry, Science and Technology as a Division of Sport and Tourism on the one hand, and Communications, Information Technology and the Arts on the other. Its ministers were largely inexperienced; Jackie Kelly gained the portfolio of Sport and Tourism after her unexpected victory in the 1998 federal election while Peter McGauran, a long serving National Party member, showed more interest in regional issues than the Arts portfolio he was given.

While government funding of tourism promotion continues apace through the Australian Tourist Commission and state tourism bodies, the downgrading of the sector and fragmentation across different responsibilities has meant that there is no clear ministerial 'ownership' of tourism and hence no concerted and coordinated prioritising of tourism as a policy area. Although governments are still happy to recite figures showing the economic and employment importance of tourism, this is at odds with the diffuse policy treatment it receives when subject to general industrial measures such as tax reform, fuel rebates and special events incentives. The reality is Cabinet indifference to tourism, as evidenced by its low profile in the 2000 federal budget. Main features concerning tourism included: record funding for the ATC ($91.7 million), continuation of the Regional Tourism Program, implementation of a Domestic Tourism Initiative, and continuing support for tourism-related agencies (DISR 2000a). To coordinate these strategies, a National Online Tourism Strategy was released in 2000. Although this may appear to be a generous package, in fact most of these 'initiatives' were merely ongoing strategies. Moreover, they were either token or desperate measures to redress underperforming aspects of the tourism industry. This included the increased ATC budget, since the extra funding was targeted towards increased international promotion due to perceived inadequacies of current marketing campaigns. From the industry's perspective, such measures may have been welcome but did little to provide substantial assistance to improve the efficiency and profitability of the industry fundamentally.

Tourism and cultural policy

Associated with this shift is a further sign of schizophrenic treatment of the area. During the Keating Labor Government (1991–96), culture received prime ministerial attention, benefiting from a number of innovative programs and new funding and support schemes. To some extent, these culminated in Keating's *Creative Nation* cultural policy (DCA 1994), in which tourism was rolled into the cultural industries and cultural tourism singled out as one of the sunrise industries of the new millennium. The focus on cultural tourism involved an emphasis on the potential of tourism to provide enrichment to visitors through exposure to cultural activities, sites, objects and experiences as opposed to mere sightseeing. Cultural tourism appeared to have the capacity to stimulate cultural production, annex tourism to diverse cultural industries, and promote the culture of the nation. It was a way to develop cultural production and export opportunities for cultural services and products. While the *Creative Nation* policy was never fully implemented due to the defeat of the Labor Government in 1996, some strategies and policies have been reinvented in other guises under the Howard Liberal-National Coalition Government.

Above all, cultural tourism has been enthusiastically endorsed at least in rhetoric by Coalition ministers, even if this has not translated into practical, on-the-ground policies and incentives. Thus, a government Facts Sheet on Cultural Tourism heralds it as a way to promote the Australian lifestyle, heritage, arts, cultural industries and leisure pursuits: 'to showcase those qualities and experiences that make us distinctly Australian and to demonstrate to the world our excellence in internationally recognised art forms' (DISR 1999). In 1998, the Bureau of Tourism Research commissioned a report designed to profile the characteristics and value of cultural tourism to the Australian economy (Foo and Rossetto 1998). The findings were enthusiastically endorsed in a joint statement by the Minister for Sport and Tourism, Jackie Kelly and Minister for the Arts and the Centenary of Federation, Peter McGauran:

> With the report showing that around 60 per cent of all tourists to Australia visit our cultural attractions, our cultural sector will obviously benefit from continuing to develop a clear understanding of the cultural tourism market ... Cultural visitors spent more time in Australia than the average visitor, and ... $300 more than the average for all inbound visitors.
>
> (Kelly and McGauran 1999)

Very often, though, cultural tourism is reduced to statistics on expenditure on arts and crafts (e.g. Buchanan 1999) or Indigenous cultural tourism (DT 1994; ATSIC 1997; ATSIC & ONT 1997). The public has been bombarded with convenient statistics. Retail shopping expenditure on arts and crafts increased by 44 per cent between 1995 and 1997 with 41 per cent of inbound visitors making a purchase in this category. According to Minister McGauran: 'This increasing international interest in Australian culture confirms the vital contribution this sector makes to Australia's exports ... [T]here is real value in increasing the partnership between the tourism and visual art and craft sectors' (McGauran 1999b). However, despite the commissioning of many reports on cultural tourism and strategies for development, cultural tourism has largely fallen between stools. On the one hand, as a niche sector it has not been effectively targeted as a specific priority for government. On the other hand, it is used as shorthand for all tourism – after all there is a cultural component to all tourist experiences – and has been lumped in with tourism policies and strategies in general (Craik 2001).

In short, while mainstream tourism is dealt with as an idiosyncratic part of industry policy, the niche area of cultural tourism is regarded as an adjunct to – or subsector of – cultural policy. This leads to double counting and inconsistencies in approaches. There is also a certain degree of incommensurability between different foci and policy strategies. For the mainstream tourism industry, culture is more of a convenient catchcry than a deeply felt commitment to the arts and cultural production, raising the spectre of opportunism and exploitation. On the other side, those involved in cultural production often view tourism with some disdain and scepticism, if not hostility. Tourism is not a main aim of strategies for cultural development. This was evidenced recently in the lack of attention afforded to it in the Nugent Report about the state of the performing arts in Australia (DCITA 1999a–b). The tourism lobby essentially is interested in 'bums on seats', bodies in beds and dollars at cash registers, while the cultural lobby is interested in cultural employment, elite cultural improvement and cultural development. In the language of citizenship, culture is ostensibly about enhancing cultural capital and its distribution across the population. Yet the elitism and the self-referential peer group surrounding major cultural institutions – and even community cultural development programs – almost inevitably nips this mission of democratisation and enlightenment in the bud. Cultural development, in practice, is targeted towards the cultural cognoscenti. In light of the cowboy mentality of the tourism industry and the elitism of the cultural industries, the degree to which genuine partnerships and sustainable programs between these two sectors can be reached is minimal or cosmetic and usually confined to short-term programs or projects. Meanwhile the treatment of tourism within industry policy compared with its treatment under cultural policy entails different aims, strategies, outcomes and unintended consequences.

Tourist trends and their implications

Tourism has been steadily growing as a component of the Australian economy. The annual number of inbound tourists doubled between 1990 and 1999 to 4.1 million (ATC 2000b). The estimated contribution to the economy is about 6 per cent of GDP and about 15 per cent of total export earnings (DISR 2000b). Tourism is said to account for about 700,000 jobs or over 8 per cent of the work-force (BTR 2000b). In Queensland, the value of tourism is reputed to be greater than the combined value of coal production, all crop production and livestock and livestock products (Tourism Queensland 1998). Despite this apparently strong performance and the continued growth of the inbound market, there is concern within the industry about the future viability of an industry dependent on foreign fads for travel, comparative exchange rates, increasingly fierce competition from other destinations and diversification and specialisation of the market.

Moreover, while growth in inbound tourism is healthy, domestic tourism – which accounts for the majority of tourist activity or 75 per cent of estimated tourist expenditure – has shown little growth (BTR 2000b). This was recognised in the 2000 Federal Budget through strategies aimed at boosting a Regional Tourism Program and supporting a joint Domestic Tourism Initiative with the states, measures designed to 'enhanc[e] awareness amongst Australians of the breadth and quality of tourism experiences right on their doorstep' (ATC 2000a). But it is fair to ask whether there is a 'natural' cap on the amount of domestic tourism. After all, internal travel amounts to switching expenditure from other domestic activities or from Australians travelling abroad and, while the latter fluctuates, there is little indication that Australians are about to abandon their propensity for overseas travel.

So we have a situation where Australia is experiencing a steady growth in inbound tourism but little growth in domestic tourism, alongside increased demands that tourism be more environmentally and culturally sustainable and more accountable to current ideas about national identity and Australian-ness. Are these two trends compatible? Or is the provision of services and products for inbound tourists inevitably at odds with those for the domestic market and for leisure and pleasure more generally?

Part of this push relates to the perceived need to diversify tourist products and package them in more sophisticated and internationally competitive ways. Tourists, it is believed, want more than the bush, the Opera House, Uluru and the Great Barrier Reef. Now, the argument goes, is the time to promote Australian lifestyle and culture more generically by packaging special types of tourist experiences of Australia's cultural assets: heritage; arts, craft and fine design; multiculturalism (ethnic communities and traditions, festivals, food and wine); Indigenous culture; live performances, special events and major festivals; lifestyle (including surfing, sport, barbeques, sheep and cattle stations); and industries (wool, forestry, mining beef, wine, niche agricultural industries, etc.) (DISR 1999). This pitch also includes diverse kinds of 'special interest' tourism.

The emphasis in these niche forms of tourism is on their educational, experiential and communicative dimensions and on the authenticity, transparency and honesty of such encounters compared with the less personal and insulated experiences associated with conventional mass tourism. Such experiences may occur in different places: outback farms and sites; cultural precincts; theme parks; heritage sites or centres; museums; galleries; performing arts venues; festivals; markets, ordinary streetlife and everyday venues. It is easy to confuse diversification and specialisation of tourist behaviour and preferences with a perceived growth in cultural tourism – or rather a shift away from general or mass tourism towards cultural tourism. Is the overall nature of tourism changing or is cultural tourism just one of the diverse special kinds of tourism that is developing and responding to changing tastes?

These trends relate to three factors: international trends in tourist behaviour; the maturation of the Australian tourism industry; and changing ideas about nation and identity. Internationally, tourism is being challenged by the changing needs, preferences and behaviour of tourists who are increasingly seasoned travellers familiar with diverse destinations and holiday types. The global traveller is a more sophisticated beast than her/his predecessor, possessing a greater knowledge of options, having plenty of experience as a tourist and accustomed to lifestyle-oriented and consumer-driven ways of life. The postmodern tourist knows what she/he wants. Very often, the global traveller eschews conventional mass tourist experiences for travel that offers something a bit different. Such tourists are particularly attracted to special interest tourism, especially cultural tourism and its ilk. The market has responded accordingly. Of course, other factors have contributed to this situation – the internationalisation of travel and tourist services and facilities, global patterns of migration and temporary movement, global communications, and concentration of airline and accommodation services. The international tourist industry is thus more complex than a decade ago, with the consequences of globalisation an everyday matter.

Reflecting these trends, the Australian tourist industry has also changed significantly over the past decade. Tourists demand higher levels of service, more flexibility and better experiences. Moves towards privatisation, increased foreign investment and deregulation have set the conditions for industry growth to be shaped by marketplace predilections. And now that Australia is no longer a one-off exotic destination, the industry has had to address ways to entice mature visitors, especially returning visitors. Part of the solution has been to annex tourism more directly to ideas, debates and activities associated with the never-ending Australian pre-occupation with national identity and national culture.

Tourism and national identity

> How do you sell a product as varied and spectacular as Australia? ... [B]y redefining Australia's personality as youthful, energetic and optimistic, stylish and unpretentious, genuine and open.
> (ATC 'Brand Australia' campaign, cited in ABC 1997, Episode 13)

The changing nature of Australian tourist experiences has already been mentioned. There has been a shift away from natural wonders, architectural monuments and wildlife towards a more nuanced image of Australia. It has been argued that this has coincided with the deregulation of the financial system and internationalisation of trade and culture that occurred in the 1980s. In tourism terms the shift was epitomised by the ATC advertisements featuring Paul Hogan inviting visitors to the land down-under where friendly informal people will 'throw another shrimp on the barbie' for the unexpected guest. This campaign, though controversial at the time, was remarkably successful in creating an image of a relaxed and friendly if largely unknown Australia.

Now tourist advocates argue that Australia needs to project a different image, one that can encapsulate the 'multidimensional aspects to Australia, including our multiculturalism, our food, our wine, our culture, our art, our beautiful natural attractions, our man-made attractions. The whole caboose, the way we live in this country' (John Morse in ABC 1997, Episode 13). Nonetheless, Morse argues that promotions must retain the most obvious icons of Australia – 'the kangaroo, the Opera House, Ayers Rock, and the Barrier Reef ... because what we see as cliches the rest of the world actually sees as very endearing icons' (ABC 1997, Episode 13). This diversification of the tourist image of Australia to incorporate both high and low culture has recognised that tourists want a range of experiences – from the sophisticated to the mundane – within a visit. Thus, 'someone who is seeking total relaxation one day might be seeking out a cultural experience the next, a sporting day the day after that, and an ecological one the day after that' (Brian King in ABC 1997, Episode 12). These 'crossover' experiences have far-reaching implications for the form of promotion and the packaging of tourist experiences.

The broadening out of Australia's tourist appeal can be seen in figures on the most popular places visited by inbound tourists in 1997 (see table below).

These attractions offer a range of experiences with some, such as the Blue Mountains just west of Sydney, providing for a variety of activities, attractions and experiences. It is important to note that some attractions do not keep records of visitation, making it difficult to identify visitor patterns. Different methods of calculating visitation paint very different pictures, as analysis of the regional figures illustrates. For example, while 624,000 visitors visited the Great Barrier Reef attractions in 1997, only 153,100 (or 4 per cent of inbound visitors) are reported as visiting the Great Barrier Reef region in 1998, although 704,200 (18 per cent of inbound visitors) visited Tropical North Queensland (BTR 2000a). In fact, the Queensland north tropics are the fourth most visited destination. And while Sydney is visited by over half of inbound visitors (56 per cent in 1998 or 58.5 per cent if the Blue Mountains are included), 81 per cent visited Queensland regions.

At the same time as coping with increased and changing patterns of visitation, the tourism industry has improved its identification of and promotion to different markets. In 1999, the ATC launched a $150 million Brand Australia

Most popular attractions visited by inbound tourists in 1997 × number of visitors

Gold Coast theme parks (artificial attraction)	846,000
Blue Mountains (natural site, scenery, lifestyle)	832,000
Great Barrier Reef (natural site, wildlife, special interest)	624,000
Fremantle (historic site, lifestyle)	365,000
Phillip Island penguin parade (natural attraction, scenery)	286,000
Parliament House Canberra (cultural monument)	192,000
Kakadu (natural site, scenery, wildlife, Indigenous culture)	106,000
Barossa Valley (wine, historic site, lifestyle)	102,000
Port Arthur Historic Site (historic site, scenery)	47,000

(Adapted from ATC 'Facts sheets. Inbound Visitor Characteristics', 2000e; source 1997 IVS, www.atc.net.au/news/facts.htm)

campaign aimed at five distinct markets (ATC 2000c). Overall, the campaign relied on promoting 'the irreverent Aussie sense of humour and spectacular images of Australia' to position it 'as a friendly, colourful and stylish destination'. The aim was to balance 'the traditional images of Australia's natural attractions ... [with] the friendly people and benefits of a holiday in Australia'. Based on research into perceptions of Australia, five slogans and market shares were identified. In North America, the slogan, 'Australia – meet the locals' drew on perceptions of the Aussie sense of humour and laid-back lifestyle; holidays that offered 'real Australian characters and promising adventure, escape and off-the-beaten track experiences' were promoted. In New Zealand, under the slogan 'And you thought you knew', the appeal was exhilarating holiday experiences, diversity and adventure. In Europe, the slogan 'Discover the other side of yourself' stressed 'freedom, escape and an enriching and unforgettable' experience. The Asian slogan, 'Australia – see you there', presented Australia as an escape from everyday restrictions, where holidays could be 'a life-changing experience of fun' and offer 'social and emotional freedom'. Finally, the Japanese campaign with the slogan, 'Australia time – a heartwarming experience', played on the image of Australia's 'safe, relaxing lifestyle, friendly people and unspoilt nature' that allow visitors to escape everyday pressures and discover their real selves.

According to John Morse, Managing Director of the ATC, the challenge is to promote global products with competitive global marketing in order to increase the depth of knowledge about what Australia can offer as the 'country that is home to the single oldest continuous culture in the world'. The key to tapping potential visitors' 'desire to know who we are and how we live' is, according to Morse, to promote an image of 'authenticity':

> That's what people love about this country. They love coming here because it's real; it's not fake. It is real and it is genuine, and it is authentic. And that's about the bush, it's about the country, it's about the people, it's about the way we are as a country. And that's such a special quality about this country.
>
> (Morse 1999)

To the ATC, the key to Australia's tourism future is projecting this diversity and vitality as 'young, vibrant, stylish and colourful'. This is illustrated by short case studies of the Sydney 2000 Olympics tourism, outback tourism, and cultural tourism.

Case study 1: The Sydney 2000 Olympics – 'Fun and Games'

> The spectacle and tourism are coming closer together. There was a time when countries used special events to showcase new trades and wares. Nineteenth century world fairs and expos – they were all precursors to today's extravaganzas.

These days, special events, like the Melbourne Grand Prix or the Brisbane Expo, are sold on their tourism potential. We're not selling goods any more, we're exporting them.

> (Wendy Carlisle in ABC 1997, Episode 11)

Sydney's winning of the bid to stage the games of the XXVII Olympiad was heralded with much fanfare. Here was the perfect opportunity to 'bask in the glare of the international spotlight' and 'to display to the world the vibrant and culturally rich nation that we have become' (ATN 2000). This premier sporting event seemed the perfect reflection of the new sense of Australian culture and identity and a heaven-sent opportunity to wallow in the national love of sporting heroes. It was also seen, predictably, as an opportunity to increase tourism:

> The 2000 Olympics will not only fast-track Sydney as one of the world's great destinations, it will also translate into more high-yield arrivals. An extra 6.3 million international tourists will arrive in Sydney during the Games and as a spin-off from the focus of attention on the State, tourist numbers are expected to increase to 7.6 million by 2003.
>
> (ATN 2000)

Such was 'the Government's commitment to tourism, and its belief in the future of tourism in this country' that the government gave an additional $50 million to the ATC and endorsed the Brand Australia campaign as the centrepiece of the strategy to maximise the long-term promotional benefits of the Games (Morse 1999). The ATC positioned the games within its 'Australia 2000 Fun and Games' theme. In contrast to these ambitious estimates of tourist activity, a somewhat sceptical note entered statements by the tourism industry in the months before the Games. Citing the minimal tourism impact of Olympics on previous host cities, analysts argued that Olympics neither massively increased tourism during the event nor inevitably after it. Experience of previous Olympic cities showed that some visitors shift the time they plan to visit to coincide with the event (switching effects) while others shift their visit to well before or after the event ('the repulse factor'). Although Barcelona experienced tourist growth following the Olympics, this had more to do with other features of this destination which was popularly perceived as a modern, go-ahead city of the future that balanced the contemporary with the historic. In fact, most Olympic cities and countries have experienced either no growth or a downturn in tourism, as in Montreal, Los Angeles, Seoul, Melbourne and Atlanta.

In reality, special events like the Olympics create a mood of near hysteria within the 'parish' and may serve to reinforce or embellish parochial images of identity, self-esteem and economic worth – as well as providing new infrastructure. The organisation of the 2000 Sydney Olympics was chaotic and marred by charges of incompetence and administrative amateurism, corruption and cronyism. Despite concerted efforts to media-manage the lead-up to the games and to eliminate all reference to negative stories, the public perception was that the management of the event was something of a joke, irrespective of the perceived success of the sporting event itself. The attention to Australia also brought attention to other pressing issues, in particular that of the treatment and situation of Indigenous Australians. To the extent that this became visible abroad, the Sydney 2000 Olympics damaged the reputation and image of Australia as a desirable destination. In short, the Games proved not to be the cornucopia that had been anticipated.

Case Study 2: Outback tourism – 'Where Dreams Come True'

> Whether it's for the wide open spaces, the magical coastline or simply for the weather, an Aussie holiday offers an unforgettable experience that's way off the beaten track. Watch a red sunset over Uluru (Ayers Rock) or sail over warm, crystal waters through the Whitsundays.
>
> (ATC 2000d)

The outback has always featured prominently in Australian tourist promotion, feted as offering 'unspoiled natural beauty', 'the most ancient landscape on earth', 'virtually untouched heritage' and including many 'natural wonders of the world' (ATC 2000d). Australia boasts thirteen World Heritage listed sites, including a number of the most popular tourist destinations – the Wet Tropics of Queensland, the Great Barrier Reef, Kakadu National Park, Uluru-Kata Tjuta National Park, the Tasmanian Wilderness and the Riversleigh Fossil Mammal Sites. This range of pristine sites alone makes for a potentially impressive itinerary.

Along with 3,429 protected areas and other lesser known outback areas, there is a huge variety of activities for the visitor, including touring on or off roads, farms and farmstays, visiting national parks, seeing wildlife (fauna, flora, marine life, bird spotting), camel trekking, camping, bushwalking, Indigenous cultural tourism, historic sites, and so on. A Queensland survey of outback tourism identified the primary pleasure as:

> experiencing the Outback and 'doing a bit of everything' – enjoying the scenery; delving into the history of the area; having some bush tucker; seeing a mine; looking at some gemstones, dinosaur evidence and/or Aboriginal art; and mixing with the locals and fellow travellers.
>
> (Tourism Queensland 1997)

As knowledge about the outback has increased, the number of tourists who include an outback component of their trip has increased. Visitors are still going to the main cities but also venturing out to other sites. This is reflected in the relative decline of Sydney as the most visited place and the inclusion of less familiar destinations. For those who do venture off the beaten track the rewards are immense. In a travellers' tale sent to the ATC, an Italian traveller describes Australia as the place 'quandro il sogno e realta' (where dreams come true). She wrote:

> We are in Australia somewhere between the Northern Territory and Western Australia ... [the] kilometres ... flow swiftly beneath us through apparently monotonous scenery which in reality is always different and fascinating. Giant baobabs some with twisted shapes which conjure up images of fairy tales heard as a child: people turned into trees, arm-like branches which stretch out into the emptiness. Large and small termites nests scattered here and there, today red like the earth they are made from, yesterday golden like the scrub which surrounds them. Fires alongside the road which spring up unexpectedly are fed by the arid vegetation and the heat of the air then equally unexpectedly die away by themselves. The bush fills the desert and brings it to life. And the infinite shades of red earth, made even redder by the last rays of the sun ... The bush, the heat, the emptiness ... Australia is a land of opposites, of contrasts: historical, ethnic, climatic, landscape ... And it is 'on the road' Australia which is the most absorbing, which makes impression and endures.
>
> (Lugaresi 1998)

But for all those who want to travel independently and experience the outback as it really is, there are more visitors who like the idea of the wide open spaces and wilderness but find the reality somewhat forbidding. Instead of the pristine and desolate outback, these visitors are satisfied by pseudo-backs, fronts masquerading as backs, or highly contrived backs. These tourists visit controlled and managed samples of the outback through venues like the Stockman's Hall of Fame in Longreach, visitor centres in national parks, organised outback tours, and Indigenous cultural tours. In short, visitor satisfaction surveys show that most visitors want an experience that is mediated, cossetted or inoculated – so this has become the primary way of accessing these sites and experiences.

As the popularity of outback tourism grows – whether soft or hard – so too does the provision of viable travel options. In Queensland, for example, the 1,700 kilometre long road from the western New South Wales border to the Gulf of Carpentaria in Far North Queensland was renamed the Matilda Highway to give a coherent identity to the towns and tourist sites along the way – Longreach (rural life, the Stockman's Hall of Fame, birthplace of Qantas airlines), Barcaldine (birthplace of the Queensland Labor Party), Winton (Banjo Paterson and 'Waltzing Matilda' country), Riversleigh (fossils) and Tambo (Tambo teddy bears) (Mathers 2000, p. 31). The Tambo teddy bears are an unlikely success story of a few enterprising women in the tiny town who decided to fight the rural decline and huge wool stockpile by making wool-based, customised teddy bears named after places and people in the locality. Such was their success that Tambo is now internationally famous and the town is well known on the tourist map. The example of Tambo suggests that future outback tourism will increasingly be based on simulacra of what the outback, rural life and Australian history are deemed to have been via reconstructions, artificial sites and highly packaged samples of outback life.

The development of outback tourism illustrates both the continuities and discontinuities of tourist experiences and ways of packaging tourist attractions. It is both a hallmark of Australia's traditional appeal and an innovation of the new image of Australia.

Case Study 3: Cultural Tourism – 'Add Culture and Stir'

Cultural tourism is tourism that focuses on the culture of a destination – the lifestyle, heritage arts, industries and leisure pursuits of the local population ... The cultural and tourism industries, and the wider Australian economy, can benefit through the development and pursuit of the dual themes of cultural identity and excellence.

(DISR 1999)

Australian tourism is experiencing a rather schizophrenic movement. On the one hand, there has been a move away from sites and sights to a diversity of attractions, interests and experiences. On the other, there has been a convergence between diverse tourist attractions and an effort to enrich tourist experiences. This ostensibly new approach to tourism offers choices for the tourist to mix-and-match a customised itinerary. The new tourist can combine conventional site visits (Uluru, Kakadu, the Opera House) with experiential components (such as Indigenous cultural tours, white water rafting, bungy jumping, farmstays, craft studio visits, shopping). By returning to the quest for educational, authentic, experiential and communicative aspects of tourist encounters, advocates and the industry are positioning culture as a central part of the phenomenon. In one sense, this is a return to the primary motivations of the Grand Tour; in another, it embraces aspects of global culture where international and standardised forms of tourism are reproduced with local inflections; and, in yet another, it taps into the desire for alternative, special interest and off-the-beaten-track kinds of travel experiences. Can cultural tourism be all these things or does this multiple specification condemn the cultural turn to become just another short-term marketing fad for the tourist industry?

Cultural tourism has been embraced with some enthusiasm by the industry because, some pundits claim, 'one in two international visitors sought at least one cultural experience during their stay' (Foo and Rossetto 1998, p. 4; Buchanan 1999; Kelly and McGauran 1999; McGauran 1999a–c; DISR 1999; Morse 1999).

The Foo and Rossetto study of the characteristics and motivations of cultural tourists was embraced by government as the cornerstone of its strategies for cultural tourism. The authors calculated that 60 per cent of international tourists in 1996 sampled a cultural attraction: historic building, site or monument (30 per cent); museum or art gallery (27 per cent); Aboriginal site or cultural display (15 per cent); performing arts or concerts (12 per cent); art or craft workshops or studios (11%); and festival or fair (5 per cent) (Foo and Rossetto 1998, p. 18). A survey of inbound visitors who identified themselves as cultural tourists concluded that they accounted for 17 per cent of all inbound visitors (Foo and Rossetto 1998, p. 60). While this paints a rosy picture of cultural tourism, it is also based on a very wide definition of cultural tourism as including all of the following:

- Festivals or fairs (music, dance, comedy, visual arts, multi-arts and heritage);
- Performing arts or concerts (theatre, opera, ballet and classical and contemporary music);
- Museums or art galleries;
- Historic or heritage buildings, sites or monuments;
- Art or craft workshops or studios; and
- Aboriginal sites and cultural displays. (Foo and Rossetto 1998, p. 7)

The breadth of this definition is expanded even further by the addition of special interest tourism as part of the cultural tourism push. In addition to the activities listed above, the ATC's list of 26 types of special interest tourism includes food and wine, Australiana, birdwatching, diving, fossicking, gay travel, golf, theme parks, weddings and whale watching. It is fair to ask whether there should be a particular focus on the cultural or educational dimension of these types of tourism in order for them to be counted as cultural tourism. Rather, government and the industry seem to have conveniently basked in the perceived 'quality' of the category of cultural tourism – and the supposed benefits of the better-heeled and educated cultural tourist – while generalising the niche form to recast the nature of Australian tourism more generally.

This enthusiasm has belatedly spread to some of the cultural industries that have found their circumstances challenged by new funding arrangements, pressures of accountability, and the push towards audience development strategies and value-added approaches to their activities. While the heritage industries have generally been enthusiastic, the arts and high culture industries remain somewhat suspicious of – and sometimes hostile to – the tourism industry. Despite this ambivalence, some cultural institutions have recognised the tourist potential of blockbuster exhibitions, special events and festivals, popular culture activities (e.g. musicals, rock music), merchandising and incentives for target audiences. Some venues have been more proactive, for example, the Sydney Opera House. Through its Discovering the Opera House program it has successfully marketed tours of the Opera House that combine a focus on the architectural elements with an emphasis on performance: 'The more people engage in the activities of the house, the more satisfaction increases for tourists' (Holgate 2000, p. 17). Recognising this, organised tours include the opportunity to watch rehearsals of the Sydney Symphony Orchestra. This strategy has spawned a market for live performances to the extent that 25 per cent of its ticket sales are now made to tourists (Holgate 2000, p. 17).

Other sectors have been more ambivalent. In the Nugent Report into the deteriorating state of Australia's major performing arts organisations, cultural tourism rated just one paragraph in the Discussion Paper and only passing reference in the Final Report (DCITA 1999a–b). While acknowledging that inbound tourists are attracted by the 'vibrant arts sector' and that they provided 'further value added by the major performing arts sector to the economy' (DCITA 1999a, p. 48), packaging and marketing performing arts for inbound tourists was not identified as one of the options for dealing with the problem of rising costs and lower audiences. This is despite the success of such strategies. The $8 million staging in Adelaide of Wagner's *Ring* cycle in 1998 'injected $10 million into the South Australian economy, with 44 per cent of the audience coming from interstate and 12 per cent from overseas' (Holgate 2000, p. 18).

Thus, although it is growing in market share and tourism promotion strategies – as well as being a platform for parochial self-congratulation about Australia's cultural coming of age – cultural tourism in Australia is generally embryonic and uneven in the range, quality and marketing of its products. There remains the question of promoting the distinctiveness of Australian culture in a way that is accessible and attractive to inbound tourists against a backdrop of global culture and the internationalisation of tourism services, facilities and products.

Indigenous cultural tourism and its prospects

Aboriginal tourism … [is] a win, win, win situation. It's a win for the Aboriginal people, in helping them to achieve economic independence. It's a win for the Australian people, generally, who can, through tourism, find out more and discover more of this rich and diverse culture. It's a win for our overseas markets. The people in the countries around the world who come to Australia, over 80 per cent of whom want to experience culture in some form or another.

(Morse 1999)

This endorsement by John Morse exemplifies the recent rhetorical pitch for Indigenous cultural tourism. Despite the use of images of Aboriginality from the earliest tourism promotion and the recommendations to develop this sector in both HKF reports (HKF 1966, 1969), attention to Indigenous tourism was minimal until the 1990s when the Department of Tourism targeted its development (DT 1994) and ATSIC developed both an Indigenous tourism strategy (ATSIC 1997) and a cultural industry strategy (ATSIC and ONT 1997). Its recognition as something unique in terms of culture, customs, art and habitus – at the same time as a culture under threat and in perpetual revision – was acknowledged overseas long before it was at home. Once that recognition occurred, the growth of Indigenous cultural tourism was rapid.

This is reflected in the growing demand by inbound tourists (15 per cent in 1996) to experience aspects of Aboriginal culture (ONT 1998). Domestic tourists have been slower to experience Indigenous cultural tourism. For example, only 34 per cent of visitors taking the Manyallaluk cultural tour (near Katherine in the Northern Territory) are domestic (Pitcher 1999, p. 194), although local school children now make up the largest proportion of visitors to Indigenous cultural tourism enterprises in New South Wales. According to Morse: 'Aboriginal tourism is going to be a fundamentally much more important part of our tourism experience than it currently is' (Morse 1999). In 1996, the estimated annual value of Indigenous cultural tourism was $5 million while the estimated value of Indigenous-owned mainstream tourism was $20 to $30 million, and the estimated value of Indigenous art and craft was a staggering $200 million (ATSIC and ONT 1997, p. 6). But despite the enthusiasm for further developing this sector, there are a number of challenges and issues that need to be addressed.

The first concerns the content of Indigenous cultural tourism: who is learning what about whom and for what purpose? John Morse (1999) argues that Aboriginal tourism is 'about sharing our cultures ... that tourism and reconciliation go hand in hand ... Tourism provides us with the opportunity for a much better understanding of the Aboriginal culture in this country'. This suggests that the main benefactors of tourism are the tourists, in learning about and better appreciating this ancient and unique culture and way of life. The primary Indigenous cultural tourist experiences include: visiting archaeological, historic and ceremonial sites; seeing rock art and other arts (acrylic painting, pottery, sculpture) and crafts (basket weaving, didgeridoo making and playing); experiencing Aboriginal ways (through bush tucker walks, corroborees) and cultural performances (dances, musicals). Although these activities are constructed for the modern tourist, they largely derive from strongly-held ideas about 'traditional' culture and 'native' people as rooted in the past and bound by unchanging and exotic laws and customs (Zeppel 1998). This is exemplified by the common adoption of 'traditional' dress or undress, body painting and traditional implements. Pretence sometimes takes on comical proportions: for example, kangaroos prepared for tourist barbeques are ostensibly hunted and killed by spears but in fact are usually purchased, hunted by conventional means (guns) or road kill (Craik 1994).

Recent research (Pitcher 1999) suggests that there may be distinct limitations to the growth of Indigenous cultural tourism. The number of Indigenous owned and controlled enterprises is small and their visitation and income is generally low. There are problems in reconciling Aboriginal ways with the demands of tourists, for example in relation to punctuality, information-giving, communication, training of guides, manufacture and sale of artifacts, and recognition of local customs (e.g. surrounding death). Another issue concerns the nature of the stories told to tourists. Although so-called Dreamtime stories are the centrepiece of much Aboriginal tourism, there are some stories which cannot be told and others that guides are reluctant to tell. But in the absence of an explanation by the guides (or in brochures) of the protocols about storytelling, some visitors feel that the guides are simply inarticulate. This is complicated by the expectation that the Dreamtime is associated with the past – a kind of timelessness – yet stories and customs have changed and been revised in the light of particular events and white contact. But tourists expect stories from the past so there is something of a mismatch between their expectations and the facts and detail that guides are prepared to share (Pitcher 1999; Craik 1998).

Pitcher contrasts the tour spiels of Indigenous and white guides on different tours in the Northern Territory. She concludes that white guides can perform in a more accessible way for tourists – for example, they present information as 'facts' and can answer the tourists' icebreaker questions (How many?, How long? etc.) (Pitcher 1999, p. 163). They can also relate Aboriginal culture to familiar reference points.

One example was a non-Aboriginal guide on a Tiwi tour who told the story of a Catholic priest, Father Gsell, who 'bought' 150 wives, many of whom 'were escaping from their prospective husbands' (Pitcher 1999, p. 184). The guide went on to explain that when the Pope found out about these wives, and asked for an explanation, he concluded that the priest 'had done the right thing but asked him to refrain from buying any more wives' (guide quoted by Pitcher 1999, pp. 184–5). Pitcher argues that in this story, the priest is the 'main protagonist' and a 'positive agent of change' whose actions the tourists seem to approve. Citing other aspects of the tour, Pitcher concludes that this kind of narrative presents Aboriginal people as disempowered, unable to manage money, ungrateful for assistance, and inconsiderate of preserving their past.

By contrast, she approves the use of local guides at Manyallaluk as being more authentic. In support she cites the results of a survey she conducted among visitors. While generally positive about their experience, respondents made numerous comments and suggestions about aspects of the tour concerning facilities, organisation, communication and food. Some found the softly spoken and shy guides hard to hear and understand, some wanted more information and supporting written material, many wanted bush tucker instead of an Aussie barbeque, some wanted more opportunity to communicate with the locals, many wanted a more tightly organised and timed tour, and so on. Above all, the tourists – and these were a self-selecting, well-educated, articulate and experienced cohort – resented the insulated nature of a tour such as this where the tourist precinct was separate from the community and no 'everyday' interaction was possible. It was also found that those on a day trip did not really get to appreciate the scenery and natural features of the area like those on overnight or longer stays. To this extent, a day trip is limited in how much it can convey, educate and enlighten.

These examples illustrate the problem of packaging and managing simultaneously the unique qualities, exotic elements and everyday life for the tourist gaze, a challenge that is more difficult in a culture that is the object of colonial and postcolonial exploitation (Craik 1994). In addition to issues associated with ownership, control and organisation, Indigenous cultural tourism faces questions of authenticity in very acute ways. Most pressing are the related issues of guaranteed authenticity that the introduction of a Label of Authenticity is designed to address (Sexton 2000), and the management of copyright and licensing issues, for example in the mass reproduction of images from paintings on T-shirts, home furnishings or carpets, a particular problem now that much 'Aboriginal' art is manufactured overseas.

Overlaying these concerns, there will be a growing debate about the ways in which Aboriginal culture is 're-tooled' for tourist consumption. This is already evident in ventures such as the successful Tjapukai cultural park in Cairns where the theme song – apparently without irony – proclaims:

> Proud to be ... Aborigine
> We'll never die ... Tjapukai
> Always be our identity
> Proud to be ... Aborigine
> You've changed our ways, our laws, our land
> That's something we can't understand
> Black and white have got to unite
> Or there'll be nothing left in the land downunder.
> (Tjapukai Aboriginal Cultural Park website)

While the park has been popular with mainstream tourists as a commercial venture, there are questions about the control and involvement of local Aboriginal people, the ways in which Aboriginal culture is being packaged for spectacular tourist displays and performances, and the dubious quality of its Aboriginal tourist art. This example illustrates that it may be necessary to customise Indigenous culture in certain ways in order to attract and entertain tourists – and secure visitor satisfaction – but in doing so, Indigenous culture may be distorted, exploited and undermined.

However, as Aboriginal cultural tourism looks destined increasingly to epitomise an image of Australia that attracts inbound visitors, it is important that Indigenous communities, governments, the tourist industry and the Australian public tackle the place of Indigenous culture in Australian life and redress problems and contradictions. Otherwise continued tourist growth may reinforce perceptions of a racist, postcolonial nation that fails to acknowledge its most distinctive element. In this sense, tourism is inextricably tied to images of nation and identity at home and abroad, but this twinning can be a double-edged sword.

Conclusion: tourism, culture, nation

Tourism has proved to be an attractive panacea for Australia as it restructures its economy and repositions and reinvents itself in an increasingly globalised way. While tourism has grown and the industry become more sophisticated, the implications of that growth raise questions about the kind of culture and nation Australia may become if it continues down the long and windy tourist track. Tourism involves casualised and low-skill employment arrangements that challenge traditional ideas about industrial rights in Australia. It is also a highly integrated industry, both vertically and horizontally, and dominated by multi-national enterprises. Although there is much rhetoric about sustainable tourism, community consultation, partnerships and ethical codes of practice, the reality is much more mixed.

Tourism is a very selective industry. It does not benefit regions, enterprises and communities in equal ways. In fact it is so selective that it can undermine the economies and well-being of regions not on the tourist bandwagon. While governments remain ambivalent towards tourism and lurch from one uncoordinated policy option to another, there is little strategic guidance of the industry as a whole – clout wins every time. And what of the tourist product? The rhetoric of tourism allows people and cultures to promote themselves in ways they think appropriate. However, tourist culture – that is, how tourism is articulated into products and services and how it is experienced by visitors – can be quite dismissive and destructive of the ideals and intentions that underpin a tourism enterprise. While Indigenous culture may be most at risk, the prospect that everyday Australian culture will become purely grist to the tourist mill and Australians objects-in-aspic of the tourist gaze should make us think. Is this really the kind of key industry or national culture that Australia wants if it is to achieve prosperity, cultural enrichment and sustainable growth in the new millennium?

📖 Guide to further reading

Zeppel (1998) provides an excellent overview of the development of Indigenous cultural tourism and issues associated with its growth, while the *National Aboriginal and Torres Strait Islander Tourism Industry Strategy* (ATSIC and ONT 1997) is a definitive blueprint for developing Indigenous cultural tourism as a partnership between government and Indigenous communities. Craik (2001) provides a comprehensive overview of cultural tourism in Australia, and Craik (1991) a detailed study of the development of Australian tourism from a cultural policy perspective. The most comprehensive government commissioned study of cultural tourism in Australia is Foo and Rossetto (1998). Buchanan (1999) is a useful survey of expenditure patterns of inbound tourists on culture. The ABC's audio series *Wish You Were Here: Australian Tourism Studies* (1997), a useful canvassing of major issues facing Australian tourist development, is available in print or online at www.abc.net.au/ola/tourism/episodes/default.htm

Websites

www.abc.net.au
   The Australian Broadcasting Corporation site contains the *Wish You Were Here* series plus news items and other relevant material.
www.atc.net.au
   The Australian Tourist Commission site holds considerable material about the industry, visitor statistics and government initiatives, and has links to other related sites.
www.btr.gov.au
   The Bureau of Tourism Research is the federal government's tourism research agency and provides details of its products and some free summaries. Excellent links to other research-related sites.
www.isr.gov.au/sport_tourism
   The Department of Industry, Science and Resources (Division of Sport and Recreation) is the federal government department currently responsible for tourism. Provides a comprehensive guide to federal government tourism policy.
www.tq.com.au
   Tourism Queensland has probably the best state government tourism agency site; it offers a comprehensive range of material including up-to-date research and an excellent set of links to other sites.

References

Aboriginal and Torres Strait Islander Commission (1997) *National Aboriginal and Torres Strait Islander Cultural Industry Strategy*, Canberra: AGPS.
Aboriginal and Torres Strait Islander Commission and the Office of National Tourism (1997) *National Aboriginal and Torres Strait Islander Tourism Industry Strategy*, Canberra: AGPS.
Adler, Judith (1989) 'Origins of sightseeing', *Annals of Tourism Research* 16, 1, pp. 7–29.
Australian Broadcasting Corporation (1997) *Wish You Were Here. Australian Tourism Studies*, Sydney: ABC.
Australian Government Committee of Inquiry into Tourism (1986) *Report of the Australian Government Committee of Inquiry into Tourism*, Volumes 1 and 2, Canberra: AGPS.

Australian Tourism Net (2000) 'Sydney Olympics 2000', www.atn.com.au/nsw/syd/olympics.htm

Australian Tourist Commission (2000a) '2000/2001 Budget', Industry Bulletin, 12 May, www.atc.net.au/news/Inside/insid41.htm

— (2000b) '1999 strong year for tourism – figures', Media Release, 20 May, www.atc.net.au/media/200500.htm

— (2000c) 'Brand Australia campaign', www.atc.net.au/brand/campaigns/brand/brand.htm

— (2000d) 'Come and say g'day', na.australia.com/us.html

— (2000e) 'Facts sheets. Inbound visitor characteristics', www.atc.net.au/news/fact.htm

— (2001) 'Australian Tourist Commission preliminary arrivals – year ending December 2000, www.atc.net.au/intell/data1/prefinal.htm

Buchanan, Ian (1999) *Cultural Tourism in Australia. Visual Art and Craft Shopping by International Visitors, 1997*, Canberra: DCITA.

Bureau of Industry Economics (1979) *The Economic Significance of Tourism*, Research Report 4, Canberra: AGPS.

Bureau of Tourism Research (2000a) 'Top 20 Regions Visited by International Visitors in Australia in 1998', www.btr.gov.au/statistics/Datacard/dc_top_20.htm

— (2000b) 'Tourism and the economy', www.btr.gov.au/statistics/Datacard/economy.html

Carroll, Peter (1991) 'The Federal government and tourism, 1945–1990' in Peter Carroll, Kerry Donohue, Mark McGovern and Jan McMillen (eds) *Tourism in Australia*, Sydney: Harcourt, Brace, Jovanovich.

Casson, Leon (1974) *Travel in the Ancient World*, London: Allen & Unwin.

Craik, Jennifer (1991) *Resorting to Tourism. Cultural Policies for Tourist Development in Australia*, Sydney: Allen & Unwin.

— (1992) 'Australian tourism: the emergence of a state-coordinated consultative policy framework' in Stephen Bell and John Wanna (eds) *Business-Government Relations in Australia: Conflict and Cooperation*, Sydney: Harcourt, Brace, Jovanovich.

— (1994) 'Peripheral pleasures: the peculiarities of post-colonial tourism', *Culture and Policy* 1, 1, pp. 153–82.

— (1998) 'Interpretive mismatch in cultural tourism', *Tourism, Culture and Communication* 1, 2, pp. 115–28.

— (2001) 'Cultural tourism' in Norman Douglas, Ngaire Douglas and Ros Derrett (eds) *Special Interest Tourism*, Brisbane: John Wiley, pp. 113–39.

Department of Communications and the Arts (1994), *Creative Nation: Commonwealth Cultural Policy*, Canberra: Commonwealth of Australia.

Department of Communications, Information Technology and the Arts (1999a) *Securing the Future. Major Performing Arts Inquiry Discussion Paper*, Canberra: DCITA.

— (1999b) *Securing the Future. Major Performing Arts Inquiry Final Report*, Canberra: DCITA.

Department of Industry, Science and Resources (1999) 'Cultural Tourism', Facts and Figures, Canberra: DISR, www.isr.gov.au/tourism/factsandfigures/culturaltourism.doc

— (2000a) 'Federal Budget 2000-2001', Canberra: DISR, www.isr.gov.au/sport_tourism/WhatsNew/index.html

— (2000b) 'Key facts – Tourism', Sport and Tourism Division website, Canberra: DISR www.isr.gov.au/sport_tourism/index.html

Department of Tourism (1992) Tourism. *Australia's Passport to Growth. A National Tourism Strategy*, Canberra: DT.

— (1994) *A Talent for Tourism: Stories about Indigenous People in Tourism*, Canberra: DT.

Edelman, Klaus and Peter Grey (1974) *Tourism in Australia*, Sydney: Committee for Economic Development of Australia.

Foo, Lee Mei and Alison Rossetto (1998) 'Cultural tourism in Australia: characteristics and motivations', Occasional Paper No. 27, Canberra: Bureau of Tourism Research.

Hall, Colin Michael and John Jenkins (1995) *Tourism and Public Policy*, London and New York: Routledge.

Harris, Kerr, Forster and Co. (1966) *Australia's Travel and Tourist Industry, 1965*, New York: HKF and Stanton Robbins & Co.

— (1969) *Tourism Plan for Central Australia*, Honolulu: HKF and Stanton Robbins & Co.

Holgate, Ben (2000) 'Culture vultures', *Weekend Australian*, 11–12 March, Review, pp. 16–18.

Industries Assistance Commission (1989) *Travel and Tourism*, Report No. 423, Canberra: IAC.

Kelly, Hon. Jackie and Hon. Peter McGauran (1999) 'Cultural tourism – a drawcard to Australia', Statement by Hon. Jackie Kelly/Hon. Peter McGauran, Minister for Sport and Tourism/Minister for the Arts and the Centenary of Federation, Media Release, 19 March, Canberra: DCITA.

Langton, Marcia (2001) 'Ignorance of Indigenous initiatives', *Australian* 25 April, p. 13.

Lugaresi, Nicola (1998) 'Australia: quando il sogno e realta (where dreams become reality)', Travellers' Tales, Australian Tourism Commission global.australia.com/pl/atc

Mathers, Jim (2000) 'Driving Queensland', *The Road Ahead* June, p. 31.

McGauran, Hon. Peter (1999a), 'Catching the wave of cultural tourism', Media Release, 20 January, Canberra: DCITA.

— (1999b) 'Increased overseas interest in Australian art', Media Release, 15 July, Canberra: DCITA.

— (1999c) 'Selling Australian culture to the world', Media Release, 17 September, Canberra: DCITA.

Morse, John (1999) 'Telstra address', National Press Club, Canberra, 12 October.

Office of National Tourism (1998), 'Aboriginal and Torres Strait Islander tourism', Tourism Facts 11, Canberra: ONT.

Pannell, Kerr, Forster and Co. (1971) *Great Barrier Reef Visitor Plan*, Melbourne: PKF.

Pitcher, Merridy (1999) 'Tourists, tour guides and true stories: Aboriginal cultural tourism in the Top End', unpublished PhD thesis, Northern Territory University.

Rojek, Chris and John Urry (eds) (1997) *Touring Cultures. Transformations of Travel and Theory*, London and New York: Routledge.

Select Committee on Tourism (1978) *Final Report*, House of Representatives, Canberra: AGPS.

Sexton, Jennifer (2000) 'Signs say label has late message', *Australian* 5 June, p. 14.

Tjapukai Aboriginal Cultural Park (1999) www.tjapukai.com.au/

Tourism Queensland (1997) 'Outback', Trends 11 www.tq.com.au/research/trends

— (1998) 'Tourism and the economy', Queensland Snapshots, September, Brisbane: Tourism Queensland www.tq.com.au/research/snapshots/economy.htm

Zeppel, Heather (1998) 'Selling the Dreamtime: Aboriginal cultural tourism in Australia' in David Rowe and Geoffrey Lawrence (eds) *Tourism, Leisure, Sport: Critical Perspectives*, Sydney: Hodder Headline, pp. 23–38.

Chapter 5

Commonality and Difference: Themes in the Arts Advocacy of H.C. Coombs

Tim Rowse

When Leslie Haylen, playwright, journalist, novelist and Labor MP representing Sydney's western suburbs, asked the House of Representatives in 1944 to consider his six-point scheme for a publicly subsidised 'National Theatre', he denied that he was peddling 'middle-class notions'. Rather, he wanted Australians to be like the valiant people of Britain, Russia and the USA, who were strong because they 'know their own story'. Aligning 'theatre' with 'nation', Haylen's words implied that if Australia's 'story' were to be told effectively theatre would be its best vehicle. He predicted that Australia's post-war migration program would set governments new challenges of social integration.

> What shall we say to the people whom we wish to settle among us? There is no common language or common understanding to unite us ... [In the past] we and the immigrants had no common meeting-ground. That meeting-ground must be found in the theatre and the playhouse.
>
> (Haylen 1944)

Contrast Haylen's thoughts on theatre and society with those of John Tasker in 1970. Tasker was a product of something Haylen's words helped to start – public subsidy for a theatre of ideas. In 1968, as founding director of the South Australian Theatre Company, he was responsible for two plays which tested the disciplines of Australian censorship, *America Hurrah!* and *The Boys in the Band*. Indeed, the first play fell foul of the police. He reflected that:

> The ... history of theatre is that of a public forum where the concerns and the problems of the day may be discussed and perhaps resolved; where the foibles

114

of mankind and society are held up for ridicule. Theatre has been a place of ritual and ceremony and mystery and terror. If we insist that every play which is presented in the theatre must be acceptable to a twelve-year-old, to a police-man who has not been to the theatre for fifteen years, to a granny out for the night with her box of Winning Post, then we debase the art of theatre to that of a sideshow.

(Tasker 1970, pp. 50–1)

Both Haylen and Tasker project social responsibilities for subsidised dramatic performance, but there are two significant differences. First, Haylen's themes are inclusion and commonality, while Tasker draws our attention to the limits of such inclusion, nominating types of people – or types of cultural disposition – who don't belong in his 'forum'. Second, the social differences which Haylen imagines to be problematic are those occasioned by multinational immigration; nowadays we term such differences *ethnic*. Tasker imagines differences which are more difficult to name, but they are not evidently ethnic. Following the work of Bourdieu, I see them as *class* differences. Bourdieu (1984) has argued that certain socially valued kinds of cultural consumption enact (and thus require) the consumers' 'cultural capital'. The nature of 'cultural capital' is subject to debate, as Tony Bennett, Mike Emmison and John Frow illustrate in this book (Chapter 9). To take the instance at hand, Tasker implied a notion of 'cultural capital' when he postulated that some people are receptive to a theatre of intel-lectual exploration and moral confrontation and others are not. The former group can be understood in Bourdieu's terms as being well endowed with cultural capital, and the latter group as lacking or as differently endowed. Tasker's words exhibit the tendency of the former group to see themselves as possessing cultural capacities which others lack, whatever the cause of that difference might be.

Certainly, it is common to find that distinction of capacity/incapacity among many of those who hold institutional power within performing arts companies, academies and funding bodies. Those mapping society in terms of the uneven distribution of certain valued cultural dispositions are inclined to an intriguingly contradictory form of self-awareness. On the one hand, they see their own cultural interests as exemplary, as an investment in what is best in the human tradition, as demonstrating what it is to be 'cultured'. On the other hand, they are conscious of the degree to which their cultural interests, however exemplary and however universal in principle, are not shared by all. Their cultural capital differ-entiates them from others, and such 'distinction' is essential to their social identity. That is, those whose social eminence, power, prestige and income are based in their possession of cultural capital are likely to be committed simulta-neously to the *universality* and the *particularity* of their cultural interests. This theoretical model of 'cultural capital' helps to make sense of something odd in Tasker's words: he evokes theatre as a 'public forum' while firmly denying entrance to certain types of 'public' on the grounds that they are indisposed to theatre's intellectual challenges and moral confrontations.

This essay is an exploration of two themes – commonality/difference and ethnicity/class – in the rhetoric of Australian cultural policy since World War II. I have chosen as my exemplar of cultural policy rhetoric Dr H.C. Coombs, founder and chair (1954–67) of the Australian Elizabethan Theatre Trust and inaugural chair of the Australian Council for the Arts (1967–73) and of the Australia Council (1973–74). My argument is that Coombs' rhetoric has characteristically tended to suppress class distinction while highlighting two other senses of cultural plurality – the 'ethnic' and, more emphatically in his case, the 'settler/Indigenous'.

It is a measure of the Bourdieuan inspiration of this essay that I wish first to characterise Coombs in class terms. In doing so, I follow Coombs himself. Although I will argue that Coombs tended to suppress (or be insensitive to or uninterested in) senses of class distinction in the *consumption* of cultural goods, he undoubtedly had a clear sense that public patronage was a class project.

Coombs and the professional-managerial class

Students of social class have proposed that the emergence of a 'professional-managerial' class has been a characteristic development within 'advanced' societies such as Australia. I have been struck by Coombs' suggestion, in the 1950s, that organised public patronage was the responsibility of senior executives and professionals. His idea prompts a hypothesis: that one of the projects through which the Australian 'professional-managerial' class mobilised was the campaign for the public provision of certain valued cultural goods. Son of a railway stationmaster and eldest of five siblings, who rose to be Governor of Australia's central bank at the age of 48, Coombs was himself the product of the recent public endowment of secondary and tertiary education. In 1974, a newspaper columnist used Coombs' career as an example of individual effort triumphing over adverse conditions, demonstrating the relative inconsequence of public sector programs of social equity. Coombs replied privately that his career 'was possible because I lived in a State with a free education system and a free university, with a government that granted scholarships, and that I was helped by affectionate parents and inspired teachers' (1974a). His riposte capped more than 30 years of advocating the state's responsibility to develop 'culture', in particular higher education, the performing arts and Aboriginal arts and crafts. Bennett, Emmison and Frow have noted the importance of public cultural provision in Bourdieu's account of 'distinction'. By persuading the state that its favourite cultural goods are too valuable to suffer the fate of other low sale commodities (that is, going out of production), the professional-managerial class further implicates the state in 'underwriting class-specific practices of distinction'

(Bennett *et al.* 1999, p. 230; and Chapter 9 below). Yet the state is increasingly called upon to justify these policies as of universal benefit. So the language of public policy must find ways to combine the themes of universality (a culture shared) and distinction (the virtue of specially cultivated appreciation). In attending to the interplay of these themes – commonality and distinction – in Coombs' career as an advocate of state patronage, I am putting forward the following proposition (which I think requires further research and evaluation) about the Australian professional-managerial class: that its characteristic policy language tends to suppress or be embarrassed by senses of class difference while celebrating other senses of cultural difference such as 'multiculturalism' and expressing a high regard for Indigenous heritage. I note in passing that Ghassan Hage has recently argued in similar terms about the 'multicultural' disposition of the professional-managerial class (Hage 1998, p. 201).

Towards a 'National Theatre'

During World War II, a number of intellectuals close to the federal government began to advocate a national cultural policy. Their words soon attracted the ABC's support – for 'a national theatre of the sincere drama of the stage which has been almost entirely neglected by private enterprise' (anon n.d.). What the ABC had been able to do for live musical performance, another government instrumentality could do for drama, ballet and opera. In considering this plea, the Labor Government faced a clamorous constituency. Popular enthusiasm for government-assisted performance – orchestral music, opera, ballet and drama – appears to have been mounting since the mid-1930s. In 1949 a *Current Affairs Bulletin* summarised the National Theatre idea as it had developed over the previous fifteen years:

> The national theatre would be complementary to the commercial and tributary theatre. It might cooperate with them on occasion. It would be formed under the auspices of the Commonwealth, but State and local governments would participate at appropriate levels, in the provision of buildings, for example. It would engage repertory companies both for city and country performances, concentrating on high standard productions of classics and the best contemporary plays. It would encourage the writing of Australian plays, conduct a school of dramatic studies, sponsor visits from overseas actors and companies, and perhaps develop a juvenile drama section. Admission would be kept at a level to bring it within the reach of all sections of the community.
>
> (anon 1949, p. 302)

The class and genre distinctions among different kinds of performance – orchestral, operatic, balletic and dramatic – were submerged by advocates' use of the word 'theatre' to refer to all of them.

In 1944 Coombs suggested that the Commonwealth form a 'Cultural Council' to coordinate existing Commonwealth efforts (such as the Art Advisory Board and the Commonwealth Literary Fund) and to develop new programs to deal with the war and its aftermath. For example, a cultural policy for country towns would be necessary if country people were to be persuaded to return to their districts from their wartime work in munitions factories. The Department of Postwar Reconstruction had shown films, fostered drama groups and exhibited new ideas about housing. Should not the Commonwealth continue to develop 'culture' as part of its stimulation of citizenship? 'Less emphasis should be placed on large scale development', Coombs suggested, 'than on assisting small groups of people who are doing a good deal, at the moment, to assist themselves and who will make possible a democratic development of culture by the masses of the Australian people' (1944). Coombs, like Haylen, saw the Labor leadership as likely to suspect 'cultural' initiatives as emanating from outside the working-class constituency, so the language of his advocacy aligned 'theatre' with 'nation' and 'democracy'.

In September 1946 Prime Minister Chifley promised in his election manifesto that 'proposals for a national theatre, put forward by enthusiastic groups, will receive sympathetic consideration from the Government'. So encouraged, the President of the Australian Theatre Movement, Locksley Shaw, suggested to Chifley on 1 November 1946 that the government take over the Movement, making it the nucleus of a theatre for fostering national culture (Shaw 1946). Chifley referred the matter to an interdepartmental committee on education chaired by R.C. Mills – the same group that was then developing ideas for a National University (Chifley 1946). In October 1947, the Mills Committee outlined a policy: a legislated National Theatre Board which would employ about sixteen actors, set up a school of the theatre and encourage ballet, opera, repertory companies and Australian dramatists. Government expenditure would be offset by ticket sales for performances in large city theatres. The public benefits would be that the Australian public would see productions of an international standard, Australian actors and audiences would be trained, and Australian writers stimulated. Theatre deserved public support as a form of moral and civic education.

Although Prime Minister Chifley wished to avoid 'creating an organisation that may ultimately prove to be a sink for public money', he left the door open a little for Coombs' and Mills' further submissions. In the winter of 1948, Australian theatregoers were getting their first post-war treat – a tour by Laurence Olivier's and Vivien Leigh's Old Vic company. Coombs found it 'an appropriate time for some action to be taken' on the National Theatre (Coombs 1948). Still cautious, the Chifley government asked Old Vic Director Tyrone Guthrie for his opinion. Guthrie's May 1949 report – after a two week visit – aroused the scorn of those for whom the whole point of a National Theatre was that it be proudly 'Australian'. To raise the audience's standard of appreciation,

Guthrie advised that nine to twelve distinguished productions be imported from Britain and the Continent over the next three years. Meanwhile theatre workers would be given scholarships to train in London. Some of them would be formed into a London-based company, with Australian directors and retaining their Australian style of speech. Thus would an Australian national company gather the prestige to found its subsequent work in Australia. Some called this an 'export-import' policy.

Acknowledging that there were 'certain weaknesses in our present situation which would militate against a high quality National Theatre being established at this stage', Coombs based his subsequent submissions to the Chifley government on Guthrie's report (Coombs 1949). The Australian National University (ANU), yet to build its campus, had just established a postgraduate training program in which promising young men and women were sent abroad. Were not the problems of theatrical and academic development similar? The government should set a date three years hence for a National Theatre to start, suggested Coombs, and it should meanwhile select and train personnel.

The similarities between the Guthrie/Coombs and the ANU developmental strategies point to a tension among supporters of a National Theatre. Some construed 'national' in terms which championed the florescence of a suppressed settler-colonial Australian culture in opposition to the claims of British cultural authority; others, including Coombs, aligned the developmental path for 'Australian culture' with what we might call its 'classical' roots in the best of British culture: great playscripts, London-based training. A remark in the 1947 report of the Mills Committee gestures towards that British heritage. 'It has been argued by two first class authorities, Sir Richard Livingstone and Professor Whitehead, that the best means of eradicating meanness and pettiness is by the representation of figures on a heroic scale, e.g. Lear and Macbeth' (Mills 1947). Could Shakespeare be performed credibly by actors with an Australian accent? In what proportions should a national theatre company mingle Shakespeare (if performed at all) with local scripts? Such questions were central to the politics of realising the word 'national' in the movement for a National Theatre.

The financial aspects of Coombs' plan, had it been realised, would have proved less controversial, as they were the fruit of his consideration of Chifley's fiscal caution. Each state should have its own National Theatre Committee, and the Commonwealth should seek state contributions to a trust fund (matching Commonwealth money) to pay for imported productions, and a scholarship fund for training. A business manager or theatrical organiser with commercial experience should be appointed, and a body of trustees selected. Here Coombs departed from the ANU model in order to preserve an element in the wartime movement for a national theatre – 'public participation':

We are confident that many business enterprises and individuals and possibly trade unions and other organisations would be prepared to contribute to a

Guarantee Fund ... The organisation for appeals of this sort could be a useful function of the State Committees ... There would perhaps be some difficulties if this move established claims to participation in the control of the scheme, but this, we believe, could be overcome.

(Coombs 1949)

Participation of this kind would be stimulated 'if the Board is granted exemption from taxation as a non-profit-making body'. So funded, it could then be commercially viable. The Chifley Government was voted out of office in December 1949 before it could act on this idea.

The Australian Elizabethan Theatre Trust

When Coombs next campaigned for an arts policy, it was to establish the Australian Elizabethan Theatre Trust, by public subscription, in the winter of 1954. He equipped himself with a new rhetoric – appealing less to the duty of government and more to the responsibilities of the new corporate elite. As well, he imagined 'the people' in terms which traded on the extraordinary popularity of the first visit to Australia by Queen Elizabeth II. In a speaking tour of the nation's city Rotary Clubs, he told the following story about the origins of the Trust idea.

> About the time of the Queen's visit to Sydney, in a conversation among a number of businessmen, surprise was expressed that the Australian people had reacted so enthusiastically to the colour and pageantry of the Queen's visit. Not that there were doubts about the fundamental loyalty of the Australian people, but rather that Australians who had a reputation for being hard-boiled and unemotional had responded vigorously to the colour and pageantry associated with the Queen's visit. We said to one another: 'Surely here is something in this which should be kept alive. When the Queen leaves Australia we should not just drop back and forget the pleasure that her visit has given us'. The question was therefore in what way could the happiness of the Queen's visit be kept alive, preferably a way which would continue to bring colour and pageantry to our national life.
>
> (Coombs 1954a)

Coombs solicited a sense of responsibility among those who managed the nation's larger public agencies and private corporations. To the Rotarians he suggested that the idea of the Trust had 'an attraction to us as heads of business enterprises'. It was 'a project which sober-thinking people are convinced has a chance of standing on its own feet'. The Trust would bring together two kinds of expertise rarely found together – managerial and artistic. Its money would be 'controlled by people with business and administrative experience interested in the theatre as onlookers, rather than as participants'. Only when public support for such leadership had been demonstrated would governments be asked to contribute.

Do these Rotarians exemplify the professional-managerial class? Only imperfectly. Coombs formulated his ideas about cultural leadership on a number of occasions in the 1950s. The key theme is succession to 'noblesse oblige'. That is, Coombs believed that the initiative in cultural leadership had passed from the wealthy and the aristocracy to a meritocracy. He evoked the meritocrats in slightly different ways on different occasions. In 1953, addressing a predominantly academic audience, he said:

> In past generations there was a privileged class in our society – a class chosen on the basis of birth – to whom were given, amongst other things, the privileges of access to learning and culture and the opportunity for leisure. That class had a motto 'Noblesse Oblige' which signified that their status carried not merely privileges but corresponding responsibilities. While perhaps few of them accepted these responsibilities fully, there is no doubt that the long list of scientists, writers, reformers, statesmen and administrators which this class has in the past produced, for example in England, is evidence of the vitality of a tradition that privileges should be balanced by an obligation to public service. The academic community of today, although differently selected, is in many ways the inheritor of many of the privileges of this class.
>
> (Coombs 1953)

Standing before the Rotarians in 1954, his appeal to the managerial competence of business persons positioned them as egalitarian inheritors of a plutocratic mission. The arts had traditionally been supported by the wealthy and the noble, he argued, but 'we in Australia have no noble and wealthy class, and I would be one of the last to suggest that we should have them for this or for any other purpose. Wealthy men are almost a thing of the past' (Coombs 1954a). In 1959, he explained to ABC television viewers the reasons for calling on the corporate elite to play such a prominent role in arts patronage.

> People in responsible positions and particularly people in industry and commerce and finance – indeed all those who are associated with enterprises which bring together great amounts of money and great income – have a responsibility to the community. It has been traditional throughout history ... that the arts have ... needed such support. They have always needed patrons. And in our type of society, with heavy taxation, it has become increasingly difficult for individuals to provide that patronage. Now, on the other hand, the influence and control of wealth and income which used to be exercised by individuals has passed to the great corporations.
>
> (Coombs 1959, p. 9)

As Governor of the Commonwealth Bank of Australia, Coombs was the CEO of a very large public corporation (more accurately, a group of linked public corporations) which mingled public duties (central banking) with commercial endeavour (notably, the Commonwealth Trading Bank). He managed a large staff among whom he encouraged, controversially, recruitment and promotion based on academic merit, not only on seniority and war service. He was thus in an excellent position to promote the claims to social eminence and social responsibility of academics, professionals, managers and men and women of capital who daily demonstrated their executive competence and spirit of community service.

In setting out the Trust's mission, Coombs was keen to emphasise the theme of executive competence. Again and again, his campaign for corporate and governmental support for the Trust in 1954 promised that the arts were to get more than just money from the corporate elite. The arts would now be better managed. The Trust would succeed where worthy amateurism had failed to sustain cultural effort. The Trust would fund only those performing arts companies whose artistic and *managerial* standards passed its tests. As he put it to industrialist Sir W. Russell Grimwade (Coombs 1954b), the Trust's money would go 'where we were satisfied about both (a) the professional quality of the performers; and (b) the adequacy of the management'.

Notwithstanding these persistent themes of meritocratic succession and managerial acumen, it is not possible to encompass all the groups evoked in the three speeches I have cited within the sociological rubric 'professional-managerial class'. That would blur an important functional distinction between the ownership of the means of production and its management; and it would also fail to take account of the distinction between owners and managers in private enterprise, on the one hand, and the professionals (including academics), on the other, whose power and eminence is rooted in public sector commitments to programs of health, education and welfare. Rather than present Coombs as a champion of a poorly defined professional-managerial class, I will argue that Coombs' career as a promoter of public cultural provision exhibits some of the inescapable complicities (political impurities, if you like) of that class. That is, my account of him illustrates the practical difficulties of that class's political and cultural self-definition.

For example, Coombs' selection of personnel to lead the Trust, including a board of directors, could be understood as a 'professional-managerial' search for respectable associations with the owners of capital and their political and judicial representatives. The Trust's president was Sir John Latham, recently retired as Chief Justice of the High Court and sometime conservative MP. The four vice-presidents were Dame Enid Lyons (first woman Minister in the Commonwealth Parliament on the conservative side, and by that time an ABC Commissioner), Sir Arthur Rymill (barrister and solicitor, President of South Australia's Liberal and Country League and Mayor of Adelaide), Sir Richard Boyer (grazier and Chair of the ABC) and Sir Robert Knox (Chair of the National

Mutual Life Association, prominent within the Chambers of Commerce of Australia since the 1930s, director of some large manufacturing and finance companies, and confidant of Robert Menzies). The notion of a professional-managerial class would stretch beyond breaking point if it were made to encompass these five people. However, the founding board, chaired by Coombs, included three senior academics, three senior public servants, two trade union-ists, and eleven company directors or general managers.

The cultural tensions within such an assemblage were soon revealed. In 1956, it was proposed that Douglas Stewart's tragedy *Ned Kelly* should be performed at the Comedy Theatre, with the Trust's help, to coincide with the Melbourne Olympic Games. However, in February 1956 several members of the Trust Board expressed doubts about the play's subject matter and the Board resolved to ask the opinion of the Olympic Festival Sub-Committee. The sub-committee's approval did not persuade all on the Trust Board, and there was further argument (Hunt 1956). Trust President Sir John Latham could not reconcile himself to the play. Coombs urged him to consider how his stand might embar-rass the Trust: 'For us to show reluctance in the face of clear and emphatic recommendations from our professional executive because some of us think the play may revive controversies best forgotten could, I feel, be gravely misunder-stood and perhaps set a precedent for a sort of "political" censorship of the Trust's artistic policy' (Coombs 1956a). Latham reluctantly yielded, telling Coombs how much he regretted 'any support or countenance to the persistent attempt to represent Ned Kelly, thief, robber, and murderer, as a misunderstood, thoughtful, and really kindly man, worthy of respect and sympathy, and fitted to be regarded as a national hero' (Latham 1956). Coombs replied that 'there is less likelihood of the Kelly myth developing in a harmful way if it is brought out into the open and looked at frankly' (Coombs 1956b).

Elusive managerialism

What did Coombs mean by 'good management'? His earliest practical answers to this question can be found in his approach to opera. In the early 1950s, Sydney opera lovers were served by the National Opera of Australia, while in Melbourne the National Theatre Movement produced operas. Coombs thought that a Trust Opera Company could draw on the resources of both and serve all capital cities with regular tours. Neither of these companies yielded readily to the Trust's vision, and the Trust's relationship with the Melbourne group – led by Gertrude Johnson and Sir Robert Knox – remained difficult for nearly all the time Coombs chaired the Trust. In 1935 Johnson had published a manifesto for a National Theatre 'presenting drama, opera and ballet and employing the graduates of the various performing arts academies in each State in theatres built on donated civic land, funded by subscription, subsidised by the ABC and, eventually, supported by the government' (Radic 1995, p. 205). The Trust was, arguably, a fulfillment of Johnson's vision, but she found that the staff and directors of the Trust saw her and her Movement as relics of the amateurism which had failed to sustain opera. In her opinion, the Trust should subsidise her work. Instead, she felt supplanted. The National Theatre Movement was thwarted by the alliance between the ABC and the Trust, a compact giving the Trust the initiative in the timing of its seasons. Johnson's Melbourne group resented the Trust's access to the Victorian Government's subsidies. The Trust never lost the self-confident view that its approach to opera reflected a higher professionalism and sounder management than amateurs, such as Johnson, could ever have provided.

And yet the goal of sounder management – to give performers a career in Australia by sustaining a year-round company – eluded the Trust. By the end of 1962, the Trust was in a similar position, financially, to that in which it had found the National Opera and National Theatre Movement in the early 1950s – broke. Maintaining its own opera company exhausted the Trust's financial reserves in the five years 1957 to 1961, so that it was unable to mount an opera season in 1961. It did not find a way, until the very end of Coombs' period in the chair, to give financial security to a national opera company. In 1967, Coombs persuaded the government to fund the Elizabethan Trust Orchestra, so breaking the Opera Company's dependence on the ABC's orchestras. Also in that year, funds from the New South Wales Government (hoping to put something in its forthcoming Opera House) and from the first subscription season made it possible, at last, for the Trust Opera to offer year-round work for its singers. In 1970, the company was renamed the Australian Opera.

The opera story is a cameo of the Trust's difficulty in making 'good management' realise its cultural goals: high performance standards and sustainable careers in Australia for talented performers. Something more was needed – government funding of both company and venues. It is to the Trust's credit that, by the early 1970s, governments were making the necessary financial commitment to the performing arts. However, if this was a triumph for the professional-managerial class upon which Coombs founded the Trust, it was a victory less of good management and more of skilful political positioning. That is, Coombs and his Trust associates aligned their theatrical causes with the interests of the state itself.

Much of the performing arts culture which Coombs and the Trust helped to generate in the 1950s and 1960s included what one might call 'urban rituals of state'. Regal and vice-regal patronage included state governors' conspicuous attendance (in the company of prime minister, premiers and their ministers) at premieres of ballet and opera, in exalted venues which served in themselves – soaring roof lines, plush interiors – as symbols of national, state and civic pride. Attaching 'theatre' to state in this fashion produced some Gilbertian moments. Towards the end of 1963, Coombs unsuccessfully lobbied for the visiting Queen Mother's itinerary to be expanded so that as well as lending her esteemed presence to a performance of the Sydney Symphony Orchestra, she would see, in a nearby venue, the premiere of Robert Helpmann's ballet *Display*. He was told that 'embarrassment and chaos' would flow from any attempt to spread the Queen Mother so thinly.[1] On 23 July 1964 patrons of the first night of the Trust's joint ballet/opera season in Her Majesty's Theatre, Brisbane experienced vice-regal ecstasy: no fewer than three governors (Queensland's, South Australia's and Tasmania's) graced the occasion.

> Every object swells with state,
> all is pious, all is great.[2]

A similar story can be told of the other great national company which owes its existence to Coombs' lobbying – the Australian Ballet. Founded in 1962 upon the expiry of a commercial ballet company, the Australian Ballet was at first uncertain of its financial future, but 'took off' politically when the Menzies Government chose it to 'represent' Australia (with the Sydney Symphony Orchestra) in the 1965 Commonwealth Cultural Festival in Britain. Having won international critical acclaim on that tour (including the Grand Prix of the City of Paris for *Giselle*), it became the first of the Australian 'flagship' companies, demonstrating, in the words of the Trust's executive director, that 'Australian theatre has a valuable ambassadorial role to play in projecting this nation's image to the world' (Haag 1965).

The challenge of drama

What about the third leg of the Trust's intervention into theatrical culture – drama? The Trust abandoned quite early the idea of starting its own national company which would tour Shakespeare and other classic drama – with the occasional worthy Australian script – to all cities and large towns. Instead, the Trust, offering guarantees against loss and paying the salaries of talented directors, encouraged repertory companies in the capital cities, many of them associated with universities. The 'Little Theatre' amateur tradition, which had flourished between the wars, was thus continued and enhanced to the point of acquiring 'semi-professional' status under the Trust.

In the Trust's promotion of drama, the tensions within Coombs' cultural leadership became clearer. Drama has much greater potential than ballet and opera to be a form of political and moral discourse and thus to challenge received ideas and representations. Trust-funded 'theatre of ideas' sometimes provoked censorship. One of the emerging features of the professional-managerial class was the readiness of some its members to see themselves as making cultural war on an artistically stuffy and morally censorious 'establishment'. Though the Trust was sometimes a vehicle for such challenges, the word 'establishment' was absent from Coombs' vocabulary. His rhetoric was characteristically integrative rather than polarising. His chairmanship required him to bridge gaps that were beginning to form in the cultural leadership he had assembled in the Trust. It is nonetheless clear that, in a number of polite skirmishes with some of the older and more conservative members of the Trust Board, such as his answers to Latham's disquiet about *Ned Kelly*, Coombs tried to clear a space for an emerging educated, well-paid, well-travelled and culturally confident constituency. The florescence of this constituency has been part of the social basis of the post-war Australian struggle over censorship. In 1948, in a debate which foretold some of the Trust's battles, the lines between respectability and artistic naturalism had been drawn over Sumner Locke Elliot's play *Rusty Bugles*. In the following decades, according to drama critic Harry Kippax, the constituency of the performing arts became enlivened with such differences.

> [W]e live in a society of competing, mutually suspicious classes of 'new rich' and 'old rich', of an old middle class blighted by inflation and a new middle class which has risen with inflation, of disappointed London-oriented imperialists and old-fashioned nationalists and optimistic internationalists, of isolated intellectuals and anti-intellectual isolationists.
>
> (Kippax 1964, p. 241)

Kippax was commending these tensions as the stuff dramatists might tackle, but his words also point to the tensions within the Trust's constituency which were making drama for its chair.

In Adelaide there were figures, some of them also eminent judges, who might have sympathised with Latham. A dissenting member of 'the Adelaide establishment', Geoffrey Dutton, recalled it in its heyday as 'solidly monarchist and even more British than Menzies' and as 'narrow, inturned, smug and racist' (Dutton 1994, p. 225). In 1960 these men started their own Festival of the Arts and so became important if sometimes ambivalent partners of the Trust. The Festival governors refused to allow Alan Seymour's *One Day of the Year* to be performed in 1960, because its investigation of generational differences in the quality of the ANZAC memory might offend the Returned Services League. The Adelaide Theatre Group, with help from the Trust, performed the play some months after the Festival. When preparing the next Festival in 1962, the governors again defended their idea of taste and propriety by announcing that they could not accept Patrick White's *The Ham Funeral*. Again the Trust differed from the governors. The Adelaide University Theatre Guild performed it in November 1961, with Trust support. This left some feathers ruffled, and Coombs had to smooth them. Sir Roland Jacobs, both a Festival governor and a Trust board member, was offended in 1963 when he thought that the Trust's Executive Director Stefan Haag was forming too cosy a relationship with the Adelaide University Guild Theatre 'behind our backs' (Jacobs 1963). He was worried that the Trust would assist the Guild to produce Patrick White's *Night on Bald Mountain*, when the 'Festival people' had just rejected it for the 1964 Festival. White's plays, were, in his opinion 'not plays that one could be proud to produce' (Jacobs 1963). Coombs replied dipl...atically that the Trust Board had just decided not to assist ... a play during the Festival period if such a proposal ... al Committee' (Coombs 1963a). At any other time, ... n its merits. The Guild performed the play in ... Festival. These Adelaide skirmishes demon- ... cultural elite: those with military, business ... fessional interests were under siege from a ... gerial class, deploying its newly-acquired ... drama which was provocatively 'modern' ...awing on rather different modernisms). ...lity on stage was particularly provocative of ...sland League for National Welfare and ... Theatre's touring production of Edward ...? in 1964, Coombs told Premier Nicklin ...ther states without provoking attending ...eferred to the police as 'the experienced ... vigilance in these matters'. He then ...ological utility. *Virginia Woolf* was a moral ...es which increasingly bedevil the institu- ...l, it gives audiences clear recognition of ...ion, it may also help them personally deal ... It was likely that 'all drama – indeed, all ...rdinarily hidden', and so be 'therapeutic ...ombs 1964a). ... the Albee plays, Coombs extolled theatre ...mpowering truth. His was a rhetoric of ... John Tasker's argument that the kind ... no business to be there anyway.

tional theatre movement in the 1940s was a yearning for an indigenous thea...e'. In 1947 Keith Macartney complained that unlike the Irish 'we still lack a truly national voice in the theatre, the most social of the arts ... The greatest drama is that which not only expresses the conception of the author and displays the art of the actors, but also gives utterance to the desires and preoccupations of its audience' (Macartney 1947, p. 93). On the eve of the Trust's formation Leslie Rees, the ABC's federal drama editor and chair of the Playwrights' Advisory Board, called for government patronage with the argument that 'the drama has a greater power than any other living art form to make direct contact with the minds and emotions of the people. Therefore, the drama's use in social criticism, its potential influence in reflecting and pointing community ideals and welding the people into a wholesome unity, cannot be overestimated' (Rees 1953, pp. 160–1). Playwright and poet Douglas Stewart thought that the playwright 'created' the nation. Shakespeare had created 'Elizabethan England – or rather, eternal England', and it was now up to Australian playwrights to form the minds and shape the lives of 'a new country such as Australia' (Stewart 1956, p. lv). This vision of theatre as a medium of collective self-knowledge seemed to be fulfilled in the Trust's commercial success in touring Ray Lawler's *Summer of the Seventeenth Doll* in 1956. First performed by the Melbourne Union Theatre Repertory in November 1955, this play quickly became an emblem of the possibility of an indigenous theatre.

Though Coombs' Australianism drew inspiration from such success, his notion of what was 'Australian' remained open. For example, his championing of Patrick White's plays suggests that he carried no torch for dramatic naturalism. White, having acquired Coombs as his Adelaide champion in 1962, was keen for him to attend the premiere of *A Cheery Soul* in Melbourne in November 1963. Coombs admired the performance of the play's star, Nita Pannell. He told her that he had found it 'the best Patrick White to date. It is, I suppose, not surprising that from the audience responses I encountered after the show, it seems to have evoked the same violent differences of opinion as his previous efforts' (Coombs 1963b). Director John Sumner, to whom Coombs also wrote a congratulatory note, was depressed by the play's reception. The critics, he complained, were 'intolerant' of 'anything outside of the obvious general public comedy that goes down well at Russell Street … any reception which requires deeper thought on the behalf of both critics and general public seems to meet with opposition in this city' (Sumner 1963). He reported White to be in a similar mood of disenchantment with the public. Coombs implied in his note to White that the two of them could share the burden of public hostility. For Coombs, an indigenous theatre could be difficult and controversial; and it did not have to adhere to an aesthetic of naturalism in order to authenticate itself as 'Australian'.

In remaining open to White's challenge to dramatic naturalism, Coombs encouraged a broad definition of the Australian heritage. In April 1964, he sent choreographer Robert Helpmann a book of A.D. Hope's poems, urging him to consider 'An Epistle from Holofernes' as a ballet.

> I do not think that we should restrict our sources to narrowly Australian themes and locations. We are, after all, a European community in our cultural inheritance and such sources as the Bible and the Greek myths belong as much to us as they do to any European country.
>
> (Coombs 1964b)

Coombs had been encouraged by Helpmann's 1963 ballet, *Display*, which he later described as drawing:

upon elements indigenous to the land of Australia in a theme which our aboriginal forebears would have recognised; it links this emotionally with the Greek myths that are the heritage of all of western civilisation; it comments justly on aspects of Australian social life, throwing light on the universal theme of the place of the non-conformist outsider in a tightly knit society; all this in a work of art marked by grace, beauty and passion.

(Coombs 1965)

Coombs was soon to go further in his pluralisation of 'Australia'. By including classical Aboriginal culture – visual and performing arts – within his idea of the nation's heritage, he challenged the convention that 'we' were European. In 1963 the Trust imported a troupe of dancers from the Northern Territory to perform in Sydney. In 1965, Coombs arranged for the Australian Institute of Aboriginal Studies to curate an exhibition, in Liverpool (UK) and later in London, of 57 bark paintings, as part of the Commonwealth Arts Festival. By the mid-1960s it had become impossible for Coombs any longer to use the words with which he had introduced Australian culture to Hugh Hunt, the Trust's first Executive Director: 'This is a young country and our history has been to a considerable extent occupied in the more practical side of life. We have not behind us a long cultural and artistic tradition' (Coombs 1955). Australia now had to be thought of as an 'old' country in its artistic traditions, and the meanings of 'we' had to be rethought.

Some of Coombs' earliest efforts to embrace the Indigenous tradition in a revised story of Australian cultural endeavour now look oddly experimental. In a speech given in the United Kingdom in 1965 he contrasted Aborigines and early settlers (Coombs 1965). The former were materially poor, but artistically rich; the latter were so desperate in their poverty that they deferred consideration of the higher things of life and were only now developing a 'culture'. As if perturbed by this declaration of difference, he then mused that although 'it will be long before the white Australian can be as free of anxiety about material things and as concerned with the quality of his aesthetic experience as his aboriginal predecessor', perhaps there were some continuities between Aboriginal and non-Aboriginal ways.

> There are those who see in our passion for the gracious ritual of cricket, the mock battles of the football field, for the long days with a wind filled sail lifting the keel under us, the influence of values which our aborigines have bequeathed us.

(Coombs 1965)

The odd suggestion that 'the Aborigines' had 'bequeathed' such values did not survive Coombs' 1966 revision of this speech. Rather than imagine continuities between the two Australian cultural heritages, Coombs was finding it necessary, by the late 1960s, to acknowledge their radical dissimilarity. In May 1969, addressing a UNESCO seminar on the performing arts, he described Australians as:

> fortunate that in the central and northern parts of Australia the rich ceremonial life of our aboriginal people persists, *despite the things that we have sought to do to it*, and the arts of painting, sculpture, music, mime and dance through which it is expressed are still flowering richly. The Council hopes to contribute to keeping these arts alive, not as decaying museum pieces but as living elements in the social life of these people; and what is perhaps from our point of view more important, as significant threads to be woven into the great fabric of our own national culture.
>
> (Coombs 1969, my emphasis)

Two years later he made the opening of a Sydney exhibition of Pitjantjatjara arts and crafts the occasion to rebuke those who 'consciously seek to shatter and destroy what remains' of Aboriginal civilisation (1971b).[3] In 1973, partly as a result of Coombs' urging, the Whitlam Government established the Aboriginal Arts Board within the Australian Council for the Arts. Wholly composed of Indigenous Australians, that Board's statements of purpose soon went beyond the mere preservation of 'classical' Indigenous culture to espouse a pan-Indigenous cultural movement. Anticipating this rapid evolution of patronage philosophy, Coombs showed in 1970 that he had moved beyond seeing the Aboriginal cultural heritage as merely a tributary of a pluralised national heritage. He told a New Zealand conference that the Australian Council for the Arts' funds were not only 'to promote the traditional arts of the Aboriginal people' but also 'to help them to adapt those arts so that they are relevant to the problems of confrontation, the problems of adjustment, the problems of living with alien people which today threaten to overwhelm the Aboriginal Australians' (Coombs 1970). He believed it to be fundamental to the Aboriginal Arts Board's work that the arts should be developed first for the artist's community, then for other Indigenous communities; and then, beyond such exchanges, the Aboriginal arts could sometimes address and enrich the rest of Australia and the Indigenous people of other lands.

In this series of statements Coombs departed more and more from seamlessly weaving the Indigenous into the ('national') settler-colonial heritage. His standpoint drew closer to that of the anthropologists whose first question of Indigenous artistic expression is: how does it help to reproduce the structures of the Indigenous social order? As Howard Morphy (1987, p. 167) points out, 'Primitive art, in Australia, and elsewhere, is first created as part of an indigenous culture, to be used and valued in a traditional way. Then it has to be created a second time, as a work of art in European terms, with a place in the European scheme of art history, a value in the art market, and a space reserved for it on the walls of art galleries'.

Conclusion

In his early advocacy of the performing arts, Coombs employed populist and nationalist images of the public. He then varied these terms by invoking Australians' demotic monarchism. His sense of cultural responsibility was class-conscious, in that he nominated a meritocracy as succeeding to the cultural leadership of wealth and aristocracy. Yet his terms for the consumption of culture remained socially integrative, implying that the meritocrats' executive competence served the cultural interests of the community as a whole. In class terms, the Trust's work was not all of a piece. Some of the Trust's achievements, I have suggested, can be seen as enriching the performed symbolism of state. Other work was consciously dissenting and outrageous. At the risk of being too schematic, I would suggest that this reflected the heterogeneity of the class alliance on which Coombs based the Trust's work. In defending contentious work against censorship, Coombs avoided making (Tasker-like) distinctions between qualified and unqualified modes of consumption, though the effect of his advocacy was to lay bare the conflicting cultural interests to which Tasker, like other critics of censorship, had to apply his activism. In advocating state support for Indigenous arts, however, Coombs' rhetoric shifted rapidly away from themes of social inclusion to an explicitly politicised nomination of cultural distinctions – not between classes or between the professional-managerial class and the 'establishment' but a radical counterposing of Aboriginal and settler-colonial traditions and interests.

The questions I have posed in this paper might be taken further by asking: how is the consumption of Indigenous Australian culture socially differentiated? Although Aboriginal motifs have been enlisted to symbolise 'the nation' (for example on the original dollar bill, the mosaic in the forecourt of Canberra's new Parliament House, the logo of the Australia Council) there is no doubt that the consumption of Aboriginal art also occasions social differentiation. The interesting question which faces a Bourdieuan analysis is: what counts as a 'competent' (in the sense of socially authorised competence) mode of consumption of Indigenous arts? What ways of interpreting Indigenous arts are now put forward – by those with the institutional power to commend or exemplify this or that way of knowing – as the most fully in touch with the artists and their civilisation? What are the authorised terms for knowing what Indigenous art is really about?

I suggest that this is an open question in Australia, one of the issues on the 'post colonial' agenda of cultural policy. Brian Kennedy, Director of the National Gallery of Australia, recently complained that the spiritual and political values of Aboriginal art and craft were being obscured by the 'aesthetic' values of that work. 'What worries me is that its aesthetics become the overriding criterion, to the point that the people looking at it do not have a sense of awareness of its relationship to land and to its stories. Are we sure what it is that we are doing by recognising Aboriginal art?' (cited in O'Loughlin 2000). His words suggest a contest between two modes of recognition. The class and institutional bases of their rivalry might be a good topic for a sociologically informed cultural studies.[4]

Notes

1   Van Praagh to Coombs, 26 November 1963; van Praagh to Coombs, 13 December 1963; Coombs to King, 8 January 1964; King to Coombs, 10 January 1964; Australian Archives CRS M448/1 item 277.
2   Zadok, paying tribute to Solomon, in Act III of Handel's *Solomon*.
3   A note on Coombs' copy of the latter cutting says 'I hope [senior NT Administration official Ted] Milliken recognises his own phrase'.
4   For an account of different traditions of reading the 'Hermannsburg School', see Green 1992.

Guide to further reading

For further references to class and cultural preferences, see the Guide to Further Reading for Chapter 9 below. The history of the performing arts in Australia is detailed in John Cargher, *Bravo: Two Hundred Years of Opera in Australia* (Melbourne: Macmillan, 1988); Katharine Brisbane (ed.) *Entertaining Australia: The Performing Arts as Cultural History* (Sydney: Currency Press, 1991); Philip Parsons (with V. Chance) (ed.), *Companion to Australian Theatre* (Sydney: Currency Press/Cambridge University Press, 1995; entries on 'New theatre', 'Amateur theatre', 'Professional theatre'), the most comprehensive reference work in the area; and Warren Bebbington (ed.), *The Oxford Companion to Australian Music* (Melbourne: Oxford University Press, 1997). Howard Morphy's *Aboriginal Art* (London: Phaidon, 1998) and Sylvia Kleinert and Margo Neale (eds) *The Oxford Companion to Aboriginal Art and Culture* (Melbourne: Oxford University Press, 2000) provide a broad introduction to Indigenous Australian art, and see references to Indigenous art in the Guide to Further Reading for Chapter 3 above. Rowse, *Arguing the Arts: The Funding of the Arts in Australia* (Ringwood, Vic.: Penguin, 1985) provides an historical account of arts funding policies as well as a critical discussion of the class-based cultural preferences of funding institutions. Justin Macdonnell's *Arts Minister?: Government Policy and the Arts* (Sydney: Currency Press, 1992) traces the contribution of Arts ministers from 1968–1987. Coombs gives an account of his own involvement in arts policy making in his memoirs (*Trial Balance*, South Melbourne: Macmillan, 1981); his analysis of the economics of the performing arts is in Coombs, 'The economics of the performing arts' (*Economic Papers* 35, September 1970/June 1971, pp. 32–46). The Australia Council website is at www.ozco.gov.au

References

anon (undated) file note, Australian Archives CRS A571/130 item 44/1171 pt 1.

anon (1949) 'Playgoers ask for more', *Current Affairs Bulletin*, 23 May, p. 5.

Bennett, Tony, Michael Emmison and John Frow (1999) *Accounting for Tastes: Australian Everyday Cultures*, Melbourne: Cambridge University Press.

Bourdieu, Pierre (1984) *Distinction: A Social Critique of the Judgment of Taste*, trans. R. Nice, Cambridge, Mass.: Harvard University Press.

Chifley, Joseph Benedict to Locksley Shaw (19 December 1946) Australian Archives CRS A432/82 item 47/291.

— to John Dedman (24 March 1948) Australian Archives CRS A432/82 item 47/291.

Coombs, Herbert Cole to Joseph Benedict Chifley (23 November 1944) Australian Archives CRS A9790/1 item 8141 pt 1.

— (cable) to Richard Mills (30 June 1948) Australian Archives CRS A432/82 item 47/291.

— (1949) Draft policy on National Theatre, Australian Archives CRS A432/82 item 47/291.

— (1953) 'The role of a regional university' (5th Albert Joseph Memorial Lecture, New England University College, 17 October). Bound Speeches of H.C. Coombs, Reserve Bank of Australia Archives, Volume One, pp. 3–17.

— (1954a) Address to the Rotary Club Sydney 27 April, Australian Archives CRS M448/1 item 266.

— to Sir W. Russell Grimwade (15 April 1954) (1954b) Australian Archives M448/1 item 266.

— to Hugh Hunt (February 1955) Australian Archives CRS M448/1 item 267.

— to John Latham (28 February 1956) (1956a) Australian Archives, M448/1 file 269.

— to John Latham (15 March 1956) (1956b) National Library of Australia, Latham papers Ms 1009 Box 72.

— (1959) 'The Governor on TV', *Currency* March (interview transcript), pp. 8–9.

— to Roland Jacobs (22 August 1963) (1963a) Australian Archives CRS M448/1 item 276.

— to Nita Pannell (20 November 1963) (1963b) Australian Archives M448/1 item 276.

— to George Nicklin (24 November 1964) (1964a) Australian Archives CRS M448/1 item 277.

— to Robert Helpmann (20 April 1964) (1964b) Australian Archives CRS M448/1 item 277.

— (1965) 'The arts in Australia', address to the Athenaeum Club, Liverpool (UK), 22 September, Australian Archives M448/1 item 142.

— (1966) 'Australia: new dimensions', Australian Citizenship Convention Canberra, Australian Archives M448/1 item 142.

— (1969) Untitled address to UNESCO seminar on the performing arts, Canberra, 26 May, National Library of Australia, Coombs Papers Ms 802 Box 21 folder 163.

— (1970) Address given by Dr Herbert Cole Coombs, 11 April, Wellington, New Zealand, at the public session of 'Arts Conference 70' arranged by the Queen Elizabeth II Arts Council of New Zealand, National Library of Australia, Coombs papers MS 802 Box 29 folder 241.

— (1971a) *Other People's Money*, Canberra: Australian National University Press.

— (1971b) Address at Argyle Arts Centre 7 December (reprinted in *Australian*, 9 December and *Northern Territory News*, 13 December).

— to Hugh Roberton 12 February 1974 (1974a) National Library of Australia MS 802 Box 41 folder 363.

— (1974b) Remarks at the exhibition of Aboriginal art, 18 February, National Library of Australia Coombs Papers MS 802 Box 26 folder 207.

Dutton, Geoffrey (1994) *Out in the Open*, St Lucia: University of Queensland Press.

Green, Jenny (1992) 'Country in mind: the continuing tradition of landscape painting' in J. Hardy, J. Vincent, S. Megaw and M. Ruth Megaw (eds) *The Heritage of Namatjira: The Watercolourists of Central Australia*, Melbourne: William Heinemann Australia, pp. 283–316.

Haag, Stephan (1965) 'Executive Director's report to members: Australian Elizabethan Theatre Trust', *Annual Report and Financial Statements*, December.

Hage, Ghassan (1998) *White Nation: Fantasies of White Supremacy in a Multicultural Society*, Sydney: Pluto Press.

Haylen, Leslie (1944) Speech in House of Representatives, 22 September, Commonwealth Parliamentary Debates 179, 1324–5.

Hunt, Hugh (1956) Circular letter to Board, 2 March. National Library of Australia, Latham Papers MS 1009 Box 72/87–8.

Jacobs, Roland to Herbert Cole Coombs (5 August 1963) Australian Archives CRS M448/1 item 276.

Kippax, Harry (1964) 'Australian Drama since "Summer of the Seventeenth Doll"', *Meanjin* 3, pp. 229–42.

Latham, John to Herbert Cole Coombs (6 March 1956) National Library of Australia, Latham Papers MS 1009 Box 72.

Macartney, Keith (1947) 'Louis Esson and Australian drama', *Meanjin* 2, pp. 93–6, 104.

Mills, Richard (1946) Interdepartmental Committee Report, Australian Archives CRS A432/82 item 47/291.

Morphy, Howard (1987) 'Audiences for art' in A. Curthoys, A. Martin and T. Rowse (eds) *Australians from 1939*, Sydney: Fairfax, Syme, Weldon, pp. 167–75.

O'Loughlin, Toni (2000) 'True values "lost in acquiring art"', *Sydney Morning Herald*, 12 April.

Radic, Thérèse (1995) 'The Australian National Theatre Movement as the catalyst for the Australian Opera: tug-boat to flagship' in N. Brown *et al.* (eds) *One Hand on the Manuscript: Music in Australian Cultural History 1930–1960*, Canberra: Humanities Research Centre, ANU, pp. 201–16.

Rees, Leslie (1953) *Towards an Australian Drama*, Sydney: Angus & Robertson.

Shaw, Locksley to Joseph Benedict Chifley (1 November 1946) Australian Archives CRS A432/82 item 47/291.

Stewart, Douglas (1956) 'The playwright in Australia', *The Australian Elizabethan Theatre Trust: The First Year*, Sydney, pp. lv–lvii.

Sumner, John to Herbert Cole Coombs (25 November 1963) Australian Archives M448/1 item 276.

Tasker, John (1970) 'Censorship in the Theatre' in G. Dutton and M. Harris (eds) *Australia's Censorship Crisis*, Melbourne: Sun Books, pp. 37–51.

Part 2
Australian Culture and its Publics

The terms 'public' and 'culture' have been combined in so many ways in recent critical debates that it is difficult to insist on a single or correct meaning for them. To speak of a 'public culture' is one thing, related to but not quite the same as the public sphere, while to speak of the publics for culture is to invoke a third meaning, one in which the concepts of public, audience and market often serve as interchangeable substitutes. Rather than opting for any one of these meanings at the expense of the others, the chapters comprising Part 2 are concerned with the different values that the concepts of public and culture have acquired in the context of the different ways in which they are combined in current Australian debates. The issues addressed include the role of the high/popular distinction in differentiating the publics for culture; the roles played by the institutions and practices of criticism and academic scholarship in organising both publics and public spheres; the functioning of different regimes of value in the strategies through which public broadcasters now address multiple publics; and the roles of class, age and gender in organising different patterns of access to, and use of, cultural resources of various kinds.

Yet, although the issues engaged with in each chapter are different, they are informed by a shared perception that the relations between questions of publics, publicness and culture are currently in the midst of significant transformations arising from a variety of pressures. It is clear, for example, that the notion of a single national culture with a single public – except, perhaps, for odd moments of national epiphany, like the closing celebrations of the 2000 Olympics – has become less and less intelligible as either a description of, or a goal for, the relations between current forms of cultural production and distribution and the patterns of cultural participation they engender. The declining role of broadcasting and its ability to constitute a national public; the development of cable television and narrowcasting; the increasing segmentation of audiences into diverse lifestyle groups: in these ways, in Australia as elsewhere, the forms of publicness associated with the cultural sphere are increasingly differentiated ones. Related theoretical debates have echoed these developments. The concept of a single public sphere as a forum for the conduct of debate on issues of general public concern has lost ground before the perception that there exists a series of differentiated public spheres – defined in terms of race, class, and gender – with their different priorities, protocols and procedures. Yet this has not detracted from the intelligibility of referring to 'public culture' as a means of specifying the civic work that culture is called on to perform through its inscription in governmental programs of one kind or another.

It is, indeed, from this understanding of public culture that David Carter and Kay Ferres take their bearings, in Chapter 6, in examining the changing public life of literature. This involves, as a preliminary argument, their taking issue with the legacy of aesthetic conceptions of literature which, in making literariness their key concern, have paid little attention to its civic functioning in public culture and as a commodity in literary markets. Rather than – as critical literary studies has been wont to – attributing to literature a capacity to transcend or subvert dominant structures, it is its circulation in public, commercial and governmental realms that interests Carter and Ferres. Perhaps the most arresting aspect of their discussion, once this initial argument is made, is the sheer range of the different forms in which literature's public life is manifested. In their concern to disaggregate literature from a single, given object into a diversity of functions exercised in the different social, civic and governmental fields in which it is used, their discussion ranges across the public issues at stake in debates about literary value and literary expertise in universities, the history of magazine and periodical publishing, the organisation of the book industry, and the emergence of literature as an object of government intervention through the programs of the Australia Council and its use as a means of civic education in the school system. The result is a rich insight into what it would mean to consider literature 'as a form of public-commercial-aesthetic *institution*' alongside the more developed analyses that already exist of the institutions of cinema, the music industry and television.

Graeme Turner's concern, in Chapter 7, is with what he sees as a significant transformation in the Australian public sphere brought about by the relentless commercialisation of cultural production that has resulted from the increasing deregulation of cultural and media markets associated with neo-liberal policy agendas that have prevailed throughout the 1990s and into the new millennium. But he brings to this concern a particular interest in the extent to which intellectuals, albeit unwittingly, may have contributed to these developments. Looking back, although not uncritically, to the policy debates of the 1970s and early 1980s, Turner notes the largely positive and enabling role played by intellectuals working in academic institutions in providing a rationale – derived from the agendas of a vigorous cultural nationalism – for the development of new forms of government involvement in the cultural sector targeted at supporting a broad range of cultural industries, popular as well as elite. By contrast, the subsequent declining influence of the agendas of cultural nationalism, allied with the sometimes uncritically affirmative conception of popular cultural practices that is often associated with cultural studies, has meant that some of the more regressive manifestations of the popular associated with an increasingly deregulated media sector – talkback radio, for example – have received scant critical attention from intellectuals. This has, Turner argues, weakened the ability of intellectuals to influence the terms in which public debates about cultural policies are conducted, and so weakened too their ability to provide effective arguments to counter the severely reduced scope for public cultural provision that is inherent in the increasing ascendancy of the neo-liberal view of markets as the only valid form of social organisation. If this is to be countered, Turner suggests, it needs to be recognised that there can be no return to grand narratives of a kind that might sustain a general critical project. He urges, instead, the need for intellectuals to develop strategies for helping reshape the future of Australian cultural institutions that will be 'more specific and focused in their application, more modestly contingent in their politics, but more explicitly ambitious in their ethical claims'.

Gay Hawkins takes up this challenge in Chapter 8 in her discussion of the changing fortunes of public sector broadcasting which, in Australia as in most other countries, has suffered a series of setbacks since the 1980s. The threat and, often, the reality of declining levels of public funding; declining audiences relative to the commercial broadcasting sector and the growth of cable and satellite television; and critiques of the ethos of public sector broadcasting – these have all taken their toll, resulting in accounts which see the future of the sector in terms of unending crisis and terminal decline. Hawkins, in looking at the recent history of the ABC, resists the lure of such 'grand narratives' preferring, instead, to develop a more differentiated approach to the institution that is responsive to the different pressures and temporalities operating upon and within it. Drawing on post-Foucauldian accounts for this purpose, she looks at the development of the new genres of 'infotainment' on the ABC and suggests that, rather than seeing these as representing a decline from earlier public service values induced by increased commercial pressures, they are more appropriately viewed as helping to form a pluralistic ethics that is better adjusted to the needs of a culturally diverse society than the ABC's earlier, and more singular, normative and pedagogic assumptions.

The nature of the ABC's publicness is also a question considered by Tony Bennett, Michael Emmison and John Frow in Chapter 9. Their concerns, however, focus on the social composition of the ABC's audience rather than its program formats, and on the nature and extent of its social reach as measured by the class composition of that audience relative to the commercial television sector. They also place these concerns in a broader perspective by comparing the patterns of class participation in Australian broadcast television with the extent to which the members of different classes participate in sports – as players or as spectators – and their degrees and kinds of involvement in different musical and literary taste cultures. Drawing on the statistical evidence of a nationwide survey of cultural practices in support of their arguments, they are left in little doubt that class continues to count, and to count culturally, so far as its roles in organising significant social divisions, and in bringing about significant inequalities in the distribution of cultural life chances, are concerned. The consequences of the distribution of different kinds of cultural capital, they argue, have been especially important in this respect. However, Bennett, Emmison and Frow are equally in little doubt that the cultural effects of class have also to be considered in their interactions with the parts played by other social variables in organising the patterns of access to, and uses of, cultural resources. The most urgent questions here, they suggest, are those posed by the current dynamics of the relations between class, culture and ethnicity in generating a new set of faultlines in Australian public and political culture between cosmopolitan urban elites on the one hand and the more restricted forms of cultural participation of working-class, rural and regional Australia on the other.

Catharine Lumby's interests in Chapter 10, by contrast, focus on the changing value of age as a marker of social and cultural identity. She takes, as her route into these questions, the 'generation panics' which, from time to time, erupted into the Australian media sphere during the 1990s. The two panics that most engage her attention are, first, those embodied in recurrent fears about the sexual exploitation of young teen girls by the popular media, and, second, the widespread concern that an unbridgeable gap was developing between the Baby-boomers and the next generation, the so-called Generation X. There is, on the face of things, an odd asymmetry between these two panics. The first, as Lumby puts it, represents a set of concerns clustering around the anxiety that young girls are 'being made to grow up too fast and that childhood is a vanishing phase in social life', whereas the second articulates the fear that 'young people are refusing to grow up, that they have failed to take on the mantle of adulthood and so constitute a generation in limbo, trapped in a perpetual adolescence'. Yet these can be seen as related phenomena, Lumby suggests, if considered from the perspective of the role that new media have played both in making it more difficult to regulate youth media practices and in dissolving the cultural salience of age as an identity marker into a more fluid and labile set of identities. If this is so, she argues, these 'generation panics' can best be interpreted as symptoms of an ongoing transformation of the public sphere from the earlier hierarchical norms of its modern phase of development into a postmodern public sphere characterised by more plural and dialogic norms of public discourse.

No equivalent dissolution of identities is in sight so far as questions concerning the relations of gender and sport are concerned. The patterns of participation in amateur sport remain rigorously demarcated along gender lines in ways that work systematically to the disadvantage of women. This is true, moreover, of all aspects of sport: from the provision of sporting facilities, the relative rates of women's and men's participation in sport, their relative levels of remuneration, representation in decision making structures, and media coverage. What most concerns Jim McKay, Geoffrey Lawrence, Toby Miller and David Rowe in Chapter 11, however, is that there are few signs of any appreciable improvement in this situation. This is not, they stress, for want of trying: there has been no shortage of government sponsored programs aimed at promoting greater gender equity in Australian sport. They suggest, however, that the form these have taken has often intensified existing inequalities owing to their being put into effect as parts of neo-liberal conceptions of government which, in their commitment to the spread of market-based principles of management, have greatly increased the commodification and professionalisation of sport in ways that have reinforced stereotypical gender divisions. Such programs have also often been only half-heartedly implemented by sports managers who too often continue to function as relay points within a culture of hegemonic masculinity which, in stressing the values of toughness and competitiveness, continues to marginalise the position of women in sport. While they are not optimistic that there are any 'quick fixes' in sight, McKay and his co-authors suggest that a clearer understanding of sport as a cultural practice and, accordingly, the need to treat sports policies as a part of cultural policies might help in loosening the commercial imperatives which now so dominate sports policies, and usually to women's disadvantage.

Chapter 6

The Public Life of Literature

David Carter and Kay Ferres

Locating literature

In this essay we want to consider the 'public life' of literature. In contemporary academic debates over cultural value, literature has often been disparaged as elitist or 'merely aesthetic', a residual fragment of high culture left over from a previous era or a minority taste that mis-takes itself as universal. In part such criticisms have been a reaction against the ways in which, over the course of the twentieth century, the academy and other cultural institutions have made 'literariness' the principal object of study and appreciation rather than the many other dimensions of literary production and consumption. They also may, ironically, reflect the extent to which 'literariness' has lodged itself within these institutions. These criticisms underestimate literature's function in public culture, in political and civil spheres, in the school, where the curriculum has exploited the civic potentials of 'English' and incorporated a range of textual objects and methods in the reading lesson, and in the marketplace, as a commodity.

Literary culture has had a central role in shaping Australian public culture and political institutions. Literary journalism has sustained debates about the national interest. In the period leading up to Federation, journals like the *Boomerang*, the *Republican*, the *Australian Nationalist*, the *Bulletin* and the *Dawn* provided a space for discussion of the form the new polity should take (Irving 1994; Lawson 1983). Although Federation has been seen as a triumph of liberal constitutionalism, some elements of a strong mid-nineteenth century republican culture survived. Federalism was a 'public thing' in the sense Alastair Davidson describes: it involved publicly visible deliberation and engaged impassioned speech not least through the mediation of the periodical press and its literary forms (Davidson 1994). In the twentieth century, in a country with a dispersed population, periodicals from the *Bulletin* to *Meanjin*, *Overland* and *Quadrant* to *Eureka Street* and *Heat* in the present have constituted public spheres in which competing versions of the good life were elaborated. Literature still plays a key role in authorising and disseminating the interventions of public intellectuals.

Further, both government and commercial interests have engaged in the development of a 'literature industry'. Government has extended protection to the literature industry by subsidising writers and publishers and promoting both a national literature and a national audience. Literature is an object of governance through the programs of the Australia Council and its state and local equivalents, through censorship, copyright and Public/Educational Lending Rights regimes, through cultural diplomacy initiatives, and, not least, through the education system. English lessons have played a key role in educating a democratic citizenry, and educational publishers have cultivated a reading public. The revitalisation of libraries and the expansion of writers' festivals are only part of a sustained, if somewhat piecemeal, program of audience development which reflects a recent policy shift from industry subsidy to market stimulation and the creation of 'capability', a capacity for innovation and 'human capital development' (Wanna and Withers 2000).

It is to these 'other' dimensions of literary meaning that we address ourselves in this chapter. In what ways does literature circulate in public, commercial and governmental realms? In what ways does it continue to sustain a public sphere? How are literature and literary cultures implicated in the public institutions which support Australian forms of democratic citizenship? In what ways can literature be considered a public good and is this at odds with its status as a commodity? How does literature participate – even play a leading role – in the twentieth-century expansion of the field of governance into the private realm? Approaching literature through such questions leads us to reconsider the industrial and commercial dimensions of literature's public life and the institutions through which literature circulates – the university, the school, the periodical press, public intellectual debate, government cultural bodies, the publishing industry and the market.

Institutions are often understood as change-resistant, even elitist, formations. Critiques of 'the canon' have cast the literary institution in this light (Bird *et al.* 1997). However, it may be more useful to think of literature as a significant site for the 'exchange of public reasons' (Gates 1996), a cultural institution which has had an important and ongoing role in the necessary contest which determines 'public good', in defining and redefining the nation and national values, and in shaping public spheres in which democratic values of freedom of expression and public deliberation can occur. We want to reaffirm literature's participation in the public and commercial spheres rather than its power to transcend or subvert dominant structures, which is perhaps the orthodox claim made for literature in contemporary criticism. Rather than see literature (or 'literariness') primarily as a form of negative critique with a deconstructive relationship to institutions, we emphasise literature's positive relation to public and commercial institutions, and its constitutive role in defining forms of public, civic and national culture.

Our argument requires a sense of literature as a 'disaggregated' object, defined in a range of very different ways by its participation in very different cultural institutions: as commodity, as professional practice, as cultural capital, as ethical and pedagogical technology (a means of expressing and debating public values), as object of governance (both industry and culture) *and* as a rhetorical and aesthetic domain (where we might define 'aesthetics' as the realm where literary form or style is invested with ethical value). Literary studies – but not literary studies alone – are still often tied to a post-romantic suspicion of any notion of state, government or nation (Bennett 1990; Carter 1999a). This suspicion has survived the shift from ethics to class to identity politics in textual analysis. But once we begin to think seriously about literature in institutional terms – as part of an industry, as a commodity with various exchange values, as an object of governmental interest – such 'anti-statism' is revealed as historically misleading and theoretically one-sided. That literature is an object of governmental interest, that the state uses it for its own purposes, says nothing in advance about political effects or ideological values. As textual analysis and cultural history have both shown, literature has certainly been used for repressive purposes in the education system, journalism and politics. But – parallel to the work that cultural policy studies have done in other areas – literature's 'positive' uses in maintaining a public sphere, authorising public debate, educating a citizenry, shaping a market and defining a national culture as the object of progressive policy making have a history which is equally long and complex. It is difficult to make sense of literature's public life in the present without taking more account of this positive history.

The persistence of the notion that literary value is 'merely aesthetic' is curious in some ways, given all the evidence over the last decade of literature's robust, diverse and contentious public life. The literary market is booming – at least in certain domains – as indicated by its increasing niche segmentation and fine-grained product differentiation, from the niche markets of genre fiction (Gelder 2000) to those of the high art novel.[1] The 'literary novel' is a more eroticised commodity than ever before and 'literary sensibility' is being invoked in the expanding genres of the essay and the memoir. Literary publishing remains high prestige and so the target of multinational takeovers despite being a high risk and on the whole low profit venture (Wilding 1999). The circuit of writers' festivals and prizes continues to expand, as does the media presence of literature (Turner 1998, pp. 362–3). Public subsidy has increased overall, especially at state and local levels, and has been maintained at the federal level.

The value of literature – the value of literary value – has been central to recent contests about public good: for example, over the role of the Australia Council's funding processes and 'political correctness'; the ethics and politics of criticism in the awarding of prizes to Helen Demidenko's *The Hand that Signed the Paper* (1994); ethical and legal values in Helen Garner's *The First Stone* (1995); the status of authorship and authenticity in a series of literary hoaxes such as those involving the ethnicity of Demidenko/Darville or Wanda Koolmatrie; and the defence by literary journalists of aesthetic values against the tide of 'cultural studies' and 'theory' in the academy (Davis 1999a; Wark 1997). Even the Prime Minister's unhappy attempt to write a new preamble to the Australian Constitution with the aid of poet and conservative spokesperson Les Murray showed literature in its public rather than merely aesthetic guise. Moreover, literature and critical discourse have played a major role in articulating multicultural, Asian-Australian, Indigenous Australian and other 'modern' versions of the nation. The 2000 Vogel literary prize was awarded to a novel about copyright issues and Aboriginal culture, themes consonant with a shift in the focus of citizenship claims which are grounded in cultural rather than individual rights (Hall 2000). If from some perspectives traditional literary education has shrunk, a modernised literary education (including film studies, performance studies, even a revitalised study of rhetoric) has greatly expanded. The English curriculum recognises the multiple dimensions of the literary object, where it is assigned to variant strands. As well, 'literature' appears across the curriculum, in subjects like civics and history. The flourishing careers of writers of 'adolescent' fiction like John Marsden and Gary Crew, and the recent success of the film adaptation of *Looking for Alibrandi* are further signs of the role of the school in cultivating new audiences for literature.

Literary studies in the university have been significantly influenced by the development of cultural and media studies, although for its part cultural studies, in any of its various guises, has been much less interested in literature than in the forms of mass communication or public institutions where the relation between culture and government is primary (Goodall 1995, pp. 147–74). There is, for example, no index entry for 'Literature' in the most recent major study of arts funding and cultural policy in Australia (Stevenson 2000). While literary studies have become cultural, sociological and interdisciplinary, their concern with the public institutional and industrial dimensions of litera-ture has gone only so far. Literary texts are rarely subjected to the kind of analysis that would locate them within a literature industry. Although there have been many revelations of 'textual politics' there has been little work done on how literature actually circulates or fails to circulate through the social structure; we have scarcely begun to talk about literature as a form of public-commercial-aesthetic institution comparable, say, to those of cinema, television, music or the fine arts (e.g., Cunningham and Turner 1997; Johnson 1997). Studies of the publishing industry are just beginning to approach the level of density of studies of other cultural or media production institutions, although 'the history of the book' (and of reading) is a significant emerging field. Studies of literature's relation to the market have tended to be simply negative, lamenting the tendency of 'market forces' to stifle innovation. The 'applied' science of literary pedagogy is all but ignored and left to educationalists. This practice looks especially odd when considered alongside the North American example of scholars like Eamonn Callan (1997) and Martha Nussbaum (1997), who argue the 'civic' case for literary studies.

Cultural studies, where it emphasises contexts and institutions, has had a useful effect in 'disciplining' literary studies, calling attention to the limits of its claims on culture and politics (Bennett 1998, pp. 21–38). But having accepted the force of arguments against the hyperbolic claims sometimes made for literature, we can see that in fact they relate to a very small, although historically significant, part of the way literature has circulated in the public, social world. Our interest, then, is in the 'work' that literature does in the public sphere outside, but also *through*, its aesthetic credentials. In the following section we examine the role of periodicals, which have typically been commercial, aesthetic and public in their interests all at once. This brief study reveals a history of literature's role in the definition of a public sphere and the shifting function of public intellectuals in Australia. Magazines afforded a space for public intellectuals with distinctively Australian preoccupations to emerge, preoccupations which found a common project – and grounds for dispute – in the cultivation of a national literature. Allied to proposals for a national theatre, this became the primary object of government cultural policy after World War II (Johanson 2000). Following these connections, we examine the contemporary presence of public intellectuals and the role of literature in cultural policy as manifested in programs of public subsidy and promotion.

Periodicals and the public sphere

Newspapers and magazines represent an extremely diverse field of professional and amateur publishing where aesthetic, commercial and public interests have combined and clashed in a great variety of forms. The domain of the periodical press is connected to the very beginnings of the 'public sphere' and literature has, ever since, been an authorising and foundational element in the shifting attempts to 're-invent the public sphere' (Eagleton 1984). To focus on the twentieth century history of Australian periodicals enables us to chart shifts in the position of literature in the public sphere – as a commodity, as leisure, as autonomous art, as an intellectual or pedagogical object – and in the nature of those who speak to and for the public sphere.

At the turn of the last century the institutions that would promote art's autonomy – art academies or high art journalism for example – were relatively weak in Australia. Aestheticism understood as a critique of bourgeois cultural values was present among writers and especially painters but it emerged in exactly the same sphere as debates about the state, the nation and the public interest, in the world of the periodical press (Lawson 1983; White 1981, pp. 89–101). The divisions between criticism and the marketplace, literature and journalism, commerce and public culture, were not yet institutionalised. Indeed the specific mix of politics, entertainment, education and culture that the general periodicals provided was a characteristic of the 'new' journalism, which made its name in the cause of the public interest.

The most famous instance, of course, is the early *Bulletin* of the 1880s–1890s (Lawson 1983). The *Bulletin* brought into being a new form of the public sphere in Australia. It did so precisely by addressing the emerging generation of educated, literate middle- and working-class readers as interested citizens, members not just of a national audience but of a national culture and polity. It wrested for this newly defined audience, from a more traditionally constituted elite, the right of debate and judgement about government and culture. The readers it addressed were 'sober judges of public affairs' in the republican sense. Thus the *Bulletin*'s seemingly incommensurate contents – party politics, business, bohemia, the bush, society, agriculture, banking, labour, literature, theatre and sport – for all were part of the discourse of government and nation it conducted. In Sylvia Lawson's phrase, 'what was literary in the *Bulletin* [was] its total writing' not just its verse or fiction (1983, p. 180). Literature, especially Australian literature, was part of the paper's conversation about nation and state, just as citizenship was a part of its talk about literature. After Federation, however, and especially after the Great War, this sense of a public sphere all but disappeared from the magazine's pages; its increasingly populist nationalism generated a negative sense of politics and government as nothing more than bureaucratic or interested interference. As a consequence its literature becomes aesthetic in the palest sense, merely decorative or sentimental. It retreated from its public being except in the form of patriotism. This collapse of the late-nineteenth-century public sphere meant that the 'bohemians of the *Bulletin*' did not develop into a distinct intellectual caste.

The public sphere which the *Bulletin* sustained depended wholly upon the commercial market for its existence. The circulation of the paper as a commodity free from 'interests' was a pre-condition of its civic discourse; and its 'literature' was similarly public in its mode. Like other magazines to the 1930s, the *Bulletin* occupied the same public-commercial sphere as the theatre (which all the papers reviewed extensively): commercial theatre and journalism both were forms that mixed popular and literary modes, art and commerce, 'seriousness' and enter-tainment, and did so because of the way they addressed a public world.

By contrast, literature's public forms after the mid-1920s would have to begin with the split between the institutions of high and popular culture. *Vision* (1923–24), for example, projected its own transcendence above nation, society and public altogether, predictably in the figure of the Artist (Kirkpatrick 1992). In the process it turned at least some of its writers, however briefly, into public intellectuals, perhaps for the first time in Australia in the modern form of the 'literary intellectual' rather than the man of letters. In the same period the older form of the news digest began to be replaced by the more self-consciously intellectual and 'governmental' form of the serious quarterly which looked forward to a new social location for the public sphere, more professional and institutionalised, less journalistic. *Australian Quarterly* (from 1929) published articles on literature alongside those on economics or international affairs.

Other magazines and papers went in the opposite direction: down-market. *Smith's Weekly* (1919–50) and *Aussie* (1920–31) captured the sense of contemporaneity and public interest which the *Bulletin* had lost by recasting national culture as a part of urban popular culture (Carter 1999b). If this redoubled the force of White Australian Empire nationalism, embedding it as a mundane cultural fact, the papers' populist address always had the potential of opening a space for 'public opinion' within the nation. They, too, were full of 'literature' in a way that linked back to the older journalistic sense of the term (Kirkpatrick 1992, pp. 110–17; Walker 1980, pp. 71–8). Readers could be offered new forms of entitlement, new forms of citizenship, for the fractious post-war world based on the generational and gendered sense of belonging that the war had created.

The social and intellectual crises of the 1930s produced a 'redistribution' of political and literary meanings. Literature again became a way of thinking politically, especially for opening up a space for talk about the national culture opposed to official patriotic rhetoric. The thirties saw the emergence of important new forms of fiction; the professionalisation and politicisation of writers' and artists' organisations (often in the one process); the formation of movements, schools and manifestos: in short, the coming into being of a self-conscious literary or 'cultural' intelligentsia (Buckridge 1998; Modjeska 1981). The careers of its members would be marked by a troubled relationship to the market, to journalism, to the academy. They were public intellectuals – in classic fashion although one largely unprecedented in Australia – who depended upon a market they despised, beseeched an academy they resented, defended the autonomy of a literature which they defined as more than merely literary, and sought a broad public which they feared as mass consumers.

Meanjin's appearance in 1940 was precisely a matter of 're-inserting' literature into public culture as a means of redefining the nature of national citizenship around modern, democratic liberalism. It was as if, given the time and place, the magazine could not do otherwise than become a magazine of cultural politics (Lee *et al.* 1990; Strahan 1984). The first issue was a 'Traditionalist Number' (1940); by number 8, the times demanded a 'Crisis Issue' (1942). *Meanjin*'s long-term success depended upon creating the space for a common, public intellectual discourse. Its readers again were citizens rather than artists – or consumers – in a context in which 'Australian' citizenship was being redefined by, for example, post-war reconstruction, the Australian Nationality and Citizenship Act (1948) and the referendum on commonwealth powers and the legality of the Communist Party (1951). The net that held the magazine together was literature, which was defined in at least three distinct but overlapping ways: in part through the idea of a *national* literature taken to be essentially democratic; but also through the notion of literature as autonomous – matching the 'committed disinterestedness' of the intellectual – and the belief that literary values were more or less naturally liberal. Literature thus appeared in its aesthetic and romantic modes but also as a civic discourse, a public good, expressing the values of democratic liberalism, freedom of expression, rationality and a common culture. The literary thus enabled the magazine's variously credentialled experts to meet less as professionals than as 'writers', 'serious readers', citizens and unattached intellectuals. Essays on Henry Lawson and poems by Judith Wright sat alongside discussions of contemporary European philosophy, urban planning, or Aboriginal culture. Although *Meanjin*'s concern was primarily with the culture of settler Australia, its discourse of nation also meant that Aboriginal culture became part of the understanding of the nation's culture. Here literature and anthropology together 'argued' Aboriginal culture into the meanings of contemporary, liberal Australia.

Meanjin, especially in the 1950s, redisposed nationalism as an oppositional discourse, able to sustain a counter public sphere where serious debate could occur about the nation, international politics, contemporary literature, communism, democracy – and the role of the writer, the critic, the intellectual and the magazine. But the fact that it could play this role was partly due to the degree that this 'oppositional' discourse had in fact *entered* government. The point is not that there was a radical nationalist faction within government but that notions of the national culture as a distinct sphere to be protected or promoted, something with economic and political significance, something to enter into all other kinds of calculations – something which indeed helped define the role of government – had penetrated throughout government, especially during the war. Projects for the establishment of a cultural council were central to the visions of post-war reconstruction, with theatre especially, but also written literature, as the primary focus for policy interest (Johanson 2000). In ways that have now become familiar to practitioners and policy makers, if still largely unrecognised in academic studies, critical cultural practices (in theatre, in literature etc.) came to be seen as *consonant with* the constitutive governmental objectives of producing democratic, educated and fulfilled citizens. If such thinking was less prominent during the years of conservative government, it remained present through consistent lobbying from *Meanjin* and other 'literary-cultural' quarterlies, and would re-emerge in the form of the Elizabethan Theatre Trust and the Australia Council (see Tim Rowse in this volume).

In the late 1950s and 1960s a new sense of public culture began to emerge, in part through a new interaction between journalism and the academy. Many of those involved in the new 'journals of opinion' – the *Observer* (1958–61) and *Nation* (1958–72) in particular – were products of and at home in both journalism and the universities: Donald Horne, Tom Fitzgerald, Ken Gott, Robert Hughes, Sylvia Lawson, Mungo MacCallum (Inglis 1989). This was a new intelligentsia, with a sense of the *modernising* potential of literary culture and a self-conscious relation to what was beginning to be called 'the media'.

The *Observer* and *Nation* were established precisely to talk about issues not discussed in the daily press or not in their ways. The essay and the critical review were their characteristic forms, once more assuming something of their traditional public role. They were pitched to an educated public that could be conceived in less hermetic forms than in *Meanjin*. It was a dispersed rather than organic audience; or, in slightly different terms, it was conceived not as a literary audience but as a variously interested public. *Meanjin* could suddenly look old-fashioned, both too amateur and too academic at once, too out of touch with anything that might be conceived as a public sphere. This was the kind of modernising spirit best summed up in Horne's *The Lucky Country* (1964) or the *Observer*'s effective takeover of the ailing *Bulletin* in 1962 when Horne tossed out everything except the name. The nation once again meant the state, not just the culture; and the sense of what culture might mean also began to change, for example with *Nation*'s essays on cinema. Literature had an important role though not necessarily a central one. Reviewers and essayists were on the lookout for the emergence of new Australian subjectivities and literature was one place they were discovered. Literature also served as a category of freedom against all the ideologies – communist, nationalist, conservative or commercial. These papers played a major role in mobilising a broad-based intelligentsia against the long-reigning Liberal Party and the 'old' Australia it was seen to represent.

What of the present? The contemporary situation is defined by two developments emerging from the late sixties: the professionalisation of Australian literature, history and other fields in the academy (marked by the appearance of professional scholarly journals and the dominance of academic authors in the cultural quarterlies); and the redefinition of the whole field of public culture by 'the media'. The literary domain is now defined by its relation to the media, to the electronic media and to the kinds of publications that are increasingly its by-product. Literature has had to become part of the media and communications industries (as its publishers are often part of larger media-communications-entertainment conglomerates). Thus an established literary magazine like *Meanjin* has had to invert its relationship to the academy, to begin from its place inside the university rather than outside. Its literariness must now be joined by a kind of 'media-ness'; it must seek new markets and publics beyond the literary audience it once had. New magazines, new publishing ventures in general, must define themselves in relation to the media. Text Publishing, perhaps the most successful new player from the 1990s, is part of a broader independent media company, Text Media. Magazines such as *Eureka Street* and *Heat* have defined a space which is partly inside, partly outside media cultures. The former, a journal of opinion and review, takes the media as one of its principal subjects; public affairs are almost always media affairs. The latter, a literary journal, assumed that its readers were media savvy, indeed that this went together with contemporary literariness. Established in 1996 with the first ever 'foundation grant' ($25,000) from the Literature Fund of the Australia Council, *Heat* managed to make high literary and aesthetic questions also a matter of politics – and (life) style.

Literature is thus now in a very different, subordinate position in relation to the media cultures compared to the relative equality of public cultural space it shared earlier with journalism and the theatre. This is a specific instance of John Frow's general remark that 'high culture ... is no longer "the dominant culture" but is rather a *pocket* within commodity culture' (Frow 1995, p. 86). The point of Frow's observation, however, is neither to mourn nor celebrate literature's shrinking significance – if that's what it is – but rather to define the new terrain, the new institutions, through which literature circulates; indeed to suggest the advantages that there might be for literature's democratic, public circulation in its new circumstances. After all, as Frow adds, what is true of high culture is also true of many forms of 'low culture'. While literature's central authority can no longer be assumed, this does not necessarily tell a simple story of its withering away. If literary texts are now produced, distributed and – perhaps – consumed in much the same way as pop culture commodities, this might also be a sign of literature's contemporary proliferation, its entry into new social relations and public spaces. The literary is still – or once again – consorting with a diversity of kinds of writing, speech and media in constituting public spheres.

Public intellectuals and the literary

One of the principal ways literary value circulates in contemporary Australia is through the interventions of public intellectuals and through debates over their status and function. These debates are also a product of the contemporary shifts in public significance and institutional location for literature indicated above. It has been a constant theme among intellectuals and commentators in recent years that the sites for serious literary, cultural or intellectual talk are shrinking (Davis 1999a, pp. 30–42). But major structural changes probably always appear this way to those whose traditional sites of authority are under threat. It is true that the stable patterns of public cultural conversation and 'book talk', bedded down in the quarterlies and the weekend review pages, have been shaken up in recent times. Book talk is not as likely to be authorised by the academy or mediated by literary critics, and it occurs in dispersed – even commercial – locations. The *Australian's Review of Books* has widened the circulation of cultural conversation and drawn on international as well as local reviewers. Radio in particular has provided many niches for publicity: on dedicated programs like

Radio National's *Books and Writing*, or *Australia Talks Books* where readers can talk back to authors, or on public interest programs like *Life Matters* and *Late Night Live*. Bookstores also publish review catalogues, and sponsor readings and reading groups. Such 'restructuring' does not necessarily equal decline, but it does signal that the public sphere cannot be reconstituted where it once was. As we have been suggesting, literature is if anything more prominent, though more dispersed and differentiated, than ever before – and the market for public intellectuals has witnessed its own mini-boom.

Public intellectuals have traditionally been one or other kind of literary intellectual. If not directly 'creative writers' or critics, they have nonetheless embodied a particular relation to literature and literariness ('literariness' here can be defined in parallel to our definition of 'aesthetics' earlier as a quality or process present when form, style or authorial persona is invested with ethical value). The public intellectual is explicitly distinguished from the 'narrow' expert or specialist and identified instead with culture in two senses, in the 'narrow' sense of art and intellectual culture and in the 'broader' sense of the national culture. Identification with the former is a qualification for identification with the latter. In the Australian media there have been both 'old' and 'new' effects in the recent modes of public intellectual discourse: on the one hand a defence of the traditional literary model of the public intellectual; on the other a process whereby intellectuals have sought out new roles made possible by shifts in the relationship between the media, the market, the academy – and contemporary politics.

One symptom has been the remarkable upsurge in the publication of books of essays by Australian writers (e.g., Garner 1996; Brett 1997; Murray 1997; Salusinszky 1997; Craven 1998; Dessaix 1998a; Fraser 1998; Manne 1998; Clendinnen 1999). If the short story was the literary fashion of the seventies and eighties, the essay was the mode of the nineties and beyond. Pressures from both the market and from literary institutions have created spaces for new forms such as the extended essay and the bestselling high-literary 'ficto-memoirs' published by Robert Dessaix, Raimond Gaita, Inga Clendinnen and Drusilla Modjeska for example. These works have affirmed their aesthetic qualities without apology – as texts and physical objects – and these qualities have been used to market them successfully to a high cultural capital, interested readership. In so doing, this market-savvy high-aesthetic mode has also reasserted the power of literary writing to address ethical issues, a power that much contemporary fiction and poetry finds increasingly difficult to manage.

On one side the effect has been to reaffirm the authority of established literary figures such as Helen Garner and David Williamson, and thereby to reaffirm the role of literary sensibility as authorising commentary over a wide range of public topics. Mark Davis, among others, has robustly criticised this effect as narrowing the sphere of valid public commentary and valid public commentators (Davis 1999a–b). But we must also recognise the newness in this *expansion* of literary modes. One of the postmodern effects of the media's redefinition of literary culture has been something like a rediscovery of certain 'nineteenth-century' modes where genres – fiction, essay, autobiography, meditation, history, documentary – are readily mixed and merged. The mixing itself becomes a sign of literariness. Many of these essayists – for example, Lily Brett and Inga Clendinnen – self-consciously occupy an intermediary space between cultures. They use the mode, and its direct address, to perform a kind of mediation of the highly differentiated public spheres which characterise multi-ethnic, globalising societies of the information age. The mode exploits both the moral authority of the writerly persona and the emotional effects of intimate, personal exchange.

We see something of this ambivalence in Dessaix's *Speaking their Minds* (1998b), a collection of interviews with prominent public intellectuals first broadcast on ABC Radio National. The primary effect of the book is to reassert the traditional authority of cultured spokespersons to pronounce on the great national and existential questions. In this mode, unsurprisingly, there is little interest in the role of academics, say, as teachers and trainers for a large section of the public; indeed little positive sense of any institutional engagement. Dessaix clearly sees the public intellectual as a persona separated from professional location in the academy. The problem here is not the book's self-conscious display of ethical concern and worrying away at the public good – far from it – but rather the narrow sense of the intellectual it defines, the implication that such cultured spokespersons represent an ideal form of the intellectual rather than one kind of intellectual comportment amongst others: good for some things but not so good for others, at home in some pockets of the media but out of place in others, good at summoning certain publics but irrelevant to others.

At the same time, however, *Speaking their Minds* represents an attempt to find a new media valency for public spokespersons. It is itself a media effect, reasserting the role of the public broadcaster in brokering public debate while testifying to the new public value invested in writing and writerly forms of media performance. Dessaix's mind-speakers include younger writers such as McKenzie Wark and Catharine Lumby who tend to be deeply suspicious of traditional claims to literary or moral authority but have taken up the essay form as a way of intervening in a public sphere defined by the mass, multiple forms of the media. Both refuse the deeply institutionalised mutual hostilities between media, academy and culture; they refuse the opposition between culture and market/media (or high and popular culture) that has traditionally defined the modern intellectual's self-image. Wark's *The Vernacular Republic* (1997) gives literature a relatively prominent place in the disputed and diverse spaces of communication without privileging it as an ideal form.

One crucial, unanticipated effect of this newly emerging public sphere – drawing on 'old' models but in new structures and media – has been the remarkable rise to prominence of historians as public intellectuals and 'writers': for example, Inga Clendinnen, Greg Dening, Henry Reynolds and Peter Read, and using the term more broadly, Gaita, Robert Manne and others. Clendinnen appeals quite explicitly to the necessity of cultivating ethical dispositions through practices of reading transferred from literary theory to *true* stories (Clendinnen 1999). The existing modes for the public intellectual are being reclaimed through the emergence of a new kind of authority founded in possession of 'deep' historical knowledge which bears a public responsibility in the present. What enables these figures rather than others – rather than any and every historian – to become public intellectuals is a transfer of values from the literary to the historical, present in the strongly projected 'writerly' qualities with which they are identified. As suggested, these writerly qualities in turn testify to certain moral or 'ethico-intellectual' capacities. In the decades from the 1920s to the 1950s, these qualities were more often evident in the ethnographic writings of anthropologists. Aboriginal demands for citizenship rights and 'uplift' in the 1930s and 1940s, and public opinion in favour of positive policies, were supported by the writings and policy advice of A.P. Elkin and Frederick Wood-Jones, among others (Attwood and Markus 1999, pp. 16–17). When this discipline foundered on critiques of its ethnocentrism, historians filled the gap.

Politicians and judges have also participated in this genre of public speech: Justices Deane and Gaudron drew attention to the 'unrestrained' language of their judgment in Mabo (1992); while Paul Keating's emotional Redfern speech (1993) and Malcolm Fraser's Vincent Lingiari memorial lecture (2000) both adopted distinctly literary rhetorical strategies. The new public modes were enabled, in part forced, by the aggressive historical activism of Keating and the no less aggressive historical 'quietism' of John Howard. They have been sustained by a market for which certain modes of history and of literature now have a similar kind of ethical and national valency. Larger commercial publishing houses have followed the lead of Fremantle Arts Centre Press and Text Publishing in recognising that certain 'new' kinds of history writing have a market potential parallel to literary forms, while there have been increasingly flexible overlaps between the academy and the magazine market. We can be sceptical of what must sometimes be moral posturing, the intellectual who knows best, but as the references to politics and the law suggest we must also be careful not to underestimate the power that such 'literary' discourse has when combined with historical and ethical agendas and when specifically national in scope.

Subsidising a national literature

The project of interesting government in the production, distribution and teaching of a national literature was taken up by members of the Fellowship of Australian Writers between the wars and then in the post-war period, at a time when the civic programs of Reconstruction and the Nationality and Citizenship Act (1948) were being debated. As a result of this lobbying, the Commonwealth Literary Fund (CLF), established in 1908 as a pension scheme for writers and their dependants, was progressively expanded after 1939 to fund lectures in Australian literature in universities and regional centres, then fellowships to writers, guarantees against loss to publishers of Australian works, and grants to literary magazines. In 1973, the activities of the CLF were taken over by the Literature Board (now Literature Fund) of the Australia Council as part of its redefinition by the Whitlam Labor Government. Whitlam's agenda to revitalise national culture and national identity was largely implemented through extending the principles of industry assistance to cultural policy.

The Australia Council, through the Literature Fund and other programs, supports Australian literature in a number of direct ways such as grants to individual writers and publishing subsidies. But its programs are also directed to literature's public life, to having literature circulate more broadly, for example through its audience development fund and support for writer residencies, writers' centres and festivals. Grants are tied mostly to individual writers or books, reflecting the ways in which the industry is understood as largely self-regulating with writers considered as independent professionals. However, the Council is not merely supporting individual creativity or cultivating taste; rather it is producing Australian literature as part of the public culture by providing minimal industry assistance, in part, as with cinema, as a kind of 'import replacement', although the market for local books is stronger and more diverse than for local cinema. Over time, practices allied with protectionism have given way to new imperatives of market stimulation and competition. Building audiences through sponsorship of writers' festivals, subsidy to the mass circulation *Australian's Review of Books*, and the support of residencies in universities, school, community groups and workplaces has brought the writer back into the civil domain.

The Literature Fund has maintained a strong presence in the Australia Council's activities, even as its programs have widened to include Aboriginal and Torres Strait Islander Arts and Community and Cultural Development. Grants distributed through the Fund have been maintained at around 7 per cent since the mid-1970s, and overall amounts closely match those delivered to other areas except for the high infrastructure performing arts. In the financial year 1998/99, the Council gave over $60 million in grants across all its programs. Just over $4 million went directly to Literature – a little more than to Dance, Music and New Media Arts, a little less than to Aboriginal and Torres Strait Islander Arts, Community Cultural Development, Theatre and Visual Arts/Crafts (Australia Council 1999). Literature is also dispersed across other categories: Theatre, the Regional Arts Fund, Emerging Artists, Aboriginal and Torres Strait Islander, Community and so forth. Despite what might appear to be the core elitism of its categories, then, there is a kind of democratising effect among the arts themselves. The small size of grants relative to other areas has probably helped literature to maintain its place. Emerging cultural industries also appear not to threaten literature's position.

Despite some low-key rhetorical grounding in notions of the arts as central to national identity – the Council's 'unique responsibility to reflect Australia's evolving national identity to its citizens and to the world' (Australia Council 1999, p. 7) – there is little attempt in Council documents to find a unifying principle for its activities. In many ways its policy statements are exemplary in their disaggregation of the aesthetic object across industrial, commercial, private and public, individual and institutional domains. Evaluations of artistic merit or excellence have a place in the Council's policies, but so do civic notions of increased access to participation in the arts, cultural diversity, freedom of expression and local or community arts development. Industrial and commercial dimensions are acknowledged through professional development programs, including marketing skills and cultural export. The arts are recognised as a complex field involving individual creativity, professional careers, training and skills, marketing and promotion, legal rights, and participation, access and equity issues. Grants and subsidies have more to do with producing professionals than preserving fossils.

Against this background, the focus of the Literary Fund itself might appear narrow and conservative. Grants largely support individual writers or books in a set range of genres (though these include biography and autobiography, essays, history and literary criticism), categories inherited from earlier models of literary assistance. But they do not necessarily represent a 'scandalous' narrowness; they function as administrative categories designed to delimit policy targets, to demarcate them from other forms of writing, to identify those areas of the industry that do require subsidy or promotion (either in order to survive or in order to fulfil other cultural objectives). In fact, in line with the Council's broader priorities, the literary programs are grounded as much in notions of the professional career, promotion in the marketplace and industrial assistance as in notions of aesthetic authority. Creativity is brought onto the same plane of calculation as notions of public benefit, career development and accountability. (It is curious that those who attack the bureaucratisation or professionalisation of literature are often also those who attack its 'mere aestheticism'.) The contentious category of 'excellence' (Rowse 1985) reappears in the form of 'literary merit'; but this can also be understood in professional rather than traditional aesthetic terms. One of the visible effects of assistance to the literature industry has been this increased professionalism and 'industrialisation', through the Australian Society of Authors for example, imposed, in part, by bureaucratic procedures.

Susan Lever (1997) has commented on the changing relations between politicians and the funding of literature, observing the shift from the Commonwealth Literary Fund's management by a committee usually comprising the leaders of the three main political parties to the 'arm's-length' operation of the Australia Council from 1975. If in one view we might lament the loss of a certain kind of direct involvement in which politicians would have regarded themselves as part of the community of readers (and Prime Minister Menzies would have expected to be familiar with all the writers under consideration), we should in Lever's terms not underestimate the achievement for a democracy of the new arrangements. Lever also cites Jose Borghino's argument that the Council has been anti-canonical 'in that it provides for writers at every stage of their careers, and deliberately sets out to look at the broad range of writers across genres, age groups, gender and ethnicity' (Lever 1997, p. 110). The Council's monitoring of its own performance in respect of these groups has often been attacked as social engineering instead of being seen as a democratising extension of liberal government in the realm of culture.

From a purist position, the Council's need to balance the potentially conflicting demands of democracy and excellence, access and merit, individual talent and cultural diversity, 'the whole community and the arts community', might be seen as its fatal flaw; but these 'faultlines' are better understood as appropriate sets of conflicting priorities. These are the technologies the Council and the Fund have at their disposal to foreground competing claims and weigh them up against each other as part of its routine administrative operation. They cannot be dismissed as 'merely bureaucratic', for they define precisely the uneven and conflictual grounds upon which any intervention – in support of public subsidy or attacking its operations – must be made. They define as completely as any high-principled theoretical attempts the diverse range of public and private domains through which literature and literary value circulate.

The point is not that the funding policies and priorities are above criticism – funding for magazines, regional bias and subsidies to multinational publishers continue to be contentious issues. But such issues do not amount to evidence that the 'governmentalisation' of literature inevitably means the institutionalisation of conservative or elitist forms. After all, the Fund has had to weather accusations by Les Murray and others that it has been biased towards a democratic rather than purely meritocratic agenda. The category of the nation itself enables a broad dispersal of 'literary merit', one which might indeed be biased towards inclusiveness or 'balance', at least across those literary kinds deemed worthy or in need of assistance.

Since the deregulatory 1980s, industry assistance has taken other forms than public subsidy or tariff protection. The 'Australian settlement' which secured forms of 'industrial citizenship' has begun to unravel as the new economy demands increased productivity and competitiveness. In the global marketplace, the 'national interest' is directed towards enhancing the Australian 'brand name'. Cultural exports are critical to this exercise. 'Australia Week', held in London in July 2000 to commemorate the passage of the legislation enacting the Constitution, was defended at home as a trade fair, rather than a repeat performance of the 'cultural cringe'. The repertoire included art exhibitions, performances, and the publication of a special issue of the literary magazine *Granta*. This was followed in September by the Sydney 2000 Olympics where the opening ceremony staged a display of Australian cultural heterogeneity. Australian culture was marketed to visitors through the arts festival held at the same time.

Media spectacle and the periodic resurgences of film culture draw international attention, but books also infiltrate the international marketplace. The taste for memoir is an international one: Dessaix's *Night Letters* and Clendinnen's *Tiger's Eye* (as well as her *Reading the Holocaust*) have found international audiences. In the domestic context, books are at the centre of a flourishing inner urban culture of coffee and civil conversation. Though the café latte and chardonnay set are regularly disparaged as elitist and out of touch, the commercial success of booksellers has had a part in urban renewal. Bookshops have embraced new media technologies and have adapted to hybrid forms of leisure and consumption. Publishers may have outsourced editing and indexing, but they have invested heavily in book design, producing the book as the eroticised object we noted above. Books like Modjeska's *The Orchard* (1994), Peter Timm's *The Nature of Gardens* (1999) and most recently, Nicholas Jose's *The Red Thread* (2000) have become desirable possessions, part of a circuit of exchange of symbolic value. A recent review of Jose's novel captures these sought-after qualities: 'Everything – the trompe-l'oeil dust jacket, the typeface, the artwork ... and the quality of the paper – contributes to a sense of restrained sensuousness, luxury tempered by elegance and good taste' (Reimer 2000).

It would be easy to dismiss this phenomenon as an effect of sophisticated lifestyle marketing, of 'taste' being elevated (once again) into a suffocating universal principle, or merely a product of generationalism (Davis 1999a). No doubt there are dimensions of all these things. Nevertheless, it is important to note the role literature is playing here, as a commodity, and important to remember the historical role of commerce in constituting a secular civil sphere. Though we tend to think of business as occupying a private sphere outside the realm of government, or at least resistant to government 'interference', commerce is an enterprise regulated by laws of contract and exchange. And in establishing its ascendancy in the secular civil sphere, commerce had to appropriate values of mutuality, hospitality, restraint and civility which were also elaborated in the fiction of writers like Jane Austen. The recent revivals of Austen's books in the cinema and on television suggests that some of the congruences of commodity culture and civil society might be redeployed in contemporary multi-ethnic societies, and that an ethics of exchange and symbolic value might have a new life in cross-cultural communication.

We began this essay by describing the public culture in which literature played a role in the 'exchange of public reasons', and participated in the deliberations about the form of the polity. We described the ecologies in which periodicals emerged and disappeared. Literariness, we've suggested, has adopted other guises in the ecologies of the new media. Public intellectuals and writers are called upon as 'brokers' of ideas and as mediators of difference. They are 'articulate', in the sense that they make connections, rather than in the sense that they bring a high moral 'tone' to debate (Ferres 2001). The liberal notion of the 'neutral' public sphere may well be unsustainable, as Alastair Davidson (1994) claims. New models of deliberation and new dispositions to address difference are starting to appear. In her Boyer lectures, Inga Clendinnen invited her audience to 'do history' with her. She resorted to 'literary' strategies to read narratives of cultural contact. Peter Read turns to new sources, including poetry and popular music, and new informants to explore, rather than resolve, doubts and ambiguities in *Belonging* (2000). The Working Dog team have reinvented a repertoire of 'civic speech', from the satire of *Frontline* to the conversations on *The Panel*, where writers, filmmakers and politicians rub shoulders with athletes, rock stars and assorted media celebrities. Perhaps the encouraging, and eccentric, sign of literature's capacity to survive in this new environment is the regular appearance of the ageing Tasmanian poet, Margaret Scott, on *Good News Week*. Her quavering voice and acerbic wit are more than a match for the brashness and bravado of Mikey Robbins and Paul McDermott. Far from shrinking away, literature is taking on a new public life.

Note

1   In 1997–98 a survey of 261 Australian book publishers showed that these organisations generated $1,242 million in turnover, of which $1,035.6 million was from book sales. Of total book sales, $623.5 million was attributed to Australian titles (ABS 2000, p. 340). It is more difficult to estimate the contribution of 'literary titles', but in 1997 and 1998 Australian publishers released around 140 new fiction titles each year (figures derived from the Austlit database).

Guide to further reading

The most recent comprehensive introductions to Australian literature are Bennett and Strauss (eds) (1998) and Elizabeth Webby (ed.) *The Cambridge Companion to Australian Literature* (Cambridge, Cambridge University Press, 2000). Davis (1999a) provides a controversial, polemical account of contemporary literary culture in Australia, while Wark (1997) discusses, also polemically, the role of literary works and authors in the 'culture wars' of the 1990s in Australia. An important new anthology of criticism is Delys Bird, Robert Dixon and Christopher Lee (eds) *Authority and Influence: Australian Literary Criticism 1950–2000* (St Lucia: University of Queensland Press, 2001). The classic older history, H.M. Green's *A History of Australian Literature Pure and Applied* (Sydney: Angus & Robertson, 1961) remains a useful account of print culture in Australia (to 1950) despite its dated critical approach. The most useful reference work is Wilde, Hooton and Andrews (eds) *The Oxford Companion to Australian Literature* (Melbourne: Oxford University Press, 1994). The established journal in the field is *Australian Literary Studies* which publishes an Annual Bibliography; other journals discussing Australian literature include *Southerly*, *Meanjin* and *Southern Review*. *Austlit* is a wide-ranging bibliographical database. Bartlett, Dixon and Lee (1999) include a number of essays on literature and the public sphere. The role of the Literature Board to 1988 is described in Thomas Shapcott, *The Literature Board: A Brief*

History (St Lucia: University of Queensland Press, 1988); more recent accounts include Lever (1997) and Galligan (1999). Among the few studies of the publishing industry are Curtain (1993), Poland (1999) and Wilding (1999), a special issue of *Continuum* (4, 1, 1990) and the journal *Publishing Studies*. Industry news and statistics are given regularly in the *Australian Bookseller and Publisher* and the *Australian Author*. Book history was featured in *Books, Readers, Reading* (*Australian Cultural History* 11, 1992) and a three-volume history of the book in Australia is in preparation through University of Queensland Press. Studies of reading include Lyons and Taksa, *Australian Readers Remember* (Melbourne: Oxford University Press, 1992); Jock Macleod and Pat Buckridge (eds) *Books and Reading in Australian Society* (Brisbane: ICPS, 1992); and Buckridge, Murray and Macleod (1995). The 1995 ABS report, *Books: Who's Reading Them Now?* updates an earlier (1990) report by Guldberg. Studies of periodicals include Carter (1999b), Lawson (1983), Lee, Mead and Murnane (1990) and Bruce Bennett (ed.) *Crosscurrents* (1981).

Websites

www.ozco.gov.au
  Australia Council
www.liswa.wa.gov.au/austlit.html
  Australian Literature Information Gateway
www.australis.org/index.html
  The Aurora Australis site offers links to Australian publishers, magazines, booksellers and other book-related sites.

References

Attwood, Bain and Andrew Markus (1999) *The Struggle for Aboriginal Rights,* Sydney: Allen & Unwin.

Australia Council (1999) *Australia Council: Annual Report 1998–99,* Sydney: Australia Council.

Australian Bureau of Statistics (2000) *2000 Year Book Australia,* Canberra: ABS.

Bartlett, Alison, Robert Dixon and Christopher Lee (eds) (1999) *Australian Literature and the Public Sphere,* Toowoomba: ASAL.

Bennett, Bruce (ed.) (1981) *Crosscurrents: Magazines and Newspapers in Australian Literature,* Melbourne: Longman Cheshire.

Bennett, Bruce and Jennifer Strauss (eds) (1998) *The Oxford Literary History of Australia,* Melbourne: Oxford University Press.

Bennett, Tony (1990) *Outside Literature,* London and New York: Routledge.

— (1998) *Culture: A Reformer's Science,* Sydney: Allen & Unwin.

Bennett, Tony, Michael Emmison and John Frow (1999) *Accounting for Tastes: Australian Everyday Cultures,* Cambridge: Cambridge University Press.

Bird, Delys, Robert Dixon and Susan Lever (eds) (1997) *Canonozities: The Making of Literary Reputations in Australia, Southerly* 57, 3.

Brett, Lily (1997) *In Full View,* Sydney: Macmillan.

Buckridge, Patrick (1998) 'Clearing a space for Australian literature 1940–1965' in Bennett and Strauss (eds), pp. 169–92.

Buckridge, Patrick, Pamela Murray and Jock Macleod (1995) *Reading Professional*

Identities: The Boomers and their Books, Brisbane: Institute of Cultural Policy Studies.

Callan, Eamonn (1997) *Creating Citizens: Political Education and Liberal Democracy*, Oxford: Clarendon Press.

Carter, David (1997) 'Literary canons and literary institutions', in Bird *et al.* (eds), pp. 16–37.

— (1999a) 'Good readers and good citizens: literature, media and the nation', *Australian Literary Studies* 19, 2, pp. 136–51.

— (1999b) 'Magazine culture: notes towards a history of Australian periodical publication' in Bartlett *et al.* (eds), pp. 69–79.

Clendinnen, Inga (1998) *Reading the Holocaust*, Melbourne: Text.

— (1999) *True Stories*, Sydney: ABC.

— (2000) *Tiger's Eye*, Melbourne: Text.

Craven, Peter (ed.) (1998) *The Best Australian Essays 1998*, Melbourne: Bookman.

Cunningham, Stuart and Graeme Turner (eds) (1997) *The Media in Australia: Industries, Texts, Audiences*, Sydney: Allen & Unwin (second edition).

Curtain, John (1993) 'Book publishing' in Cunningham and Turner (eds) *The Media in Australia* (first edition), pp. 102–18.

Davidson, Alistair (1994) '*Res Publica* and citizen' in Headon *et al.* (eds) pp. 161–74.

Davis, Mark (1999a) *Gangland: Cultural Elites and the New Generationalism*, Sydney: Allen & Unwin (revised edition; first published 1997).

— (1999b) 'Assaying the essay: fear and loathing in the literary coteries', *Overland* 156, Spring, pp. 3–10.

Dessaix, Robert (1996) *Night Letters* Sydney: Pan Macmillan.

— (1998a) *And So Forth*, Sydney: Pan Macmillan.

— (ed.) (1998b) *Speaking their Minds: Intellectuals and Public Culture in Australia*, Sydney: ABC.

Eagleton, Terry (1984) *The Function of Criticism: From The Spectator to Post-Structuralism*, London: Verso.

Ferres, Kay (2001) 'Articulate citizens' in Kay Ferres and Denise Meredyth, *An Articulate Country: Reinventing Citizenship in Australia*, St Lucia: University of Queensland Press, pp. 140–56.

Fraser, Morag (ed.) (1998) *Seams of Light: Best Antipodean Essays*, Sydney: Allen & Unwin.

Frow, John (1995) *Cultural Studies and Cultural Value*, Oxford: Clarendon.

Galligan, Anne (1999) 'Government grants and the role of subsidy', *Southerly* 59, 1, pp. 123–35.

Garner, Helen (1995) *The First Stone*, Sydney: Pan Macmillan.

— (1996) *True Stories: Selected Non-Fiction*, Melbourne: Text.

Gates, Henry Louis Jr (1996) 'Critical race theory and free speech' in Louis Menand (ed.) *The Future of Academic Freedom*, Chicago: University of Chicago Press, pp. 119–59.

Gelder, Ken (2000) 'The obscure(d) world of Australian popular fiction', *Australian Book Review*, July, pp. 34–7.

Goodall, Peter (1995) *High Culture, Popular Culture: The Long Debate*, Sydney: Allen & Unwin.

Hall, James (2000) 'Bigtime plot twist for smalltime storyteller', *Australian* 11 October, p. 3.

Headon, David, James Warden and Bill Gammage (eds) (1994), *Crown or Country: The Traditions of Australian Republicanism*, Sydney: Allen & Unwin.

Inglis, K.S. (ed.) (1989) *Nation: The Life of an Independent Journal of Opinion 1958–1972*, Melbourne: Melbourne University Press.

Irving, Helen (1994) 'Who were the Republicans?' in Headon *et al.* (eds), pp. 69–79.

Johanson, Katya (2000) 'The Changing Role of Australia's Cultural Council 1945–1995', unpublished PhD thesis, University of Melbourne.

Johnson, Heather (1997) *The Sydney Art Patronage System 1890–1940*, Grays Point, NSW: Bungoona Technologies.

Kirkpatrick, Peter (1992) *The Sea-Coast of Bohemia: Literary Life in Sydney's Roaring Twenties*, St Lucia: University of Queensland Press.

Lawson, Sylvia (1983) *The Archibald Paradox: A Strange Case of Authorship*, Ringwood, Vic.: Penguin Allen Lane.

Lee, Jenny, Philip Mead and Gerald Murnane (eds) (1990) *The Temperament of Generations: Fifty Years of Writing in Meanjin*, Melbourne: Melbourne University Press.

Lever, Susan (1997) 'Government patronage and literary reputations' in Bird *et al.* (eds), pp. 104–14.

— (1998) 'Fiction: innovation and ideology' in Bennett and Strauss (eds), pp. 308–31.

Manne, Robert (1998) *The Way We Live Now: The Controversies of the Nineties*, Melbourne: Text.

Modjeska, Drusilla (1981) *Exiles at Home: Australian Women Writers 1925–1945*, Sydney: Angus & Robertson.

— (1994) *The Orchard*, Sydney: Pan Macmillan.

Murray, Les (1997) *The Working Forest: Selected Prose*, Sydney: Duffy & Snellgrove.

Nussbaum, Martha (1997) *Cultivating Humanity: A Classical Defence of Reform in Liberal Education*, Cambridge, Mass.: Harvard University Press.

Poland, Louise (1999) 'Independent publishers', *Journal of Australian Studies* 63, pp. 110–18.

Reimer, Andrew (2000) 'When East meets West', *Age* 7 October, p. 11.

Reynolds, Henry (1999) *Why Weren't We Told? A Personal Search for the Truth About Our History*, Ringwood, Vic.: Viking.

Rowse, Tim (1985) *Arguing the Arts: The Funding of the Arts in Australia*, Ringwood, Vic.: Penguin.

Salusinszky, Imre (ed.) (1997) *The Oxford Book of Australian Essays*, Melbourne: Oxford University Press.

Shapcott, Thomas (1988) *The Literature Board: A Brief History*, St Lucia: University of Queensland Press.

Strahan, Lynne (1984) *Just City and the Mirrors: Meanjin Quarterly and the Intellectual Front 1940–1965*, Melbourne: Oxford University Press.

Stevenson, Deborah (2000) *Art and Organisation: Making Australian Cultural Policy*, St Lucia: University of Queensland Press.

Turner, Graeme (1998) 'Film, television and literature: competing for the nation' in Bennett and Strauss (eds), pp. 348–63.

Walker, R.B. (1980) *Yesterday's News: A History of the Newspaper Press in New South Wales from 1920–1945*, Sydney: Sydney University Press.

Wanna, John and Glen Withers (2000) 'Creating capability: combining economic and political rationalities in industry and regional policy' in Glyn Davis and Michael Keating (eds) *The Future of Governance: Policy Choices*, Sydney: Allen & Unwin, pp. 67–93.

Wark, McKenzie (1997) *The Virtual Republic: Australia's Culture Wars of the 1990s*, Sydney: Allen & Unwin.

White, Richard (1991) *Inventing Australia: Images and Identity 1688–1980*, Sydney: Allen & Unwin.

Wilding, Michael (1999) 'Australian literary and scholarly publishing in its international context', *Australian Literary Studies* 19, 1, pp. 57–69.

Chapter 7

Reshaping Australian Institutions: Popular Culture, the Market and the Public Sphere

Graeme Turner

Shaping our popular culture

As John Frow and Meaghan Morris have pointed out, Australia has a long history of remarkably explicit public debate about the policies, processes and purposes of state-sponsored nation formation (1993, pp. xiii–xiv). A key strategy throughout this history, until recently, has been the use of cultural policy as a means of protecting local or national cultural production against competition from outside – particularly where there is a significant disparity between the infrastructure support available to the Australians and to their competitors. The book bounty (a means of subsidising local book production, now defunct) and the various systems for allocating grants to elite artists are early examples of such a strategy. What is notable about the period since the 1970s is the increasing extent to which cultural policy has interested itself in activities aimed at developing industries which contributed to Australian popular, as well as to elite, culture. The expansion of government support for a broader field of local publishing (popular as well as literary fiction, biography, history), the extension of arts funding programs to include community art forms (still contentious), the inclusion of television within the funding regimes assisting the film industry and, most significantly, the provision of government assistance to the production and marketing of contemporary popular music, are all examples of this. Such interventions flowed from the view that governments should support a broadly dynamic culture, tolerant of the full range of popular and elite forms. This view was entirely consonant with theoretical and political trends within the universities, a growing and increasingly sophisticated interest in popular culture and popular forms as well as a strategic concern with the formations of specifically Australian popular cultures.

Today, it is less common to encounter discussions which assume the context of some form of national popular culture, either in the universities or within cultural policy frameworks.[1] David Carter's review of Ken Wark's *The Virtual Republic* notes the difficulty Wark faces in attempting to 'restore' or even 'conserve the concept' of the nation, 'or at least the "space" it roughly describes in the face of those who want to dissolve it into a bottom-line, end-of-the-day market, boost it into One Nation or, like John Howard, do both at once' (1998, p. 230). Even Wark's 'modest or sceptical nationalism' runs against the grain of current academic or policy debates. Within such contexts, the idea of the nation has declined in influence over the last decade, and with it has declined the point and legitimacy of many of the earlier, cultural, nationalist arguments for government intervention in the framing of the national culture (Turner 1994). The consequent disarticulation of 'the national' from 'the popular' has occurred in conjunction with, or may indeed have enabled, a significant reorientation of the category of popular culture itself.

In what follows, I am going to examine some of the reasons why this should matter. Such an examination begins by pointing out the historical importance of debates between intellectuals within the universities to the formation of Australian popular culture. It continues by outlining how debates which may look like they are of concern only to those working in relatively enclosed academic disciplines have influenced the shape of Australian cultural institutions, before suggesting how these disciplines may contribute to the shaping of an Australian popular culture for the future. In the final section of this chapter I present three short case studies – of talkback radio, popular music and current affairs television – as examples of popular cultural forms in need of critical scrutiny from the academy.

The nation, the popular and the market

How popular cultural forms have been understood within the academy, as well as within the cultural industries, has significantly influenced the shape and remit of contemporary cultural institutions within Australia. Critical arguments about the cultural importance of the 'quality' films produced by the Australian film industry, for example, were in part responsible for the concentrated investment in the visually arresting period dramas of the late 1970s – *Picnic at Hanging Rock, My Brilliant Career* and so on (see Dermody and Jacka 1987 and 1988; Moran and O'Regan 1989). A quite different set of propositions about the cultural function of popular cinema and locally produced entertainment were inscribed into the prospectuses which attracted commercial investment to the more populist genre features of the 1980s, such as *Mad Max* 2 and *Crocodile Dundee* (Moran and O'Regan 1989, pp. 118–45; Morris 1988, pp. 241–69). While they may not have originated in the universities, both sets of propositions were widely promulgated, debated and developed there in the 1970s and 1980s through the emerging disciplines of screen studies, cultural studies, film history, media studies, Australian studies and so on. Frequently, those involved in such debates in the universities also contributed directly to related debates within government and the industry aimed at shaping the policy framework. More broadly, it is certainly possible to detect a close alignment between the outcomes of debates within the universities and arguments about the funding and regulatory regimes for Australian cultural industries over the 1980s and early 1990s.

This alignment, in turn, has affected the kinds of interests pursued within the academy. To continue using the film industry as an example, we know quite a lot about the generic markers of the body of film texts the post-1970s Australian film revival produced, as well as the objectives and ramifications of the various policy settings which enabled these projects to attract funding from Australian investors.[2] We know a lot less about how these texts might have in fact contributed to the specific character(s) of Australian popular culture(s) – yet this was the primary argument for their existence in the first place. Significantly, the cultural objectives which underpinned the original arguments for public support of a national film industry – that is, of creating a distinctive national culture – are precisely the ones that have been set aside in our subsequent accounting for the success or otherwise of the institutions such arguments helped to put in place.

One reason for this, and I admit there are many, is that the academy has, by and large, become comfortable with, and has assisted in the development of, the Australian film industry's reluctant acceptance of the logics of the market. Now, more than ever, it is customary for the Australian industry to approach the idea of an Australian popular culture through an assessment of the effective operation of the mechanisms of commercial consumption (sales of tickets, say) rather than through the, admittedly more complicated and less quantifiable, cultural nationalist perspective (examining how the texts play their part in a process of nation formation) (Reid 1993). As a result, it has become quite difficult to imagine how those assumptions about the cultural function of popular film narrative which were current during the 1970s and 80s could apply to local productions of the 1990s such as *The Matrix* or *Mission Impossible II*. One relevant consideration, referred to earlier and central to my interests in this next part of the argument, is the fact that the category of 'the popular' itself has undergone significant reshaping in recent years. In what follows, I want to suggest that this reframing of the category of the popular carries consequences for the kinds of contribution the academy makes to future debates about the shape and remit of our cultural institutions and cultural industries.

When I speak of the 'academy' here, I have in mind the broad alliance of disciplinary and sub-disciplinary orientations including literary studies, Australian history, screen studies, media studies, communication studies, Australian studies, cultural studies and cultural policy studies, which from time to time have directly interested themselves in arguing a connection between cultural institutions or cultural industries and the national culture. The idea of 'the national culture' is not necessarily problematised within such arguments – frequently because it is invoked for strategic or polemical reasons rather than as the consequence of any theoretical investment in the nation as an ideal (see Cunningham 1992). Indeed, invocation of the national culture in these contexts is often marked by a conven-ient slippage between the comparatively elitist cultural assumptions which legitimate government support for, say, Australian literature, and the compara-tively populist assumptions which would encourage government support for the production of commercial feature films.[3] The slippage is, for the most part, in the service of a principled inclusiveness which carefully avoids dealing with hierarchies of taste in order to subscribe to what has become cultural studies' orthodox, so-called 'anthropological', definition of culture as 'the whole way of life'. Indeed, certain of the directions pursued by cultural studies are central to my argument, so from here on I will concentrate my discussion of developments within the academy on those within cultural studies.

Cultural studies' definition of culture as 'a whole way of life' explicitly included popular culture. This was achieved, however, by disconnecting the term from some of its earlier meanings and associations. Among these earlier associations were a definitional connection between 'popular culture' and a simple grassroots populism, or a crass, market-driven, meretriciousness – each connection bearing pejorative class or aesthetic implications. The renovation of the definition of popular culture stripped away such pejorative implications in order to resituate it as the ground upon which *all* contemporary culture was formed (Bennett *et al.* 1986). In turn, this 'ground' was usually located within a national or perhaps regional model of society; popular culture became the site where shared meanings were constructed and contested by and for a specific national culture or region. Broadly inclusive, radically democratic in its impli-cations, this new model of popular culture embraced the potential paradox of supporting a politics that was both anti-capitalist and populist.

In recent years, this version of popular culture has been challenged by (at least) two interrelated formations. In the first of these, the popular is once again defined in terms of the market. This time however, I would argue, such an orien-tation is not seen as a bad thing; rather, according to this model, a dynamic popular culture is the natural consequence of the free choice provided by an unfettered market. The new element here lies in the fact that the celebration of this formation of popular culture is also a celebration of the dynamism and diversity created by a globalising capitalism which proposes an equivalence between the act of consumption and an act of citizenship.[4] For some cultural critics, this is a particularly enabling position. Gay Hawkins' contribution to this volume is able to write back against what she sees as a defeated and passive narrative of decline in accounts of public broadcasting by mobilising the notion of the 'freely choosing subject', an optimistic reading of the cultural potential of the individual that (following Nikolas Rose) regards the rise of the consumer as 'a new way of making citizens'. The second formation reinforces aspects of the first by regarding the transnational market for popular cultural forms, especially media products, as a positive, democratising force which has enabled the breaching of 'artificial' barriers (such as national borders) to cultural and commercial exchange. Aligned closely with theories of the postmodern and substantiated by the citation of examples of globalising cultural industries such as telecommunications or e-commerce, this elaborates an image of a post-national, mass-mediated, often virtualised, public sphere.[5] When brought into close convergence, what these two views of popular culture can produce is an enthusiastic advocacy for the vitality and democratic inclusivity of a wholly commercialised public sphere which markets its benefits without fear, favour, or regulatory inhibitions to citizens of all nations.

The modulations which have produced this formation of the popular have been gradual, and implicated in a range of complicated and not necessarily consistent theoretical developments. While there is much within each of these theoretical developments to earn one's interest and assent, while each development may have had no such end view in sight, and while there may be significant countervailing or parallel trends within cultural studies itself, their cumulative effect is a radical repositioning of one of the dominant strains within cultural studies' view of the popular. The originary story of cultural studies has it as a version of cultural criticism which was engaged on a mission of recovery, correcting the elitism implicit in the prevailing protocols of cultural criticism, in the prevailing understandings of popular culture and, ultimately too, in the prevailing assumptions informing the structure and objectives of cultural policy. While the scale of its contribution might be debated, it seems undeniable that the development of cultural studies – together with media studies, film studies, and the new humanities in general – has assisted in achieving that correction. For the most part, their newly renovated versions of the popular were variously inclusive and sophisticated. While they recognised the function of discourses of the popular in constructing assent and serving established interests, they nevertheless endorsed the legitimacy and potential progressiveness of popular pleasures as well as the resistant strategies of consumption available to popular audiences. The notion that popular culture only succeeded because it was consumed by 'cultural dopes'[6] was thoroughly debunked by a generation of scholars who were themselves enthusiastic consumers of popular cultural forms. Once the battle for the redefinition of the popular had been won – and this seems to me to have occurred by the end of the 1980s – cultural studies was free to move towards a new kind of critical engagement: in Australia this was to include, among other things, the formation of cultural policy.

We now face a situation where the continuation of the critical project of the new humanities in general and cultural studies in particular may actually be hampered by some of the tolerances its previous successes helped to create. In practice if not in principle, the tolerance for the popular which has emerged as the default setting also encourages the cultural critic's tolerance for the commercial. John Fiske's work is the usual target for this kind of criticism. In some of his late 1980s work, it is frequently argued, Fiske's championing of the active reader's ready resistance to anything but messages which serve their own interests turned capitalism into something of a paper tiger (McGuigan 1992). Fiske does not deserve to be the scapegoat for this tendency, however. Enthusiastic pluralism flourished during cultural studies' fashion for theorising the postmodern; the 'free floating signifier' of postmodernism made the 'ideology critique' of 1970s marxism look daggy and naff. And the proliferation of modes of, and opportunities for, consumption consequent upon certain trends towards globalising markets redefined democratic and individual freedoms. Somehow along the way, politics turned into shopping. The convergence I described earlier, where 'the popular' as a commercial domain merges in slightly new ways with 'the popular' as the ground for democratic citizenship, has conquered scepticism about capitalism's compatibility with the interests of 'the people'. 'Choice' has become the term that facilitates the merger between commercial and democratic logics.

This may seem like a return to what is now a familiar and predictable critique of cultural studies' cultural populism. I agree with those who would say that cultural populism is no longer (perhaps never was) the dominant mode of practice within cultural studies and I am not interested, here, in pursuing a debate internal to cultural studies (see Turner 1999). In any case, we do have accounts of this situation which see it as a structural matter rather than an issue of political positioning. David Chaney, for instance, describes the convergence I have been talking about in terms of formal parallels between 'the character of mass national markets and mass national political publics': 'The practice of citizenship involves the same form of relationship between the individual and collective opinions as that between the individual consumer and patterns of taste and fashion' (Chaney 1994, p. 104). But I am more concerned about what we do with this situation. What I wish to pursue here is my view that the range of what can easily be uttered within the field has been altered by a redefinition of popular culture that, possibly more implicitly than ever before, has become reconciled with the dominance of the market in the formation of the public sphere. I am interested in and concerned by the practical consequences for public intellectuals working within such a theoretical orientation.

It would be hard to claim that Australian cultural studies' 1980s enthusiasm for particular kinds of popular culture texts – the playful, the transgressive, the self-reflexive, the progressive – has had much effect on the nature of the material the media industries produced or on the choices audiences made. *Australia All Over* is still the most listened to radio program in Australia, as it has been for many years, followed closely by John Laws syndicated talkback (nothing playful, progressive or self-reflexive about either of them). The merging of democratic and capitalist discourses which celebrate the newly commercialised public sphere has been accompanied, paradoxically and unpredictably, by the successful marketing of the expression of regressive and reactionary populisms across the media. Of course, many of these populisms are not new, either in form or substance, but worryingly few have become targets of the new humanities' critique. While some academics have been interested in addressing and understanding the appeal of the new talk shows in the US, such as *Oprah* and *Rikki Lake* (see Lumby 1997), there is an enormous range of significant and influential Australian popular cultural material which we have left almost entirely alone. The tabloid press, talkback radio shock jocks, the 'new lads' men's magazines such as *Ralph*, gossip and celebrity magazines like *Who*, most of whom employ or at least flirt with the discourses of a reactionary populism, have not yet been the object of much serious analysis or critique.[7]

I would contend that this is not surprising. There are now significant factors which discourage academic work on the kind of territory I have described. On the one hand, to attack such forms of popular culture as regressive or distasteful risks the appearance of complicity with the elitist taste-based agenda the earliest forms of cultural studies set out to discredit. On the other hand, to endorse such products as a legitimate form of popular expression risks appearing complacent about their politics – which are in most cases antipathetic to those of virtually all forms of cultural studies. Caught between a rock and hard place, many have chosen to say nothing on these subjects. While the academy's treatment of the popular retained its principled scepticism about the legitimacy of discourses of the market, this dilemma was less profound. In all the cases I mention, there is no question that these forms have substantial popular support in terms of audience figures, readership, sales and so on. There is also no question this popular support emerges from a broadly based political shift in favour of the ideologies in question. Consequently, and given the repositioning of the popular I describe, which accepts the notion that the market reflects legitimate choices made by consumer/citizens, it is now more difficult for a cultural studies intellectual to criticise popular cultural forms which articulate ideologies he or she opposes.

In many cases, the expressions of reactionary populism which have prospered under conditions supported by the incorporation of the category of the popular into the rhetorics of the market are themselves symptoms of structural problems, institutional asymmetries of power, and the failure or decline of government regulation. As such, they constitute strong provocations for analysis and for the process of reshaping Australian institutions. However, as I say, they are also instances where broad popular support, at least in terms of the weight of the market, is in place. Against such support, it is difficult for cultural criticism to investigate alternative structures without appearing to undermine cultural studies' commitment to 'the popular'. The strength of this commitment, then, may function as a disabling factor in the academy's contribution to the remaking of our cultural institutions.

How do we respond to this? Perhaps one response is to acknowledge that cultural critique can no longer be driven solely by a broadly programmatic critical or political project. Instead, the work of cultural critique may have to be highly case-specific, detailed and contingent – bent on exploring alternatives while offering what may be ethical or evaluative judgements on the practices it examines. As Gay Hawkins suggests in her essay 'TV Rules', and as I have outlined elsewhere in relation to tabloidisation (Hawkins 1998; Turner 1999), we may need a new kind of critical practice which more explicitly acknowledges that its judgements are derived from particular cultural sources, from particular regimes and contexts of value, and constitute a response to a specific provocation.

Cultural industries and the market

Enough generalities. It is time to move on to some specific provocations which might explain what has given rise to this argument as well as indicating the kinds of critique which might be mounted. Let me refer to three examples. These are instances where the flourishing of reactionary populism has so far been more or less neglected by the academy. They are also cases where the dismantling of specific, national-interest, regulatory and policy regimes has been justified through precisely the discourses of the popular/market I have been discussing. And they are cases where detailed analysis can substantially assist in the exploration of alternative structures and responsibilities for the respective institutions.

The first example is drawn from commercial radio, where a series of regulatory changes initiated in the late 1980s and driven by the objectives of the National Radio Plan (1989–90) have produced what I regard as a significant weakening of the sector's contribution to the national culture in the provision of news and current affairs programming. Without going into the details or the reasons for the specific directions pursued by the National Radio Plan here (cf. Turner 1993), no one would deny that it revolutionised the commercial radio market in Australia. Introduced at a time when commercial radio was starting to address niche markets (as in 2WS in Sydney, for instance) and pursue primarily local advertising (or, as some were saying at the time, leading the trend towards the 'demassification of the media'), the National Radio Plan produced a radical change of direction for the industry. The National Radio Plan indirectly but effectively raised operating costs across the sector – thus increasing competition for audiences and for advertisers. The consequences were profound. Some metropolitan and regional AM radio stations closed, some metropolitan FM stations merged with their competitors, and hitherto informal networking arrangements were formalised. Radio stations began to compete with television networks as well as with other radio stations for a larger share of national (rather than local) advertising accounts. The market conditions for commercial operators became brutal, their capacity to survive within this environment a genuine problem, and the government ultimately had to accept 'market realities' and agree to a major deregulation of the industry.

Among other things, deregulation relieved licensees of the obligation to produce their own local news service. As a consequence, independent news production in radio has declined substantially. In Brisbane, where I live, competing stations share newsrooms or operate networked rip-and-read services. There is now only one commercial station (4BC) with its own news-room, and there are no completely locally produced news bulletins. Without a newsroom or local bulletins there is little need to employ journalists. There is no current affairs radio programming in the commercial sector in Brisbane at all. These developments constitute major changes to the service commercial radio has provided but they have been invisible within the academic literature; I only discovered their existence when I embarked on an ABC-funded survey which directly compared ABC radio and television news and current affairs provision with the commercial sector (Turner 1996).

Worse is to come. The increased competition made niche marketing insupportable as a commercial strategy, and networks were forced to seek mass-marketable programming for their audiences and for their high profile adver-tising clients. One consequence was the reinforcement of the commercial power of the sure-fire drawcards, the talkback shock-jocks, who expanded into the space once occupied by (among other things) current affairs. In a sense, John Laws has replaced current affairs on the largest commercial radio network in the country. As was made abundantly clear during the 1999 'cash for comment' inquiries, Laws is a radio personality, not a journalist, and so operates without any of the journalists' ethical and professional constraints. Until the eruption of the cash for comment scandal, there had been very little written about talkback, the dominant form of commercial broadcasting in Australia for the last five or six years. Even now, there is still very little academic research or analysis in print. The only sustained example is Stephen Mickler's critique of the racist law and order campaign mounted by Howard Sattler in Perth. Mickler confronts the problem of the elite critic having to deal with the reactionary populist content of these programs – that of the host and his callers – by attempting to understand the political attraction of the positions they articulate (Mickler 1992; see also Rowe 1992). His is an illustrative and impor-tant example, explicitly arguing a critique of racist populism; a less ethically focused critique of the format would struggle to defend itself against accusations of elitism or of a misunderstanding of the commercial character of the talkback host's relation to their audiences. Mickler doesn't attack the genre of talkback. By inves-tigating a group of claims made on this program, he is able to outline specific instances where this particular broadcaster, presumably in search of higher ratings, distorted and misrepresented the facts in order to raise the level of racial tension within the community. The case study reveals that the program actively works against the objective of constructing a well informed community.

In the case of the decline in news and current affairs on commercial radio, I am unaware of a single discussion of this policy issue within Australian media research. Indeed, given the considerations I have just described, it is difficult to imagine what might be the framework within which such a discussion could be enclosed. It would be inappropriate to mount a critique of commercial radio for its gradual withdrawal of resources from news and current affairs since the regulatory regime within which they must operate has actively encouraged this strategy. Furthermore, deregulation effectively dismissed any recourse to some notion of national cultural responsibility as an unaffordable luxury within the prevailing economic climate. Nevertheless, the principles which were displaced by deregulation, inconsistent as they may be with the current formation of popular culture in the academy as well as with the market orientation of policy, are precisely those which will have to be rearticulated within new accounts of the future of radio in Australia. One of the hopeful signs to emerge from the 'cash for comment' hearings was that this was an issue for a number of participants, including representatives of the federal government.

In my second example, the cultural form is again effectively disarticulated from the national and abandoned to the logic of the market for what seems in this case to be political opportunism. Up until the late 1980s, the Australian popular music industry operated successfully within an almost entirely commercial environment. There were two crucial government interventions: the local music quota which was instituted in 1949, and the requirements for the local production of advertising which were established to protect local television production in the 1950s. Popular music was the last to join the queue of cultural industries which were scrutinised and organised by government. Marcus Breen has charted the progress of the Labor Government's interest in popular music, noting how unique a political opportunity it represented for the government at the time (1999). Economically viable, with considerable export potential, Australian popular music was a bandwagon to climb on rather than a basket case to revive. While it was initially exploited for the political potential of its market demographic (resulting in youth-oriented policy programs such as Priority One), popular music was ultimately developed within the Trade portfolio where it became one of the jewels in the crown of the newly dynamic Austrade. Increasingly, as it lost its connections with the nationalist agenda (the triumphalism of the local music industry, of local bands making good overseas and so on) and the realm of social policy (the Priority One connection), popular music was once again abandoned to the mercy of the market. Within such a context, local content regulations seemed old-fashioned and interventionist so they were replaced by a code of self-regulation for the radio industry which significantly reduced the level of support for local music. In a related development, the requirement for locally produced advertising also offended against the federal government's alignment with post-GATT capitalism, and the revenue available to local recording studios began to decline. No longer defended in terms of its contribution to Australian popular cultures, valued only for its export potential, the popular music industry today is more exposed than ever to the pressures of 'commercial realities'. While the cultural effects of these 'realities' may be regretted down the track, they are not likely to be contested at the level of policy or government regulation.

As a side issue, and in a knock-on effect of the same group of deregulatory radio policies mentioned in the first example, the industry's major outlet for new popular music – radio stations with a teen music or Top 40 format – has disappeared as well. This has happened, moreover, at a time when the turnover for the industry remains strong and when the champion of the local product, Mushroom Records, has a distribution deal with Sony which offers its brightest international prospects so far. However, in a hopeful sign of what still might happen when the academy and the policy makers communicate with each other, the demise of teen radio has indeed been pursued within media and cultural studies. My own work on teen radio and Mick Counihan's account of the fate of HITZ-FM are among a number of studies which, first, flowed through into media features and commentary and, second, helped to provoke the ABA's 1996 study, *Music, new music and all that: Teenage radio in the 90s* (Cupitt, Ramsay and Sheldon) which contains suggestions about the future disposition of new licences and niche marketing in an expanded radio spectrum. This may be the exception which proves the rule, however. In this instance, critique was not discouraged by the intellectual context I have been describing because this was, once again, a case where the academy could revert to its more comfortable role of leaping to the defence of popular taste. Nevertheless, as the debates over parallel importing and CD pricing demonstrates, popular music is one area where we can see, from time to time, a close, case-related involvement from the academy in the shaping and critique of cultural policy.[8]

The third example is the most troubling because it refers to a cultural form which is powerful, pervasive, and nowadays almost beyond the reach of policy or regulatory structures. Current affairs on commercial television provides one of the most inflamed instances where the market actively encourages the production of reactionary, even victimising, program material. The examples I have in mind – *A Current Affair*'s exploitation of the Paxton family and its hidden video exposure of the late Benny Mendoza – are predatory and malicious, but they scored high ratings. Once a genre of programming which attracted a lot of critical attention from cultural and media studies, recent trends in current affairs have either been ignored or protected by a generic defence of populist and 'anti-bourgeois' programming. Such a defence – and it has its merits – regards such programming as a deliberate and empowering challenge to elite or patriarchal definitions of what counts as important or acceptable content in a range of genres from news to talk shows. I have dealt at length with the necessity of finding a way to acknowledge this argument while still being able to criticise these programs elsewhere (1999), so I won't go into it in detail here.

However, while some criticism of these shows may be taste-driven and thus enclosed within debates which are not our key concern at this point, there is one aspect of the institutional climate within which they operate that is worth highlighting, as it is relevant and usually ignored. As it happens, this is also a case where the academy's analysis of media practice could help to isolate key features of the institutional environment which demand to be changed. In his essay on the media and democracy, which discusses the difficulties in reconciling the contradiction between the news media's commercial considerations and their democratic responsibilities while acknowledging the fact that 'neither public service media nor private corporations can be seen as automatically enhancing the democratic cause', Rod Tiffen offers a list of six 'democratic tests' which should be applied to media performance (Tiffen 1994, p. 64). These include appropriate practices of disclosure, absence of sanctions against public dissent, the existence of sufficient processes of redress, an implied preference for the democratic process, access and diversity, and the enhancement of collective choice. Tiffen regarded the Australian media as performing best on the first two (disclosure and defending dissent), and with mixed success on the fourth and fifth (normatising democracy, and access and equity). He was most categorically critical of the avenues available for redress. There, he said, 'the media have rarely managed to enhance the debate on policy beyond reporting conflicts between the parties and the most prominent pressure groups' (pp. 66–7). It is the failure in this area of policy, virtually untouched by cultural studies so far, that is most relevant to the issue of the predatory practices of such programs as *A Current Affair*. The incommensurability between the program's power to mobilise public opinion and that of the Paxton family (for instance) to either resist or seek compensation against its effects is what enables such programs to operate with complete disregard for the individual in the pursuit for ratings. As Tiffen helps us to realise, we need better protection for victims of the media than we now provide.[9]

The market and the public sphere

I commenced this discussion by drawing attention to the productive interaction between cultural institutions and the academy in the revival of the Australian film industry. The dialogues established between the discourses of cultural criticism, the discourses of policy documents, and the discourses of the film text during the mid-1970s to the mid-1980s may well be unique. But they do indicate the creative potential of academic knowledges. They were engaged critically, strategically and through a wealth of detailed case studies over a long period of time, substantially influencing policy directions and permeating the broader discourses through which Australian film was discussed within the culture. While contemporary analogies for that kind of influence are hard to produce, it remains a model for the academy's intervention into the public sphere as the commercialisation of that public sphere makes the renovation of our major cultural institutions ever more necessary.

It is a model that was built upon an earlier tradition of cultural criticism, however. Perhaps this tradition should have been less comfortable with its constituent contradictions: its vigorous proposal of a national cinema sitting awkwardly with the reluctance to acknowledge popular cinema genres, for instance. Alternatively, perhaps the fact that it remained comfortable with these contradictions for some years actually enabled important interventions – interventions in the name of a national culture that stood for more than the concept of a national market. Film policy may be less innocent and less theoretically compromised today; it is also less culturally significant. It has understood how comprehensively it is implicated in the move towards a commercialised public sphere, and how narrow is the latitude allowed for creative intervention that is not wholly in accord with the dictates of the market.

One of the keys to the cultural shifts in the last decade has been the pre-eminence achieved by the institutions of business, by discourses of the economy, and by the broad deployment of the concept of the market as a strategy for social organisation (see Turner 1994). The alignment of these forces with a rational-ising and globalising capitalism has proved almost irresistible. Free market economics represents itself as fundamentally democratic while it turns regulated environments into markets; the consumer benefit of proliferating choice is offered right across the society as a means of closing down government services, demolishing regulatory structures, and minimising the commercially inhibitory effects of existing policy frameworks. Obvious as the point may be, it has to be said that this trend directly denies the point of having publicly funded cultural institutions at all. If the core function of our cultural institutions, and even of some of our cultural industries, is to provide us with the things the market does not find profitable, then we may be approaching the day when the failure of the market to provide for the culture will be seen as a regrettable 'reality' rather than as a cause for government intervention. This is the climate within which the reshaping of Australian cultural institutions will occur, a climate within which the political orientation is towards their abolition or diminution.

To change this climate will not be easy – particularly for those in the academy who feel themselves implicated in such an orientation in their own work, or in their own institutional context. So many of the enabling 'grand narratives' – socialism, cultural nationalism, social democracy – have lost their purchase. As the new humanities has keenly pursued the work of theoretical clarification in conjunction with what is called 'the real world' of cultural policy, many have had to accept that the days of the broadly critical project – of moving through a series of institutional domains with barely a break in its theoretical stride – have gone. Consequently, to participate in discussions about the future shape of cultural institutions in Australia today may require very different, far less expansive or exorbitant, critical strategies to those used in the past. They will have to be more specific and focused in their application, more modestly contingent in their politics, but more explicitly ambitious in their ethical claims.

Notes

1 Instead, we find arguments which contest the need for such a connection. Leading the way in this regard was Elizabeth Jacka's 'Australian cinema: an anachronism in the 1990s', first published in 1988 and reprinted in Graeme Turner (ed.) (1993). In later work, Jacka and Stuart Cunningham have taken up the notion of a 'strategic nationalism',

which is the use of the idea of the nation for strategic political outcomes rather than as any ideal form of social of cultural organisation.

2 The most recent review of these issues and their related problematics, and indeed of the pair of discourses referred to earlier in this paragraph, can be found in O'Regan (1996).

3 I would see this ambiguity as implicit in much of the institutional history of the first fifteen years of the Australian film revival. Ben Goldsmith (1997) has examined this kind of contradictory funding regime in his account of the AFDC.

4 John Fiske's work is the most common location of this even though he does maintain a critique of capitalism while drawing attention to the agency of the individual subject. Possibly the most significant influence on optimistic accounts of the resistant within consumer capitalism comes from Michel de Certeau's (1984) apparent celebration of the 'tactics of the weak against the strong'.

5 The writers I have in mind here come from a broad range of disciplinary locations in the political economy of the media industries (Graham Murdock, James Curran, Richard Collins), theorists of the postmodern (David Harvey, Iain Chambers and Arjun Appadurai) and cultural studies or television theorists (Ien Ang, John Hartley) – and would not necessarily accept the commonalities I am proposing between them.

6 The term popularised from Stuart Hall's work.

7 There are some signs of interest. The most substantial so far is Catharine Lumby's second book, *Gotcha: Life in a Tabloid World* (1999), and myself, Frances Bonner and David Marshall have recently completed a book on the production of Australian celebrity which deals with some of these topics (2000).

8 The work of Marcus Breen as a journalist, as a consultant with CIRCIT, and finally as an academic researcher is an instance of this kind of involvement and this becomes apparent in his account of the popular music industry.

9 It is a point made in the draft report of the Productivity Commission's 1999 inquiry into broadcasting regulation as well, in response to submissions made by academics working in media and cultural studies.

📖 Guide to further reading

An insight into an earlier mode of academic engagement in Australian cultural policy issues can be found by reading Cunningham (1992), or by returning to Dermody and Jacka (1987 and 1988). For the kinds of arguments which defend the increasingly demotic range of the contemporary media it is useful to read John Hartley's *Popular Reality: Journalism, Modernity, Popular Culture* (London: Edward Arnold, 1996) and Catharine Lumby (1999). For a critique of the uses of the national in Australian popular culture see Graeme Turner (1994), and for a useful account of the shift in cultural studies which has seen the merging of the notion of the democratic state and the market, see Chaney (1994). An early discussion of the 'cash for comment' inquiry can be found in Turner, 'Talkback, advertising and journalism: a cautionary tale of self-regulated radio', *International Journal of Cultural Studies* 3, 2, pp. 247–55.

References

Bennett, Tony, Colin Mercer and Janet Woollacott (eds) (1986) *Popular Culture and Social Relations*, Milton Keynes: Open University Press.

Breen, Marcus (1999) *Rock Dogs: Politics and the Australian Music Industry*, Sydney: Pluto Press.

Carter, David (1998) 'Wark wars', *UTS Review* 4, 1, pp. 228–33.

Chaney, David (1994) *The Cultural Turn: Scene-setting Essays on Contemporary Cultural History*, London: Routledge.

Cunningham, Stuart (1992) *Framing Culture*, Sydney: Allen & Unwin.

Cunningham, Stuart and Elizabeth Jacka (1993) *Australian Television and International Mediascapes*, Cambridge: Cambridge University Press.

Cupitt, M., G. Ramsay and L. Sheldon (1996) *Music, New Music, and All That: Teen Radio in the 90s*, Sydney: Australian Broadcasting Authority.

de Certeau, Michel (trans. Steven Randall) (1984) *The Practice of Everyday Life*, Berkeley: University of California Press.

Dermody, Susan and Elizabeth Jacka (1987 and 1988) *The Screening of Australia*, Vols 1 and 2, Sydney: Currency Press.

Frow, John and Meaghan Morris (1993) *Australian Cultural Studies: A Reader*, Sydney: Allen & Unwin.

Goldsmith, Ben (1997) 'Producing Culture for the Nation', unpublished PhD thesis, University of Queensland.

Hawkins, Gay (1998) 'TV Rules', *UTS Review* 4, 1, pp. 123–39.

Jacka, Elizabeth (1993) 'Australian cinema: an anachronism in the 1990s' in Graeme Turner (ed.) *Nation, Culture, Text: Australian Cultural and Media Studies*, London: Routledge.

Lumby, Catharine (1997) *Bad Girls: The Media, Sex and Feminism*, Sydney: Allen & Unwin.

— (1999) *Gotcha: Life in a Tabloid World*, Sydney: Allen & Unwin.

McGuigan, Jim (1992) *Cultural Populism*, London: Routledge.

Mickler, Stephen (1992) 'Gambling on the first race: a comment on racism and talkback radio 6PR, the TAB and the WA Government', Louis St John Memorial Trust Fund, Centre for Research in Culture and Communication, Murdoch University.

Moran, Alison and Tom O'Regan (1989) *The Australian Screen*, Melbourne: Penguin.

Morris, Meaghan (1988) *The Pirate's Fiancée: Feminism, Reading, Postmodernism*, London: Verso.

O'Regan, Tom (1996) *Australian National Cinema*, London: Routledge.

Reid, Mary Anne (1993) *Long Shots to Favourites: Australian Cinema Successes in the 90s*, Sydney: Australian Film Commission.

Rowe, David (1992) 'Just warming 'em up: radio talkback and its renditions', *Continuum* 6, 1, pp. 14–29.

Tiffen, Rod (1994) 'The media and democracy: reclaiming an intellectual agenda' in Julianne Schultz (ed.) *Not Just Another Business: Journalists, Citizens and the Media*, Sydney: Pluto Press, pp. 53–68.

Turner, Graeme (1993) 'Who killed the radio star: the death of teen radio in Australia' in Tony Bennett, Simon Frith, Lawrence Grossberg, John Shepherd and Graeme Turner (eds) *Rock and Popular Music: Policies, Politics, Institutions*, London: Routledge, pp. 142–55.

— (1994) *Making it National: Nationalism and Australian Popular Culture*, Sydney: Allen & Unwin.

— (1996) 'Maintaining the news: a comparative analysis of news and current affairs services provided by the ABC and the commmercial sector', *Culture and Policy* 7, 3, pp. 127–64.

— (1999) 'Tabloidisation, journalism and the possibililty of critique', *International Journal of Cultural Studies* 2, 1, pp. 59–76.

Turner, Graeme, Francis Bonner and David Marshall (2000) *Fame Games: The Production of Celebrity in the Australian Media*, Cambridge: Cambridge University Press.

Chapter 8

The ABC and Rhetorics of Choice

Gay Hawkins

Two words dominated debate about the state of public service broadcasting (PSB) in the 1990s: *crisis* and *decline*. All around the world, wherever publicly funded television and radio operated, these terms were repeatedly invoked to summarise the effects of a myriad of technological, policy and economic changes. While PSB has always been subject to multiple influences there is no question that the nineties was a period of massive structural transformation. New technologies and the rise of multichannel environments, decline in government funding and support, loss of audiences, the drift to commercialism: all these trends and more were assessed as threatening the very heart of broadcasting services designed not for profit but for informing, educating and entertaining the national public.

In Australia the ABC was not immune from such changes, far from it. It copped all of the above plus a few extras peculiar to its specific history and location. The Labor Government that had ruled for most of the 1980s entered the 1990s with Prime Minister Keating describing the ABC as 'the most self-indulgent and self-interested outfit in the country' (quoted in Inglis 1997, p. 10). For political leaders, courting commercial media proprietors was now far more crucial to electoral success than keeping the ABC on side. But this kind of animosity was nothing compared with what the conservative Coalition Government had in store when it was elected in 1996. Not only did it rapidly and dramatically extend the funding cuts and restructuring begun by Labor; it also upped the ideological attacks. Bob Mansfield, former chief executive of McDonald's, Optus and Fairfax, was commissioned to conduct a major review into the role and function of the whole corporation. While his report reflected strong support for the crucial role of the ABC in national public life (much to the surprise and relief of the ABC and its advocates), it did recommend a revised charter and a series of structural changes to the organisation. These included the outsourcing of all production except news and current affairs, axing the international services Radio Australia and Australia Television, and the merger of radio and television divisions in order to facilitate cost savings and the transition to digital technologies which allowed for the same material to be used in different sites (Mansfield 1997).

Compared with those made in other countries, Mansfield's recommendations were moderate. In New Zealand a conservative government had transformed the public service broadcaster into a state-owned commercial enterprise indistinguishable from other channels. In Britain the BBC resisted strong pressure during the 1980s to privatise or become a subscription based service, only to enter the 1990s with a new management team keen to appease a Conservative Government. This took two main forms. The first involved a half embrace of the free market with a massive emphasis on increasing revenue from commercial overseas activities like BBC World Service Television. The second involved increasing efficiencies through dramatic and savage internal restructuring. In Canada two decades of funding cuts meant that by the end of the 1990s the CBC had half the staff, advertising during the national news bulletin (a previously protected programming space) and only 14 per cent of the English-language audience.

In this international context the Mansfield Report seems almost innocuous. However, there were some significant silences, especially about ABC Online, the ABC's burgeoning multimedia and internet services. These were described as specialist activities and peripheral to the core business of mass broadcasting. This has proved to be a very shortsighted assessment in the light of subsequent developments, which have not only seen the global rise of the internet but also ABC Online become one of the most successful and popular websites in Australia.[1]

Many of the structural and economic changes recommended by Mansfield were already in train within the organisation long before his report and they continued long after it had been handed down. Quite simply, the ABC underwent enormous transformation during the nineties, which kept the lobby group 'Friends of the ABC' run off its feet. But beyond all the public debate about declining budgets, massive job losses, technological change and government attacks there was another debate not so much about money and management but about meaning. What was the purpose of this public cultural institution at the end of the twentieth century? Who should it serve and how? Had the organisation lost its way? Newspaper columnists bemoaned the decline in programming standards and the rise of crass, commercially oriented shows. Others complained about declining Australian content and an over reliance on British imports. Then there was the spectacular fuss about the screening of the Sydney Gay and Lesbian Mardi Gras in 1994. This was evidence, according to conservatives, of the ABC being captured by politically correct minorities and abandoning its moral duty to the nation. These sorts of criticisms raised questions about the ABC's cultural authority. They revealed an anxiety about whether the institution was still committed to promoting certain supposedly universal aesthetic and moral principles; about whether it could still generate respect and deference; and about whether its traditional cultural functions and status were still intact.

They weren't. And while many saw this as a tragedy, as the definitive evidence of crisis and decline, I want to argue that the transformations in the ABC's cultural functions and authority that peaked during the early 1990s were important, necessary and long overdue. One of my aims in this chapter, then, is to resist the lure of narratives of loss. I want to write *against* the story of public service broadcasting in the 1990s lurching toward its inevitable and tragic demise. For the problem with this story, as narrative theory reminds us, is that it limits the production of meaning as much as it enables it. Not only does it order messy and multiple changes into a chronology of cause and effect but it also represents the ABC as a monolithic unity, as a unified coherent whole in which all the forces of change line up together.

My motivation in resisting this narrative is political and emotional. It should be obvious by now that I don't think this particular story is useful for analysing the ABC during the 1990s let alone the future. While I get mad about the relentless economic and ideological attacks on the ABC, I don't mourn at all its abandonment of certain sorts of cultural authority. I like the way that it has developed one of the most popular websites in Australia, I liked it screening Mardi Gras and, yes, I even liked *That's Dancin'*, the show often identified as the beginning of the end. I simply can't think of the ABC in the twenty-first century as a pale, commercialised shadow of its former great self. The institution has changed, of course, but assessing these changes just cannot be done via the logic of narrative and its particular system of judgement which implies past good, present bad, future unimaginable.

Governmentality

In this chapter I want to develop an alternative approach, one that avoids not only perpetuating narratives of loss but also the dangers of reductionism which diagnose changes in PSB as an effect of fundamental economic and political processes. The perspective I want to develop is more modest and more influenced by Foucault's (1991) concept of governmentality than by established traditions in media theory. A governmental approach is concerned with understanding 'the forms of action and relations of power that aim to guide and shape (rather than force, control or dominate) the actions of others or oneself' (Cruikshank 1999, p. 4). Governing, then, is about the myriad of processes, techniques and strategies that seek to regulate and administer populations. These processes are not exclusive to large-scale state organisations. They occur across an enormous range of sites from the shopping mall to the doctor's surgery to the bedroom and they often involve internal and voluntary relations of rule: ways we act on ourselves. Foucault's concept of governmentality radically decentres political power and highlights the variety of forms of rule and their objectives. The emphasis is on *how* authority and rule are enacted rather than *why*. It also focuses on the types of knowledge that governing depends on: the problematisations and assumptions about subjectivity and populations that are used to justify actions and practices.

In relation to the media, governmental approaches are scarce. The tendency to represent 'the media' as a unified and coherent field driven by the logic of profit and/or ideological domination persists even in the face of the rise of cultural studies and its emphasis on the active audience. Yet even the most cursory glance reveals that media play an important role in the administration of populations and that the forms of this administration are complex, shifting and various. A governmental perspective allows us to think about how these mediated forms of social regulation work in ways that do not involve control or manipulation but, rather, the production of a complex network of power/knowledge relations in which various forms of personhood or ways of being are made thinkable and therefore manageable (Rose 1999, p. 22).

This perspective also radically decentres 'the ABC' because its focus is not on the unity of the organisation, on its coherence and singularity, but on its heterogeneity, conflicts and multiplicities. Different sections of the ABC are implicated in governing in different ways. The assumptions about viewers vary according to different ways of problematising their relation to the organisation and the different forms and techniques of authority that are deployed. The Children's Programming Unit, for example, privileges a pedagogic relation with its audiences on the assumption of their vulnerability and need for protection. As a special population children are known or understood quite differently from others and what counts as good or responsible programming emerges in the interplay between ways of knowing children and ways of addressing and regulating them. Governmentality, then, is a way of thinking about institutions not in terms of unity and narrativisation but as dispersed sites where certain practices are put into play on the basis of particular assumptions about the presons that use or inhabit them. It is an approach concerned not with 'the whole story' but with localised examples. An approach that investigates small sites as domains of action and value; not as evidence of some underlying or totalising logic but as spaces where particular problematics of governing are played out.

The problematic that I am interested in involves, in the broadest terms, the relationship between the ABC and new forms of subjectification or personhood. From the late 1980s two policy shifts occurred. The first focused on the idea of 'choice'. Evidence of declining audiences led to a push for more popular programming and the extension of options for audiences. More variety in television shows and less highbrow and elitist fare was seen as the solution to a drift away from the ABC to the commercial channels. The second policy shift was concerned with the problem of difference: what was the ABC's responsibility to multiple publics, to the emergence of identity politics predicated on the fact of racial, ethnic and sexual diversity? Each of these shifts made trouble for some of the ABC's longstanding policies, particularly notions of quality and the pedagogic duty of this televisual form. More significant, however, was the way in which the recognition of multiple publics and the rise of a rhetoric of 'choice' generated a quite different set of ethical claims about the relationship between the ABC as a public authority and the individuals and groups who used it. These ethical claims were based on new assumptions about the nature of personhood or subjectivity. To see viewers as having the right to 'choice' assumed that they were able to enact that right sensibly and with as little interference as possible. To see the viewer as in need of having their 'difference' affirmed assumed a relationship between identity and the truth of the self that the ABC was obligated to maintain through the provision of appropriate programming.

Both these examples can be read as evidence of the emergence of new ethical inscriptions within sections of the ABC in which the viewer is understood as a freely choosing subject interested in maximising identity and quality of life.

'Freely choosing subjects'

I've borrowed this term from Nikolas Rose (1992), whose work on forms of subjectification represents a significant engagement with and development of Foucault's (1991) account of governmentality. Rose's project has been to reframe political thought; to develop alternative accounts of rule, authority and techniques of governing appropriate to deep transformations in contemporary politics and social life. While Foucault's accounts of governmentality are brief and underdeveloped, one of his final recommendations before his death was to pursue the relations between the administration of the social and personal existence, or the conduct of conduct. Rose has taken up this challenge and produced an inventive and empirical analytics of government that foregrounds the multitude of practices aimed at shaping the conduct of populations, groups and individuals and the sorts of knowledges and truths that are developed to rationalise such practices.

Rose argues that many contemporary forms of government involve knowledges and techniques that mobilise and shape individual capacities and conduct in ways quite different from earlier forms. In the broad move from corporatism to advanced or neo-liberalism, which is his primary focus, numerous shifts have occurred in the ethos or arts of governing. Very briefly, neoliberalism describes a reconstruction of government away from the idea of the state as a protector of the population's needs and interests, as a source of welfare from cradle to grave, towards the idea of the enabling state. 'Enterprise' is a key term in this process. The aim of governing should be the empowerment of individuals to become responsible for their own well-being (Rose 1999, pp. 140–2). The state is represented as a partner, not a parent. Neoliberalism, then, involves: the radical pluralisation of social technologies of rule sometimes referred to as the de-statisation of government; new relations between expertise and politics; and new specifications of the subject of government (Rose 1996, pp. 54–7). The subject of neoliberal programs of rule is the entrepreneurial individual, the individual endowed with freedom and autonomy.

> The enhancement of the powers of the client as customer – consumer of health services, of education, of training, of transport – specifies the subjects of rule in a new way: as active individuals seeking to 'enterprise themselves', to maximise their quality of life through acts of choice, according their life a meaning and value to the extent it can be rationalized as the outcome of choices made or choices to be made … Within this new regime of the actively responsible self, individuals are to fulfill their national obligations not through relations of dependency and obligation to one another, but through seeking to fulfill themselves within a variety of micro-moral domains or communities.
>
> (Rose 1996, p. 57)

It is possible to read Rose's argument as nothing new, as saying something that many have already said – contemporary forms of government have replaced the citizen with the consumer – but this misses the fundamental point. For Rose, it is not that the rise of the consumer represents the death of the citizen, the loss of that most valued and precious of political subjects. Rather, his argument is that the freely choosing subject, the entrepreneurial self, is a *new* way of making up citizens. Rhetorics of choice presume a person able to self-regulate, an actively responsible self committed to making appropriate calculations about his or her conduct in the interests not only of 'national obligations' but also in the interests of identity, lifestyle or personal fulfilment. These techniques of the self, these ways of relating to and investing in ourselves, cannot be thought of as disconnected from wider regimes and programs of government. The ways in which the truth of identity has become connected to notions of freedom and choice is a recent problematisation. And it foregrounds the issue Foucault (1988) argued was the most crucial aspect of governmentality: the relationship between regimes of government and regimes of personal conduct.

This argument has great value for thinking about reorganisations in PSB. For a start, it calls into question accepted media studies analyses of these changes. The shift from citizen to consumer is a standard trope in the PSB narrative, and one of the primary indicators of decline. Implicit here is the assumption that the consuming subject is a lesser and essentially inferior person in comparison with the citizen. Apart from generalised Left suspicion of choice and markets, this critique evokes a sense of anxiety about a shift in the relation between PSB and viewers. Unlike the citizen, the freely choosing subject is not understood as vulnerable and ethically incomplete but as active and self-regulating. The duty of the public service broadcaster is not to improve and inform but to facilitate autonomous self-actualisation.[2]

Rhetorics of choice with their presumption of an entrepreneurial subject represent an important shift in the policies of most public service broadcasters from the mid-1980s on. Within ABC-TV the rise of this rhetoric is most evident in two developments. The first involved experimentation with the new genre of infotainment that began in the late 1980s triggering ongoing attacks on commercialism. These attacks eventually led to the establishment of the Senate Select Committee on ABC Management and its Operations in the early 1990s.[3] The second involved the rather reluctant recognition of cultural diversity and identity politics evident in developments like the establishment of the Aboriginal Program Unit in 1987, the commissioning of mini-series with multicultural themes and the landmark screening of Sydney's Gay and Lesbian Mardi Gras in 1994. In all these domains the meanings for 'choice' and the ways in which the relationship between choice and subjectivity was configured took specific forms which shall be examined later. First though, it is necessary to briefly reflect on the origins of these neoliberal rhetorics of choice and their implications for the other, more traditional, policies shaping the ABC.

Impacts of the Dix Report

Within the ABC the rise of rhetorics of choice is most often attributed to David Hill, appointed as Managing Director in early 1987 and the initiator of an aggressive restructuring of the organisation. Hill was openly committed to making the ABC popular, to attracting bigger audiences through more 'mass appeal' programming (Hill 1994, p. 28). As easy as it may be to construct Hill as the phobic object, as the manager everyone loved to hate, the seeds of these transformations can be traced back much earlier to the impacts of the 1981 federal government inquiry: *The ABC in Review: National Broadcasting in the 1980s*. Also known as the Dix Report, this document represents one of the most thorough and important assessments of the state of the ABC since its establishment. From the mid-1980s, as the ABC began to reel under increasing government cutbacks, internal management restructures, shifts in broadcasting regulations and declining audiences, several changes occurred which laid the foundations for a more pluralistic approach to both audiences and programming. These changes, often broadly described as corporatisation, were a result of recommendations in the Dix Report. They involved the creation of a Board and Director General structure (like the BBC), a new charter, provision for revenue raising procedures from retailing to co-productions, greater commitment to Australian content and overall restructuring of the organisation.

But the Dix Report was more of a landmark because of its assessment of the ABC as fundamentally conservative on issues of cultural diversity. Dix identified a serious failure within the ABC to respond to changes in Australian society, particularly the growth of multiculturalism and the needs of youth audiences, Aborigines and isolated regional viewers. The organisation was judged as suffocatingly anglocentric, as evident in everything from the over reliance on British programming to the tone of on-air announcers. Far from being at the forefront of innovative broadcasting, the Dix Report implied that the ABC at the beginning of the 1980s was technologically and socially backward – monocultural, monolithic and moribund; and very ill-equipped to deal with rapid transformations in broadcasting and cultural landscapes.

Overall, the emergence of rhetorics of choice in the ABC during the 1980s can be read as a response to two of Dix's primary recommendations: 'The organisation must become more entrepreneurially minded, it must overcome its distaste for the commercial' (Dix Report 1981 Vol. 1, p. 15) and 'The ABC has a duty to provide programs to Australian society as a whole *and* its constituent community groups' (p. 7, my emphasis). In this context it is possible to see the shift to more popular programming and the emergence of a new politics of difference as related. The commercialism shift was about opening up or diversifying programming choices with the explicit aim of winning back audiences and it triggered the long running debate about the ABC's relationship to ratings. However, this shift also implicitly assumed that ABC viewers desired and were able to manage this choice.

The recognition of other axes of difference beyond the usual 'women, rural, children' trilogy that for so long was the ABC's attempt at mopping up a few of those othered by its deeply institutionalised exclusions is most evident in various innovative and interesting multicultural, queer and Indigenous programming over the last fifteen years. This very different recognition of minority publics not only assumes a relationship between identity and the truth of the self, but also radically pluralises value. As the fuss over Mardi Gras revealed: what's offensive and tasteless to you is affirming and pleasurable to me. While these two different moves towards diversification each had their own politics, both presumed a viewer actively seeking and able to manage choice. And both destabilised long held assumptions within the ABC about its cultural duty and authority and the nature of cultural value.

Value and difference

My point is not that the emergence of discourses of choice has obliterated other policy discourses within the ABC: the organisation remains radically heterogeneous. Rather, that this new configuration of the relationship between the ABC and its audiences has generated real tensions with other policies, particularly those focused on questions of quality and the pedagogic role of public service broadcasting. One of the ways to examine these tensions is to begin with the relation between value and difference. This relation forms part of the discursive context for the rise of the freely choosing subject because this new way of thinking about personhood not only enables a recognition of difference but also, in the same moment, foregrounds the inherent instability of claims to universal value. The idea of the freely choosing subject, or the entrepreneurial self, involves important shifts in the relation between difference and value. And it is these shifts that disrupt long held assumptions about what constitutes quality and about the pedagogic duty of PSB. It is difficult to sustain claims about quality and pedagogy, for so long the touchstone of all that was special about PSB, in the face of substantial shifts in normative knowledges of the audience. Once the audience is represented not only as a series of multiple publics but as actively entrepreneurial in their pursuit of identity then it is difficult for public broadcasters to confidently and paternalistically claim: 'we know what's best for you'.

So how was the relationship between value and difference managed prior to the 1980s? Like most PSBs around the world, the history of the ABC until the early to mid-1980s was a history of the management of two dominant policy paradigms: the responsibility to provide an adequate and comprehensive service to all, and to provide a service based on clear moral and aesthetic principles that were presumed to educate and improve viewers and to be universal. 'Quality' is the broad code name for this second paradigm. The relationship between these paradigms has always been shifting and at times uneasy.

'Quality' has functioned as a very distinctive discourse of value within PSB. By discourse of value I mean the institutional and discursive practices which work to rank, distinguish and attribute status to certain cultural forms and practices and the audiences that recognise and enjoy these. For value always implies a valuing subject or community, a 'value-for' as Frow (1995, p. 143) argues, and this means that valuing is always a transaction and always involves an ethical dimension, a regulation of conduct calculated to realise certain moral or aesthetic objectives.

Historically, several key assumptions shaped the ABC's discourse on quality. The first concerned the relationship with commercial television. The ABC's difference, its distinction, was predicated on a fundamental rejection of the logics of commercialism. 'Quality' meant not commercial. Value here was produced in a relation of negation and opposition. Good TV (and the first step in understanding value is 'locating and understanding the intelligibility of the good in a particular locale' – McHoul 1996, p. 207) was not driven by market forces or by pandering to audiences. Its tone, as a viewer quoted in the Dix Report declared: 'was quieter, more serious, sophisticated, mature, not sensational' (1981 Vol. 3, p. 67). However, the problem with this method of valuing was that it left the ABC, and many other PSBs, in a continual quandary over how to be both distinctive and popular. After all, the service was obliged to be comprehensive, to meet the needs of all the nation, and such notions of quality often proved to seriously undermine the demand for wide appeal. Managing the distinction between popular and commercial was at the heart of this dilemma.

Both Simon Frith (1983) and Ien Ang (1991) have discussed this tension in relation to the history of the BBC, focusing specifically on the place of entertainment as a key site where the competing and contradictory demands of quality versus popularity were regularly played out. Frith points out that entertainment was for a long time viewed with suspicion, it was seen as the 'ground bait' used to attract viewers who could then be reformed and improved. Ang develops a similar argument describing how, within BBC policy, the living room was predominantly seen as a classroom with edification privileged over pleasure. This particular ethics of amusement, which consistently valued the middlebrow over the vulgar and information and aesthetics over fun, positioned commercial television as the trivial, low, hedonistic other driven by a crude populism which had no lasting value. It also presumed a very distinctive relationship between pleasure and value that had profound implications for how the audience was understood and rendered manageable by PSB. Put simply, PSB's notion of quality as 'not commercial' has been fundamentally predicated on a reductive binarism between pleasure and value in which value has been seen to involve a necessary sublimation of pleasure.

The privileging of instant gratification, hedonism and escape associated with commercial television positioned the viewer as a child, unable to sublimate pleasure in the interests of higher values such as aesthetics or education. This ethics of immediate pleasure produced primitive and classically mass cultural responses in audiences. In contrast, the PSB viewer was engaged in a quite different technology of the self predicated on the capacity to manage and delay pleasure in the interests of a more mature and complex and *civilised* response. This rejection of pleasure in the interests of value involved sublimation (denial of the affective and the sensual) and a hierarchical ranking of televisual forms and audiences, in which those who watched quality were implicitly constituted as better or superior.

Assumptions about the ABC's pedagogic role have historically had implications more for questions of difference than for those of value. This pedagogic role, often described in terms of PSB's authoritarian paternalism, presumes a homogeneous national public. PSB's whole philosophy of service and responsibility to 'the people' renders them an *a priori* pedagogic object. In the history of the ABC duty to the 'Australian people' or 'the nation' has been a central component of the institution's political rationality. This pre-given notion of 'the people', continuist and fixed in time, has been invoked not only to justify and explain the necessity and object of this broadcasting service (the people are the immanent subjects of national broadcasting policy) but also as a central rhetorical strategy in various narratives of nation emanating from the ABC. For Homi Bhabha (1994) pedagogic relations between nation and people exist in an increasing tension with what he terms performative representations of nation.

Historically, the pedagogic denies difference in several ways. First, it depends on the attribution of a representative unity to the people which is driven by an obsession with boundaries and margins. Second, it denies the 'prodigious living principle of contemporaneity' (Bhabha 1994, p. 145). That is, it is irretrievably backward looking in its temporality. And finally it presumes a notion of collective identity or citizenship predicated on an assimilationist notion of commonality rather than the fact of fundamental difference and heterogeneity.

The performative, or what Bhabha terms the nation's 'enunciative present' – all those messy signs of everyday life and diversity that have become increasingly visible – disrupts pedagogic assumptions. For not only does it open up a space within the nation for minority discourses, it also generates profound ambivalence and movement within national narratives. The performative opens up the nation to the never-ending play of difference; it disrupts the implicit power to generalise and totalise through its recognition of otherness. Increasingly, this has been contained by new national narratives of pluralism or multiculturalism which hold together the pedagogic and the performative in an uneasy tension. The point is that any recognition of the nation as fragmented, as a series of diverse and multiple publics, challenges pedagogic authority.

Neoliberal gardening

The Comedy Company, 60 Minutes and *Australia's Most Wanted* have a rival. From next Sunday, in the important 7.30 pm timeslot, the ABC is presenting David Hill's contribution to the ratings war: a 13 part series about – wait for it – ballroom dancing. (The Guide, *Sydney Morning Herald*, 26.6.89)

In turning now to the case of infotainment, the aim is to track how the problematics generated by the rise of the freely choosing subject are played out in a specific site. Beginning with a quote about *That's Dancin'* may seem odd, considering that my focus is that strange televisual hybrid, infotainment, rather than 'pure entertainment', as The Guide classified *That's Dancin'*. However, this quote nicely foregrounds some of the issues raised by the emergence of this new genre on the ABC. First there is the tone, that slightly sneering disdain about a popular form. Then there is the connection between Hill and ratings, a connection that was an ongoing component of criticisms of Hill during his period as Managing Director. Then there is the challenge to the ABC's long held distance and differentiation from the commercial channels with *That's Dancin'*'s explicit pitch to mass appeal. And as for dropping the 'g' on dancing … no wonder this show was cited over and over as a sign of the ABC 'losing the plot' (*The Bulletin* 7.6.94).

Infotainment shows began on the ABC around the same time as *That's Dancin'*, 1988, and they generated the same sort of flak. *Holiday* (a co-production with the Australian Tourism Commission), *The Home Show, The Investigators,* *For Love or Money* and *Everybody* are probably the most memorable and they followed the pioneering of this genre on Channel 9 with *Burke's Backyard* in 1987. Ten years later and infotainment was still thriving on the commercial channels with an enormous glut of shows and no obvious signs of decline. Often described as 'know-how TV' or 'lifestyle TV' these shows are cheap to make (especially when compared to drama), fast paced and increasingly connected to a magazine via cross promotion. They give new meaning to the idea of direct address and often involve various forms of subtle and not so subtle product promotion.

While *The Investigators* was an enormous ratings winner, infotainment on the ABC is generally not the success story of the commercials. Although the ABC got into this genre early, *Gardening Australia* and a string of local and imported cooking shows are now the only survivors. The *Home Show* triggered the Senate Inquiry on ABC Management and Operations because of accusations of back-door advertising. *Holiday* couldn't compete with the rise of glossier commercial versions with bigger budgets and *Everybody* seemed earnest and worthy in comparison with the far raunchier *Sex/Life* on Channel 10.

There is an interesting and complex story to tell about the institutional politics behind the rise of infotainment on the ABC which would investigate this genre's connections with earlier forms of information programming, but I want to focus on other interrelated questions, using the example of *Gardening Australia*. First, in what ways does this show constitute choice as a form of subjectification? Second, how can infotainment on the ABC be understood as a distinctively public service way of approaching this genre? And, finally, how does this show manage the relationship between value and difference?

If we had to identify the dominant mode of address on *Gardening Australia* it would be advice. Nearly every segment combines information with instruction: this is the perfect soil, rose garden, compost heap, etc., and this is how you achieve it. The intimacy and informality of the announcers means that they occupy an ambiguous space between amateur and expert. Amateur in the sense that gardening is a widespread site of everyday creativity marked by informal means of exchange of anything from knowledge to clippings, and expert in the way that authority and skill are invoked in order to promote particular forms of gardening practice and conduct over others. For example, it is assumed on *Gardening Australia* that the proper or well-managed garden has a compost heap. And in this assumption the actively responsible subject is produced, the subject not only willing to learn and seeking personal fulfilment in gardening but also willing and able to initiate 'good' waste regulation techniques. This is *Gardening Australia's* version of ethics.

According to Rose (1992) the rise of the expert is a key aspect of neoliberal forms of governing. He argues that the guidance of selves is no longer a matter of large scale authorities – religion, morality, 'the state' – but rather the province of experts of subjectivity 'who transfigure existential questions about the purpose of life ... into technical questions about the most effective ways of managing malfunction and improving "quality of life"' (1992, p. 142). (It would be hard to get a better description of infotainment than this quote!) There are some problems with Rose's argument about experts, particularly his rather too-neat fit between the operations of expertise and the ends of government. However, there is great value in the way he conceptualises the relationship between subjectivity and choice. The ideal or most highly valued political subject aspires to autonomy and personal responsibility and finds meaning and identity in acts of choice which are not random or irrational but are constrained by particular sorts of allegiances and carefully regulated in the interests of achieving definite objectives: economy, order, virtue or whatever (Rose 1992, p. 143).

Despite the strong generic logic of the infotainment format it is possible to argue that these shows were and are different on the ABC. I am not convinced by the claims that infotainment was a sign of the ABC 'going commercial' or that these shows compromised or contaminated the public service objectives of the national broadcaster. These assessments may be common but they are also glib and inadequate. As we know from the history of the ABC, light entertainment has always been a feature of its television programming, as have information shows. While this programming is little researched or understood, it is important to note that entertainment has never been excluded from PSB, nor is it antithetical to PSB objectives. However, this does not deny the fact that PSB does entertainment differently from commercial stations (as I've argued earlier) or that this form occupies a different place within the overall hierarchy of programs. What is important to understand is how the rise of the very specific genre of 'infotainment' is related not only to rhetorics of choice but also the wider institutional regimes of value surrounding entertainment within the ABC.

As outlined above *Gardening Australia* privileges advice as its dominant mode of address. So too does *Burke's Backyard*, but I think that the form of this advice is different on the ABC. The pedagogic relation that underpins all forms of the giving and receiving of expert information is much more ethically based on *Gardening Australia* than on *Burke's Backyard*. By this I mean that the ways in which practices and choices are regulated on *Gardening Australia* is much more often connected to questions of the 'good': recycling, responsible waste management, growing your own vegetables, protecting the environment, reduction of water use, etc. While there are elements of this on *Burke's Backyard*, highlighting the ways in which the boundaries between commercial and PSB television have definitely blurred, there is still a sense in which the commercial version of infotainment defines choice more in terms of consumer awareness (cf. the road testing pets segment on *Burke's Backyard*) than in terms of ethical practices of the self.

This distinction leads us to questions of value: aesthetic and ethical. *Gardening Australia* naturalises middlebrow taste, its gardens are ordered, pretty, well-maintained, rarely grand. Vulgarity is kept carefully at bay, there are no wild and wacky garden designs, no gnomes or green concreted yards with a lonely oleander in one corner. Aesthetically viewers are invited into a middle-class community where a pretty restricted set of gardening styles prevails. Sure, there are the occasional glances up to grand bourgeois gardens but there are very few glances down, except in the peculiar case of vegetables. Growing vegetables and the do-it-yourself ethos this values is much more difficult to classify; it certainly cannot be pinned down to a neat class division. If anything, growing vegetables fore-grounds questions of ethics rather than aesthetics. It is about certain kinds of relationships to food rather than beauty, literal rather than metaphorical taste. This ethical dimension in *Gardening Australia* shows how complicated the politics of difference are. For while I would argue that *Gardening Australia* denies difference in its privileging of a middlebrow aesthetic, in its denial of the vast diversity of garden forms and styles, it is also at the same time ethically pluralistic. It is open to various styles of conduct and meaning around the vegetable patch: veggies as part of an ethos of self-sufficiency and economy; recognition and tolerance of 'other' veggies (in this case a selection of Asian greens) as part of our multicultural heritage and veggies as part of a green push for chemical-free food.

Take a recent segment on growing olives. In this segment Peter Cundall, the show's host, introduces viewers to Attilio Minnucci, a small landholder in Tasmania's Huon Valley. As Peter and Attilio wander through an olive grove, Peter tells viewers Attilio's story. It's a story of migration, of coming to Tasmania in 1952 and experimenting with olives to find the right ones for the climate. The two then discuss aspects of olive cultivation with the conversation moving between Peter's expert advice and Attilio's more experientially based recommen-dations. The segment ends with Peter urging viewers to plant olives: 'the average Australian backyard is big enough for at least one or two and, after all, Attilio's family have been growing them for five hundred years'. A semiotic reading of this segment would focus on the way in which it reproduces the fairly tired sign of olives standing for Italianicity in particular and ethnicity in general. However, beyond this is an ethical subtext in which difference is both recognised and positively valued. Attilio's story and knowledge are affirmed in this segment in a way that positions viewers as being open to that which they don't know. Peter Cundall sets the tone here with his keenness to hear Attilio's advice, to defer to his amateur expertise. This is an ethics of inclusion predicated on generosity.

How then to make sense of *Gardening Australia*? John Frow (1995, p. 60) argues that one of the crucial elements in all systems of cultural value is the way they organise the play of self and other. In relationship to *Gardening Australia*, then, we can see that aesthetically it others an enormous variety of gardening styles. It is blind to certain forms of gardening diversity and difference: the unashamedly vulgar, scorched-earth regimes, seriously neglected messes. If these are dealt with it is only ever as problems or quaint examples of what to avoid. This is not to say that what's excluded is a 'working class' gardening aesthetic, as if that were some kind of unified and coherent field and as if there were some neat alignment or fit between a class and particular cultural forms. All that can be said is that these silences and exclusions generate a politics of difference, which is also always a politics of value. *Gardening Australia* legitimises a middlebrow notion of what counts as beautiful in the backyard. And in this sense it resonates with a long history of entertainment on the ABC. As I have already outlined, PSB has a distinctive regime of value around entertainment which privileges the middlebrow over the vulgar and information and aesthetics over hedonistic or populist fun. Infotainment on the ABC represents a new site for the extension and innovation of this regime of value. Despite strong generic links with *Burke's Backyard*, the way in which *Gardening Australia* connects information and entertainment is different from the commercial channels precisely because of its specific institutional context and history.

This aesthetic homogeneity is undercut, however, by *Gardening Australia's* ethical diversity. If ethics is about how to define and regulate ourselves according to a moral code, how to conduct and judge our lives, then *Gardening Australia* valorises various types of ethical practices in relation to gardening. It has a pluralistic ethical vocabulary. In this way it is open to various identity projects, various technologies of the self. The garden becomes a site of self-fulfilment, personal choice and responsibility, a space where we can express ourselves according to various moral codes. This logic reorders the relation between PSB and viewer not in terms of a paternalistic or authoritarian reform of the population but in terms of a regulated freedom in which we are governed by the choices we make (Rose 1992, p. 160).

Choosing the ABC

The example of infotainment on the ABC is illuminating, for this minor television genre allows us to think of the relation between governing and the conduct of the self in very productive ways. While many have condemned the ABC for embracing programs that are supposedly the exclusive preserve of the commercials, *Gardening Australia* shows us that there is a distinction between what the ABC and commercial channels mean by 'lifestyle'. While both broadcasting services accept that contemporary forms of personhood demand extensive technical knowledge and skill in the everyday arts of living, the regimes of ethical and aesthetic value that are attached to these various conducts are different on the ABC. The ways in which 'choice' functions as a form of subjectification on the ABC explicitly excludes consumption. The freely choosing subject addressed on *Gardening Australia* is not a shopper seeking useful knowledge of the market but a person whose identity, pleasure and measure of quality in life involves gardening. The issue here is not simply that the ABC is legally prohibited from promoting products. Rather, it is that the forms of choice privileged on *Garden-*

ing Australia are regulated according to the wider discursive history of public service broadcasting. Making the right 'choice' in this context means choosing a middlebrow aesthetic. This is very much in keeping with a long history of entertainment on the ABC that has carefully and consistently kept vulgarity at bay. This means that the exclusions and forms of aesthetic judgement at play in *Gardening Australia* in no way challenge the cultural authority of the ABC. Quality is protected.

However, in the realm of ethics this version of infotainment is valuably pluralistic. There are many different forms of ethical conduct promoted on *Gardening Australia* with many different objectives. These reveal the radical possibilities of choice in the sense that different subjectivities are acknowledged and addressed. They also reveal the ways in which choice as an ethical rather than an aesthetic practice can fundamentally disrupt the ABC's pedagogic authority. The sorts of advice and expertise offered on *Gardening Australia* presume a variety of ethical practices in the backyard: the water-saving garden, the therapeutic garden, the productive garden, etc., and in this recognition of diversity various publics or ethical communities are recognised. The 'Australian people' or 'the nation' as a monolithic pedagogic object becomes impossible to sustain and instead we see how citizenship can be conceived of in terms of a positive valuation of difference

Discourses of choice don't signify the collapse of the ABC. As the case of infotainment reveals, this discourse has contradictory effects which both reproduce and disrupt the traditional authority of the organisation. More significant, however, is the way in which 'choice' represents the ABC's attempts at managing a new problematic of government; audiences who are no longer constituted as ethically incomplete but as ethically diverse.

Notes

1 For a discussion of the Mansfield Report see the special forum in *Media International Australia*, No. 84, May 1997.
2 See Hindess (1996) for a discussion of the complex and various meanings of 'autonomy' in liberalism. Hindess argues that autonomy is represented as both essentially human and as artefactual, as a product of particular governmental practices.
3 The findings of this Senate Select Committee are written up in the report *Our ABC: Report of the Senate Select Committee on ABC Management and Operations* (1995) Commonwealth of Australia, Canberra.

📖 Guide to further reading

For an excellent introduction to debates about the ABC set in the context of Australian television more generally, see Tom O'Regan, *Australian Television Culture* (Sydney: Allen & Unwin, 1993). M. Price, *Television, the Public Sphere and National Identity* (Oxford: Oxford University Press, 1995) relates these issues to the role of television in the public sphere, while M. Raboy (ed.) *Public Service Broadcasting for the Twenty-First Century* (Luton: John Libbey and University of Luton Press, 1996) provides a broader international perspective. *Media International Australia* (no. 83, 1997) 'Your ABC, our ABC, no ABC' is a special issue on the ABC. For the ABC's home page, see www.abc.net.au

References

Ang, Ien (1991) *Desparately Seeking the Audience*, London: Routledge.

Australian Broadcasting Corporation (1980–1997) *Annual Reports*, Canberra: AGPS.

The ABC in Review: National Broadcasting in the 1980s (1981) Canberra: AGPS (commonly referred to as the Dix Report).

Bhabha, Homi (1994) *The Location of Culture*, London: Routledge.

Cruikshank, B. (1999) *The Will to Empower,* New York: Cornell University Press.

Dean, Mitchell (1999) *Governmentality*, London: Sage.

Dix Report, see *The ABC in Review* above.

Foucault, Michel (1988) 'Technologies of the self' in L. Martin, H. Gutman and P. Hutton (eds) *Technologies of the Self: A Seminar with Michel Foucault,* Amherst: University of Massachusetts Press, pp. 16–49.

— (1991) 'Governmentality' in Graham Burchell, Colin Gordon and Peter Miller (eds) *The Foucault Effect*, Hertfordshire: Harvester Wheatsheaf, pp. 87–104.

Frith, Simon (1983) 'The pleasures of the hearth' in *Formations of Pleasure,* London: Routledge and Kegan Paul, pp. 101–23.

Frow, John (1995) *Cultural Studies and Cultural Value*, Oxford: Clarendon.

Hill, R. (1994) 'Has the ABC lost the plot?' *Bulletin*, 7 June.

Hindess, Barry (1996) 'Liberalism, socialism and democracy: variations on a governmental theme' in Andrew Barry, Thomas Osborne and Nikolas Rose (eds) *Foucault and Political Reason*, London: University of Chicago Press and UCL Press, pp. 65–80.

Inglis, Ken (1997) 'ABC shock crisis threat', *Media International Australia* 83.

Mansfield, Bob (1997) *The Challenge of a Better ABC*, Canberra: AGPS.

McHoul, Alec (1996) *Semiotic Investigations*, Lincoln: University of Nebraska Press.

Parliament of the Commonwealth of Australia (1995) *Our ABC: Report of the Senate Select Committee on ABC Management and Operations*, Canberra: Commonwealth of Australia.

Rose, Nikolas (1992) 'Governing the enterprising self' in P. Heelas and P. Morris (eds) *The Values of the Enterprise Culture*, London: Routledge, pp. 141–64.

— (1996) 'Governing "advanced" liberal democracies' in Andrew Barry, Thomas Osborne and Nikolas Rose (eds) *Foucault and Political Reason*, London: University of Chicago Press & UCL Press, pp. 37–64.

— (1999) *Powers of Freedom*, Cambridge: Cambridge University Press.

Rose, Nikolas and Peter Miller (1992) 'Political power beyond the state: problematics of government', *British Journal of Sociology* 43, 2, pp. 173–205.

Chapter 9

Social Class and Cultural Practice in Contemporary Australia

Tony Bennett, Michael Emmison and John Frow

Discussing the role of class in Australian social, cultural and political life has always involved taking issue with those traditions which maintain either that Australia does not have classes or, if it does, that no one pays them much attention. When sociologists write about class, for example, they usually begin by acknowledging the force of this national trait, accounting for its origins and continuing influence in terms of the distinctive dynamics of Australian social development and, at the same time, discounting it as prejudice, as myth, by marshalling the evidence – that has never been wanting – pointing to the existence of enduring and deep-seated social inequalities. This is how Bob Connell and Terry Irving (1992) begin their *Class Structure in Australian History*, offering an account of the belief in Australian classlessness which relates it to the specific history of class formation in Australia and the racial dynamics of a frontier society. John Western (1991) performs a similar role, clearing the ground for a discussion of the structure of class relationships in contemporary Australia by engaging critically with those traditions of Australian political culture which mistake egalitarian aspirations for outcomes.

This aspiration against class – for, in its utopian forms, that is what this belief amounts to – has always had a particular salience in debates about, and attitudes toward, Australian culture. Inequalities in the distribution of productive resources, and in the income and wealth derived from these, have usually been more readily conceded than the further contention that class might matter culturally. The absence of an aristocracy and landed gentry, and the absence – indeed, active opposition to – the forms of deference associated with European class practice and experience, have contributed, Connell and Irving suggest, to a

193

widespread belief in the levelling of cultures and manners (1992, pp. 11–12). This has given rise to a cultural egalitarianism which, if it accepts that cultural practices are marked by class, is likely to see this as just a matter of taste, ranking all cultural practices equally and seeing little connection between cultural questions and the economic, social or political aspects of class power.

The effects of this tendency to downplay the significance of class have been compounded in recent years by the considerably diminished significance that is now accorded questions of social class in contemporary social theory. There are a number of reasons for this: postmodernism has tumbled classes from their earlier role as the leading actors in grand narratives of historical development, while developments in feminism and studies of race and ethnicity have stressed the centrality of other social differences and divisions, detaching these from their earlier subordination to class divisions. What Jan Pakulski and Malcolm Waters (1996, p. 10) call the 'proposition of behavioural and cultural linkage' that had, in earlier formulations of class theory, connected class membership to questions of cultural consciousness, lifestyle and identity, has also been called into question. The proliferation of consumer-generated taste cultures has, it is argued, undone earlier divisions between class-marked cultures, replacing them with a multiplicity of lifestyles and cultural identities which increasingly lack any anchorage in, or relation to, clear social referents outside the commercial processes which generate them.

True though all of this may be, the vocabulary of class has been very much to the fore in the major Australian public debates of the late 1990s. It was activated, in complex and contradictory ways, by the rhetorical strategies of Pauline Hanson and the One Nation Party in their appeal to an older sense of white, Anglo-Celtic, working-class solidarities in opposition to what Ghassan Hage (1998, p. 201) characterises as the classed (largely middle-class and professional) figure of the cosmopolitan multiculturalist. A similar set of class coordinates was evident during, and in the immediate aftermath of, the republican debate. In the wake of the constitutional referendum held in November 1999 a number of commentators characterised the vote as manifesting a division between two distinctive class formations in Australian society. Paul Kelly wrote in the *Australian* (8.11.99) of a split between 'two different societies – a confident, educated, city-based middle class and a pessimistic, urban and rural battler constituency hostile to the 1990s change agenda' (p. 1). Dennis Shanahan, writing in the same issue, posited a division 'between the more affluent inner-city dwellers, who feel more secure about the economy and the future, and the less-well-off rural and regional people, who are faced with uncertainty about jobs and threatened by change' (p. 4). Moreover, these class divisions were typically invoked in a cultural form as a clash between ways of life marked in the distinction between 'the chardonnay set' and the 'beer and sausages' ethos of the battlers.[1]

This is, of course, a fairly crude form of class analysis, which takes account neither of the heterogeneity of both the republican and the monarchist vote, nor of the complexity of actual class formations and of their intersection with other dimensions of social difference such as age and gender. It does nevertheless pick up one of the dominant patterns of cultural practice which emerge from a study we conducted in the mid 1990s (Bennett, Emmison and Frow 1999).[2] For our evidence – derived from a nationwide survey of 2,756 adult Australians – demonstrates a clear differentiation between an *inclusive* mode of cultural practice, in which people participate actively in a wide range of activities and possess broad competencies across both 'high' and 'low' culture, and a *restricted* mode, in which participation is relatively passive and confined to relatively narrow areas. The inclusive mode is most strongly correlated with high levels of education, with urbanity, with youth and with women rather than men; its core class is the professional class. The restricted mode is associated with low levels of education, with rural and regional Australia, with age, and with men rather than women, and it is most clearly exemplified in the manual working class. We might call this – again simplifying drastically – a contrast between the 'knowledge classes' which have arisen since the 1960s, and the 'old classes' which were formed in the agricultural and industrial economies that are now in various stages of decline.

Our evidence points, then, to a strong cultural divide between an older, less educated, less urban, and lower income group which (to take a few cogent examples) doesn't frequent restaurants, chooses its friends from amongst its neighbours rather than its work colleagues, and isn't particularly interested in international travel; and a younger, higher income, better educated and more urban group whose cultural interests and practices are more varied, and more confident, than those of the group to which it is diametrically opposed. We must stress that things are always more complex than this, and that this pattern looks somewhat different in each area of cultural practice. What does remain constant, though, is the central role of education in forming this pattern of cultural distinction and organising its relationship to social classes. The form that this connection takes, however, varies across different regions of cultural practice. Here we look at three – participation in sports, musical tastes, and reading practices – before returning to consider how these relations of class and culture inform the changing forms of social division in contemporary Australia.

Class, sports and the body

Cultural practices and choices are always positional: they help us to define who we are in relation to those with whom we identify and those from whom we wish to differentiate ourselves. They are thus always over-determined by positional struggles, and perhaps nowhere with more intensity than in those areas of symbolic differentiation where differences are the most arbitrary and therefore the most willed. In many ways the most fundamental of these is the social imaginary of the body, the ground for all those formations of the self that proceed by way of attention to, training of and pleasure in the body.

Our most salient examples of class-differentiation in relation to the body come from two dimensions of sport: first, the pattern of oppositions formed between those who do and those who do not play sport; second, the pattern of oppositions between those who participate in sport and those who are spectators. When, with regard to the first of these questions, we consider the class composition of sports participation we find a pattern in which a particular class or a small cluster of classes predominates in the playing of a sport. The full table of participation by class in the ten most popular participant sports is given in Table 1.[3]

Table 2 identifies, for each class, the sports in which they predominate. The salient feature of this list is the absolute predominance of the two most highly educated classes, professionals and managers, in five sports, and their shared predominance in three others. These are clear indicators of the formative role of cultural capital – that is, of those officially valued cultural and intellectual skills which, selectively distributed by the education system, serve as the means for occupational advancement and preferment – in guiding participation in sport.

Table 1 Participation in sports by class (aggregated column percentages)

	Employer	Self-employed	Man-ager	Profes-sional	Para-profes-sional	Super-visor	Sales/clerical	Man-ual	Mean
Tennis	14.0	18.4	18.8	29.4	17.3	16.5	16.2	14.2	16.4
Golf	17.7	18.0	28.3	12.0	14.4	13.8	8.4	10.3	13.1
Swimming	7.6	9.2	9.7	20.2	14.5	11.6	14.3	7.8	11.3
Walking	6.0	6.7	8.4	9.4	7.0	4.8	10.6	4.6	6.7
Squash	4.4	5.1	9.3	6.6	9.0	9.9	5.3	5.1	5.7
Touch F'ball	3.7	3.9	1.7	4.8	7.7	4.4	3.6	10.7	5.4
Cricket	3.1	4.9	8.7	6.7	5.2	6.7	3.4	6.0	4.9
Netball	0.0	1.6	2.3	3.0	5.3	2.3	12.6	3.0	4.7
Aerobics	1.9	2.5	1.4	6.3	3.4	1.5	7.6	2.2	3.7
Lawn Bowls	2.4	4.9	8.6	1.9	1.2	4.7	4.1	2.7	3.5

Table 2 Classes predominating in particular sports

professionals:	tennis, swimming
sales/clerical workers and professionals:	aerobics
managers:	golf, cricket, lawn bowls
managers, paraprofessionals and supervisors:	squash
sales/clerical workers:	netball
sales/clerical, professionals and managers:	walking

One final pattern is a negative one: the class with the highest degree of cultural capital, that of professionals, scores below the mean on only three sports: touch football, netball and lawn bowls. This datum allows us to construct the upper and lower extremes of a hierarchy of cultural value ranging from tennis and swimming at the top to touch football and netball at the bottom. However, the complexity of the relations between class and culture does not allow any simple categorisation of the intermediate sports.

When we look at the other end of the participation spectrum, perhaps the most striking aspect of the group (36.6 per cent of our sample) which declares that it never plays sport is the strong negative correlation with level of education that is seen in Table 3. To put this correlation in positive terms, the more educated you are, the more likely you are to participate in sports. In class terms, employers and manual workers are the strongest non-players, while managers are at the opposite end of the scale, followed by professionals (Table 4).

Women score higher on this negative scale than men (40.3 per cent to 32.8 per cent). As might be expected, there is a regular correlation between non-participation and increasing age, and those with no children at home are much less likely to play a sport. People without formal education and those who attended state schools are above the mean for non-participation, and those from private schools are well below it. The poorer you are, the less likely you are to play a sport. Those from the suburbs and the country play less sport than those who live elsewhere, while migrants and Aborigines play less than the non-Aboriginal Australian-born. As Jim McKay (1991, p. 11) summarises it, 'sport is participated in by predominantly young, affluent and relatively well-educated male Australians'.

If we turn now to the distinction between playing and watching sports some equally striking results appear. Consider, for example, the breakdown of the overall spectatorship of sports by the different social classes given in Table 5.

Table 3 Non-participation in sport by level of education

Primary	Some secondary	Completed secondary	Vocational/ apprenticeship	Part tertiary	Completed tertiary	Mean
57.4	47.5	33.7	36.0	28.3	25.3	36.6

Table 4 Non-participation in sport by class

Employer	Self-employed	Man-ager	Profes-sional	Para-profes-sional	Super-visor	Sales/ Clerical	Manual	Mean
42.6	33.0	18.3	28.7	33.4	33.7	34.0	41.4	36.6

Table 5 Watch sports regularly at live venues, by class (means for all sports)

Employer	Self-employed	Man-ager	Profes-sional	Para-profes-sional	Super-visor	Sales/ Clerical	Manual	Mean
4.4	4.5	5.1	3.1	3.9	6.2	4.9	6.6	5.0

Table 5 represents almost a reversal of the corresponding pattern for *participation* in sport, at least at the outer limits. If we take the corresponding percentage means for all sports played, the comparative rank order of classes for participation and for spectatorship is as given in Figure 1.

Those classes, like the professionals and paraprofessionals, which had scored very high on the playing of sport, score very low on watching it, whereas manual workers, who play little sport, watch it a great deal. The reversal is not, of course, complete: employers neither play nor watch much sport, and managers, supervisors, and sales and clerical workers retain a relatively strong position on both scales. But the value hierarchy which led from the most educated to the least educated classes has been substantially reversed. Here, again, that dichotomy between, on the one hand, inclusive and more active forms of cultural practice and, on the other, more restricted and passive modes of cultural involvement that we spoke of earlier is strongly in evidence. The same is true of the distribution of musical tastes, albeit in a different form which attests more to the strength of the inclusive/restricted opposition than – as we have seen is the case with sport – the distinction between active and (relatively speaking) passive forms of cultural practice.

Class and musical tastes

Musical tastes have figured prominently in investigations of the relationship between class and culture. At least two rival versions of the relationship currently vie for attention. One, whose provenance can be traced to Herbert Gans's work (1966, 1974) on 'taste cultures' and their publics, sees an isomorphism between class and taste structures. At one end of the social scale stands an economically privileged class whose cultural tastes are largely centred around 'highbrow' genres: in the case of music a preference for opera, classical music and symphony orchestras coupled with a simultaneous rejection of the popular or commercial musical genres favoured by the majority. Perhaps the clearest formulation of this position is that of Pierre Bourdieu (1984) for whom musical tastes can be viewed as the markers *par excellence* of participation in a bourgeois class culture.[4]

The value of such elite-to-mass taste dichotomies has recently been questioned by researchers who have proposed a different relationship governing the

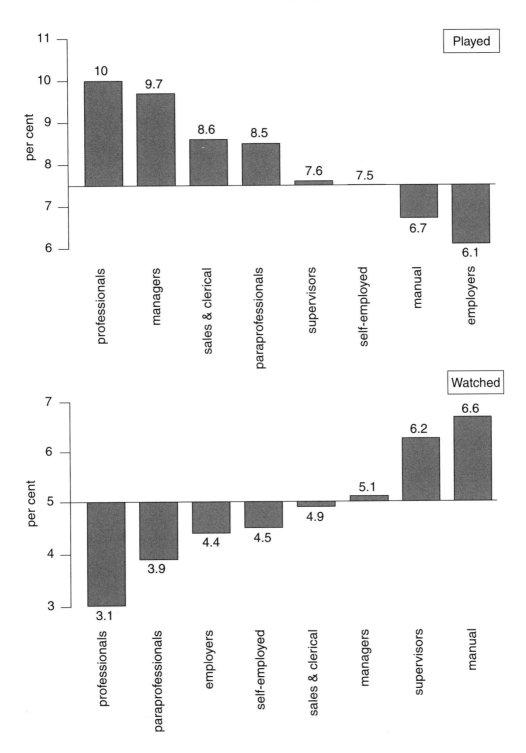

Figure 1 Percentage means for sports played and sports watched at live venues, by class (relations to the overall mean)

social distribution of tastes. In this latter view (DiMaggio 1987; Peterson 1992; Peterson and Simkus 1992; Peterson and Kern 1996) the members of the higher social classes are viewed more as omnivorous cultural consumers, favouring not only the traditional elite musical genres but also the popular musical forms which the earlier theoretical position saw them as necessarily rejecting. These omnivorous tastes are held to flow from the more diffuse cultures and networks in which the members of these classes participate (DiMaggio 1987; Relish 1997). By contrast, cultural tastes are held to become progressively more 'univorous' or restricted the lower down the class ladder we go.

What light does our research throw on these contrasting accounts of the relations between class and musical tastes? There is certainly evidence suggesting support for an elite-to-mass model. For example in Figure 2 we present the findings concerning attendance at opera according to class location as represented by the combined percentage of each class who indicated that they attended 'often' or 'sometimes'. Here the resulting class gradient flows from those richest in economic capital, by virtue either of direct ownership of, or administrative control over, productive resources, to those lacking both.

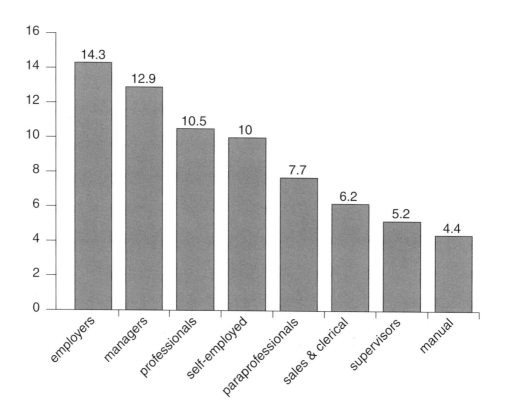

Figure 2 Attendance at opera by class

However it is not difficult to find contrary evidence which suggests that such class-based patronage may have more to do with conspicuous consumption of prestigious events than with any deep-seated aesthetic appreciation of the genre. In answer to a question concerning their favourite musician, singer or composer, employers thus revealed very little interest in 'elite' performers and recorded a strikingly similar profile to that of manual workers in the pattern of their responses (see Figure 3).

Is a more clear-cut pattern of relations between class and musical taste evident when we look at the class distribution of genre preferences? In Figure 4 we look at how our respondents' first preferences for classical and country and western music – genres representing the poles of the musical taste hierarchy – vary by class location. As we can see, when aesthetic criteria – as opposed to claims to prestige through patronage of elite art forms – come to the fore, the class gradient takes on a rather different character. The key data here are those of the extremes of the figure: the preference of manual workers for country and western music coupled with their minimal interest in classical music, and the inverse of these relationships in the case of professionals. Again, these data offer some support for Gans's and Bourdieu's models, with the proviso that it is the cultural rather than the economic capital of professionals – and the absence of both in the case of manual workers – which is at the root of these relationships.

However what these figures do not reveal is that the favourite musical genre for *all* social classes is neither country and western nor classical music but the archetypal 'middlebrow' form: 'easy listening'. Moreover, two other genres – 'top-40 pop' and 'rock' – both have higher mean preference ratings than country and western and classical music. The widespread support for these popular musical forms suggests it may be more useful to theorise Australian musical tastes

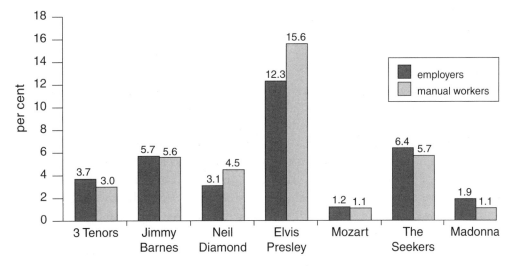

Figure 3 Similarities in musical tastes of employers and manual workers

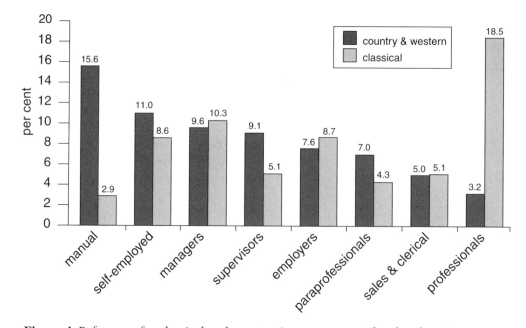

Figure 4 References for classical and country & western music by class location

through the omnivore-univore distinction than the 'snob-to-slob' or elite-to-mass model. For Richard Peterson, the defining characteristic of a music omnivore is someone whose musical tastes embrace quite distinct classifications: an individual, that is, who likes musical genres conventionally regarded as 'highbrow' as well as those seen as 'middlebrow' or 'lowbrow'. A musical highbrow, on the basis of our survey results, emerges as someone whose first, second and third preferences in music combine – in any order – opera, classical and light classical genres. Easy listening, musicals and big band music constitute our middlebrow genres. Finally, we define the lowbrow category as comprising a preference for country and western, rock and top-40 pop, again in any order.

An omnivore, then, is someone whose musical preferences cross these taste boundaries. Seen in these terms there are, in fact, several possible types of omnivore to be found, depending on how these movements are mapped. We use the term 'highbrow' omnivore to refer to someone whose three preferred musical genres consist of any *two* highbrow genres and any *one* of the various lowbrow genres. A 'lowbrow' omnivore, by contrast, is someone whose three favourite types of music are a mixture of any *two* lowbrow genres and any *one* of the highbrow music types. Finally there is the complete or 'ideal type' omnivore: someone whose three favourite music genres are drawn from *each* of the highbrow, middlebrow and lowbrow categories. To simplify the following analysis we shall deal only with the numerically most numerous 'lowbrow' and 'ideal type' omnivores.

Table 6 shows the rank order by class location for both lowbrow and ideal-type omnivores. The most surprising aspect of these findings – running quite

Table 6 Class composition of omnivore types

Percentage of class category classified as omnivore type (Rank order by class location)

'Lowbrow' omnivore		'Ideal type' omnivore	
Sales and clerical	33.9	Paraprofessionals	16.5
Manual	33.7	Managers	13.2
Paraprofessionals	27.9	Enployers	11.1
Supervisors	25.5	Supervisors	8.8
Self-employed	19.2	Sales and clerical	7.6
Managers	18.7	Self-employed	7.2
Employers	17.9	Professionals	6.7
Professionals	11.7	Manual	3.8

contrary to the expectations engendered by Peterson's theories – is that, with the exception of manual workers, professionals contain the lowest number of ideal-type omnivores.

How can we account for this apparent inconsistency? Is Peterson wrong in suggesting that people with the most cultural capital are the most likely source of omnivorous taste? One way of resolving this question is to deal separately with two categories which are analytically fused in Peterson's work. For Peterson 'the elaborated musical taste code of the omnivore member of the elite can *acclaim* classical music and yet, in the proper context, show *passing knowledge* of a wide range of musical forms' (Peterson 1992, p. 255; emphasis added). Peterson appears, in short, to slip between talking about 'preferences' and 'knowledge'. Omnivores acclaim classical music – this is the form of music they 'really' like best; but they are also knowledgeable about many other genres. However the question of whether or not they *like* these other genres to the same extent is not really considered. Our data suggest that those most eligible for omnivore status on the basis of their higher cultural credentials do not in fact *like* the range of genres that Peterson predicts. But are they *knowledgeable* about these musical forms? Two further questions from our survey can help us answer this question. Our respondents were asked if they were familiar with a range of musical works and if they could identify the name of the performer, composer or songwriter with whom the work is associated. Ten works of classical music and seventeen works designed to cover the range of contemporary popular genres were provided. The relevant data from these questions are given in Tables 7 and 8.

From Table 7 we can see that professionals clearly have the greatest familiarity with the world of classical music. They are the least likely to know none of the works, and three times as likely as the average to be familiar with eight or more. A familiarity with works of popular music (Table 8) is more widespread, but professionals are again the ones whose knowledge is most extensive. Fewer professionals than any other group report not knowing any items on the list; they

Table 7 Knowledge of musical works: 'high culture' (row per cent)

Class category	None	1–2	3–4	5–7	>8
Employers	30.1	19.6	21.8	21.1	7.5
Self-employed	29.2	18.4	24.6	22.2	5.7
Managers	15.4	19.8	20.9	34.1	9.9
Professionals	10.8	14.9	21.3	30.2	22.9
Paraprofessionals	23.5	15.0	26.6	30.1	4.7
Supervisors	28.0	23.7	24.9	17.1	6.2
Sales & clerical	29.6	20.8	25.6	19.6	4.4
Manual	44.6	25.7	18.3	9.6	1.9
Mean	**28.8**	**20.4**	**23.2**	**20.5**	**7.1**

Table 8 Knowledge of musical works: 'popular culture' (row per cent)

Class category	None	1–3	4–6	7–8	9–11	>12
Employers	13.5	20.3	20.3	25.6	19.6	0.8
Self-employed	13.7	22.7	23.0	16.3	18.6	5.7
Managers	7.7	20.9	19.8	27.5	18.7	5.5
Professionals	5.1	13.3	24.1	25.1	24.4	7.9
Paraprofessionals	7.0	17.4	28.2	22.5	18.3	6.6
Supervisors	8.4	13.7	27.4	24.0	21.5	6.2
Sales & clerical	6.0	17.1	27.5	21.3	21.5	6.5
Manual	15.0	21.7	25.3	16.8	16.6	4.7
Mean	**9.7**	**18.3**	**25.3**	**21.0**	**19.9**	**4.7**

are marginally more likely than others to be familiar with twelve or more works, and almost a third (32.3 per cent) recognise nine or more.

Our examination of the musical interests of Australians has pointed to a crucial difference between their tastes and their knowledge – something never recognised as an issue by Bourdieu and analytically blurred in Peterson's work. 'Omnivorousness', we argue, is better understood in terms of a knowledge base rather than any deep affinity for a range of music genres. Peterson is partly correct in his view that univorous tastes are more likely to be found among those nearer the base of the socio-economic order, but we have also found this to be a characteristic of professionals' musical tastes as well. Manual workers and professionals may not like the same types of music, but what both have in common is a tendency to make their selections from amongst aesthetically similar genres: more highbrow in the case of professionals, more lowbrow in the case of workers. Both have, in our terms, tastes which are more restricted than other classes. Where they differ is in their command of musical cultures. Manual workers remain more restricted than other classes in the knowledge they have of both classical and popular music; in contrast, professionals have a much more inclusive knowledge of both of these realms.

Although sport and music are generally not considered to be cultural domains with obvious affinities, on the basis of the evidence we have reviewed so far it is tempting to speculate about the possibility of some unexpected homologies, particularly in relation to the participation of professionals. With regard to sport, professionals are active players but unlikely to be found as spectators at live sports venues. Our research also indicates that professionals are the class with the most active musical lives: musical instruments are most likely to be found in the homes of professionals and they are twice as likely as other Australians to play them on a regular basis. With regard to the consumption of music, professionals, as we have seen, are knowledgeable about many different genres although their actual tastes are much more restricted. Although we have no data on this issue we think it likely that professionals might also – for much the same reasons which generate their expansive musical knowledge – exhibit a similar scholastic familiarity with the world of sport: that is, to be able to name such things as national team captains, recount landmark results in the sporting calendar or the trophies for which different sports compete and so on. In short it is possible to think of professionals very much as the 'knowledge class' in that the manipulation and collection of information applies not only to their work but to their cultural pursuits as well.

Class, reading and literature

Similar tendencies are evident in the class distribution of literary tastes. The class which is dominant in terms of its economic position – employers – tends to be middle of the range in terms of the aesthetic weighting of its literary preferences. If professionals exhibit the highest levels of involvement in literary culture, manual workers have very little connection with the literary world. Table 9, comparing rates of ownership of different types of book, offers a good measure of these differences. The high rate of difference – 70 per cent compared with 49 per cent – between the means for professionals and employers is especially revealing: it makes clear the lack of a close fit between the distribution of literary forms of cultural capital and the distribution of economic forms of class power.

Similar patterns are evident when we consider the class distribution of genre preferences. Table 10 assigns genres to classes on the basis of the class with which they are most strongly associated compared with the average for all other classes. It is notable that, except for poetry (a somewhat ambiguous genre, encompassing aesthetic forms, religious verse, and doggerel), which is most strongly associated with employers, the high literary genres (classical authors, contemporary novels, historical writing and biography, for example) are most clearly associated with professionals. The genres of popular fiction which enjoy

Table 9 Ownership of type of book by class

	Employers	Self-employed	Mana-gers	Profes-sionals	Para-profes-sionals	Super-visors	Sales/clerical workers	Manual workers
Literary classics	52.1	46.9	57.0	79.8	47.1	40.3	47.3	28.2
Art books	36.1	38.8	46.1	52.2	33.6	31.5	33.6	22.8
History books	58.3	59.2	75.6	76.1	53.0	56.5	52.8	43.7
Biographies	53.3	55.2	75.3	78.0	50.0	51.7	49.0	35.6
Poetry	45.1	45.1	49.9	65.0	36.3	39.9	43.3	29.7
Mean	**49.0**	**49.1**	**60.8**	**70.2**	**44.0**	**43.9**	**45.2**	**32.0**

the highest status – crime and science fiction – are most strongly associated with managers and supervisors, while those genres which are most likely to be disparaged as trite or worthless are liked most by sales and clerical workers (romance fiction) and manual workers (horror and erotica).

It is important, when considering figures of this kind, to take account of the gender make-up of these different class categories, especially the marked predominance of men (65 per cent) among employers, the self-employed, managers and manual workers; and the predominance of women among supervisors and, in particular, sales and clerical workers (81 per cent). This raises the question, when gender and class are considered together, of their respective roles in determining reading practices. Table 11 throws some light on this question. The first column tells us how likely it is that men of a particular class will read a particular genre compared with women from the same class. In the case of managers, where 32.7 per cent of men read crime fiction and 38.8 per cent of women, men are 84 per cent as likely to read crime fiction as women. The plus sign for male-to-female ratios of preferences in this column indicates that this ratio is significantly higher than the male-to-female ratio of the sample average for all classes, given in the second column. The high male-to-female ratio of preferences for humour among the self-employed is thus merely a more extreme manifestation of the male preference for this genre that is evident at the level of the whole sample. A minus sign indicates that the ratio of men to women readers is significantly less than that for the sample as a whole. Whereas men for example are, on the whole, more likely to include thrillers in their favourite reading than women, this is not true for managers, where women's preference for this genre outweigh men's. An equals sign indicates that there is no significant difference between the class-specific and the sample ratios.

There is, of course, little to be served by emphasising the role of class in organising reading practices at the expense of the role of gender: both are important. But Table 11 does allow us to distinguish the ways in which – for different classes – class and gender interact. It tells us that, in the case of both types of deviation from the sample norm discussed above, reading is subject to a specific class effect that is manifested in the distinctive articulation of gendered preferences that it organises. That said, the meaning and significance of this class effect is sometimes obscure. What aspects of the class situation of working-class women would account for their particularly strong liking for horror stories? Why should occult literature be so popular with male paraprofessionals? If the answers to these questions are not clear there are, in other cases, some speculations that might be advanced. It seems likely, for example, that, for women managers, a preference

Table 10 Genre preferences by class

	Strongest class preference	Average of other class preferences	Strongest preference as % of average preference
EMPLOYERS			
Poetry	5.2	3.1	168
SELF-EMPLOYED			
Humour/comedy	18.1	15.3	118
MANAGERS			
Crime/murder/mystery	34.3	25.0	137
Thriller/adventure	40.6	35.6	114
PROFESSIONALS			
Classical authors	13.7	4.4	311
Contemporary novels	28.8	12.4	232
Political	5.5	3.0	183
Historical	19.0	10.6	179
Craft/hobbies	16.0	10.6	151
Biographies	26.2	18.4	142
Educational	14.9	10.8	138
Scientific	6.8	5.2	130
PARAPROFESSIONALS			
Occult	3.2	1.7	188
Travel, exploration	19.2	12.8	150
SUPERVISORS			
Science fiction	13.3	9.2	145
SALES AND CLERICAL			
Romance	28.8	9.9	291
Historical romance	13.2	7.7	171
Cooking	18.9	11.4	166
MANUAL			
Horror	7.2	3.4	212
Gardening	17.6	9.2	191
Sport & leisure	19.1	12.1	158
Erotica	4.9	3.4	144

Table 11 Genre preferences by class and gender

	Male as % of Female (class specific)	Male as ratio of Female (sample average, all classes)
EMPLOYERS		
Poetry	36 (=)	34
SELF-EMPLOYED		
Humour	188 (+)	132
MANAGERS		
Crime/murder/mystery	84 (=)	79
Thriller/adventure	81 (−)	115
PROFESSIONALS		
Classical authors	44 (=)	44
Contemporary novels	33 (=)	29
Political	721 (+)	418
Historical	230 (+)	176
Craft/hobbies	78 (+)	55
Biographies	53 (=)	57
Educational	57 (−)	98
Scientific	734 (+)	591
PARAPROFESSIONALS		
Occult	135 (+)	94
Travel, exploration	322 (+)	173
SUPERVISORY		
Science fiction	266 (=)	279
SALES AND CLERICAL		
Romances	7 (=)	7
Historical romance	8 (=)	7
Cooking	39 (+)	25
MANUAL		
Horror	95 (−)	126
Garden	115 (=)	116
Sport & leisure	797 (=)	815
Erotica	228 (−)	414

for thrillers is part and parcel of a habitus in which, in order to operate effectively within a predominantly male class milieu, tastes and preferences are regularly masculinised. The forms of identification (usually male) associated with thrillers may also resonate well with the situation of women exercising senior forms of responsibility in the workplace: a form of 'power reading' which functions as the literary equivalent of power dressing. The most systematic set of class effects, however, is registered in relation to professionals in the unusually strong male bias toward factual and documentary genres – political, historical, and scientific – that this class exhibits. Of course, women professionals retain a marked prefer-

ence for aesthetic literary genres, but this is no more true of women professionals than it is of women as a whole.

Class publics, cultural policies and social divisions

Class, then, to borrow a phrase from Erik Olin Wright (1997), counts; and it
counts culturally. The pattern of the distribution of forms of cultural participation and of the cultural tastes and preferences that go along with them is one
which, while it has many other aspects, has a clear class logic. This is governed
by two main principles. First, the range of cultural interests and activities
increases in direct proportion to the extent to which class position depends on
the acquisition of selectively transmitted educational skills and qualifications.
This principle, as we have seen, is a general one applying to pretty well all forms
of culture irrespective of whether they are classified as highbrow, middlebrow or
lowbrow, or whether they are mainly intellectual pursuits or bodily practices.
But – to come to the second principle – the extent of these differences tends to
increase when it comes to intellectual and aesthetic forms of high culture.

We can confirm this by considering the class composition of the publics that are
recruited by various kinds of publicly subsidised arts and culture and comparing
these with the clientele for private arts markets and the audiences for commercial
media. This is the work performed by Table 12 where the category of *subsidised
culture* refers to a set of cultural activities – usually of a high cultural status – which,
while receiving varying levels of government funding and also falling within the
official purview of arts or cultural policies, usually also have to apply entry charges
or seek sponsorship to supplement their income from the tax roll. The organisation
of this set of activities is thus a hybrid one in which principles of public ownership
and subsidy, and the operation of market forces and private sponsorship, are
combined in varying permutations. The activities in question are attending public
musical performances, public lectures, orchestral concerts, chamber music, ballet,
musicals, opera, theatre and cultural festivals. The category of *public culture* refers
to activities associated with a range of public spaces – art galleries, museums,
botanical gardens, public libraries – which still rely mostly on government funding,
even though some museums now apply entry charges to supplement their support
from public sources. The figures for *public broadcasting* focus on the make-up of
the audiences for ABC television and SBS. These involve a different set of relations
again since, although both ABC television and SBS (even with sponsorship) are
mainly reliant on public funding, their reception takes place in the private sphere
of the home. We also include the ABC in view of the requirement that is placed on
it to include serious drama, classical music, opera, documentary and current affairs
in its programming.[5] As a counterpoint to the different forms of public culture
represented by these three categories, we also look, under the category of *private
culture*, at the class distribution of the ownership of a selective range of

Table 12 Class compositions of public and private cultural sectors

	Subsidised culture: participation in often or sometimes	Public culture: visiting often or sometimes	Public broadcasting (ABC, SBS): watching mainly or regularly	Private culture: ownership of high-culture objects and artifacts	Commercial culture: watch commercial television mainly or regularly
Employers	18.9	27.1	32.0	23.5	40.5
Self-employed	18.4	33.2	34.3	22.6	41.1
Managers	22.1	43.2	38.6	28.2	39.9
Professionals	25.9	51.2	43.2	37.5	24.1
Paraprofessionals	17.4	39.7	27.0	23.7	46.6
Supervisors	16.1	33.1	26.4	19.8	48.1
Sales/clerical	16.6	31.9	21.8	20.8	54.8
Manual	10.0	22.1	22.1	12.8	55.8
Professionals as % manual	**259**	**232**	**195**	**293**	**43**

high-culture objects and artifacts: limited-edition prints, sculptures, art posters, large collections of books, literary classics, art books and pianos. Finally, as an example of the operation of mass culture markets, we look at the class composition of the audience for commercial television.

The effects of class are most marked in relation to, first, the realm of private culture, and second, that of subsidised culture. In both cases the highest rates of participation are associated with professionals and the lowest with manual workers. Indeed, this is true for most of the groups, thus confirming the general division we have noted between the new 'knowledge classes' and older class formations rooted in industrial and agricultural economies. What are we to make of figures of this kind? On one reading, they present a good case for the public subsidy of aesthetic and intellectual forms of high culture in suggesting its capacity – by broadening access – to make class count for somewhat less than it might otherwise in this region of cultural practice. On another reading, however, it might be argued that the degree of class differentiation in the rates of use of the publicly funded cultural sector is large enough to call into question the rationale for public support in these areas. Don't – on these figures – public broadcasting, public culture and publicly subsidised culture tend in the same direction as private cultural markets in delivering an appreciable class advantage to the professional, managerial and employing classes? And, if this is so, what ground can there be for the continuing subsidy of these cultural activities?

These are not hypothetical questions. They have been at the centre of debates focused on the equity and access objectives of cultural policies since the 1970s.

As such, the responses they have elicited have varied. These have included the largely optimistic 1986 House of Representatives report *Power, Patronage and the Muse* which, while recognising class-based divisions in the cultural sphere, viewed increased funding (if properly targeted at the culturally disadvantaged) as a means of attenuating, if not overcoming, these divisions. This was countered by the more sceptical tone of the Department of Finance's 1989 discussion paper *What Price Heritage?* which favoured the introduction of user-pays principles to help cover the private benefit the middle classes derived from their high rates of use of the public cultural sector. More recently, access and equity objectives have tended to be translated into the language of audience development that charac-terised the cultural policies of the final years of the Keating Government, as well as those of the Coalition Government.

As our figures lack the crucial dimension of a comparison through time that would make it possible to assess the effects of different policy environments, they do not allow definitive answers to these questions. But they do make it clear that, whatever might be the intentions of governments in the matter, an active and broad use of publicly subsidised cultural resources does distinguish the cultural practices of the 'knowledge classes' from those of most other classes and, thereby, serve as a means of marking the social distinction that they derive from the cultural capital acquired during the course of their educational and profes-sional careers. It is clear, also, that this is largely the light in which the members of other classes see the matter. As Figure 5 shows, professionals are the only class who think that the arts should receive more funding. While managers are more or less equally divided on this question, a substantial majority of all the other classes believe that public arts funding is already at too high a level.

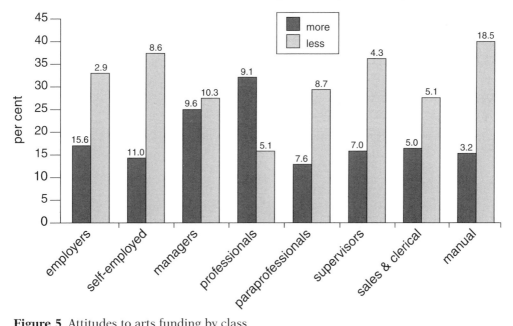

Figure 5 Attitudes to arts funding by class

There is a strong tendency, noted by Tim Rowse (1985) in *Arguing the Arts*, for arts constituencies and lobby groups to discount figures of this kind in favour of more general arguments for arts support that are not so vulnerable to the light that statistics can throw on the social articulations of arts practices and their audiences. This is, in our view, unacceptable. Although the conclusions to be drawn from it may vary, the range of class variation – in views, tastes, attitudes and practices – that we have charted is sufficient to urge the need for questions of social class to be given more explicit, and more sustained, attention in arts and cultural policy debates. But there are also political issues at stake here. For the class-marked divisions in attitudes, tastes and cultural practice we have been concerned with are precisely those which, as we noted at the outset, have proved so politically consequential in the republican debate, the phenomenon of Hansonism and, before that, the decisive shift of electoral support from Labor under Paul Keating to John Howard and the Coalition.

Ghassan Hage throws useful light on these questions, while also adding a new dimension to them, in suggesting that these political tendencies can, in part, be attributed to the emergence of an increasing gap – simultaneously one of class and of culture – between two forms of cultural capital that have shaped and regulated access to the dominant styles and rhetorics of governing in post-war Australia. The first of these democratised the role that access to British upper-class culture had previously played in constituting a more or less 'natural' Australian governmental aristocracy. The accomplishment of the laborist radical nationalisms of the 1960s and 1970s, Hage argues, was to make the possession of any Anglo-Celtic background and a commitment to a common ethos of mateship sufficient for this purpose. If, in their different ways, Hansonism, the defeat of republicanism and the Howard ascendancy have constituted a rallying to and around this position, this has to be understood, Hage argues, as a reaction against the white cosmopolitan forms of multiculturalism which, in the 1980s and early 1990s, came to define a new ideal of the dominant forms of Australianness in whose name the country should be governed. Hage insists on the need to understand the class characteristics of this formation. He argues that the white cosmopolite, representing a governmental project committed to cultural diversity, tolerance, multiculturalism and enmeshment with Asia, is 'no longer simply any White person, but necessarily a classy one' (Hage 1998, p. 201). And again:

> Just as important as his or her urban nature, the cosmopolite is a *class* figure *and* a White person, capable of appreciating and consuming 'high-quality' commodities and cultures, including 'ethnic' culture. (201)

It is, of course, the 'knowledge classes' Hage has in mind here – classes which, given the shifting emphases of immigration policy since the 1980s, have become increasingly international in their composition, a reflection of the 'steady movement of highly skilled, highly trained professionals' which, according to

David Held *et al.* (1999, p. 304), has characterised contemporary forms of global migration. Our own figures confirm this. Migrants from northern Europe, the UK, and Asia all contribute significantly to the make-up of Australia's professional and managerial classes – more so than those born in Australia – whereas migrants from southern Europe are over-represented in the employer, supervisory and manual working classes. This is reflected in their cultural practices. If we look at participation in the different forms of high culture represented in Table 13 we see that migrants from northern Europe, Britain and – to a lesser extent – Asia are far more likely to be cosmopolitan cultural grazers than are those born in Australia.

Some of the detailed aspects of Hage's analysis are, of course, debatable. It is, for example, arguable that, far from witnessing the ascendancy of a common culture of Anglo-Celtic mateship, the Whitlam years testified to the emerging political influence of new forms of cultural capital rooted in the expansion of public education and the growth of the professional class. Be this as it may, there is little doubt that Hage is right in suggesting that how well Australia is able to manage the intersections between relations of class and relations of ethnicity is likely to prove one of the major political challenges of the twenty-first century. And this can only be assisted by a fuller understanding of the role that cultural practices play in the constitution of both sets of relations and in mediating the connections between them.

Table 13 Public/private culture by country of birth

	Australia	United Kingdom	Northern Europe	Southern Europe	Asia	Australia as % N. Europe
Subsidised culture	10.6	14.4	19.6	14.1	14.7	54%
Public culture	32.4	43.9	41.3	26.2	33.7	78%
Public broadcasting	24.4	35.9	36.2	33.1	35.1	67%
Private culture	21.4	25.5	24.3	16.2	17.0	88%

Notes

1 The cultural style and ethos of the leaders of the republican movement did much to foster this sense of a class division. See, for a perceptive discussion of its limitations in this respect, Morris (1998).

2 We have not, for this chapter, detailed the methods used in this study. Discussions of these can be found in chapter 1 and the methodological appendices of Bennett, Emmison and Frow (1999).

3 We identified eight classes, defined briefly as follows. *Employers*, comprising 5 per cent of the sample, were those with a workforce of three or more employees. The *self-employed* (15 per cent) either worked on their own account or employed up to two

other workers. *Managers* (3 per cent) were those responsible for the exercise of managerial functions across a range of fields of employment: finance, production, personnel, distribution, sales, services and farming. *Professionals* (11 per cent) comprised a wide range of workers whose occupations depended on their possession of certified competencies: scientists, engineers, doctors, teachers, social workers, lawyers, artists and cultural producers, etc. *Paraprofessionals* (9 per cent) were also dependent on educational qualifications for their positions, but usually of a more technical kind. They included nurses, police officers, and engineering and building technicians. *Supervisors* (13 per cent) comprised those exercising routine supervisory functions over both blue- and white-collar workers. *Sales and clerical workers* (24 per cent) comprised white-collar workers without supervisory responsibilities, while *manual workers* (20 per cent) were blue-collar workers without supervisory responsibilities.

4 Bourdieu summarises the relationship this way: 'nothing more clearly affirms one's "class", nothing more infallibly classifies, than tastes in music. This is of course because, by virtue of the rarity of the conditions for acquiring the corresponding dispositions, there is no more "classificatory" practice than concert-going or playing a noble instrument' (Bourdieu 1984, p. 18). Bourdieu's own empirical investigations reported in *Distinction* demonstrate that, at least in France of the 1960s, there was a remarkable affinity between an individual's preference for certain works of classical music, their social origins and educational capital.

5 It should be noted, however, that since SBS was not available in many areas of Australia at the time the Australian Everyday Cultures survey was administered, our SBS audience figures are not nationally representative.

Guide to further reading

Bourdieu (1984) remains the classic sociological account of the systems of cultural preference by which social difference is formed and maintained. Its central concepts of cultural capital and habitus have been widely influential in providing a theoretical framework to explain the unequal distribution of access to legitimate culture. DiMaggio (1987) refines Bourdieu's approach, suggesting that cultural classification systems in the modern world, reflecting the growth of the culture industries with commercial principles of classification and the autonomisation of art worlds, are becoming more differentiated and less hierarchical than Bourdieu's account implies. Connell and Irving (1992) remains the major historical account of class in Australia. Working from a marxist perspective, the authors trace the development of the contemporary hegemony of an industrial ruling class from shifting patterns of class relations since convict settlement and early colonial capitalism. The major sociological account of contemporary class formations in Australia is that offered in Janeen Baxter, Michael Emmison, John Western and Mark Western (eds) *Class Analysis and Contemporary Australia* (Melbourne: Macmillan, 1991). The authors draw on extensive survey materials and on the theoretical work of Erik Olin Wright and John Goldthorpe, and pay particular attention to the complex relation of non-class variables such as gender to the shaping of social class. Bennett, Emmison and Frow (1999) draws on a comprehensive survey of the

Australian population to offer a wide-ranging analysis of systems of cultural preference and practice in Australia. Drawing its inspiration from Bourdieu, it is nevertheless critical of Bourdieu's theoretical framework and seeks to elaborate a more differentiated account of the social variables governing cultural consumption. It also seeks to extrapolate a range of implications for the development of cultural policy.

Websites

www.ausport.gov.au/topstat.html

A site containing comprehensive statistical information on Australian sport with useful links to many databases dealing with sports attendance, adult and child participation, household expenditure on sport and recreation, etc.

www.mca.org.au

Website of the Music Council of Australia, whose mission is the advancement of Australian musical life in all its aspects. Useful links to community music organisations, discussion groups and a wide variety of resources.

www.amws.com.au

Australian music website. Essentially a series of links and pages that exist as a tribute to Australian music.

www.acn.net.au

Website for Australia's Cultural Network: an online gateway to Australian cultural organisations, websites, resources, events and news.

References

Bennett, Tony, Michael Emmison and John Frow (1999) *Accounting for Tastes: Australian Everyday Cultures*, Cambridge: Cambridge University Press.

Bourdieu, Pierre (1984) *Distinction: A Social Critique of the Judgment of Taste*, trans. Richard Nice, Cambridge, Mass.: Harvard University Press.

Connell, Robert W. and Terence H. Irving (1992) *Class Structure in Australian History: Poverty and Progress*, Melbourne: Longman Cheshire.

Department of Finance (1989) *What Price Heritage? The Museums Review and the Measurement of Museums' Performance*, Canberra: Commonwealth of Australia.

DiMaggio, Paul (1987) 'Classification in art', *American Sociological Review* 52, pp. 440–55.

Gans, Herbert (1966) 'Popular culture in America: social problem in a mass society or social asset in a pluralist society' in Howard Becker (ed.) *Social Problems: a Modern Approach*, New York: John Wiley.

— (1974) *Popular Culture and High Culture: An Analysis and Evaluation of Taste*, New York: Basic Books.

Hage, Ghassan (1998) *White Nation: Fantasies of White Supremacy in a Multicultural Society*, Sydney: Pluto Press.

Held, David, Anthony McGrew, David Goldblatt and Jonathan Perraton (1999) *Global Transformations: Politics, Economics and Culture*, Cambridge: Polity Press.

House of Representatives, Standing Committee on Expenditure (1986) *Patronage, Power and the Muse: Inquiry into Commonwealth Assistance to the Arts*, Canberra: AGPS.

McKay, Jim (1991) *No Pain, No Gain? Sport and Australian Culture*, Sydney: Prentice Hall.

Morris, Meaghan (1998) 'Lunching for the republic: feminism, the media and identity politics in the Australian republicanism debate' in David Bennett (ed.) *Multicultural States: Rethinking Difference and Identity*, London: Routledge.

Pakuski, Jan and Malcolm Waters (1996) *The Death of Class*, London: Sage Publications.

Peterson, Richard (1992) 'Understanding audience segmentation: from elite and mass to omnivore and univore', *Poetics* 21, pp. 243–58.

Peterson, Richard and A. Simkus (1992) 'How musical tastes mark occupational status groups' in M. Lamont and M. Fournier (eds) *Cultivating Differences: Symbolic Boundaries and the Making of Inequality*, Chicago: University of Chicago Press.

Peterson, Richard and R. Kern (1996) 'Changing highbrow taste: from snob to omnivore', *American Sociological Review* 61, October, pp. 900–7.

Relish, M. (1997) 'It's not all education: network measures as sources of cultural competency', *Poetics* 25, pp. 121–39.

Rowse, Tim (1985) *Arguing the Arts: The Funding of the Arts in Australia*, Ringwood, Vic.: Penguin Books.

Western, John (1991) 'Class in Australia: the historical context' in Janeen Baxter, Michael Emmison, John Western and Mark Western (eds) *Class Analysis and Contemporary Australia*, Melbourne: Macmillan.

Wright, Erik Olin (1997) *Class Counts: Comparative Studies in Class Analysis*, Cambridge and Paris: Cambridge University Press in association with the Editions de la Maison des Sciences de l'Homme.

Chapter 10

Generation Panics: Age, Knowledge and Cultural Power in a New Media Era

Catharine Lumby

A few months before my 35th birthday, at an age when my doctor was reminding me that my childbearing years would soon come to an end, I became a 'young' feminist. The catalyst was the publication of my first book, *Bad Girls: The Media, Sex and Feminism in the 90s* – a book which specifically eschewed the idea that feminism could or should be divided up along generational lines. But what I had to say in the book had little to do with its popular reception. What mattered was that it arrived in the shops at a time of enormous public interest in a purported stand-off between 'old' and 'young' guard feminists. After two decades of relying on a handful of senior feminist commentators – Anne Summers, Germaine Greer, Dale Spender, Moira Rayner – the media was desperate to find exemplars of the brave new feminist wave.

The sudden interest in what an ageing 'new' generation of feminists think can be traced, in large part, to the impact of a book by Helen Garner which was published in March 1995. On the face of it, *The First Stone* was Garner's analysis of the fallout from allegations of sexual harassment made by two young female students against the master of their university college. But in cultural and political terms it was much more. The real subject of *The First Stone* was Garner's concern that the role of 'eros' in human relations – a quality she defines elsewhere as 'a quick spirit that moves between people' and a 'moving force that won't be subdued by habit or law' – was being abandoned or overlooked by younger feminists in the mistaken belief that all human interactions can be codified and patrolled (Garner 1996, p. 174).

By the time the furore had died down, *The First Stone* had spawned a host of outraged books, articles and public exchanges. The bitter flavour of the debate can be inferred from an essay Rosi Braidotti wrote in *Bodyjamming*, a collection of essays edited by Jenna Mead in response to *The First Stone*. Garner, Braidotti writes, is guilty of 'a gentle but steady consumption of other people's lives, experiences, features, names and pain for the purpose of nurturing her writing', commenting that:

> good artists are major cannibals who consume others in one big chunk ... Mediocre artists are vampires who bleed their beloved victims over prolonged periods of time so gently that they hardly notice it at first. In my opinion Garner is no cannibal.
>
> (Braidotti 1997, p. 133)

The extraordinary anger and dissension unleashed by Garner's book is of interest to me here for the way a complex debate about gender, sex and ethics was so frequently and effortlessly recast as a generational struggle over who 'owned' feminism. Despite the very different agendas and ideological positions which grounded three 'young' feminist books published in the same period, authors Kathy Bail, Virginia Trioli and myself were all, at various times, asked to account for the 'victim' feminism which had supposedly infected young women in the 1990s and, in more general terms, to 'explain' our generation to older feminists (Bail 1996; Trioli 1996).

Writing about popular debates over feminism at the time, Mark Davis observed:

> In part victim panics are a story about young women fucking up and getting it wrong, again, and feminists with a certain media presence making themselves available to blow the whistle. A favourite tactic of several local media feminists is to dichotomise between their feminisms and what follows by casting themselves as the movement's mothers, presenting feminism as something over which they have ownership.
>
> (Davis 1999, p. 84)

What Davis' overview of *The First Stone* debate in his book *Gangland* captures is not simply the way an obsessive focus on generationalism marred and constrained a series of potentially productive discussions, but the strident, forced quality that attended assertions of seniority, authority and generational difference. He writes further that: 'Generationalism, lately, has become a way of lashing out' (Davis 1999, p. 20).

On one level the way debates about feminism are played out in the popular media will always be a pale and distorted reflection of the politics which motivate such exchanges. But on another, the debate over *The First Stone* illustrates the anxiety which now coalesces around what has been a key category of identity in Western society and culture since, at least, the mid-twentieth century: age (or generationalism). It's an uncertainty, I will argue, which heralds some major shifts in the discursive boundaries which organise the relationship between age, knowledge and cultural power.

My analysis of the discursive function of generational frameworks in defining cultural power derives, in part, from Foucault's analysis of the social function of childhood in *Discipline and Punish*, where he argues that 'the internal search for childhood' is the hallmark of the emergence of the disciplinary society (Foucault 1979, p. 193) and that the management and surveillance of childhood is deeply linked to the management and surveillance of the family: an institutional corner-stone of Foucault's disciplinary society. The family, for the Foucault of *Discipline and Punish*, is 'the privileged locus of emergence for the disciplinary question of the normal and the abnormal' (Foucault 1979, p. 216). Reflecting on Foucault's claim, Anne McGillvray observes: 'Whose body is more docile, whose geopolitics are more controlled, whose "calm knowledge" is more rigorously investigated than those of the child? The child is the matrix of the norm' (McGillvray 1997, p. 4).

In the second half of the twentieth century, disciplines devoted to surveilling and managing children were, as I outline below, increasingly brought to bear on adolescence, which was seen as both an extension of childhood and as an inde-terminate zone between childhood and adulthood which necessarily focused anxiety about where the boundaries between the two lie.

A second point of departure for my analysis is the work of John Hartley, in which he sketches a new model for understanding the public in the age of popular mass media (Hartley 1992, 1996). In *The Politics of Pictures* he writes that 'the media are simultaneously creative and participatory. They create a picture of the public, but it goes live, as it were, only when people participate in its creation, not least by turning themselves into the audience' (Hartley 1992, p. 4). Hartley's claim here is one I examine at length in *Gotcha: Life in a Tabloid World* (Lumby 1999). Briefly, he is arguing that the mediation of the public sphere has fundamentally altered the way publics are formed and that it is now largely through popular media flows into the domestic space of the home, rather than through their repre-sentation in and by courts, parliaments and elite media discourse, that individuals and communities form a sense of identity and of their relation to others.

In this chapter, I will argue that it is no longer merely the conventional child-hood and adolescent years which concentrate social anxiety about the relationship between age, knowledge and cultural power, but that broader changes in the way knowledge and ideas circulate in popular culture have profoundly eroded the status of age as a marker of personal, social or cultural identity. One of the conse-quences of this erosion is the eruption in Australia of what I've chosen to term 'generation panics' – specifically of recurrent outbreaks of heightened public concern about issues which symbolise this destabilisation of age as a social and cultural marker. These 'generation panics', I'll argue, following recent literature which has revived the term 'moral panics' (with key reservations outlined below), constitute a hyperbolic assertion of social and cultural hierarchies which are in the process of dissolving (Thompson 1998).

In establishing this argument, I will focus on two prominent instances of generation panics which emerged in Australia during the 1990s. The first concerns recurrent fears about the corruption and exploitaton of teenage girls by the popular media, particularly through the use of young models and sexualised images of young teen girls. The second revolves around fears over a culturally and socially corrosive gulf between the Babyboomer generation and the generation which followed it, popularly known as Generation X. In the case of the first generation panic, anxiety is focused on the fact that young girls are supposedly being forced too quickly into the adult world – that they're being made to grow up too fast and that childhood is a vanishing phase in social life. In the case of the second generation panic, the relevant fear is that young people are refusing to grow up, that they have failed to take on the mantle of adulthood and so constitute a generation in limbo, trapped in a perpetual adolescence.

These panics, I'll argue, are only superficially contradictory and are actually markers of the same vectors of change which are profoundly rearranging Australian social and cultural life. Of particular interest here is the role of the popular mass and new media in 'democratising' the public sphere by opening up new channels of information and, in the process, breaking down conventional social hierarchies. Indeed, I'll argue that the central reason generational differences have become such a locus of social anxiety is that age is perhaps the last marker of social and cultural identity whose naturalised status still goes largely unquestioned.

Seen and not heard

Just as the media cannot leave the constitutionally anomalous royal family alone, so they cannot stop fiddling with those whom John Hartley characterises as 'the last colonised class'. Young girls, Hartley argues, are the textual mark of the tension between alternative types of journalism; they are used as teaching aids in both 'positive' and 'negative' journalistic visualisations of social identity and civic propriety (Hartley 1998, p. 53).

In his essay titled 'Juvenation: news, girls and power', Hartley takes a closer look at the contemporary fuss over advertising and fashion images of young-looking girls in both Australia and the UK and argues that age has become a critical category in policing the boundary of the social – an 'intense and active semiotic hotspot' for producing and patrolling normative constructions of identity (Hartley 1998, p. 54). One of his key contentions then is that 'youth' have been getting younger, at least in representative terms, and that the term now covers people roughly from the age of eight to eighteen (rather than mid-teens to mid-twenties).

Yet, in a book first published a year before Hartley's article, Australian academic Mark Davis wrote that 'many people under the age of thirty-five or so feel stuck in a never-ending "apprenticeship", constantly being told they are "not ready"' (Davis 1999, p. 8). Davis' thesis in *Gangland* is that the Babyboomer generation are responsible for introducing an insidious bracket creep into the relationship between age and social and cultural power. As a generation who have always prided themselves on their youthful radicalism and who are used to hogging the relatively small Australian cultural stage, Davis suggests, the Babyboomers are unwilling to pass the mantle of cultural and political authority on to their successors and, as a result, the definition of 'youth' has been gradually redefined upwards in Australian cultural life.

On the face of it, Hartley's and Davis' claims are contradictory. But if we look more closely at the underlying trends which are driving the shifts they observe, then we might argue that both are symptoms of the same economic and technological diversification in the production and consumption of popular culture. Before I go on to unpack and expand on this claim, it's worth revisiting the discursive origins of the term 'youth culture'.

The categorisation and study of the behaviours and needs of a social group located in a liminal position between childhood and full adulthood dates back, at least, to 1905 when G. Stanley Hall published his seminal text, *Adolescence*. In that book, Hall identified the onset of puberty as marking the beginning of a critical period in human development when maturation was fuelled by psychological and physical turmoil (Hall 1905). From its earliest mobilisation, the term carried with it a sense that adolescence was a time fraught with social as well as personal risk. Analysing G. Stanley Hall's book, Kenneth Thompson writes:

> Hall maintained that individual maturation recapitulated the development of the species and that the transition from childhood to maturity corresponded to the leap from barbarism to civilisation … The condition of youth provided a yardstick against which the progress or decay of society could be measured. The idea of youth as a 'barometer' and agent of progress quickly took hold.
>
> (Thompson 1998, p. 44)

As Marcel Danesi notes, it is important to distinguish the evolution and subsequent cultural resonance of the term 'adolescence' from that of the terms 'teenager' or 'youth'. The first, he says, refers to the 'behaviours set in motion by the onset of the reproductive capacity', while teenager 'refers to a socially constructed category superimposed on the life continuum by modern consumeristic culture' (Danesi 1994, p. 6). If we follow Danesi's distinction, it wasn't until the mid-1940s that the teenage years began to designate the parameters of a distinct social group and market (Palladino 1996, p. xvi). And it was only in the 1950s that, as Danesi puts it, the teenager emerged in Western consciousness as a 'persona' (Danesi 1994, p. 15).

In material terms, the extension of mass schooling and the increase in average disposable income and leisure time in the decades after World War II in the west were highly influential in extending the period children remained under the control of parents and teachers and, ultimately, in establishing their status as an unstable, unformed group in need of close expert scrutiny. The resultant surveillance of young people by professional groups such as psychologists, psychiatrists and educators was mirrored in the marketplace by the obsessive interest market researchers and advertisers demonstrated in capturing, influencing and understanding the teenage market, where the notion that teenagers need guidance in establishing their identity has informed cultural products aimed at teenagers as well as those aimed at their guardians. The 1950s, in particular, saw the popularisation of a discourse of concern about the teenage years and the 'generation gap', evidenced by the publication of guides to dealing with adolescents with titles like Baruch's *How To Live With Your Teenager* (1953) and Landis' *Understanding Teenagers* (1955), magazines like *Seventeen* which aimed to guide teenage girls through the minefield of adolescence, and epitomised by the film *Rebel Without A Cause*.

The 1960s saw a plethora of research in the fields of sociology, psychology, and communications, which focused on deviance and delinquency among teenagers – notable studies included the Eppels' study of the moral values and dilemmas of adolescents, *Adolescents and Morality* (1966), and Eysenck's *Crime and Personality* (1964). The bulk of academic research on young people and the media which followed these studies also focused on the corrupting effects of television programs and other media products (Reeves and Wartella 1985; Cumberbatch and Howitt 1989).

Sociologist Stanley Cohen's groundbreaking work in analysing moral panics over seaside clashes between the Mods and Rockers in 1960s Britain (Cohen 1972) laid the foundation for a theoretical turn in studies of youth culture, and was followed by a host of work, exemplified by the seminal essay collection *Resistance Through Rituals: Youth Sub-cultures in Post-war Britain* (Hall and Jefferson 1976), which explored the way young people expressed and constructed themselves through culture. While this early work on youth culture in cultural studies has subsequently been criticised for focusing too narrowly on what David Buckingham has termed the 'spectacular' aspects of working-class culture, as well as for sidelining female and non-Anglo subcultures (Buckingham 1993, p. 12; McRobbie 1980), it undoubtedly marked an important shift away from understanding 'youth' or 'adolescence' as a fixed state of existence. Rather, as David Buckingham noted in his introduction to a series of case studies of youth audiences, the cultural studies trend has increasingly been to situate 'media use within the wider context of social relationships and activities, which are by definition diverse and particular' and to see audience identity as something 'you do rather than something you are' (Buckingham 1993, p. 13).

The real significance of the cultural studies tradition, for the purposes of this chapter, is that it highlighted the role culture, and in particular popular media culture, plays in mediating the boundaries between childhood and adulthood. Age, in this sense, emerges not only as a biological and a social category, but as a cultural one, in which flows of information, ideas and images act as force fields which attract and repel different generational groupings.

In *Centuries of Childhood*, Philip Aries links the importance of age in Western societies to the need to overwrite the rhythms of the natural world with those of capitalism. He remarks that the demands of bureaucratic, industrial economies make it hard for anyone not to 'know' their age (Aries 1973). Following Aries, the authors of a book mapping the history of the study of childhood, *Theorising Childhood*, argue that childhood has not always existed in its present European form and that childhood is 'less a fact of nature and more an interpretation of it' (James, Jenks and Prout 1998, p. 62). Any account of what it might mean to be a child, they argue:

> must be situated against the backdrop of the particular ways in which cultural conceptions of age and status are entwined and embedded in the particular structural arrangements of a society ... The experience of being a child cannot simply and unproblematically be read off the immaturity of the body.
> (James, Jenks and Prout 1998, p. 63)

In the print media era this cultural production of age groups was quite explicit, with materials primarily marked, catalogued and made available on the basis of age. It is a practice which survives, to some extent, in the classification of broadcast television programs, movies, videos and video games, but which has been substantially eroded by the sheer proliferation of media formats and by the advent of technologies which allow the illicit copying of programs and products. With the arrival of cable television, the VCR and computer technologies the job of policing the access children and young people have to information has become increasingly difficult. There's more of it and lots of it is buried in forms that adults are unfamiliar with. The apotheosis of this undermining of the graduated and hierarchical world of print media is the internet, a medium on which it is notoriously difficult to regulate or censor information flows.

The relatively rapid shift, since the early 1990s, from a world still dominated by old media to a culture defined by new media is rendering the social body and its competing identities increasingly labile. New media forms are not simply carriers of information, they are carriers or vectors along which social relations travel. To make this claim is not to suggest that media forms determine identity. I'm arguing, rather, that dominant social markers of identity, including age, compete with and are incorporated into another logic altogether – the logic of the production of appearances in the mediated public sphere. The anxieties which coalesce around the destabilisation of conventional generational boundaries, in this light, grow directly out of a tacit recognition that the play of appearances in the virtual realm of the media has its mirror in the expanded and abstracted terrain of contemporary social relations.

As noted above, in recent years there has been a revival of interest in the efficacy of the 'moral panic' model for understanding eruptions of public concern over youth culture. In his book, *Moral Panics*, Kenneth Thompson brings a broader theoretical orientation to the field of moral panics studies by integrating it with related concepts drawn from sociology and media and cultural studies. One of the most useful features of the book is Thompson's concern to tease out the way different theories of moral panic have located the media's role in escalating public anxiety. He contrasts the tendency of US moral panic theorists to locate the media as merely one of many 'interest groups' with an investment in circulating moral panic narratives, with the Birmingham School's structural analysis of the media's role as the key to the signification spiral of a given panic. Thompson goes on to ask what relevance recent changes in the form, content and scope of the contemporary media and of the public sphere more generally have for the field of moral panics, noting that 'the rapidity of social change and growing social pluralism create increasing potential for value conflicts and lifestyle clashes between diverse social groups, which turn to moral enterprise to defend or assert their values against those of other groups'. They do this, he writes, 'within a public arena which offers many media outlets for amplifying their fears and articulating demands for social control and regulation to defend those values' (Thompson 1998, p. 11). In this light, moral panics might be understood as attempts to redefine or fix collective identity and interests in an increasingly pluralistic world. And while they certainly constitute a reactive mode of establishing identity, they are nonetheless important markers of points of change and dissolution on the cultural and social body.

Modelling reality

A British documentary screened on the ABC on 24 November 1999 revolved around a BBC investigative reporter's undercover journey into the modelling industry, posing as a fashion photographer. The journalist's particular interest lay in the potentially deleterious effects the modelling lifestyle has on the physical and psychological health of the young teenage girls who are drawn into it – particularly on the effects of partying, drug taking and predatory men. Key sections of the documentary, titled *MacIntyre Undercover*, consisted of grainy footage shot by the reporter, Donal MacIntyre, using a camera he concealed beneath his jacket to record supposedly casual conversations with fashion industry players and their 'prey'. Throughout the documentary his tone is one of grave moral concern for the young models, a concern which he assumes his audience will automatically share.

The screening prompted a flurry of familiar stories in the Australian media about the exploitation of young girls by the modelling industry and the dangers of exposing teenage girls generally to popular culture (Williamson and Temple 1999). Since the rise of the 80s supermodel, modelling has become one of the hottest topics in Australian teen girls' magazines like *Dolly, Girlfriend, Cosmopolitan* and *Cleo*. The magazines routinely feature stories on individual models, articles on how to get into the industry, and run or promote modelling contests readers can enter. The apparent fascination teenage girls have for modelling has spawned a concomitant popular discourse around the risks this fascination with modelling poses to adolescent females. In *Reviving Ophelia*, a bestselling book subtitled 'Saving the selves of adolescent girls', Mary Pipher sums up a persistent popular claim about the impact of models on teenage girls:

> as real women grow heavier, models and beautiful women are portrayed as thinner ... Girls compare their own bodies to our cultural ideals and find them wanting. Dieting and dissatisfaction with bodies have become normal reactions to puberty. Girls developed eating disorders when our culture developed a standard of beauty that they couldn't obtain by being healthy. When unnatural thinness became attractive, girls did unnatural things to be thin.
>
> (Pipher 1996, p. 184)

Other common concerns circulate around the dangers of promoting sexual precocity in teenage girls through exposure to the 'adult' worlds of make-up and fashion. In 1997, for instance, a furore erupted over a cover girl contest run by *Dolly*. NSW Liberal MLC Marlene Goldsmith sparked the debate by claiming that *Dolly* encouraged 'children to see themselves as sexual objects' and allowed 'paedophiles to get a sense that their activities are legitimate'. A range of state and federal ministers and child protection advocates joined Goldsmith in her campaign against the use of young models. Senator Jocelyn Newman, then Minister Assisting the Prime Minister on the Status of Women, said the overtly sexual portrayal of a slender teenager was 'disturbing' and sent 'all the wrong messages' to young women. NSW Women's Minister Faye Lo Po' also attacked *Dolly*'s sexual depiction of the model and what she described as the near-pornographic nature of the texts and pictures in the magazine. NSW Child Protection Council Chief, Judy Cashmore, agreed that the magazine 'gives messages to paedophiles that it's OK to see kids in that [sexual] light' (Corbett and Symons 1997).

The overwhelming focus of Australian popular debate about teenage girls today revolves around the question of what forms of knowledge they have acquired through the media – particularly what they have come to know about grooming themselves for the male gaze – and how the acquisition of this knowledge has the potential to limit or damage their ability to acquire genuine 'self-knowledge'.

In *Out Of the Garden*, a study of marketing and children's media, Stephen Kline maps historical trends in the publication of children's literature, tracing the evolution from heavy-handed instruments of pedagogy, to products designed to please as well as instruct the child, to the birth of a mass market in comics and magazines. He writes:

> Whereas books were fiction for children – to be read to, chosen for, and offered as gifts to children – the comic was the first cultural product cheap enough to be bought by them ... Comics symbolised the intrusion of the consumer-sovereignty dilemma into the world of children's culture. Distribution in the mass market thus ultimately transformed the differences in taste, purpose and values between adults and children's fiction into a breach in socialisation – the first sign of a cultural generation gap that liberal thinking parents found ideologically problematic. (Kline 1993, p. 104)

Kline's analysis is a reminder that demands to protect a supposedly powerless and naïve group, such as teen girls, are always shadowed by desires to control them. But the question which remains unanswered is why young-looking models (and their putative effects on the young women who consume their images) are causing so much concern at this particular moment in cultural history? Why, as John Hartley puts it, have images of pre-teen and teen girls become such a 'semiotic hotspot'?

To answer that question I propose following the threads of an argument Hartley mounts elsewhere when he analyses the controversy sparked by US photographer Sally Mann's photographs of her own naked children engaging in everyday activities and concludes that Mann's images offend:

> a governmentalist tradition which cannot handle the idea of what it preconceives as a vulnerable, impressionable, untutored, inexperienced population being in fact able to think, act, feel and grow for itself. And so it has produced an image of the public as an infantilised and unenlightened female, for ever in need of correction and protection, hidden out of sight and away from the light – away from the glare of publicity. When someone ... actually produces images of this youthful femininity, showing it to be anything but infantilised (and far from sentimentalised), the results can seem shocking, precisely because they transgress the established boundary between public and private.
>
> (Hartley 1996, p. 17)

Seen in this light, the sexualised or 'knowing' images of girls and young women produced for them in popular media operate on two levels. On one hand, they are a socially challenging reminder that children (and young teenagers) already have relationships to self which are independent of adult constructions of their needs and vulnerabilities. And such images arguably have a particularly heightened 'shock' value at a time when parents and others in a positions of authority feel that they are unable to monitor the access young people have to information and ideas flowing out of the 'adult' world through the new media technologies.

This is not to argue, of course, that images of young girls are unmediated representations of youthful femininity or that such femininity is expressed in the shape of a uniform social identity. The point is rather that images of juvenated femininity, whatever their context, are potentially confronting because they symbolise the destabilisation of the liberal masculinised public sphere by images, ideas and social groups which have been conventionally excluded. As I've argued elsewhere (Lumby 1997, 1999), the virtual public sphere constituted by the media is one which exchanges the linearity of rational debate for a seductive stream of images and an ordered governmentalist tradition of politics for looser local, domestic and consumerist formations of identity. The young girl is, in both historical and culturally symbolic terms, the antithesis of the reasonable and informed citizen which underpins the Athenian blueprint for the liberal public sphere. And in these terms, the popularity of images of juvenated femininity are a constant reminder of the way the masculined liberal public sphere has been invaded, in both cultural and political ways, by images, identities and voices which were once more rigorously patrolled.

Generation vexed

Despite being widely hailed (and condemned) as a book promoting the cultural tastes and values of Generation X and attacking those of the Babyboomer generation, Mark Davis' 1997 book *Gangland* wasn't so much an argument for generationalism as an argument against it. Davis observed:

> Generation X isn't an expression used by anyone in the age group it refers to. Generationalism itself, as a marker of intrinsic difference, is an idea distinctly out of fashion except, it seems, among those who like to think of themselves as *the* generation, and who use the idea to keep a little distance between themselves and whoever follows.
>
> (Davis 1999, p. 15)

Generationalism, in Davis' terms, is a key regulatory category around which Western culture is organised. In 1990s Australia, he suggests, the discourse of generationalism was frequently mobilised to devalue the cultural interests and values of anyone younger than the Babyboomer generation – 'to set up young people, even demonise them, as "outsiders"' (Davis 1999, p. 16).

In a late-1990s essay on the mobilisation of social concern and fascination with the so-called 'Generation X' in Australia, media studies scholar Jason Sternberg proffers the term 'lifestyle panic' to describe the simultaneously all-encompassing and yet fragmenting nature of the phenomenon. He writes:

> The Generation X panic attempted to encompass almost every aspect of young people's lives – that is their lifestyles – into one overarching mega-panic. For example, while the panic surrounding the Mods and the Rockers was largely concerned with two 'deviant' youth subcultures, the panic over Generation X has broken up and attached itself to several new and pre-existing smaller

(although no less important) panics concerning topics such as sexuality, political involvement and suicide.

(Sternberg 1997, p. 80)

One of the distinguishing features of this 'lifestyle panic', according to Sternberg,
is that is was played out not only in the conventional 'hard news' media but also
in media trade publications, entertainment media and fiction (Sternberg 1997,
p. 81). Sternberg goes on to point out that the label was invented by a novelist and
parlayed through the popular media (as a series of lifestyle tropes and attitudes)
direct to market researchers, who self-consciously devised questions to test young
consumers' identification with a fictional category. What Sternberg's analysis
highlights is that Generation X is a generational category devised in a time when
the hallmarks of generationalism are marketing tools well before they have had
an opportunity to settle into life as badges of alternative cultural identity.

McKenzie Wark has argued that it's not just Generation X which is a media
product, but that 'the whole idea of generationalism, the idea that there are
common experiences that define an age cohort, is a media artefact' (Wark 1999,
p. 219). Wark's argument rests on the claim that the mass media have synchronised flows of information and therefore the images and stories people tend to
use to describe historical experience. He elaborates:

The mass broadcast vectors of radio and television produce the phenomena of
people experiencing the same images simultaneously. Radio and television work
their way into everyday life. The images and stories they carry propose templates
for reading experiences in everyday life ... What a generation shares is not the
same experiences, but rather different experiences read via the same images.

(Wark 1999, p. 219)

It follows from Wark's analysis, however, that the shift from a mass media environment to a new networked media environment in which media production is
increasingly niche marketed and media consumption is fragmented would have
an important impact on young people's perception of 'belonging' to a generation.
And, indeed, it's the sense of not belonging – a detachment from universalist
politics, and a failure to take an interest in big picture issues – which is sometimes said to define the 'trouble' with Generation X (Davis 1999).

As Sternberg argues, 'with its mysterious connotations, Generation X would
therefore seem to be a useful phrase in that it gives a name to an age-based
cohort which appears to be shifting its patterns of media consumption in
complex and not always easily understood ways' (Sternberg 1998, p. 123). This
unpredictability has given rise to a media moral panic about the supposed
'dumbing down' of youth. Indeed, the failure to follow conventional trends in
media consumption by moving 'up' from entertainment-orientated youth culture
formats to 'hard' news and current affairs formats in their twenties has been a

key focus of concern over the cultural habits of Generation X (Sternberg 1998). Yet, is the panic at heart a panic over generational differences in cultural values and tastes, or is the underlying fear a fear that generationalism is itself dissolving in the face of an increasingly pluralistic media sphere – and in the process taking with it commercial as well as political identities?

If we return to the discursive origins of youth culture and generationalism in the late 1940s we find that the flipside of the extension of surveillance of young people into the adolescent years was the invention of a youth market. Indeed, writing in 1942, the sociologist Talcott Parsons argued that peer group cultures were localised expressions of generational patterns of consumption (Parsons 1942). And, as Kenneth Thompson points out, this ambiguous image of youth culture as 'both a symbol of an emerging affluent consumer society and as a threat to moral discipline and order' was a hallmark of media representations from the 1950s on (Thompson 1998, p. 46). In this light, generational panics around Generation X might equally be understood as panics over 'the future of the third stage of capitalism: the transition from a modern to a postmodern society' (Sternberg 1997, p. 86).

Generating youth

To claim someone is panicking is to stake a claim to higher, more rational ground. When we accuse others of panicking we are suggesting that they are not thinking clearly – that they are acting the way women, crowds and animal herds behave: irrationally, impulsively and hysterically. To accuse others of panicking is to declare oneself in control – to state: 'They're panicking and I'm *concerned.*' This rhetorical configuration alerts us to one of the greatest potential limitations of the moral panic as a theoretical tool. A term which claims to diagnose collective outbreaks of 'othering', it can unwittingly be used to construct its own 'other' in the process. In this sense, moral panic is a term which is grounded in a conventional liberal model of public communication and one endorsed by Kenneth Thompson when he writes:

> At its best, the media's dramatisation of issues may promote rational and informed debate, provided the format of discussion meets certain criteria: sufficient length for in-depth treatment, well-informed participants to put different sides of the argument, with firm but sympathetic chairing. In such circumstances, it is unlikely to give rise to a moral panic. At its worst, the media's treatment of an event or issue can be so sensationalized as to arouse fears of risk and threat that lead to disproportionate demands for action.
>
> (Thompson 1998, p. 29)

Thompson's separation of media coverage into 'rational and informed debate' and 'sensationalized' coverage is ultimately anchored in a hierarchy of sense-making that assumes there is a privileged, rational outside to the media sphere – a place from which a calming voice of authority could emanate. Ironically, it is arguably the very same desire for the maintenance of social order which mobilises moral panics in the first place.

Yet, the instances of what I've dubbed 'generation panics' might equally be seen in a more productive light than Thompson's analysis suggests. Indeed, if we return to John Hartley's claim that children are the 'last colonised class' (Hartley 1998, p. 53), we might begin to see generational panics over images of youth in the media as markers of a transition from the modern to the post-modern public sphere. Understood in this way, generation panics are also the symbolic markers of the dissolution of the top-down model of public discourse in which authorised figures speak and the infantilised masses listen. At the end of the twentieth century, Western public spheres have become a forum for voices and interests which were conventionally excluded from public debate. As a social group who are frequently spoken of, but rarely heard, children, and by symbolic extension, 'youth', are perhaps the last frontier in the democratisation of public discourse.

📖 Guide to further reading

In broad terms, there is a vast body of interdisciplinary literature on youth and youth subcultures, much of which has been generated by scholars working in the field of cultural studies over the past three decades. The seminal text on youth subcultures is Hall and Jefferson (1976). This spawned a rich body of work in the field including Paul Willis *Learning to Labour: How Working Class Kids Get Working Class Jobs* (Farnborough: Saxon House, 1977), Dick Hebdige *Subculture: The Meaning of Style* (London: Routledge, 1973) and Angela McRobbie *Feminism and Youth Culture* (Basingstoke: Macmillan Education, 1991). While much of this work has focused on how youth identities, inflected by class, race and gender, work to resist and transform dominant cultural and political ideologies, it has been equally concerned with what Lawrence Grossberg defines as the ambivalent valuation of youth in *We Gotta Get Out Of This Place: Popular Conservatism and Postmodern Culture* (New York and London: Routledge, 1992) – the way in which youth is an uncertain and contested social category. David Buckingham's (1993) work on youth culture and media consumption is also useful here for his exploration of the way media use helps create shifting forms of identity.

In terms of work which has focuses on the narrower theme of this chapter – Australian youth culture, generationalism and media consumption – a number of works are relevant. Hartley (1996) contains an important analysis of the way popular youth-related media has transformed the public sphere and, with it, traditional hierarchies based on age and gender. The same theme is developed in Lumby (1997). Davis (1999) is important for his analysis of the way dominant hierarchies of cultural value reflect interests organised along generational lines, and Wark (1999) is key for his claim that the very idea of generationalism itself is a media artifact.

References

Aries, Philip (1973) *Centuries of Childhood*, Harmondsworth: Penguin.

Bail, Kathy (ed.) (1996) *DIY Feminism*, Sydney: Allen & Unwin.

Braidotti, Rosi (1997) 'Remembering Fitzroy High', in J. Mead (ed.) *Bodyjamming*, London: Vintage, pp. 121–47.

Buckingham, David (1993) 'Introduction' to Buckingham (ed.) *Reading Audiences: Young People and the Media*, Manchester and New York: Manchester University Press

Cohen, Stanley (1973) *Folk Devils and Moral Panics: The Creation of the Mods and Rockers*, Herts: Paladin.

Corbett, B. and E. Symons (1997) 'Sex symbol at 13 and Dolly isn't kidding', *Daily Telegraph*, 5 March, p. 3.

Cumberbatch, G. and D. Howitt (1989) *A Measure of Uncertainty: The Effects of the Mass Media*, London: John Libbey.

Danesi, Marcel (1994) *Cool: The Signs and Meanings of Adolescence*, Toronto: University of Toronto Press.

Davis, Mark (1999) *Gangland: Cultural Elites and the New Generationalism*, Sydney: Allen & Unwin (first published 1997).

Foucault, Michel (1979) *Discipline and Punish: The Birth of the Prison*, London: Vintage Books.

Garner, Helen (1996) 'The fate of *The First Stone*', *True Stories*, Melbourne: Text Publishing, pp. 169–78.

Hall, S.G. (1905) *Adolescence*, New York: Appleton-Century-Crofts.

Hall, Stuart and Tony Jefferson (eds) (1976) *Resistance Through Rituals: Youth Subcultures in Post-war Britain*, London: Hutchinson.

Hartley, John (1992) *The Politics of Pictures: The Creation of the Public in the Age of Popular Media*, London and New York: Routledge.

— (1996) *Popular Reality: Journalism, Modernity, Popular Culture*, London: Arnold.

— (1998) 'Juvenation: news, girls and power' in C. Carter, G. Branston and J. Allan (eds) *News, Gender and Power*, London and New York: Routledge, pp. 47–70.

James, A., C. Jencks and A. Prout (1998) *Theorising Childhood*, Cambridge: Polity Press.

Kline, Stephen (1993) *Out of the Garden: Toys, TV and Children's Culture in the Age of Marketing*, London and New York: Verso, 1993.

Lumby, Catharine (1997) *Bad Girls: The Media, Sex and Feminism in the 90s*, Sydney: Allen & Unwin.

— (1999) *Gotcha: Life in a Tabloid World*, Sydney: Allen & Unwin.

McGillvray, Anne (1997) 'Introduction' in Anne McGillvray (ed.) *Governing Childhood*, Hampshire: Darmouth, pp. 1–24.

McRobbie, Angela (1980) 'Settling accounts with subcultures: a feminist critique', *Screen Education*, 34, pp. 37–49.

Palladino, Grace (1996) *Teenagers: An American History*, New York: Basic Books.

Parsons, Talcott (1964) *Essays in Sociological Theory*, New York: Free Press (first published in 1942).

Pipher, Mary (1996) *Reviving Ophelia*, Sydney: Transworld.

Reeves, B. and E. Wartella (1985) 'Historical trends in research on children and the media 1900–1960', *Journal of Communication* 35, 2, pp. 118–33.

Sternberg, J. (1997) 'Generating X: lifestyle panics and the new generation gap', *Media International Australia* 85, November, pp. 79–90.

— (1998) 'Rating youth: a statistical review of young Australians' news media use', *Australian Studies in Journalism* 7, pp. 84–136.

Thompson, Kenneth A. (1998) *Moral Panics*, London: Routledge.

Trioli, Virginia (1996) *Generation f: Sex, Power and the Young Feminist*, Melbourne: Minerva.

Wark, McKenzie (1999) *Celebrities, Culture and Cyberspace*, Sydney: Pluto Press.

Williamson, B. and W. Temple (1999) 'Model agency in sex scandal', *Daily Telegraph*, 24 November, p. 5.

Chapter 11

Gender Equity, Hegemonic Masculinity and the Governmentalisation of Australian Amateur Sport

Jim McKay, Geoffrey Lawrence, Toby Miller and David Rowe

I really have regarded being captain of the Australian cricket team as the absolute pinnacle of sporting achievement, and really the pinnacle of human achievement almost, in Australia.

Prime Minister John Howard (cited in Winkler 1997, p. 6)

Introduction

Sport is, without question, a key cultural institution in Australia. By every available measure, it is a significant component of Australian society – as pastime, industry, locus of political power, source of media content, subject of everyday speech, and marker of ethnic, racial, sexual and national identity (see, for example, Adair and Vamplew 1997; McKay 1991). Many countries display a deep sporting affiliation, but few claim to be, in the self-consciously ironic title of Richard Cashman's book (1995), a 'Paradise of Sport'. Yet in this sporting 'paradise' there is familiar evidence of class, racial, ethnic, sexual and gender inequalities of both opportunities and outcomes (Vamplew and Stoddart 1994). For instance, sport in Australia (as in most other countries) has a profoundly masculine inflection, operating as a major means through which ascendant forms of masculinity are asserted, promoted, tested and defended against 'rival' articulations of masculinity and femininity (Connell 1995). Meaghan Morris (in Turner 1992, p. 653), for instance, notes sport's cultural and gender power in wryly describing Australia's 'dreaded tradition ... of men, sport and beer'. This is not, of course, to argue that women have been entirely absent from the sporting

233

landscape or have failed to gain some access to sport's masculinist citadel (Cahn 1994; Hargreaves 1994). However, while sport has been an often-unacknowledged aspect of women's leisure, it is also apparent that at the amateur, semi-professional and elite levels, women have been subordinate in many crucial respects. These include the provision of sporting facilities, rate of participation, remuneration, representation in decision-making positions, media coverage and corporate sponsorship. Hence, as is the case with other popular social and cultural institutions, structures of power (albeit uneven and contested) can be readily shown to exist, while also being subjected to denial by those with a deep affective investment in the institution and its *mythos*.

Two vivid reminders of sportswomen's marginal status in Australia occurred in 1999. First, following the world championship victory of the Australian women's field hockey team, an announcement appeared on the official Parliament House noticeboard indicating that Prime Minister John Howard would be attending a reception in their honour. However, the notice incorrectly stated that the event was going to be held for the Australian women's *cricket* team. When the Australian netball team subsequently won its third consecutive world championship, the Prime Minister congratulated the team's captain for her squad's effort, but mistakenly referred to her charges as the women's *hockey* team. The media portrayed the Prime Minister's error as a minor gaffe. However, it is inconceivable that any Prime Minister would be so easily forgiven for mistaking, say, the national men's cricket and rugby union teams.

In this chapter we examine the major articulations between Australian amateur sport and gender, with special reference to recent gender equity policies implemented by the Australian Sports Commission (ASC), which is primarily responsible for planning and funding amateur sport on a national basis. Of the various elements of sporting mythology, the amateur ideal persists, despite accelerating degrees of commodification and professionalisation. Playing sport 'for the love of the game' still exerts a powerful appeal within sporting culture, despite (perhaps because of) the increasingly serious nature of sport as industry and as career.

Our analysis draws on Bob Connell's notion of *hegemonic masculinity* to understand the articulation of gender identities, relations and symbols in sport. This concept refers to the 'culturally idealised form of masculine character', which stresses 'the connecting of masculinity to toughness and competitiveness', the 'subordination of women', and 'the marginalisation of gay men' (Connell 1990b, pp. 83, 94). We also deploy the concept of *governmentality*, which originated with Roland Barthes' (1973) attempt to describe the tendency of capitalist states to calibrate and manage the conduct of their citizens in spheres that were not traditionally subjected to direct intervention by the state. Subsequently, Foucault referred to governmentality as:

> the ensemble formed by the institutions, procedures, analyses, and reflections, the calculations and tactics that allow the exercise of this very specific albeit

complex form of power, which has as its target population, as its principal form of knowledge political economy, and as its technical means apparatuses of security.

(Foucault 1991, p. 102)

For Mitchell Dean and Barry Hindess (1998, p. 9), the process of governmentality is 'shot through with multiple and heterogeneous ways of making the world thinkable and calculable' (for a critical summary of governmentality and its uptake, see Miller 1998b). This emphasis on both the multifarious and specific aspects of governmentality is important for our analysis, because it helps to illuminate how the gender regime of Australian sport, in the name of equity, access and efficiency, is being institutionally reconfigured in a manner that barely disturbs – and, indeed, substantially reconfirms – fundamental structures of gender inequality.

We will, therefore, first trace the process by which sport has shifted over the past twenty years from a predominantly non-profit (or at least rudimentarily entrepreneurial) activity in civil society, with all its attendant chauvinisms (and 'organic' social meanings), to one that has been taken up and moulded by a range of governmental and commercial imperatives. These dictates are sometimes synchronised, as when social-movement pressures for gender inclusiveness meet 'enlightened' audience demographics for media advertisers (Andrews 1998), and sometimes conflictual, as when gender equity policies are attacked by 'hysterical' white male sportswriters (McKay 1997). Our analysis commences with a brief institutional history of Australian sport, specifically in relation to its gendered structures of labour and power. We then analyse sport's gendered regime in the crucial arena of the 'media sports cultural complex' (Rowe 1999), concluding with an appraisal of the potential of current state equity policies to address and redress gender inequalities in sport.

Commercialisation, professionalisation and state intervention in Australian sport

To state the obvious – as Ellis Cashmore (1996, p. 174) has done – '(p)eople enjoy watching and appreciating a contest and, in some circumstances, are willing to pay to do so. The trend has been that they are prepared to pay more and more'. It is clear that, as capitalism has grown, so has competitive sport, becoming a 'big business' itself in a world where products (including sport) can be bought and sold to the highest bidder. Sport – once a barely rationalised, amateur pursuit emanating principally from nineteenth-century Britain – has now become firmly embedded within capitalism as a moneymaking venture (Rowe and Lawrence 1990, 1998).

A captive audience is the basis for consumer capitalism's 'hard sell' – and it is important to advertisers of mass-produced commodities that the audience base is as wide as possible – which means that women must also be persuaded to watch TV sport, especially men's TV sport. Thus, televised sport undoubtedly changed in order to 'incorporate' women. Mechanisms for enticement include: a reduction in 'rough' play, more colourful clothing, more spectacular camera shots, and the promotion of athletes as sex symbols (something, again, essential for promoting audience interest – particularly among heterosexual women – see Miller 1998a). But it is not only those selling products (particularly the large corporations) who can make profits from sport: clubs, 'middle agents', journalists, referees, coaches and a host of other functionaries all prosper from sport (see Rowe 1995). Players, in particular, know that they sell their labour power in a capitalist marketplace that is fickle. Since the sport-productive life of an athlete is relatively short, it is economically rational for many athletes – particularly those operating at the top level – to seek the greatest reward in the quickest time for their labour. The professionalisation of sport has meant that players train hard, are subject to physically and psychologically tough coaching regimes and self-discipline, and are in a very competitive arena where poor form can mean substantial loss of earnings, and where good form can mean dramatically improved financial remuneration and social prestige. The contracts offered in Australian rugby league during the 1995–6 pay-TV driven 'Super League War' (Rowe 1997) made millionaires of many players, professionalising and commercialising the sport along the lines of US major sporting competitions. With such large sums at stake, it is apparent that amateur and semi-professional values and practices have ceded a great deal of ground to full-blown professionalism. The state has mostly stood by and adopted its traditional role during an innovative period of capitalist accumulation: policing property rights. At the same time as this commodification has been underway, sport has undergone a revolution in its governance.

The mythic history of Australian cultural nationhood has drawn heavily on the notions of moral uplift that rested on the exalted status of amateur sport in the British Empire. While the aristocratic bias of the amateur sports ethic was historically matched only by the persistence of betting, gaming and 'pay for play' in sports like horseracing, boxing, rugby league and cricket (Adair and Vamplew 1997), a sense of national vigour, health, the outdoors, and rugged physical masculinity was reasonably well sustained until the mid-1970s, by which time most major sports around the world had professionalised and corporatised. Quite suddenly, the image of Australians being 'naturally' good at sport and nourished by success at imperial sports like cricket, tennis and swimming was threatened by the success of the socialist state sport systems of the former Soviet Bloc and China, as well as 'socialism-by-stealth' from American college campuses. The response by successive Australian governments was intervention in the market of sporting prowess in the 'national interest'. Thus, what had been a comparatively organic, civil society model of amateur sport (albeit with a relationship of 'disciplinarity' with the school curriculum) became a quasi-moral imperative to provide champions in all sporting endeavours. Australia's 'failure' to win a gold medal at the 1976 Montreal Olympics was an especially strong catalyst for state investment in elite sport. This state expenditure was complemented by the provision of a satisfactory investment climate for commercial media organisations and other sport-related businesses to promote sporting contests and to sponsor athletes. Before proceeding to a discussion of relevant state expenditure and policy priorities, it is necessary to highlight Australian sport's overwhelmingly male dominance.

Gender inequalities in Australian sport

Numerous studies have documented that Australian sport is pervaded by systematic gender inequalities. In the area of grassroots participation and attendance, for example, national surveys have shown that males have higher overall participation rates in organised sport and physical activities (see McKay 1990, 1991, 1992 and McKay *et al.* 2000 for comprehensive analyses of sport participation according to gender, age, ethnicity, race and socio-economic status). If we turn to sport's gender-based division of labour, it is no surprise that sport substantially mirrors the patterns of both vertical and horizontal segregation found in the wider public realm. Case studies of sport have found that women do an unequal share of ancillary labour such as cooking, cleaning, chauffeuring and fund-raising (Boyle and McKay 1995; Dempsey 1992; Thompson 1999). In this way women facilitate the sporting activities of their brothers, children and male partners at the expense of their own leisure time. Such studies have shown that a strong constraint on females' involvement in sporting organisations, particularly in later life, is the commonsense view that men are more entitled to leisure because they have earned the right to it through greater involvement in the paid workforce. This belief is particularly pertinent when considering positions of authority in sporting organisations. For instance, some sports clubs still limit full membership status to men and only accept women as associates. This means that men dominate executive positions, voting rights and budgets, and regulate women's access to bars, equipment and facilities. Gendered structures of power in sport are also evident in institutionalised patterns of sexual harassment and the often intensely homophobic and misogynistic nature of sporting subcultures (Baird 1994; Bricknell 1999; McKay and Middlemiss 1995).

One reason sport is such a resonant symbol of hegemonic masculinity is that it literally *embodies* the seemingly natural superiority of men over women. Over the past few centuries, physical strength has lost much of its importance in sustaining ideologies of masculine superiority, while the prevalence of automation, cybernation and robotics has almost eliminated the mandatory, diurnal exercise of physical prowess. Norbert Elias and Eric Dunning (1986, p. 10) have argued that the process of 'sportization' in modernity has, especially for men, enabled an increasingly regulated display of the physical aggression and score-settling rendered illegitimate by the wider 'civilizing process'. For Connell (1983, p. 27), sport is, therefore, an important site for the simultaneously embodied and symbolic display of hegemonic masculinity. The valorisation of men's corporeal power invokes routine comparisons between the qualitative and quantitative differences of sportsmen and sportswomen (Kane 1995), perhaps most notably in the invasive bodily practice of 'gender-verification' of sportswomen at the elite level. Women's bodies, in symbolic terms, are always the 'other', because if sport and masculinity are as deeply intertwined as we propose, then the idea of sport and femininity as having any kind of equivalence is necessarily subversive. Sport continues to be a site where struggle occurs over what constitutes the 'legitimate body' as well as over the ways in which bodies might be 'used' (Loy *et al.* 1993).

This point leads us to address the cardinal role that the media play in symbolising gender differences. Again, a plethora of studies has shown that sportswomen receive coverage that is massively disproportionate to their participation and achievements. For instance, Mikosza (1997) found that coverage of sportswomen in Australian newspapers had declined from 10.7 per cent of the total in 1996 to 7.5 per cent in 1996 (also see Phillips 1996; Rowe 2000; Toohey 1997). This neglect is astonishing considering that sportswomen have won numerous individual and team championships at the international level: between 1948 and 1996, women won 40 per cent of Australia's gold medals at the Olympic Games despite competing in only 25 per cent of the total events and comprising just 24 per cent of Australia's representatives; between 1911 and 1990 women captured 35 per cent of Australia's gold medals at the Commonwealth Games, even though they were allowed to participate in only 31 per cent of the sports available and constituted just 27 per cent of all Australian athletes.

In addition to this obvious quantitative difference, there is a discernible qualitative discrepancy in how sportsmen and sportswomen are depicted, with the media tending to admire the former for what they *do* and the latter for how they *look*. The thoroughgoing sexual objectification of the female sporting body in a manner akin to that of soft pornography, with the predominantly passive female athlete functioning as the object of the male gaze, is most prominent in 'cheesecake' presentations in the *Golden Girls of Athletics, Golden Girls of Sport* and Matildas (women's soccer) calendars and the magazines *Inside Sport* and *Sports Monthly* (Mikosza and Phillips 1999). As Jefferson Lenskyj (1998, p. 31) notes, the formula in publications such as these is based on the binary antithesis of men's sports/women's bodies. The other major way in which female sporting sexuality is brought to the fore as an active force in the media is via 'moral panics' about lesbianism (Burroughs *et al.* 1995; Lenskyj 1995; Miller *et al.* 1999; Stevenson 2001).

As Stoddart (1994) and others have noted, the most common justification given by the commercial media for the quantitative under-representation and qualitative sexualised elaboration of women's sport is that, when compared with men's sport, it is a less dramatic, compelling spectacle and so is less popular and commercially lucrative. Academic audience research (such as Sargent *et al.* 1998) tends to support this position in finding that even women generally prefer to watch men's sport than women's sport. The explanation for this disparity in media sport appreciation, we argue, lies within the gendered power structure of sport that we have outlined above.

The twin logics of Australian amateur sport policy

Until about twenty years ago most amateur sporting organisations in Australia were administered by 'old boys', relied heavily on grassroots support, and were subject to minimal direct regulation by the state. However, since the 1980s both the Australian Labor Party (ALP) and the Liberal-National Coalition have implemented policies that have radically transformed amateur sport. In 1981, the Liberal Prime Minister, Malcolm Fraser, opened the Australian Institute of Sport (AIS), which is often referred to as 'the gold medal factory'. The Australian Sports Commission (ASC) was created by the ALP in 1984 and incorporated the AIS five years later. Today, the ASC has a multi-million dollar budget and is responsible for the national planning and funding of amateur sport, including gender equity programs. Like virtually all federal policies implemented by the ALP during its reign from 1983 to 1996, the planning and funding of amateur sport was shaped profoundly by the ALP's dismantling of the traditional Keynesian mode of governance. Drawing on the concept of governmentality, Mark Beeson and Alan Firth (1998; see also Hampson and Morgan 1999; Pusey 1991; Rowe 1998; Yeatman 1990) argue that a cardinal feature of the Hawke-Keating Governments was the ascendance of neoliberalism, a political rationality that emphasised the importance of creating an economically efficient and effective workforce for competition in the global economy by fostering 'market-like relations' (p. 221) in the economic, state and civil spheres. Hence, it is not surprising that during the past ten to twenty years, sporting metaphors and images have been regularly invoked by politicians, business leaders and advertisers to promote neoliberal slogans related to 'excellence', 'enterprise', 'the level playing field', 'no pain, no gain', and so on, as well as to justify the principles of social Darwinism, self-discipline, scientific management, competitive individualism, and the need to have a fit and healthy population (McKay 1991; McKay *et al.* 1993). Consequently, nearly all 'amateur' sporting organisations (NSOs) are now dependent on either the private and/or state sector for support and have executives and managers who are responsible for advertising, marketing and public relations. As Kikulius *et al.* (1992) argue in a more general context, the pressures to corporatise and professionalise have meant that the day-to-day operations of NSOs have gone from being discussed around the kitchen table to being managed from the boardroom or executive office. Two recent policies underline the anachronistic nature of 'amateurism': the ASC's Olympic Athlete Program that annually allocates millions of dollars of public funds to over 30 national sports organisations, partially on the basis of their likelihood of winning medals at the 2000 Games, and the Australian Olympic Committee's announcement that it would pay swimmers $35,000, $21,000 and $9,000 for gold, silver and bronze medals respectively at international events.

However, in line with our earlier emphasis on specificity and complexity, it is vital to note two points. First, in an age of privatisation, corporatisation and deregulation, where the state has increasingly withdrawn resources from the public sector, sport has received unprecedented commitments from the state. The ASC was almost alone in being cushioned from the 1996 cuts experienced by other federal government organisations, with Sydney's hosting of the 2000 Olympics guaranteeing even more state funding (Cashman and Hughes 1998). In 1998, after pressure from lobby groups and influential members of his party, the Prime Minister announced that tickets for the 2000 Games would be exempt from the proposed goods and services tax. In summary, since the early 1980s, there has been a definite trend toward a neoliberal form of governance of amateur sport with organisations coming under immense pressure to commodify and professionalise their operations. In the process, traditional grassroots sport has been transformed from a relatively amateur-based pastime into a full-blown corporate entity. However, this transition has been both complex and incomplete. For instance, despite extending and intensifying the ALP's neoliberal agenda since assuming office, the avowedly anti-interventionist Howard Government has also injected vast sums of tax money into amateur sport, in anticipation of the positive ideological spin-offs from the 2000 Olympics. The Prime Minister even reversed his intention to officially open the Games, proclaiming that his act would 'prevent party politics intruding into this great sporting event. Ensuring the Games will be a great unifying occasion is much more important to me than any personal satisfaction I might derive from performing the opening ceremony'. In the euphoria following the Australian Olympic team's success at the Sydney Games, Prime Minister Howard declared that his government would continue its current level of funding for sport. But that was before the post-Olympic decline of the Australian economy became readily apparent. In any event, funds for each sport are still tied to performance (that is, to winning medals), so sport has no special exemption from the processes by which virtually all cultural institutions have been inexorably – if unevenly – industrialised and marketised.

The second point we want to stress is the complex and contradictory way in which policies directed at sportswomen have evolved in Australia. In 1972, the US federal government passed Title IX of the Education Amendments Act, which was specifically aimed at eliminating and mitigating discrimination against girls and women in intercollegiate and interscholastic sport. This proved to be an important impetus for the emergence of a variety of national and international organisations advocating greater women's rights in sport, as well as a model for similar policies in other western nations (Hall 1994; Hargreaves 1999). The International Working Group on Women and Sport (IWGWS) has mounted perhaps the most impressive global example of this social movement. In 1994, nearly 300 delegates from over 80 countries met in Brighton, England, for the 'Women, Sport and the Challenge of Change' conference that was supported by the British Sports Council and the International Olympic Committee. Some important outcomes of the event were the formation of the IWGWS, the launch of an 'International Strategy of Women in Sport', and a 10-point proclamation that subsequently became known as the 'Brighton Declaration'. Since then, over 200 organisations throughout the world have formally adopted the Brighton Declaration and a second world conference on women and sport attended by about 400 delegates from over 70 countries was held in Windhoek, Namibia in 1998.

As is the case in most liberal-democratic states, Australian governments have attempted to redress the enormous gender inequalities in sport (and in other institutions) by implementing 'affirmative action', 'gender equity' and 'equal opportunity' policies for sportswomen. These compensatory schemes have usually entailed establishing women's sport promotion units, introducing special training schemes for women coaches and administrators, pressuring the media to cover more women's sport and to present 'positive images' of sportswomen, and obtaining more corporate funding. As already indicated, most gender equity initiatives in Australia were implemented by Labor governments. However, there was always a tension between the ALP's commitment to gender equity and Equal Employment Opportunity (EEO) and the regimes of masculinity and neoliberalism in the state sector that are inimical to such initiatives. As Jill Blackmore has observed:

> In an era of globalization, social justice discourses premised on citizenship rights have been replaced by discourses of how diversity can improve national productivity. The state has been reconstituted to mediate 'the market' rather than defend, least of all advocate, the public good.
>
> (Blackmore 1999, p. 204)

Moreover, bureaucratic organisations are some of the prime sites where hegemonic masculinity is constructed in postindustrial societies. For instance, in commenting on the demise of 'tradition-centered patriarchal authority', Connell argues that:

> Over the period in which both the modern state and the industrial economy was produced, the hegemony of this form of masculinity was challenged and displaced by masculinities organized much more around technical rationality and calculation ... This did not eliminate other masculinities. What it did was marginalize them: and this created conditions for new versions of masculinity that rested on impulses or practices excluded from the increasingly rationalized and integrated worlds of business and bureaucracy.
>
> (Connell 1987, pp. 130–1)

Thus, amateur sporting organisations in Australia have been subjected to dual, competing pressures: to become more efficient, commercial, professional and global in their practices, but also to display a greater commitment to equity. A significant question, therefore, is the extent to which gender equity initiatives can effect more equitable gender relations in sport, when this institution is such a potent validator of masculinity and is also so deeply embedded in the neo-liberal mode of governance that characterises both the public and private sectors. We now examine the limits and possibilities of such policy initiatives in more detail by examining the ASC's attempts to increase the proportion of female coaches and administrators in sporting organisations.

Gender equity policy in Australian amateur sport

In Australian NSOs, women comprise 17 per cent of the national coaching directors, 10 per cent of the presidents, 12 per cent of the national development officers, and 18 per cent of the executive directors (ASC 1998). Moreover, sports management in Australia displays the patterns of horizontal and vertical segregation mentioned earlier, with men usually located in the 'hard' sectors (e.g., finance, marketing, policy planning, talent identification, sports science, elite sports, Olympic sports, and men's events) and women in the 'soft' areas (e.g., affirmative action, youth sports, people with disabilities, women's events, human resources, and public relations – see McKay 1997).

Research on attempts by the ASC to redress this specific gender imbalance shows that current gender equity policies in sport are unlikely to lead to more equitable relationships between men and women. McKay (1997) found that the implementation of gender equity policies had been rendered largely ineffective. On the one hand, most managers followed procedures of 'benign neglect' or 'minimum compliance', meaning that gender equity was invariably seen strictly as 'a women's issue'. On the other hand, a smaller group of managers either subtly undermined gender equity initiatives or (consistent with Blackmore's thesis) framed them in ways that allegedly improved efficiency. In both scenarios, gender equity policies were seldom viewed as an opportunity to demonstrate the organisation's substantive commitment to social justice. It is in such intra-organisational environments, where the day-to-day 'business' of sport is done, that the full extent of this continued hierarchical and segmented 'gendering' of the institution of Australian sport is revealed as a product of a policy of governance conditioned by twin, apparently contradictory logics.

According to Ann Hall (1994, p. 54), the failure by governments in Australia, Canada, the United Kingdom and the United States to implement meaningful gender equity policies in sport has placed women in the schizoid political predicament of whether to promote *sport for women* or *women in sport*. Hall sees the former as 'a more radical feminist perspective' which 'promotes its aims through sport', and views the latter as 'a distinctly liberal approach which seeks to improve the lot of women already in sport through a sports organization for women'. Referring specifically to the Canadian situation, Hall argues that a combination of the masculine domination of sport, the traditionally conservative political views of sportswomen and neoliberal state policies have depoliticised the gender equity initiatives of Sport Canada, the federal agency responsible for amateur sport. She argues that policies have gradually been shifted toward a traditional liberal-feminist concern with getting more women to the same 'starting line' as men, without questioning institutionalised patterns of aggression, injury, sexual harassment and violence against women, homophobia, and differences of social class, ethnicity/race, age and disability (see Burstyn 1999). Furthermore, Hall notes that there has been a tendency for the women's sporting organisations she has studied to emulate the hierarchical aspects of bureaucratic organisations, with professional experts skilled in marketing, business administration and management supplanting grassroots volunteers. In an earlier study, Hall also predicted that gender equity issues would be co-opted by the rational-bureaucratic culture and masculine discourses that dominate sporting organisations:

> From a radical feminist perspective … the problem of change for the betterment of women (and men) is how to create change so that the values of people in power are not necessarily the values of a fundamentally homogeneous group of specifically white, middle-aged men of privilege. If women who are imitation men are placed in these positions, fundamental change will not occur.
>
> (Hall *et al.* 1989, p. 42)

As McKay (1997) has noted, there are striking parallels with the scenario outlined by Hall in the Canadian context and the evolution of gender equity policy in Australian amateur sport. Under the ALP, the pursuit of gender equity in sport readily recommended itself to two strategies – to make women's sport more commercially appealing (a matter of 'good business sense') and to make it more administratively sophisticated (a question of governmentality). Now, it would be a retrograde step to dismiss these measures because they do not cater to the 'needs of all women' – this is an impossible task. As Connell (1990a, p. 536) notes, gender equity initiatives in general provide some leverage for some women even if they are not connected with 'a more radical form of engagement with the state'. For instance, many of the programs and publications of the ASC have presented alternatives for women, albeit to a restricted audience. Nevertheless, the fact that gender equity policies were framed by neoliberal logic, or ignored and undermined by senior management during the ALP's long term in power, meant that the initiatives only ever received tacit support. The deficiency of the ALP's policy is evident in the fact that after nearly two decades of 'initiatives', the ASC's own research shows that women are still vastly underrepresented in virtually every aspect of Australian sport (ASC 1998). Moreover, the prospect that this situation will improve in the short to medium term is doubtful, given that, since it was elected in 1996, the Howard Government has implemented conservative social policies (in areas such as individual work contracts, child care, taxation, health, education and social welfare) that are at best indifferent to the 'condition' of women.

Conclusion: reshaping the gender regime of Australian amateur sport

The Australian state has long been implicated in both fostering business enterprise and protecting it from external competition and internal unrest. Today, guided by neoliberal ideologies that emphasise free-market policies, it has extended this agenda into cultural institutions such as the arts, education and sport, which were hitherto relatively insulated from this aspect of governmentalisation. In this chapter, we have argued that the neoliberal project, in tandem with the discourses and practices of hegemonic masculinity, has actually constrained rather than advanced women's opportunities to become full sporting citizens in amateur sport. Even in the unlikely event that current gender equity policies did increase the number of women managers, this would not necessarily change the regimes of hegemonic masculinity and neoliberalism that currently regulate everyday life in sporting organisations. Moreover, little or nothing would be done to alleviate the stresses that many professional women experience in combining work and family responsibilities (Hochschild 1997; McKenna 1997; Wajcman 1998) – an issue that seldom informs either the masculine or neoliberal practices that currently underpin workplaces in both the private and public spheres (Braithwaite 1999; Gatens 1999; Yates 1999). If organisations attempt to recruit more women, but retain gender equity policies that are based on sameness rather than difference, then it is unlikely there will be much impact on what Cockburn (1991, p. 219) calls the 'white male heterosexual and largely able-bodied ruling monoculture'. As Wieneke puts it with respect to EEO policies in Australia:

> The underlying theoretical assumption in the redistributive EEO or liberal reform model is that male-constructed and male-dominated organisational structures and processes are the yardstick against which success or failure to provide 'equal employment opportunities' for women are measured. There is no questioning of the nature of the structures themselves and the contexts within which they are created, nor of the part they play in constructing and maintaining the very inequality we are attempting to eliminate.
>
> (Wieneke 1992, p. 137)

In applying this argument specifically to Australia, it is necessary to canvass ways in which sport can be reconfigured so as not to reproduce current asymmetries of gender power – or, worse, to exacerbate them – but to open itself to a greater degree of cultural democracy. Given the obstacles that have been placed in their way, it is remarkable that so many Australian females have been attracted to and stayed involved in sport. But until policies are implemented that squarely redress the systemic disadvantages that girls and women face both inside and outside of sport – including unequal access to both school-based and community sport programs, sexual harassment, homophobia, neglect and patronisation in the popular sports media, and invisibility in organisations that are neither women- nor family-friendly – Australian women will, indeed, have completed only 'half the race' (Stell 1991).

The necessary foundation for such a policy program is the recognition of sport as a major *cultural* institution. As we have shown, while retaining its strongly masculine ambience, sport has passed through different institutional phases: first, it was treated as non- or even anti-institutional (natural, ungoverned or ungovernable); it was then systematically organised into rule structures that were framed and policed by amateur, civil-societal associations; and, later, it was subjected to the double disciplines of the market (as an economic institution) and of government (as an object for political intervention). In the process, sport has rarely been taken seriously as a *cultural* formation that requires a careful, systematic calibration of its complex state, industrial and social structures and practices. This is not an argument that sport has been marginalised by government or starved of funds. Far from it – the state has increasingly intervened in sport and raised its funding at all three levels of government. It has not, however, matched the embrace of the democratically inspired 'anthropological' approach to culture with a thoroughgoing dismantling of its hierarchical structure based on the traditional privileging of approved forms of art.

When the arts came to be of interest to Labor in the early 1990s, in terms of capital accumulation and interest-group politics, sport was not on its agenda. As Deborah Stevenson (2000, p. 34) has argued, cultural policy formation at this time was influenced by 'advances in the interdisciplinary field of Cultural Studies' and so preferred the conception of 'cultural' to that of 'arts development'. Yet key discussion documents that were to frame new cultural policy had a very familiar complexion in their classification of the culture that merited support. As Stevenson (2000, p. 35) explains, 'Tellingly, though, no mention is made of a very important area of cultural practice that at the time fell within the same portfolio – sport.' It was not surprising, then, that *Creative Nation*, the ensuing, much-heralded Commonwealth Cultural Policy (produced under the former Labor Government), seemed to regard sport not as a primary component of Australian culture but as its virtual *antithesis*. Sport was one of the cultural activities that was not selected for analysis and there were no policy recommendations concerning it. Indeed, sport was regarded as a force that helped to undermine Australian culture, because 'The proportion of private sector sponsorship of the arts and humanities compared to sport has fallen substantially' (Commonwealth of Australia 1994, p. 12).

Creative Nation as a product of the Department of Communications and the Arts did not simply reflect the bureaucratic priorities of reshuffled portfolios (that saw Sport and the Arts first joined and then separated). The ideological split was longstanding, despite the organisational structure and the policy rhetoric repositioning culture as a way of life rather than as a set of canonical texts and practices. In any case, the document also dealt with areas extending well beyond the (then) portfolio and departmental structure, such as tourism, heritage and indigenous culture. This writing of sport out of the most significant national cultural policy of the last three decades is symptomatic of the difficulties we have outlined in instituting effective equity programs within Australian sport. Despite the recent injection of funds into sport, all political parties have viewed it as marginal to their national cultural policy initiatives. It was not until the Whitlam era that sport was accorded a semblance of status at the federal level (the ASC is a semi-autonomous statutory body). Since then, most of the federal ministers responsible for sport have been junior politicians with little say in Cabinet decision-making processes. State governments have increased their commitment to sport during the 1990s, but mainly to steer policy toward public and private investment, rather than to stimulate any critical assessment of its wider purposes and functions.

If we look at the rise of cultural policy studies in the academy across Australia during the 1980s and 1990s, sport has been excluded for the most part. This is in keeping with the priorities of cultural policy studies – attacking the cultural Left's interest in social-movement politics and recommending a turn to institutionalism in its stead. This exclusion is consistent with the traditional tendency of Australian intellectuals to differentiate themselves from sport and with the nature-culture divide, where the body is an ordinary part of life and the arts are of added value, a logic that marks out the arts as part of learning and sport as part of nature.

Located somehow outside the boundaries of approved Australian culture in this way, it is not surprising that sports 'policy' has been preoccupied with the 'feel-good factor' of winning (preferably gold) medals and the economic imperatives of the sports and media industries. Thus, it is no accident that the vast majority of funds for research into sport by Australian academics has been allocated to sports scientists and physical educators for projects that are designed to identify athletic talent, enhance elite performance, detect the use of illegal performance-enhancing drugs, promote health, and uncritically extol the purported character- and nation-building virtues of participation in sport and physical education. Moreover, the ASC has actually criticised two of the few social science research projects that it has funded (McKay 1997). This lack of recognition of sport as a *cultural* institution has, as we have seen, been compounded by the proprietorial and exclusionist gender practices of many major public and private sports organisations. It is this gendered culture of sport – historically produced and institutionally reproduced – that is in need of continuing attention and contestation over the full range of cultural policy fronts.

📖 Guide to further reading

Connell (1995) uses a social constructionist and pro-feminist perspective to examine topics such as the dynamic and multiple nature of masculinities, men's bodies, violence, sexuality, the gender politics of various men's movements, and the prospects for attaining gender justice in Western societies. Dean and Hindess (1998) bring together a range of positions reflecting the influence of Foucault's work on contemporary approaches to the study of government; topics include: the corporatisation of education, the ethos of state bureaucracies, sexual harassment in the military, the regulation of the unemployed, people living with HIV/AIDS, gay communities, indigenous governance, governing material culture, managing national economic policy and the new contractualism.

M. Ann Hall in *Feminism and Sporting Bodies: Essays in Theory and Practice* (Champaign: Human Kinetics Press, 1995) argues for a relational approach to gender in sport in examining topics like sporting bodies, epistemological, theoretical and methodological aspects of studying women in sport, and the limits and possibilities of various sportswomen's advocacy groups. Hargreaves (1994) combines historical and sociological data to trace the development of females in sport from Victorian times until the present. Topics include the intersections between gender and social class, the development of female sports and physical education in the UK, patterns of containment and resistance in sportswomen's push for equality, the social construction of female bodies, institutionalised patterns of sexual discrimination, women's involvement in the Olympics, and the sexual politics surrounding homophobia, racism, globalisation, morality and empowerment.

McKay (1997) used in-depth interviews with managers to analyse how gender equity programs were implemented in Australian, Canadian and New Zealand sporting organisations. It was found that a combination of masculine structures of power in the organisations and neoliberal state regimes resulted in gender equity initiatives being framed mainly in terms of what they could do to improve managerial efficiency and effectiveness. In a similar vein, McKay, Hughson, Lawrence and Rowe (2000) challenge the conventional wisdom that Australian sport is an egalitarian institution by providing a comprehensive empirical overview of social inequalities in sport according to gender, social class, ethnicity and race. Drawing on data from five high technology, multinational corporations with model equal opportunity policies, Wajcman (1998) argues that although the entry of some women into the corporate elite has made the gendered nature of organisational life more transparent, women still continue to be excluded and marginalised from male networks. Wajcman uses feminist theories of equality and difference to show how these processes operate at both work and home.

⌨ Websites

www.ausport.gov.au/partic/wshome.html
  Australian Sports Commission
www.de.psu.edu/wsi/brighton.htm
  Brighton Declaration on Women and Sport
bailiwick.lib.uiowa.edu/ge/index.html#200
  Gender Equity in Sports
www.harassmentinsport.com/
  Harassment and Abuse in Sport Collective
www.udel.edu/HESC/bkelly/iapesgw/
  International Association of Physical Education and Sport for Girls and Women
www.triathloncanada.com/women/forward.htm
  The Windhoek Call for Action
www.de.psu.edu/wsi/index.htm
  WomenSport International

References

Adair, Daryl and Wray Vamplew (1997) *Sport in Australian History*, Melbourne: Oxford University Press.

Andrews, David L. (1998) 'Feminizing Olympic reality: preliminary dispatches from Baudrillard's Atlanta', *International Review for the Sociology of Sport* 33, pp. 5–18.

Australian Sports Commission (1998) *Facts Sheets*, Belconnen, Australian Sports Commission www.ausport.gov.au/wofamenu.html

Baird, Katrina (1994) 'Attitudes of Australian women sports journalists', *Australian Studies in Journalism* 3, pp. 231–53.

Barthes, Roland (1973) *Mythologies* (trans. Annette Lavers), London: Fontana.

Beeson, Mark and Ann Firth (1998) 'Neoliberalism as a political rationality: Australian public policy in the 1980s', *Journal of Sociology* 34, pp. 215–31.

Blackmore, Jill (1999) *Troubling Women: Feminism, Leadership, and Educational Change*, Philadelphia: Open University Press.

Boyle, Maree and Jim McKay (1995) '"You leave your troubles at the gate": a case study of the exploitation of older women's labor and leisure', *Gender & Society* 9, pp. 556–75.

Braithwaite, Valerie (1999) 'Designing the process of workplace change through the Affirmative Action Act' in M. Gatens and A. MacKinnon (eds) *Gender and Institutions: Welfare, Work and Citizenship*, Melbourne: Oxford University Press.

Bricknell, Louise (1999) 'The trouble with feelings: gender, sexualities and power in a gender regime of competitive sailing', *Journal of Sport & Social Issues* 23, 4, pp. 421–38.

Burroughs, Angela, Leonie Seebohm and Liz Ashburn (1995) '"Add sex and stir": homophobic coverage of women's cricket in Australia', *Journal of Sport & Social Issues* 19, 3, pp. 266–84.

Burstyn, Varda (1999) *The Rites of Men: Manhood, Politics and the Culture of Sport*, Toronto: University of Toronto Press.

Cahn, Susan (1994) *Coming on Strong: Gender and Sexuality in Twentieth Century Women's Sport*, New York: Free Press.

Cashman, Richard (1995) *Paradise of Sport: The Rise of Organised Sport in Australia*, Melbourne: Oxford University Press.

Cashman, Richard and Anthony Hughes (1998) 'Sydney 2000: cargo cult of Australian sport?' in D. Rowe and G. Lawrence (eds) *Tourism, Leisure, Sport: Critical Perspectives*, Sydney: Hodder Education.

Cashmore, Ellis (1996) *Making Sense of Sport* (second edition), London: Routledge.

Cockburn, Cynthia (1991) *In the Way of Women: Men's Resistance to Sex Equality in Organizations*, London: Macmillan.

Commonwealth of Australia (1994) *Creative Nation: Commonwealth Cultural Policy*, Canberra: Department of Communications and the Arts.

Connell, R.W. (1983) *Which Way Is Up? Essays on Class, Sex and Culture*, Sydney: Allen & Unwin.

— (1987) *Gender and Power*, Sydney: Allen & Unwin.

— (1990a) 'The state, gender and sexual politics: theory and appraisal', *Theory and Society* 19, 5, pp. 507–44.

— (1990b) 'An iron man: the body and some contradictions of hegemonic masculinity' in M. Messner and D. Sabo (eds) *Sport, Men, and the Gender Order: Critical Feminist Perspectives*, Champaign, IL: Human Kinetics Press.

— (1995) *Masculinities*, Sydney: Allen & Unwin.

Dean, Mitchell and Barry Hindess (1998) 'Introduction: government, liberalism, society' in M. Dean and B. Hindess (eds) *Governing Australia: Studies in Contemporary Rationalities of Government*, Cambridge: Cambridge University Press.

Dempsey, Kenneth (1992) *A Man's Town: Inequality Between Women and Men in Rural Australia*, Melbourne: Oxford University Press.

Elias, Norbert and Eric Dunning (1986) *Quest for Excitement: Sport and Leisure in the Civilizing Process*, Oxford: Basil Blackwell.

Foucault, Michel (1991) 'Governmentality' (trans. Pasquale Pasquino) in Graham Burchell, Colin Gordon and Peter Miller (eds) *The Foucault Effect: Studies in Governmentality*, London: Harvester Wheatsheaf.

Gatens, Moira (1999) 'Institutions, embodiments and sexual difference' in M. Gatens and A. MacKinnon (eds), *Gender and Institutions: Welfare, Work and Citizenship*, Melbourne: Oxford University Press.

Hall, M. Ann (1994) 'Women's sport advocacy organizations: comparing feminist activism in sport', *Journal of Comparative Physical Education and Sport* 16, pp. 50–9.

Hall, M. Ann, Dallas Cullen and Trevor Slack (1989) 'Organizational elites recreating themselves: the gender structure of national sports organizations', *Quest* 41, pp. 28–45.

Hampson, Ian and David E. Morgan (1999) 'Post-Fordism, union strategy, and the rhetoric of restructuring: the case of Australia, 1980–1996', *Theory and Society* 25, 5, pp. 747–96.

Hargreaves, Jennifer (1994) *Sporting Females: Critical Issues in the History and Sociology of Women's Sports*, New York: Routledge.

— (1999) 'The "Women's International Sports Movement": local-global strategies and empowerment', *Women's Studies International Forum* 22, 5, pp. 1–11.

Hochschild, Airlie (1997) *The Time Bind: When Work Becomes Home and Home becomes Work*, New York: Metropolitan Books.

Jefferson Lenskyj, Helen (1998) '"Inside sport" or "on the margins"? Australian women and the sport media', *International Review for the Sociology of Sport* 34, pp. 19–32.

Kane, Mary Jo (1995) 'Resistance/transformation of the oppositional boundary: exposing sport as a continuum', *Journal of Sport & Social Issues* 19, 2, pp. 191–218.

Kikulius, Lisa, Trevor Slack and Bob Hinings (1992) 'Institutionally specific design archetypes: a framework for understanding change in national sport organizations', *International Review for the Sociology of Sport* 27, pp. 343–69.

Lenskyj, Helen (1995) 'Sport and the threat to gender boundaries', *Sporting Traditions* 12, 1, pp. 47–60.

Loy, John W., David L. Andrews and Robert Rinehart (1993) 'The body in culture and sport', *Sport Science Review* 2, 1, pp. 69–91.

McKay, Jim (1990) 'Sport, leisure and social inequality in Australia' in D. Rowe and G. Lawrence (eds) *Sport and Leisure: Trends in Australian Popular Culture*, Sydney: Harcourt Brace Jovanovich.

— (1991) *No Pain, No Gain? Sport and Australian Culture*, Sydney: Prentice Hall.

— (1992) 'Sport and the social construction of gender' in G. Lupton, T. Short and R. Whip (eds) *Society and Gender: An Introduction to Sociology*, Sydney: Macmillan.

— (1997) *Managing Gender: Affirmative Action and Organizational Power in Australian, Canadian and New Zealand Sport*, Albany: State University of New York Press.

McKay, Jim, John Hughson, Geoffrey Lawrence and David Rowe (2000) 'Sport and Australian society' in Jake Najman and John Western (eds) *A Sociology of Australian Society*, Melbourne: Macmillan.

McKay, Jim, Geoffrey Lawrence, Toby Miller and David Rowe (1993) 'Globalization, postmodernism and Australian sport', *Sport Science Review* 2, 1, pp. 10–28.

McKay, Jim and Iain Middlemiss (1995) '"Mate against mate, state against state": a case study of media constructions of hegemonic masculinity in Australian sport', *Masculinities* 3, 3, pp. 38–47.

McKenna, Elizabeth Perle (1997) *When Work Doesn't Work Anymore: Women, Work and Identity*, New York: Hodder & Stoughton.

Mikosza, Janine (1997) *Inching Forward – Newspaper Coverage and Portrayal of Women's Sport in Australia: A Quantitative and Qualitative Analysis, 1996 and 1997*, Canberra: WomenSport Australia.

Mikosza, Janine and Murray Phillips (1999) 'Gender, sport and the body politic: the framing of femininity in the *Golden Girls of Sport Calendar* and *The Atlanta Dream*', *International Review for the Sociology of Sport* 34, pp. 5–16.

Miller, Toby (1998a) 'Scouting for boys: sport looks at men' in D. Rowe and G. Lawrence (eds) *Tourism, Leisure, Sport: Critical Perspectives*, Sydney: Hodder Education.

— (1998b) *Technologies of Truth: Cultural Citizenship and the Popular Media*, Minneapolis: University of Minnesota Press.

Miller, Toby, Jim McKay and Randy Martin (1999) 'Courting lesbianism', *Women and Performance: A Journal of Feminist Theory* 11, 1, pp. 211–34.

Phillips, Murray (1996) *An Illusory Image: A Report on the Media Coverage and Portrayal of Women's Sport in Australia*, Belconnen: Australian Sports Commission.

Pusey, Michael (1991) *Economic Rationalism in Canberra: A Nation-Building State Changes its Mind*, Cambridge: Cambridge University Press.

Rowe, David (1995) 'Big defence: sport and hegemonic masculinity' in A. Tomlinson (ed.) *Gender, Sport and Leisure: Continuities and Challenges (Topic Report 4)*, Brighton: Chelsea School Research Centre.

— (1997) 'Rugby league in Australia: the Super League saga', *Journal of Sport & Social Issues* 21, 2, pp. 221–6.

— (1998) '"My fellow Australians": culture, economics and the nation state', *Australian Studies* 13, 1, pp. 68–90.

— (1999) *Sport, Culture and the Media: The Unruly Trinity*, Buckingham: Open University Press.

— (2000) 'To serve and to sell: media sport and cultural citizenship', *Proceedings of the Sport and Human Rights Conference*, Sydney: University of Technology, pp. 182–91.

Rowe, David and Geoffrey Lawrence (eds) (1990) *Sport and Leisure: Trends in Australian Popular Culture*, Sydney: Harcourt Brace Jovanovich.

— (eds) (1998) *Tourism, Leisure, Sport: Critical Perspectives*, Cambridge: Cambridge University Press.

Sargent, Stephanie Lee, Dot Zillmann and James B. Weaver (1998) 'The gender gap in the enjoyment of televised sports', *Journal of Sport & Social Issues* 22, 1, pp. 146–64.

Stell, Marion (1991) *Half the Race: A History of Australian Women in Sport*, Sydney: Angus & Robertson.

Stevenson, Deborah (2000) *Art and Organisation: Making Australian Cultural Policy*, St Lucia: University of Queensland Press.

— (2001) 'Women, sport and globalization: competing discourses of sexuality and nation', *Journal of Sport & Social Issues*, in press.

Stoddart, Brian (1994) *Invisible Games: A Report on the Media Coverage of Women's Sport*, Canberra: Sport and Recreation Ministers' Council.

Tatz, Colin (1995) *Obstacle Race: Aborigines in Sport*, Sydney: University of New South Wales Press.

Thompson, Shona (1999) *Mother's Taxi: Sport and Women's Labor*, Albany: State University of New York Press.

Toohey, Kristine (1997) 'Australian television, gender and the Olympic Games', *International Review for the Sociology of Sport* 32, pp. 19–29.

Turner, Graeme (1992) 'It works for me: British Cultural studies, Australian cultural studies and Australian film' in Lawrence Grossberg, Cary Nelson and Paula Treichler (eds) *Cultural Studies*, London: Routledge.

Vamplew, Wray and Brian Stoddart (eds) (1994) *Sport in Australia: A Social History*, Cambridge: Cambridge University Press.

Wajcman, Judy (1998) *Managing Like a Man: Women and Men in Corporate Management*, Oxford: Polity Press.

Wieneke, Christine (1992) 'Does equal employment opportunity serve the women's movement? A case study from Australian higher education' in Hilary Hinds, Ann Phoenix and Jackie Stacey (eds) *Working Out: New Directions for Women's Studies*, London: The Falmer Press.

Winkler, Michael (1997) 'Brylcreemed heroes', *The Age*, 15 November, p. 6.

Yates, Lynne (1999) 'Feminism's fandango with the state revisited: reflections on Australia, feminism, education, and change', *Women's Studies International Forum* 22, 5, pp. 555–62.

Yeatman, Anna (1990) *Bureaucrats, Technocrats, Femocrats: Essays on the Contemporary Australian State*, Sydney: Allen & Unwin.

Part 3
Programs of Cultural Diversity

The complexity of the public support Cathy Freeman enjoyed after she had been rebuked, at the 1994 Commonwealth Games, for carrying the Aboriginal flag as well as the 'white flag' would be missed, Meaghan Morris has argued, if it were not also recognised that 'no *migrant* athlete feeling unrepresented by the "Anglo-Celtic" flag would be so celebrated for making a comparable gesture' (Morris 1998, p. 242). Ghassan Hage makes a similar point when he suggests that Aboriginal blackness now has a distinctive national value, representing a particular kind of national belonging, that has no equivalence in the value accorded the cultures of Australia's varied diasporas (Hage 1998, p. 57). It is, of course, no more Morris's purpose than it is Hage's to prioritise one set of differences, those between white and black Australia, over another, those between Australia's 'ethnic' minorities and the Anglo-Celtic 'mainstream' which still – in public discourse – makes the strongest, in the sense of loudest, claim to call Australia home. Nor is it ours. The point rather concerns the distinctive configuration of the ways in which questions of diversity are posed in Australia in view of the complex ways in which histories of movement, occupation, and displacement meet and intersect here.

While, if taken literally rather than as an aspiration, debates about post-nationalism are no doubt premature, and while the rhetorics of globalisation are exaggerated in suggesting a general, worldwide transformation in the speed and extent of the international flows of peoples, capital, trade and culture, there are some contexts in which the textures of national cultures have been significantly rewoven as their boundaries have become increasingly porous. Australia is one of these contexts, as the effect of post-war immigration from a variety of southern European and Asian societies has produced greater diversity within Australia while the availability of a more varied set of mediascapes – to use the term proposed by Ajun Appadurai (1996) – has also given rise to a more varied repertoire of identities, social imaginaries, and, more simply, ways of being

253

Australian. The ideal of nationalist imaginaries – one land, one nation, one people, one culture – has, as a consequence, become one that has had to be reworked in the context of successive redefinitions of Australia as a multicultural society and the varied formulations of 'unity through diversity' that these have entailed. At the same time, the resistance of Indigenous Australians to having their claims to a distinctive culture dissolved into a unifying nationalist imaginary of one land, one nation, one people, one culture has grown immeasurably. This is especially true of the build-up to, and the period since, the Mabo and Wik judgments and is evident in the separate set of relations between the land, a people and its culture, and the corresponding claims for the recognition of distinctive cultural rights and entitlements, that Indigenous demands now enunciate.

These are, then, two different forms of diversity, both of which have challenged the earlier assimilationist projects of White Australia, albeit that the principles on which they rest are quite different. James Clifford touches on these questions when he notes that the 'cosmopolitanisms articulated by diaspora discourses' are not only 'in constitutive tension with nation-state/assimilationist ideologies' (Clifford 1997, p. 287) but are also in tension with the basis for Indigenous challenges to such ideologies. Whereas the diasporic horizons that now inform the politics of many post-war migrant communities within Australia are structured by histories of displacement, travel and settlement, those of Indigenous movements characteristically 'stress continuity of habitation, aboriginality, and often a "natural" connection to the land' (287) even though, of course, their actual historical experience has also often been one of displacement, travel and resettlement. The differences between these two principles are reflected in the complex and shifting patterns of alliance, and sometimes conflict, between the social, political and cultural organisations representing Indigenous Australia and those representing different migrant communities. They have also been reflected in the clearly differentiated departments of government that have been established, at the federal and state levels, for the development and implementation of policies relating to multicultural Australia on the one hand and Aboriginal Australia on the other.

The increasing influence of the vocabulary of cultural diversity as a means of registering connections between a wide range of oppressed and excluded minorities and their rights to maintain and develop distinctive cultures and identities has, of course, much to recommend it. It serves as a means of recognising what have often been related histories of struggle against the homogenising tendencies of nationalist imaginaries and of fostering common platforms for future struggles by bringing them within the framework of the human rights agendas which increasingly – as a condition of international legitimacy – enjoin national governments to respect and promote the cultural rights of minorities. It is equally important, however, that these advantages are not purchased at the price of failing to recognise where, and why, specific forms of diversity – diasporic, Indigenous, those based on regional identity or sexual

preference – differ from each other: differ in their histories; differ in the challenges, to politics and policy, that they pose; and differ in the kinds of urgency
that attach to them in particular historical circumstances.

It is, then, these differences that are to the fore in the chapters in Part 3,
although they all share a sense of pressing urgency, given the degree to which the
after-effects of One Nation and the markedly mono-cultural aspirations of the
Howard administration have reverberated through the body politic. In an essay
first published in the early 1990s, Jon Stratton and Ien Ang offered a relatively
optimistic assessment of the effects of multiculturalism as having provided 'a
framework for a politics of *negotiation* over the very content of the national
culture, which is no longer imagined as something fixed and historically given
but as something in the process of becoming' (Stratton and Ang 1998, p. 157).
They went on to qualify this in remarking that official multiculturalism also
tended to 'freeze the fluidity of identity' in seeking to knit 'unruly and unpredictable cultural identities and differences into a harmonious unity-in-diversity'
(157). Subsequent assessments – their own included – have often been sharper
as the dilution of the agendas of multiculturalism under the Coalition has
significantly redefined the terms and conditions under which the content of the
national culture can be negotiated.

The changed tenor of these debates is reflected in the two main questions that
preoccupy James Jupp in Chapter 12: 'What was multiculturalism?' and 'Where
is it now?'. Jupp's purpose in using the past tense here is not to write a requiem
for Australian multiculturalism but, rather, to trace a historical shift in its
currency and main points of social application. Contending that multiculturalism initially had relatively little to do with questions of cultural diversity,
Jupp argues that when it was first adopted as government policy by the Whitlam
administration, its location within the Department of Immigration indicated that
its overriding purpose was to manage those who – as migrants to Australia –
occupied a liminal zone between the nation's inside and its outside. Its function,
as he puts it, was largely that of 'an immigrant settlement and integration policy'.
While it retained this aspect in its subsequent development into and through the
1980s, that decade also saw greater stress placed on the need to recognise, and
support, those distinctive forms of cultural diversity associated with settled
migrant communities. In assessing the effects of this 'second phase' of multiculturalism – a phase which connected its agendas much more clearly to those
of arts, media and cultural policies – Jupp judges that they have been uneven.
This involves the contention that SBS has proved more successful in catering to,
and promoting, demands for greater cultural diversity than has the Australia
Council. While not disputing the Council's good intentions, Jupp – echoing
Deborah Stevenson's assessment (Stevenson 2000) – sees the Council as always
having to straddle, somewhat awkwardly, the competing criteria of excellence
(usually defined in terms of white and Anglo cultural norms) and multicultural
relevance. Jupp's more general argument, however, and it is a more optimistic

one, is that it has been through the grassroots programs of local semi- and non-governmental institutions, rather than through programs at the Commonwealth level, that cultural diversity has been most actively, and most successfully, nurtured and celebrated.

Jupp has his doubts about the extent to which the celebration of Australia's cultural diversity that was the *leitmotif* of the Bicentenary has proved to be of enduring significance. Chris Healy shares this assessment arguing, in Chapter 13, that the pluralist and inclusive versions of national heritage which dominated the celebrations of 1988 should be seen, in retrospect, more as the culmination of the earlier process through which the national heritage had been expanded to include hitherto neglected constituencies (women, the working classes, ethnic minorities) than as the harbinger of things to come. Indeed, for Healy, the Bicentenary represented the exhaustion of such conceptions of heritage as, collapsing from overuse, they were – and have continued to be – challenged by countervailing practices of heritage that they have proved unable to contain. He assesses the Aboriginal boycott of 1988 as having been especially important in this respect in making publicly manifest Aboriginal conceptions and practices of heritage which rejected the all-encompassing inclusiveness of the Bicentenary's 'tactical pluralism'. Its influence in this regard has been subsequently extended by the radically transformed set of relations between Aboriginality and heritage that has been produced, amongst other developments, by the Mabo and Wik cases. For these have produced a new place for questions of Aboriginality and heritage as an inter-cultural zone between Aboriginal and white Australia. Healy sees this zone playing a crucial role – in the distinctive definition of heritage that he offers – in reshaping how 'historical understandings or habits of memory are deployed in relation to governance'. A related challenge is posed by the more traditional understandings of national heritage which – excluded from the multicultural, republican and postcolonial projections of the future that emerged from 1988 – re-appeared in the 1990s, and with a vengeance, as One Nation reclaimed this ground for its own. While not wishing to valorise the understandings of nation and history which underlie the vernacular practices of heritage which gave One Nation and John Howard's attacks on 'black armband history' their powerful cultural appeal and resonance, Healy makes a powerful case for the development of new ways of dealing with such historical understandings that will draw them into productive exchange and dialogue with other tendencies.

Questions concerning the relations between national heritage and the practices of cultural institutions loom no less largely in Nicholas Thomas's concerns in Chapter 14. And his perspective is similar to Healy's in the emphasis it places on the role which museums – in organising 'a habit of memory that is nationalised' – play in socialising a population and, thereby, contribute to the 'business of government'. Thomas's focus, however, is more specific in the spotlight it brings to bear on the complex, and often contradictory, roles that are played by 'Indigenous presences' within such processes. In considering these, Thomas takes issue with those schools of criticism which interpret museum displays of Indigenous peoples' artifacts as radically decontextualising because they sever those artifacts from their everyday use in Indigenous cultures. This is, Thomas argues, an effect of the museum *per se*, by no means limited to its consequences for the exhibition of Indigenous peoples' artifacts, and, as such, should not distract our attention from the fact that this so-called decontextualisation is the result of a work of distinctive practices of recontextualisation which always animate the museum object in powerful ways, investing it with signifying new possibilities. Yet Thomas wants also to argue that Indigenous peoples' artifacts have a certain 'presence' arising from 'their material characteristics, and the objectified intelligence that they carry' which may set them at odds with the larger narratives that are implied by the exhibition contexts in which they are displayed. It is from this perspective that Thomas examines both Australian museum exhibitions of Aboriginal art and New Zealand exhibitions of Maori culture. His conclusions echo those of Chris Healy in the value he places on those ways of contextualising the objects of Indigenous material culture which allow their latent presence – the refractory histories that they embody – to speak against the grain of all-encompassing national narratives, even those inclusive ones which construct the nation in the form of a patchwork quilt of different communities held together by a connecting thread of shared values.

The exhibition of Aboriginal art in Australian art galleries has, as Thomas has argued elsewhere (Thomas 1999), played an important role in enhancing the prestige of Aboriginal culture, particularly among educated elites. Yet there is, as Meaghan Morris notes, recalling her comments on Cathy Freeman, often 'an appalling gap between the cultural prestige accorded to Aboriginality and the living conditions and prospects of many Aboriginal people' (Morris 1998, p. 24). Helen Molnar would agree. She would also take the further step of contending that the prestige enjoyed by certain forms of Aboriginal culture – especially those that have been subjected to high-art forms of appropriation – does not extend to all of them. The case she cites in Chapter 15 is that of Aboriginal languages which – through the disruption of Aboriginal communities and the legacy of colonial conceptions of Aborigines as a dying race with, therefore, a dying culture – have been either actively discouraged or allowed to languish. As a consequence, the hundred or so Aboriginal languages now remaining have fewer and fewer speakers, posing a threat to their long-term viability and that of the distinctive ways of life, customs and knowledges connected with their development. It is for this reason, among others, that Molnar places such importance on the role of Indigenous media in re-establishing Indigenous communication networks that had been disrupted by colonisation and, in so doing, providing a basis – in language and in everyday life – for new Indigenous cultural dynamics. Even so, the story she has to tell is a sorry one of the all-too-frequent misalignments between Aboriginal cultural needs on the one hand and policy responses to those needs on the other.

   Robin Trotter's concerns in the final chapter focus on questions of regional diversity, and the contradictory dynamics affecting regional economies – and, related to these, distinctive regional cultures and identities – as they come to form parts of more globalised systems of exchange. She explores these questions by examining how cultural tourism has reorganised the economies and cultures of a number of Queensland regions. Cairns, as the centre for eco and adventure tourism – for reef, rainforest and rock – in Far North Queensland; Townsville's redefinition of itself as a cultural centre; the role of the Stockman's Hall of Fame and of the Matilda Highway in the tourism strategies of Central West Queensland; and the development of Ipswich as a regional museum centre and a key hub in the Queensland information economy: each of these, Trotter argues, has involved the development of a distinctive set of relations between the region concerned, the state capital, Brisbane, and the national and international economies. This has also had distinctive consequences for regional identities in Queensland. As regional tourist destinations develop interstate and global markets, she argues, 'regional identities are increasingly severed and dislocated from state and national frames of reference', while major metropolitan centres simultaneously – in aiming to place themselves on the world market as part of a cosmopolitan network of world cities – draw 'less and less on the regions for cultural identity'. It is in these ways, Trotter concludes, that tourism has become a major force in the ongoing transformation of the relational frameworks within which regional identities are shaped and formed.

References

Appadurai, Arjun (1996) *Modernity at Large: Cultural Dimensions of Globalisation*, Minneapolis: University of Minnesota Press.

Clifford, James (1997) 'Diasporas' in Montserrat Guibernau and John Rex (eds) *The Ethnicity Reader: Nationalism, Multiculturalism and Migration*, Cambridge: Polity Press.

Hage, Ghassan (1998) *White Nation: Fantasies of White Supremacy in a Multicultural Society*, Sydney: Pluto Press.

Morris, Meaghan (1998) 'Lunching for the republic: feminism, the media and identity politics in the Australian republicanism debate' in David Bennett (ed.) *Multicultural States: Rethinking Difference and Identity*, London and New York: Routledge.

Stevenson, Deborah (2000) *Art and Organisation: Making Australian Cultural Policy*, St Lucia: University of Queensland Press.

Stratton, Jon and Ien Ang (1998) 'Multicultural imagined communities: cultural differences and national identity in the USA and Australia' in David Bennett (ed.) *Multicultural States: Rethinking Difference and Identity*, London and New York: Routledge.

Thomas, Nicholas (1999) *Possessions: Indigenous Art/Colonial Culture*, London: Thames & Hudson.

Chapter 12

The Institutions of Culture: Multiculturalism

James Jupp

The creation of a multicultural society in Australia through the post-1947 immigration program is accepted as a desirable reality by the major political parties (Jupp 1996, 1998a). But it has been subjected to a steady stream of criticism by a vocal minority, which finds an echo in public opinion as recorded by the few polls which have canvassed the issue. These critics have been given consistent publicity by some of the media. The greatest media barrage was produced by the maiden speech of Pauline Hanson (Independent MHR for Oxley) on 10 September 1996 (Hanson 1997; see also Sheehan 1998). There has been only a limited academic critique of multiculturalism (Castles *et al.* 1988; Kukathas 1993; Hage 1998) and not much academic defence of it either, with most discussion coming through government agencies or politicians (OMA 1989; NMAC 1995, 1999; Theophanous 1995). It is quite untrue to say that multiculturalism 'has never been defined', as Leonie Kramer among others has claimed, but such definitions tend towards 'motherhood statements'. Many consistent critics pay little attention to these definitions or to the evolution of public policy since Australia was first officially declared a multicultural society by the Whitlam Government in 1973. They prefer to repeat alarmist claims, often derived from American controversies.

Critics of multiculturalism may be divided between those taking a polemical or ideological stance against 'divisiveness' and those who regard official policy as a way of obscuring inequalities or even racism. Supporters of multiculturalism usually produce a liberal democratic defence rather than favouring cultural relativism. In this view society should accommodate or even 'manage' diversity. While many polemicists are active in politics or public controversy, a division between 'academics' and 'publicists' can be artificial. Professor Blainey, for example, has conducted most of his criticism since 1984 in popular media. In the opposite camp, Dr Theophanous has argued his position in academic texts but was also a Labor politician. While the critics are usually conservative and argue for the supremacy of mainstream culture and national identity, a radical critique has also developed following the pioneering study of Stephen Castles, Mary Kalantzis, Bill Cope and Michael Morrissey in 1988. Academics such as Ghassan Hage or Jon Stratton see multicultural policy as obscuring the dominance of 'whiteness' and, therefore, as a weapon in the hands of those denying or suppressing the claims of minorities (Hage 1998; Stratton 1998). The impact of this approach on public policy has been negligible compared with the influence of the more conventional conservative critique.

Multiculturalism in Australia has not necessarily been very concerned with culture in the conventional sense. At the national level it has usually been administered through the Department of Immigration, which has little interest in cultural issues other than the teaching of English to new arrivals. While an Office of Multicultural Affairs functioned within the Department of Prime Minister and Cabinet between 1987 and 1996, it was promptly abolished as one of the first acts of the Howard Government. The function was returned to Immigration without a budget and survives as a small section with the limited role of servicing the National Multicultural Advisory Council and having an input in various spasmodic campaigns for tolerance. The Office had already moved its focus away from cultural and educational policy towards immigrant settlement and access to public services. A major collection of research papers published by it in 1989 had nothing directly related to cultural issues and policies (Jupp 1989). This relative indifference was reflected in the three Commonwealth multicultural agendas of 1989, 1995 and 1999. The first two devoted two pages each to arts policy while the latest had nothing at all.

The heyday of official multiculturalism at the national level was between the Galbally report on migrant services in 1978 (Galbally 1978) and the launching of the second multicultural agenda by the Keating Government in 1995 (NMAC 1995). Since then there has been a marked decline of enthusiasm, a reduction of staffing, funding and functions at the Commonwealth, state and non-governmental organisation (NGO) level, and a less than encouraging atmosphere from politicians, public servants and populist journalists. The major NGO advocating multiculturalism, the Federation of Ethnic Communities' Councils of Australia (FECCA), has also lost much of its drive although it continues to be funded from the budget of the Department of Immigration. While some of this reflects caution induced by the impact of One Nation – which wanted multiculturalism 'abolished' – it also suggests that the enthusiasm of the 1970s has waned in the face of different priorities and reduced public interest. An optimist might argue that multiculturalism is so widely accepted as to be uncontroversial, but that has certainly not been the tenor of political debate in the late 1990s.

What was multiculturalism?

There is some confusion in the Australian debate on multiculturalism because of the intrusion of partisan political arguments and the importation of ideas from North America and Europe which are not necessarily relevant to the local scene. What is attempted here is an account of the development of public policy in Australia with particular reference to the cultural dimension in the conventional sense of the arts, media and creative writing. Cultural maintenance, in the sense of preserving languages and other imported cultural manifestations, has been a concern of organised ethnic groups but has had a diminishing impact on public policy. Policy was developed largely under the influence of the Department of Immigration and had its origins in fears of social disharmony created by mass immigration from non-British sources. This was a quite different motivation from that behind the parallel development of Canadian multiculturalism. Over the years there was a consistent and bipartisan development of policy, which began to be fractured in the 1980s with the reassertion of conservative ideas derived from the United States and reinforced by the ideology of economic rationalism. As multiculturalism and immigration were closely bound together in the public eye, the increasing unpopularity of immigration, caused largely by high unemployment, also undermined previously widespread support. In recent years the drive for multicultural approaches in the arts was thus countered by reduced enthusiasm for multiculturalism as an official national policy. Nevertheless that policy has never been officially repudiated and was reaffirmed by the Liberal–National Coalition at the end of 1999.

The official adoption of a policy of multiculturalism followed a decade when attitudes and policies were coming to grips with new realities different from those based on previous experience with British immigration. Multiculturalism queried the belief that all other cultures were inferior to, and incompatible with, the 'mainstream' culture of white British Australia. It accepted that immigrants would continue to speak their own languages and would try to pass on to their children a sense of pride in their origins. Those who had come as refugees would still follow closely the politics of their homelands, even while being anxious to become Australian citizens. Finally, with the official ending and denunciation of White Australia by the Whitlam Labor Government in 1973, it was accepted that physical appearance or non-European origin were not a suitable basis on which to exclude people from the Australian community. The social and economic integration of immigrants continued in parallel with the adoption of multicultural approaches.

Australia was officially declared as 'multicultural' in 1973, but it took some time to give concrete meaning to the term. Multiculturalism as public policy in Canada has never been officially managed by agencies concerned with immigration. In Australia, by contrast, there has always been a close association between the two policy areas. Multiculturalism has been developed through advisory councils attached to the Department of Immigration. The minister responsible for multiculturalism has always been the Minister for Immigration. Even after the creation of the Office of Multicultural Affairs within the Department of Prime Minister and Cabinet in 1987, the Department of Immigration retained the term 'Ethnic Affairs' in its title. In 1996, when the Howard Coalition Government transferred the Office back to the Department, it was renamed the Department of Immigration and Multicultural Affairs. Previously, the Australian Institute of Multicultural Affairs (1979–1986) had fallen within the Immigration portfolio though it was governed by its own legislation. This did not prevent its abolition by the Hawke Government. As immigrants are, by definition, 'outsiders', this institutional affiliation has tended to underline the marginal and exotic nature of cultures other than those adapted from the United Kingdom or adopted from the United States. The relative weakness of the Department of Immigration has also limited the extent to which it could coordinate multicultural policies across a wide range of institutions, levels of government and differing publics and interests.

Developing a theory of multiculturalism rested with a handful of people who were also concerned with immigrant settlement. These included the Minister for Immigration in the Whitlam Government, Al Grassby, the chairman of the Australian Ethnic Affairs Council, Professor Jerzy Zubrzycki, and the Professor of Sociology at La Trobe University, the late Jean Martin (Hage and Couch 1999). Zubrzycki's paper, *The Questing Years* (1968), focused on issues which are still relevant today, including the non-recognition of overseas qualifications, migrant concentration in manual employment and the teaching of English. He advocated cultural pluralism which 'stands for the retention of ethnic identity and continued participation of individual settlers in minority group activities' and rejected 'attempts to promote an amalgamation of cultures ... and assumptions of Anglo-Saxon superiority and conformity'.

Grassby took up similar themes in 1973, developing the concept of the 'family of the nation' and drawing heavily on the Canadian model. Grassby favoured the 'indefinite' preservation of distinct ethnic groups and ethnic heritages. Further work on this theme was undertaken by a succession of councils advisory to the Minister for Immigration. Among issues developed by these councils were the teaching of English, the recognition of qualifications, the sensitisation of service deliverers to ethnic variety, translating and interpreting services, training, and funding support for organised ethnic groups. These were all aimed at integrating migrants. Very little support was given to ethnic minority cultures or languages, despite the wishes of many ethnic community activists.

Australia as a Multicultural Society (Australian Ethnic Affairs Council 1977) called for 'a society in which people of non-Anglo-Australian origin are given the opportunity, as individuals or groups, to choose to preserve and develop their culture, their languages, traditions and arts ... while at the same time they enjoy effective and respected places within one Australian society, with equal access to the rights and opportunities that society provides and accepting responsibilities towards it'. These themes were reiterated in the report *Multiculturalism for All Australians* (Zubrzycki 1982). This stressed rights and duties within a democratic society and was the first of these reports to include Aborigines within its ambit. Aborigines have, however, always had separate institutions and interests despite some cooperation with ethnic organisations on issues such as racism or language policy.

The link between immigration and multiculturalism was cemented by the Galbally report on migrant programs and services in 1978. This urged the creation of the Australian Institute of Multicultural Affairs, the use of ethnic-specific welfare workers, and the creation of migrant resource centres. All these were to be funded through the budget of the Department of Immigration. The report also recommended the introduction of broadcasting in various languages. This led to the creation of the Special Broadcasting Service (SBS) in 1978, which began television transmission in 1980. The Galbally report strongly emphasised English language learning, including the introduction of full-time on-arrival courses for adult migrants through the Adult Migrant Education (later English) Program. These courses were free of charges, which is no longer the case.

Multiculturalism, then, developed as an immigrant settlement and integration policy. It was not originally concerned with Aborigines, who were the responsibility of different agencies. It was concerned with the second generation children of immigrants but this aspect was inadequately developed when compared with the Canadian situation. Most policy development for the younger generation has emerged from the education systems and has been pluralist and sometimes confused, varying from state to state. The admonition, made as recently as 1999, that multiculturalism and immigration were distinct policy areas was not borne out by the administrative arrangements.

The major lobby group supporting multiculturalism has been the Federation of Ethnic Communities' Councils of Australia (FECCA) founded in 1979. This was funded by the Department of Immigration from 1983 but later became the responsibility of the Office of Multicultural Affairs, returning to Immigration in 1996. FECCA acknowledges the distinctiveness of the Australian-born of non-English-speaking background (NESB). But many of its efforts have been directed towards immigrant settlement and most of its activists (though not all) have been immigrants. FECCA produced a series of policy papers on national language policy, SBS, folklife, arts and culture, and a national cultural policy in the 1980s, but has become much less active in those areas in recent years. Its interest in cultural policy was greatest in the mid-1980s, prompted by the threatened amalgamation of SBS and the ABC (which FECCA successfully opposed) and by Commonwealth inquiries into multicultural education and folklife. Papers presented to its Perth conference in 1985 called for changed acquisition policies by collecting agencies. Museums responded to this and to a conference held in Melbourne in 1988 by the Museums Association and Library

Council of Victoria (Birtley and McQueen 1989; Galla 1993). Encouragement was also given to museums dealing specifically with multiculturalism, such as the Migration Museum of Adelaide, the Jewish museums of Melbourne and Sydney or the Chinese Museum of Melbourne. A more sweeping paper called for a national cultural policy which reflected the multicultural reality of Australia. This concluded that 'it is time for action to match the rhetoric of multiculturalism within the Arts, Heritage and Cultural institutions of Australia and make the marginal accepted by the mainstream' (Gardini and Skardoon 1985, p. 19).

By 1989, multiculturalism was officially defined as having three main dimensions:

- *Cultural identity: the right of all Australians* ... to express and share their individual cultural heritage, including their language and religion
- *Social justice*: the right of all Australians to equality of treatment and opportunity, and the removal of barriers of race, ethnicity, culture, religion, gender or place of birth
- *Economic efficiency*: the need to maintain, develop and utilise effectively the skills and talents of all Australians, regardless of background (Jupp 1989, p. iii).

Multiculturalism has several facets and levels of application. Because it also aims to be 'for all Australians', aspects of multiculturalism can be found in the policies of a range of agencies. All state governments have some institutions dealing with ethnic affairs. The largest is in New South Wales and the most recent is in Queensland. While most have kept the words 'ethnic' or 'multicultural' in their titles, the NSW commission changed its name to the Community Relations Commission in 1999. These have a concern with language services and education which are state functions and have also developed policies in the fields of health, housing and local government. Those services falling within the immigration powers of the Commonwealth include:

- the provision of on-arrival services and information for new immigrants
- English as a second language training for adults and children
- translating and interpreting services and
- immigrant welfare.

Commonwealth responsibilities under other powers include broadcasting and community and race relations. The Commonwealth, especially through the Australia Council, has also assumed a broad responsibility for cultural support, which it shares with the states.

As the 1999 multicultural agenda puts it: 'Australia is, and will always be, a multicultural society irrespective of our immigration intake, and multiculturalism remains an important means of addressing the challenges and opportunities of cultural diversity' (National Multicultural Advisory Council 1999, p. 3).

Where is multiculturalism now?

Until the early 1980s multiculturalism was fairly uncontroversial although attitudes towards immigration had changed by the mid-1970s, from broadly favourable to more critical. Multiculturalism has been consistently criticised by Professor Blainey among others. His reiteration of this critique in the *Bulletin* in August 1994 is a helpful starting point for analysing some of the basic arguments (Blainey 1994). Blainey argued that he was right to warn against Asian immigration and multiculturalism, even though few of the disasters he predicted years earlier have actually happened. He believed that multiculturalism must be rejected if it is based on pure cultural relativism, which has never been the case in Australia. Blainey is right (but scarcely controversial) in pointing out that the core of Australian life and institutions is still essentially of British origin and that ethnic minorities are small and often peripheral (see also Hage 1998). Prime Minister Keating similarly endorsed institutions which are primarily of British origin by saying that 'all Australians share the same civic obligations to accept the basic structures and principles of Australian society, and the same civil rights'. The new agenda launched by John Howard on 5 May 1999 also specifically identified the British inheritance as central to Australian institutions (National Multicultural Advisory Council 1999, p. 48).

In her maiden speech in 1996 Pauline Hanson repeated many of Blainey's arguments, though adding her own agenda items on Aborigines, the United Nations and foreign aid. Governments were 'encouraging separatism' through Aboriginal funding. Arguing that ordinary Australians had been kept out of the debate, she wanted 'our immigration policy radically reviewed and that of multiculturalism abolished'. Migrants of Asian origin 'have their own culture and religion, form ghettos and do not assimilate … A truly multicultural country can never be strong or united'. In her view 'abolishing the policy of multiculturalism [would] save billions of dollars and allow those from ethnic backgrounds to join mainstream Australia'. She did 'not consider those people from ethnic backgrounds currently living in Australia anything but first-class citizens, provided of course that they give this country their full, undivided loyalty' (Hanson 1997, pp. 2–11). Many similar attacks have been launched by print and radio journalists such as Paul Sheehan (Sheehan 1998), Alan Jones, Stan Zemanek, Frank Devine and many others whose voices reach millions while they complain that debate is being suppressed!

Hanson's case did not rest on the concept of racial inferiority but on the incompatibility of different cultures. This 'cultural' approach now finds a stronger echo in public opinion than the original racist arguments for White Australia. But there is very little study of cultural variety in Australia. Governments are the main source of research funds on immigration and ethnicity and they have defined the problems as mainly economic or social (OMA 1992). Australian social scientists have yet to produce the range of cultural analysis common in North America, except in Aboriginal studies (Jupp 1998b). Indeed, the two major research agencies in this area were abolished by the Hawke Government in 1986 and by the Howard Government in 1996 for essentially partisan reasons.

One of the popular criticisms of multiculturalism is that some cultures endorse behaviour which is not compatible with Australian (or Western) values or practices. The Muslim attitude to women is frequently quoted, backed up by the titillation of genital mutilation (a practice so rare in Australia that very few cases have ever come to light). There has been little encouragement for moral relativism in official Australian multiculturalism. The Law Reform Commission argued that its major inquiry was 'not only about extending the boundaries of the legal system to give greater recognition to cultural diversity, and to ensure equality of treatment and opportunity. It is also about establishing appropriate limits on the right to cultural freedom' (Law Reform Commission 1992, p. 1.18).

The 'cultural defence' is normally rejected by judges except in some traditional Aboriginal cases. This defence argues that the defendant's culture justifies behaviour which is not endorsed by the law. Different marriage practices are endorsed through the marriage celebrant system and non-Christian schools are financially supported on the same basis as their far more numerous Christian counterparts. The long-term trend is towards secularisation. Moreover, majorities of migrants from some major 'non-Christian' societies (such as India, Sri Lanka, Lebanon, Korea, Egypt, Iraq or Indonesia) are Christians, many of them also English-speaking. Their cultures, while not necessarily 'European', are partly westernised, a tendency likely to be strengthened as the skill and education levels of immigrants are raised by public policy.

Government programs and agencies

Multicultural programs and agencies in Australia are primarily concerned with easing immigrant settlement, with securing equity for ethnic minority members, and with moderating the risk of social disharmony (OMA 1992). There has been a plethora of enquiries into multicultural and settlement programs over the past twenty years, with scarcely a year passing without a round of community consultations and recommendations. The argument that multiculturalism has never been debated or put to the people is nonsense and designed to create resentment. Among the more important enquiries have been those producing the three 'agendas' of 1989, 1995 and 1999. Both the Galbally report of 1978 and the Review of Migrant and Multicultural Programs of 1986 devoted some space to multiculturalism and consulted widely with ethnic communities. This was much less true of the two inquiries into Australian Studies and Australian Folklife in the late 1980s (CRASTE 1987; Dept. of Arts 1987). In part this represented departmental preoccupations, as the first two were the responsibility of the Department of Immigration while the latter two fell within the overall ambit of the Departments of Education and Arts. The Commonwealth Department of Education was seen as hostile to multiculturalism by its critics and this was especially true under the ministry of John Dawkins. His attitude towards the national policy on language was especially resented (Ozolins 1993). There was certainly a contrast between his preoccupations and those of his predecessor, Susan Ryan. But her orientation was towards defining culture in specifically 'Australian' terms, which also led to a neglect of multicultural aspects. The report *Windows on Worlds* of 1987 had only five pages on multicultural studies out of 230 and no recommendations, although the committee did commission a useful summary on multiculturalism (Brennan 1986).

Of more potential significance was the report, also launched by Ryan in 1987, called *Education in and for a Multicultural Society*, and the National Policy on Languages developed by Jo Lo Bianco for the Department of Education in the same year (Lo Bianco 1987). While neither of these was centrally concerned with creative culture, they were designed to change the entire orientation of the education systems away from their Anglocentric past. But most of these reports of the late 1980s had little lasting impact and the National Advisory and Co-ordinating Committee on Multicultural Education did not long survive Ryan's departure from the ministry. The final abolition of the Commonwealth Schools Commission by Dawkins removed another agency which had shown an active interest in multicultural and language education.

Multicultural agencies exist at the Commonwealth and state levels and in some large municipalities in Sydney and Melbourne. With the exception of New South Wales and Victoria such units are small, with a major interest in providing information, interpreting and translating. As at the national level, they are advised by committees drawn from the various ethnic communities and have a close, if not always uncritical, relationship with the state Ethnic Communities' Councils (EECs). The Federation of Ethnic Communities' Councils of Australia (FECCA), together with the Ethnic Communities' Councils, which are its state-level constituents, are the major representative groups in ethnic affairs. These are funded from taxation as are many other interest groups. They are important advocates of multiculturalism but have less influence in other areas of public policy (Jupp and Kabala 1993). In recent years FECCA has been subject to several internal crises, the latest of which saw the suspension of affiliation by the Victorian ECC early in 1999. In the same year the funding for the New South Wales ECC was withdrawn by the state Labor Government.

State initiatives are most important in providing services in education and health. In recent years the trend has been for the Commonwealth to become less engaged and the states more so, in part reflecting the ideological preferences of the Commonwealth Coalition. In Victoria and New South Wales all government departments are obliged to publish details of their services for a non-English-speaking clientele. Policy increasingly focuses on positive aspects of diversity rather than on perceived social problems:

The Government of Victoria regards the cultural diversity of our community as one of the State's greatest assets. It is a richness which is recognised as contributing much to Victoria's economic prosperity, cultural life and community fabric. Promoting policies and programs which deliver culturally appropriate services to enable Victorians greater contribution to and participation in public life is integral to this vision.

(Victoria State Government 1998)

State multiculturalism, unlike Commonwealth government programs, is not directly concerned with immigration policy. It applies, especially in the school systems, to the locally born as well and to those who have been in Australia for many years. This has led to innovative language policies in Victoria and South Australia.

Most of the 'multicultural' services criticised for spending 'billions' are simply concerned with settling NESB immigrants into society and ensuring some equity for them. Agencies such as the Human Rights and Equal Opportunity Commission are much more involved in women's and Aboriginal issues than with multiculturalism. Reaffirmed Commonwealth support at the end of the 1990s did not extend, however, to recreating a central agency, as the third agenda had recommended (National Multicultural Advisory Council 1999, rec. 30). Instead the government approved a part-time council, with its secretariat located in the Department of Immigration and without the right to fund contracts.

Broadcasting and the Australia Council

The most expensive multicultural agency is the Special Broadcasting Service, the main provider of non-English language programming on television and radio. The major coordinating and funding body for cultural activity at the national level is the Australia Council. Organised ethnic communities have usually defended SBS while being critical of the Australia Council. The exhaustive Connor review of multicultural broadcasting concluded in 1985 that 'the perception that the ABC has been insensitive to the needs and interests of some sections of Australian society, especially ethnic communities, is still very strong' (Connor 1985). The Dix Report on the ABC in 1978 had already noted that 'the view of the world which the ABC presents to the community is overwhelmingly monocultural' (ABC in Review 1981). FECCA took up this argument, meeting with the minister (Michael Duffy) and organising meetings to oppose the merger of the two broadcasters. In response to the largest of these meetings, in Melbourne in 1986, Prime Minister Bob Hawke reversed his minister's policy and SBS remained independent. Despite several similar crises in recent years, the two public broadcasters remain distinct. SBS has extended its range and a second national radio channel was launched in the 1990s to cope with the increasing number of languages in use in Australia. FECCA has continued to see

SBS as a major multicultural institution, criticising only its control by Anglo-Australians at the higher management levels.

Relations with the Australia Council have been more problematic. Because funding is often at the heart of cultural politics, the Australia Council has been criticised for its allocation of resources to ethnic or multicultural organisations and individuals. Galbally recommended that 'the Australia Council develop closer links with ethnic communities and that it reassess its budgetary allocation in order to ensure that ethnic arts receive a more equitable amount' (Galbally 1978, rec. 50). This raised the whole issue of what constitutes 'high' and 'folk' culture and 'ethnic' or 'mainstream' culture. For example, a report commissioned by the Office of Multicultural Affairs recommended that 'the Federal Government liaise with representatives from the Australia Council's Performing Arts and Community Cultural Development Boards in order to come to a practical position regarding folkloric work. If it is heritage art, then from where should it receive its funding?' (Castles and Kalantzis 1994; Australia Council 1993, rec.13) It went on to recommend greater consultation across the boards of the Arts Council 'so that individual artists, groups and companies that wish to maintain a dual identity and role are not compromised philosophically and artistically by the current lack of sympathetic policy' (rec. 14).

On several occasions since the 1980s the Australia Council has attempted to develop an acceptable multicultural policy. As so much creative work is done by Australians of non-English speaking background this is inevitable and desirable. In 1982 the Council adopted a multicultural arts policy across its boards and by 1986 was distributing $1.3 million, which was only 3 per cent of total allocations. Multicultural arts were defined as 'the practice of artistic traditions (popular, folk, or high arts) of immigrants and people descendant from non-English speaking backgrounds' (Jupp 1986, para 13.58). Aboriginal culture then and now has been discretely funded through a range of institutions and usually at a more generous level. Under the chairmanship of Donald Horne in 1990, the Australia Council developed the Ideas for Australia program which included policies for cultural diversity. Its report noted that:

> in the Australia Council there is some representation of ethnic minorities. There are none at the top of the ABC. There is on the board of SBS, but its most influential managers are mostly of English-speaking cultural and linguistic background ... It is a problem to find experts and peer judges for arts whose established tradition is somewhere else in the world and which is carried in languages and modes of expression which are perceived as outside the stream of Australian history
>
> (Totaro 1990, p. 24).

In response to these criticisms and problems, the Australia Council began revising its policies in the 1990s (Blonski 1992). It attempted to secure some uniformity across its boards, some of which had been much more sympathetic to multiculturalism than others. Overall policy was developed by a Multicultural Advisory Committee (ACMAC) set up in 1990 and including representation from the boards and from the National Aboriginal and Torres Strait Islander Arts Board. A full policy statement was issued in 1993 (Australia Council 1993). In a draft discussion paper in 1999, ACMAC noted that 'over the past decade the field, and even the definition and use of the term multiculturalism has broadened to encompass a wide variety of arts practice and content'. Despite this, many of the issues remained the same as in previous decades, including promoting access, equity, and inclusiveness and reducing marginalisation; convincing those in positions of leadership of the value of the Council's multicultural work; identifying barriers to diverse art production; and enabling feedback within the arts community.

Semi- and non-governmental institutions

With the reduction of Commonwealth support for multiculturalism after 1996, responsibility moved towards state governments. It also rested where it had always been, among non-governmental institutions such as churches, clubs and associations. Of course many of these continued to look for support from public funds. These were more forthcoming from the state rather than the Commonwealth level if activity had a cultural rather than a welfare orientation. The Commonwealth continued a modest subsidy for 'weekend schools' run by ethnic communities and for insertion classes for languages within the school systems, with the main beneficiary being Italian. While rarely described as 'multiculturalism', the greatest expenditure normally goes to religious institutions. The distinction between 'religion' and 'culture' is highly contestable for the non-Christian religions. The Commonwealth supports Jewish and Muslim schools on the same basis as for other religions and state governments often provide free or cheap land for mosques and temples, as previously for churches. Compared with this level of provision, the relatively small sum available for private cultural activity scarcely deserves the criticism which is often launched against it.

The most obvious manifestations of privately organised multicultural events are the various festivals. Those which are specifically dedicated to multicultural performance include Carnivale in Sydney and the National Multicultural Festival in Canberra. Two of the most successful ethnic festivals are the Lygon Street Festa for Italians and the Antipodes Festival for Greeks in Melbourne. All of these are organised partly through the ethnic communities and expect and receive usually modest public funding. It is especially interesting that Australian folk festivals, which were once the preserve of 'rural nostalgia', are now completely open to other ethnic influences. The Woodford Festival, which claims to be the largest in the world, now has a program which includes 'traditional Australian', Aboriginal and ethnic performers (Woodford 1999). Its public sector sponsors in 1999 included the Australia Council, the Council for Aboriginal Reconciliation, the Queensland Arts Office and Multicultural Affairs – Department of Premier and Cabinet. Similarly varied festivals are now held all over Australia. The role of the Commonwealth in all this is negligible.

Most ethnic activity takes place through the initiative of clubs and associations, which also receive little if any public funding. These include major clubs such as the Castellorizian or Marconi in Sydney, the Veneto in Melbourne or the Hellenic in Canberra and Brisbane. Many clubs also take part in soccer competitions or other sporting and social activity. The public sector input is largely confined to the granting of liquor and gambling licences. Whether the clubs fulfill important 'cultural' activities is a matter of taste and definition. Some are indistinguishable from general community clubs, while some try to preserve an 'ethnic' ambience. Commonwealth grants to organisations through the Department of Immigration are restricted to the support of immigrant welfare and settlement and do not go to commercial clubs. State government grants usually go to subsidise newsletters or other minor expenses. Most organisations receiving such funding are small and with limited resources, unlike some of the major clubs. The myth that 'billions' are being spent on subsidising alien cultures is simply a lie. As the 1999 agenda put it: 'many of the criticisms of multicultural funding are based on incorrect perceptions of the dollars involved which, while not inconsiderable, are much lower than the wildly exaggerated amounts sometimes claimed' (National Multicultural Advisory Council 1999, p. 11).

Mainstream, ethnic and multi-cultures

A central dilemma for cultural policy has been to determine between the conflicting claims of mainstream, ethnic and multicultural creative activity. The boundaries between different cultures are rarely clear cut, especially as globalisation and homogenisation have become so influential. Are rodeos, line dancing or country music manifestations of Australian culture or just locally adapted American imports? Is a Chinese pianist playing Chopin an example of multiculturalism? Is Scottish dancing ethnic or a long-standing Australian tradition? Aboriginal art and dance are clearly both ethnic and uniquely Australian. But is this true for Aboriginal country or pop music? Henry Lawson or Les Murray are uniquely Australian. But must the labels of ethnicity or multiculturalism be applied to Andrew Riemer or David Malouf simply because they are not of British or Irish origin? These are not just abstract issues. Funding often depends on the category to which cultural activity is allocated by decision-makers. Opera in Italian or French or ballet first performed for the Russian Tsars is not treated the same way as Croatian folk dancing or Greek *rembetika*.

One of the greatest obstacles to be overcome by creative performers seeking funds has been the equation of 'ethnic' and 'folk'. The intricate classical music and dance of India, for example, may be treated as though it were folk art and thus undeserving of funding support from those who finance the European classics. In the late 1940s, as Australia started to become multicultural, East European refugees actively promoted their folk dancing, costumes and musical traditions because these were seen as national manifestations which the communists were either suppressing or, more correctly, were using for their own political purposes. The revival and codification of folk culture had been a major feature of nineteenth-century nationalism, especially in the Austro-Hungarian empire and in the non-Russian periphery of the Tsarist empire. Most Displaced Persons came from these areas and felt an obligation to organise around this folk revivalist culture in the expectation that they would eventually return to their homelands. The strongest continuing manifestations of this urge are still noticeable among Ukrainians, Croatians, Latvians and Hungarians, long after the first immigrant generation has become too old to dance.

East European culture was, then, fixed in the perception of policy makers as centred around formalised folk dancing. It was ethnic rather than multi-cultural because each manifestation was specific to a nationality or even to a region. The plethora of 'multicultural festivals', of which that in Canberra is among the largest and best supported, have centred on folk dancing ever since. If the Ministers concerned, Barry Cohen and Chris Hurford, had had their way, almost the entire $2 million allocated to multiculturalism in the Bicentennial budget would have gone to a huge folk festival to be held in Melbourne in sweltering January 1988. But the ethnic communities themselves finally revolted and the money went instead to a Bicentennial Multicultural Foundation, which is still doing useful work on the proceeds. Otherwise the 1988 celebration had very little ethnic culture on display. It was, nevertheless, criticised in *Quadrant* for denying Australia's mainstream cultural heritage (see Bennett *et al.* 1992).

The Bicentenary did inspire much work relevant to multiculturalism but not as a direct result of its multicultural program. This became bogged down in competition with different ethnic organisations for funds and a lack of direction from the Bicentennial Authority. The Aboriginal program, which was allocated more funds, did not perform much better. The celebration of Australian Federation in 2001 was even more focused on majority concerns, as befits the commemoration of the activities of Anglo-Australian men who looked to or came from the United Kingdom. There was almost no multicultural or ethnic element in the grants for historical and educational research given by the Centenary of Federation Council, a point made during 1999 by Nick Xynias of the Queensland Ethnic Communities' Council. Perhaps this was not surprising as the relevant committee was chaired by Geoffrey Blainey.

Cultural melting pot or mosaic?

Because Australian culture is derivative and part of a much broader English-language culture, it is hard to determine which of its aspects are specifically 'Australian', which are 'global' and which are 'multicultural'. Canada faces this dilemma even more acutely, as it has two 'founding cultures' but lives next door to the most powerful culture in the world. Britain is once again discovering that 'English' culture is not the only one worthy of support. New Zealand hovers uncertainly between a dual- and a multi-cultural ideal. Above all, the United States cannot be sure that it will remain an 'English-speaking society' indefinitely. That a strong English-only movement has tried and sometimes succeeded in legislating for monolingualism suggests a basic insecurity in the face of the Spanish language cultures which are starting to dominate (once again) in parts of the South–west.

Americans have an often ambivalent picture of their culture as distinct while at the same time drawing on many others. This confusion is present in Australia but without as strong a basis in reality. Australia is still a predominantly English-speaking 'white' society, as Ghassan Hage has recently pointed out. Official multiculturalism has done very little to alter this reality, despite the fears and phobias of its critics (Hage 1998). It has also attempted to apply rigid public service criteria to activities and processes which are often vaguely defined, contested and controversial. These criteria are not simply shaped by the requirements of public accountability, but also by influences from those who believe that multiculturalism is an illegitimate use of public funds or that the state should not have a directive cultural role.

By far the greatest external cultural influences on Australia have always been from Britain and the United States and these have been almost uninfluenced by public institutions. Box-office receipt figures for 1999 show that 84 per cent were for American films, 11 per cent for British, 3 per cent for Australian and 2 per cent for others – the latter category including any films which might be designated 'ethnic' or 'multicultural'. Statistics for television viewing tell the same story. With little variation across Australia, the commercial channels attract 80 per cent of viewers, the ABC 16 per cent and multicultural SBS only 4 per cent or less. A glance at programming shows the commercial channels to be predominantly American, the ABC still British and only SBS multicultural. Most Australian programming is for sport, news, children's and game shows on all channels. Radio and the print media are less Americanised, with reprints more likely to be from the British press than from the United States. But such phenomena as all-pop stations or talkback radio are modelled on American media though staffed by Australians.

The all-pervasive American influence ranges from sport to the universities. Basketball rivals soccer in its following, while academic sabbatical leaves to England are now taken predominantly in the arts, with the United States more popular in most other disciplines. Thus multiculturalism is in no sense responsible for undermining 'Australian' culture, which is already undermined. What it has done, on a very modest scale, is to sustain the cultures brought to Australia by a variety of immigrants since 1947. It has had less success in gaining majority acceptance that such cultures are a legitimate component of the national culture. In practice a distinctly 'Australian' culture is also a minority culture which needs protection. Perhaps the alliance between 'ethnic' and 'folk' performers is a recognition of this. If 'white Australian' culture needs protecting, so does Aboriginal culture which is often Americanised as well. This latter is, however, much more likely to be accepted by public institutions and public opinion than the protection of European or Asian cultural forms. These 'migrant' cultures are often expected to disappear along with other languages, whereas Aboriginal culture is uniquely Australian.

Public institutions respond to the political atmosphere and to what they presume public opinion to be. Multiculturalism has been very popular in the private sphere where it has brought a cornucopia of different foods, the option of tuning in to a variety of performances and the possibility of viewing ethnic cultures at the plethora of festivals. But minority cultures, languages, politics and religions are much less acceptable. Because most institutional centres of policy making are controlled by Anglo-Australians, there has been a tendency to move the focus towards areas which are of concern to the majority and to governments. These include immigrant settlement and welfare, education and literacy, Aboriginal issues, national identity and citizenship, social cohesion and access and equity. This process began under the Commonwealth Labor governments of 1983–1996 but was accelerated by early and continuing measures by the Howard Government. These virtually withdrew the Commonwealth from any direct concern with the cultural and linguistic aspects of multiculturalism. There was no longer an agency at the centre concerned with this policy area. This did not inhibit the states, NGOs and the private sector from continuing to support multiculturalism in all its aspects. However, the enthusiasm of the 1980s was dissipated, the partisan consensus was suspended and public agencies responded accordingly.

The 25 years since Australia became officially multicultural are littered with abandoned programs and practices. The Australian Institute of Multicultural Affairs (1979–1986), the Office of Multicultural Affairs (1987–1996) and the Bureau of Immigration, Multicultural and Population Research (1989–1996) were all abolished and their staff, research material and libraries disbanded. Multicultural education, the national language policy, free English tuition, ethnic affirmative action, monitored access and equity and subsidy for 'weekend schools' were either abandoned or severely curtailed. Yet SBS continued and its scope was extended, state governments and some local councils increased their activity, the Australia Council and the museums adopted multicultural policies, festivals flourished at the state and local levels, autonomous associations of ethnic and multicultural creative artists were formed, the ethnic press expanded with daily and bi-weekly papers for the large Chinese, Greek, Italian and Vietnamese readership, and clubs and associations grew in numbers and wealth.) The viability of multiculturalism depended on who controlled these activities and on the support and enthusiasm of their constituencies, rather than on the often inconsistent policies of politicians and bureaucrats.

📖 Guide to further reading

Castles and Kalantzis (1994) look at the concept of excellence and how it can be judged in a multicultural society. They argue that excellence, once established in a variety of cultural forms, is a useful tool for the marketing of culture and the projection of an image of Australia overseas. Stratton in Hage and Couch (1999) develops the concept of 'whiteness', a term originating in the United States, and applies this concept to the Australian situation, arguing that 'whiteness' is not simply based on observable colour, but on the definition of a central core and 'othered groups' who are seen as peripheral. Australian multiculturalism is thus a method for managing cultural diversity rather than for developing difference and is especially unfavourable to moral diversity, remaining relatively unchallenged as a public policy. Jupp (1998a) describes the development of public policy and institutions under federal and state governments since the early 1970s and the extent to which cultural maintenance is the responsibility of ethnic communities, rather than of governments. The National Multicultural Advisory Council (1999) states the official position of the Howard Government and claims that multiculturalism is a vital dimension of Australian culture. It must, however, be dynamic and not static and develop within the broader context of accepted Australian values and practices. Ozolins (1993) traces the development of the National Policy on Languages following the Lo Bianco Report of 1987 and the subsequent impact of 'economic rationalism' on language policy, with its emphasis on 'languages of commerce'. He also considers the role of Aboriginal languages within the overall policy. Theophanous (1995), then a national Labor politician, looks at the development of the Special Broadcasting Service, which he regards as a success, and that of the ABC and other media, which he regards as flawed. He also analyses the Keating Government's cultural statement of 1994, *Creative Nation*.

🖱 Websites

The following institutions all have major interests in Australia's multiculturalism with dedicated websites as indicated.

www.immi.gov.au
   Department of Immigration and Multicultural Affairs
www.fecca.org.au
   Federation of Ethnic Communities' Councils of Australia
www.sbs.com.au
   Special Broadcasting Service
www.eacnsw.com.au/
   NSW Community Relations Commission
www.ozco.gov.au/
   Australia Council
www.multicultural.vic.gov.au
   Victorian Multicultural Commission
www.immi.gov.au/multicultural/cma
   Council for Multicultural Australia

References

The ABC in Review: National Broadcasting in the 1980s (1981) Canberra: AGPS (commonly referred to as the Dix Report).

Australia Council (1993) *Policy on Arts for a Multicultural Australia*, Sydney: Australia Council.

Australia Council Multicultural Advisory Committee (1999) *Policy and Implementation Discussion Paper*, Sydney: Australia Council.

Australian Ethnic Affairs Council (1977) *Australia as a Multicultural Society*, Canberra: AGPS.

Bennett, Tony *et al.* (eds) (1992) *Celebrating the Nation: A Critical Study of Australia's Bicentenary*, Sydney: Allen & Unwin.

Birtley, Margaret and Pamela McQueen (eds) (1989) *New Responsibilities: Documenting Multicultural Australia*, Melbourne: Museums Association of Australia (Victoria).

Blainey, Geoffrey (1994) 'Cover story: the multicultural verdict', *Bulletin*, 30 August, pp. 22–5.

Blonski, Annette (1992) *History of Ethnic Policies in the Australia Council*, Sydney: Australia Council.

Brennan, John (1986) *Multiculturalism as Concept and Policy*, Canberra: CRASTE.

Castles, Stephen and Mary Kalantzis (1994) *Access to Excellence*, Canberra: AGPS.

Castles, Stephen, Mary Kalantzis, Bill Cope and Michael Morrissey (1988) *Mistaken Identity: Multiculturalism and the Demise of Nationalism in Australia*, Sydney: Pluto Press.

Committee to Review Australian Studies in Tertiary Education (1987) *Windows onto Worlds*, Canberra: AGPS.

Connor, Xaxier (chair) (1985) *Serving Multicultural Australia: the Role of Broadcasting*, Canberra: AGPS.

Department of Arts, Heritage and the Environment (1987) *Folklife: Our Living Heritage*, Canberra: AGPS.

Department of the Arts, Sport, the Environment, Tourism and Territories (1991) *A Plan for Cultural Heritage Institutions to Reflect Australia's Cultural Diversity*, Canberra: AGPS.

Galbally, Frank (chair) (1978) *Migrant Services and Programs*, Canberra: AGPS.

Galla, A. (1993) *Heritage Curricula and Cultural Diversity*, Canberra: AGPS.

Gardini, Anthony and Pamela Skardoon (1985) 'Towards a national cultural policy which reflects the multicultural reality of Australia', Paper presented to the National Congress of the Federation of Ethnic Communities' Councils of Australia, Perth, 22–24 November.

Gunew, Sneja and Fazal Rizvi (eds) (1994) *Culture, Difference and the Arts*, Sydney: Allen & Unwin.

Hage, Ghassan (1998) *White Nation: Fantasies of White Supremacy in the Multicultural Society*, Sydney: Pluto Press.

Hage, Ghassan and R. Couch (eds) (1999) *The Future of Australian Multiculturalism*, University of Sydney: Research Institute for Humanities and Social Sciences.

Hanson, Pauline (1997) *The Truth*, Ipswich, Qld: Author.

Jupp, James (chair) (1986) *Don't Settle for Less*, Canberra: AGPS.

— (ed.) (1989) *The Challenge of Diversity*, Canberra: AGPS.

— (1996) *Understanding Australian Multiculturalism*, Canberra: AGPS.

— (1998a) *Immigration*, Melbourne: Oxford University Press.

— (1998b) 'Ethnic, multicultural and immigration studies' in *Challenges for the Social Sciences in Australia*, Canberra: AGPS, pp. 113–18.

Jupp, James and Marie Kabala (eds) (1993) *The Politics of Australian Immigration*, Canberra: AGPS.

Kukathas, Chandran (ed.) (1993) *Multicultural Citizens*, Sydney: Centre for Independent Studies.

Law Reform Commission (1992) *Multiculturalism and the Law*, Sydney: Australian Law Reform Commission.

Lo Bianco, Joseph (1987) *National Policy on Languages*, Canberra: AGPS.

National Multicultural Advisory Council (1995) *Multicultural Australia: The Next Steps*, Canberra: Australian Government Publishing Services.

— (1999) *Australian Multiculturalism for a New Century*, Canberra: Ausinfo.

Office of Multicultural Affairs (1989) *National Agenda for a Multicultural Australia*, Canberra: AGPS.

— (1992) *Access and Equity Evaluation Report and Research*, Canberra: AGPS.

Ozolins, Uldis (1993) *The Politics of Language in Australia*, Cambridge: Cambridge University Press.

Sheehan, Paul (1998) *Among the Barbarians*, Sydney: Random House.

Stratton, Jon (1998) *Race Daze: Australia in Identity Crisis*, Sydney: Pluto Press.

Theophanous, Andrew (1995) *Understanding Multiculturalism and Australian Identity*, Melbourne: Elikia Books.

Totaro, Paulo (1990) *Cultural Diversity: Media and the Arts*, Sydney: Australia Council.

Victoria State Government (1998) *Victoria's Commitment to Diversity*, Melbourne: Department of Premier and Cabinet.

Winternitz, Judith (1990) *Australia's Hidden Heritage*, Canberra: AGPS.

Woodford Folk Festival (1999) *Program*, Woodford, Qld.

Zubrzycki, George (1968) *The Questing Years*, Canberra: AGPS.

— (1982) *Multiculturalism for all Australians*, Canberra: AGPS.

Chapter 13

'Race Portraits' and Vernacular Possibilities: Heritage and Culture

Chris Healy

Even people's confidence in their nation's past came under attack as the professional purveyors of guilt attacked Australia's heritage and people were told they
should apologise for pride in their culture, traditions, institutions and history.

(Howard 1988, p. 7)

The spectre of heritage

'Heritage' is a term both broad and slippery. Beyond the literal meaning of
property passed between generations, its contemporary evocations include
'inherited customs, beliefs and institutions held in common by a nation or
community ... [and] natural and "built" landscapes, buildings and environments
held in trust for future generations' (Davison *et. al.* 1998, p. 308). Even this
elemental definition strongly associates cultural institutions and heritage. Most
cultural institutions articulate inherited customs and beliefs through a sense of
heritage which, in turn, certifies their authenticity and legitimacy. Parliamentary
conventions, halls of fame and honour boards, much judicial ritual, the use of
uniforms, anniversary commemorations of all sorts and university degree-
conferring ceremonies are strong examples of such practices. At the same time
the more material and codified notion of heritage as things held in trust explicitly organises the work of many cultural institutions. Museums, the Australia
Heritage Commission, sites registered on the National Estate, libraries, archives,
some aspects of education, academic research, urban planning and large parts of

tourism all partake in 'the heritage industry' (Hewison 1987). Already the conjoining of 'heritage and cultural institutions' seems to gesture toward a sheep-run of territory and a king-tide of question.

Nevertheless, at the risk of drowning in generalities, here I want to consider heritage even more broadly as a constitutive and organising rhetoric across the field of cultural institutions and practices. In this chapter heritage refers to the mobilisation of historical understanding or social memory in *institutional* and *citizenly* forms. This sense of heritage encompasses how the nation relies on heritage – emerging ideally, in Anderson's evocative phrase, from deep roots in an 'immemorial past' (Anderson 1991, p. 11) – and the ways in which heritage is evoked in media, political and commemorative spaces. It includes, but is not reducible to, 'preserved things' or 'the things we want to keep' as the Hope inquiry into the Australian National Estate defined the term (Hope 1974). Yet I also want to use the term to suggest an older ethical and evaluative meaning along the lines of Ernest Scott's praise of 'the splendour of our heritage and the greatness of our possibilities' (cited in Davison *et. al.* 1988, p. 308) without lapsing into the not-yet-archaic racial-nationalism expressed in Henry Parkes' celebration of heritage in the form of a 'crimson thread of kinship'. There are advantages in thinking broadly about heritage as one of the key modes in which 'the past' is put to use in cultural institutions. Heritage can be regarded as a crucial element of the institutional and citizenly collective commonsense that underpins public culture (Morris and McCalman 1998, p. 7). Understood in this way heritage directs us to institutions and utterances in and through which historical understandings or habits of memory are deployed in relation to governance. However, it is not just any conjuring of 'the past' or evocation of history which falls within the territory of heritage but specifically the deployment of history in imagining and defining citizenship and governance.

My starting point in this chapter is a proposition – Australia is in the midst of a mundane heritage crisis or, at the very least, a moment of significant instability in the taken-for-grantedness which heritage can offer. Three reference points organise and orient my remarks here. First, I consider the legacy of the 1988 Australian Bicentennial celebrations. I draw attention to the pluralist and inclusive versions of national heritage which predominated during those celebrations. These tropes were built on a tradition of cultural criticism which confidently uncovered and disavowed pre-existing 'myths' of Australian heritage but was vague as to the images, narratives and evocations which could replace these myths in civic culture. Thus 1988 as a 'race portrait' seems, from this distance, not only anxiously white but genuinely insecure and inaffective. Second, I turn to consider the consequences of the Aboriginal boycott of the Bicentenary. My argument in this section is that, post-1988, Aboriginal people and their supporters have built a new and powerful place for Aboriginality and heritage in public culture (Thomas 1999). These transformations of Aboriginality and heritage are elaborated in relation to the Royal Commission into Aboriginal

Deaths in Custody and *Bringing them Home* and include the decisions of the High Court in the Mabo and Wik cases. My argument is that, like native title itself, the new civic role for Aboriginality and heritage exists productively between Aboriginal and non-Aboriginal heritage (conceived as relatively distinct spheres). Third, I turn to formal political disputations around heritage in the so-called 'Battle for History' and the rise of the One Nation Party as further evidence of a (mundane) heritage crisis. One Nation (like the opposition to Mabo, Wik and reconciliation from within the federal government) was shaped by paranoid heritage myths and relied heavily on a singular and exclusionary notion of national heritage. The success of this political assemblage derived, in part, from the absence of credible political alternatives affectively rooted in national heritage. But the phenomenon of One Nation was built on the unsustainability of the pluralist, non-nationalist heritage proffered in 1988. In this sense One Nation is, like John Howard's sense of 'future directions', a protest against the perceived 'theft' or degradation of Australian heritage.

Having suggested some of the dimensions of a heritage crisis I conclude by offering some suggestions about how heritage in the vernacular might be one way of thinking about a post-pluralist heritage. Vernacular heritage is a loose way of describing historical meaning which is shared by relatively small groups of people; it might be locally specific in terms of idiom and themes or it might be familiar principally to those who share a common language or set of experiences, but it is certainly particular and lived rather than general and abstract. My suggestion is that thinking about heritage in the vernacular may offer productive possibilities for cultural institutions. This is important because heritage will remain a key point of insecurity and longing as globalisation, market challenges to public culture, new information and media economies and so on are reshaping the institutions of culture. Heritage matters today not because there is too much of it, not because an earlier model needs to be reconditioned, not because it's impossible, but because the desires stoking its production address an urgent problem: 'how to combine distinctive national traditions and conditions with a new and disciplined openness to the world' (Goodman 1992, p. 193).

'Race' portrait 1: 1988 as happy postmodernism

Heritage both reached a conclusion of sorts and may have become something new in Australia during 1988. The exhaustion of certain notions of heritage was, in part, the result of the shifting valency of heritage as, first and foremost, national and democratic through the post-war period. Although there is a long history of heritage in Australia (Davison 2000), the coincidence of new kinds of history making and cultural dynamism in the 1960s and 1970s was far from arbitrary. Whitlam's 'new nationalism' described a government for the future which promulgated not only preservationism in the shape of the Australian Heritage

Commission but, more broadly, conceived of history as available, in the form of heritage, to articulate and affirm a *bran nue dae* for Australia. The national past held all the magical and tragic powers of myth and was supplemented by a faith that the future could be built on a new and truer cultural nationalism. This configuration of heritage drew on and elaborated the single most important innovation of twentieth-century historical scholarship: an expansion of history's purview to include those who had previously been regarded as ephemeral historical subjects – peasants, the working classes, women, the colonised and (so–called) minority identities. Democratised history gave to heritage a relentless positivity at the end of the last century; its representations should be communal, they should include everyone's story, the next one, and then some ... In the post-war period these histories were put to work in an ever-expanding array of citizenly and governmental forms to substantiate and celebrate a national history all our own. Despite the efforts of a generation of conservative rule attached to the mother-country which obscured 'collective remembrances' rooted in Australian soil, the heritage culture of the 1960s and 1970s began to re-discover and re-invent the signs and sounds of a nation – in preservation, collections policies and stamps; in popular ceremonies, anthems and civic rituals; in film, in song and in story. By the 1980s this cultural work had modernised and revivified Australian heritage as constitutive of a new bedrock for the Australia nation.

In what ways then did the many forms of this nationalised, modern and democratic heritage come to a terminus in 1988? My suggestion is that 1988 made apparent some of the tensions and limits in this inclusive, pluralist and demonstrative configuration of Australian heritage. Amongst people who have written on historical representation and the Bicentenary there is a remarkable unanimity of opinion that inclusiveness and pluralism were the key organising principles (Janson and Macintyre 1988; Bennett *et al.* 1992). The bicentennial 'heritage portrait' was a grand hug-in of spatial togetherness in the form of symbolic journeys, collective spectacles and hi-tech panoramas. Whether in analyses of the Australian Bicentennial Authority, the New South Wales 'First State 88' exhibition, stamps, *Images of Australia*, ephemeral material, *Australia Live* or the Bicentennial Exhibition, analysts have concurred as to the centrality of 'cultural diversity and racial reconciliation' (Burchell 1987, p. 22). David Goodman and Peter Cochrane called this strategy 'tactical pluralism', referring to the Australian Bicentennial Authority's attempt to include 'all the groups clamouring for recognition within the scope of the celebrations' (Cochrane and Goodman 1988, p. 33), However, this unanimity of analytical opinion did not guarantee any common set of judgements as to the significance of these Bicentennial phenomena. One conservative writer complained that Australia appeared as a 'land of incoherent diversity' (quoted in Cochrane and Goodman 1988, p. 33), while other commentators bemoaned the lack of a critical edge or wondered why 'many began to feel that in their empty, undiscriminating openness, there were few possibilities of liberation' (Goodman 1992, p. 198). Still others despaired that 1988 represented a 'pallid official amnesia' (Murphy 1988, p. 54) or pondered the ramifications of such happy postmodernism representing Australia as a 'space wide open' for tourism and foreign capital (Morris 1988). It is possible to identify three features that may help us to make sense of 1988 as both disappointing and ineffectual. First, the absence of any strong nationalism. Second, the exhaustion of a particular (nationalist) mode of cultural criticism. And third, not so much the pallidness of 1988 but the fact that it was downright white. I'll briefly discuss each of these propositions.

If the heritage products of 1988 lacked a strong nationalism, this is explicable in terms of forces both intrinsic and extrinsic to the field of heritage. The impact, reach and pace of the (ongoing) internationalisation of economic and cultural life in Australia since 1983 has been profound. While this has produced new moments for nationalist outpouring (we might think of Bob Hawke's rapture at the 'national triumph' of winning the America's Cup, or the globalisation of sport in general), the balance between articulating the nation as the first among many and understanding the nation as an occasionally significant moment in a global field has shifted decisively to the latter. For many people, the disappointment of a globalised nation was made symbolic in 1988 in the Coca-Cola signage that adorned the spinnaker of one of the First Fleet re-enactment vessels that sailed into Sydney Harbour in January of that year – a new Australia sailing under a new flag. Powerful though that sign might have been, more broadly there were serious narrative difficulties in founding nationalism in a replay of (somebody else's) imperial adventure, and precious little nationalist meat in the immediate 'beginning' which supposedly grounded the celebration.

These very real problems were exacerbated by the seeming inability of 1988 to generate affective images and narratives of the national. The problem was not in the volume of either mediatised or popular articulations of history or heritage. Nor was the problem one of excluding critical or argumentative engagements with history. On the contrary, the Bicentenary 'fostered a wide interest in "history" in every sense of that term … [It] pluralised, or rather multiplied, historical consciousness in Australian cultural life' (Morris 1998, p. 12). But this inclusiveness was shadowed during the Bicentenary by a particular model of cultural criticism. Meaghan Morris has suggestively identified some of the problems of coupling banal pluralism with ritual unmasking in her discussion of Russell Braddon's 1988 series, *Images of Australia*, broadcast on ABC television. This series was a quest for national identity which took the form of 'a journey through disillusion' (Morris 1988, p. 181). Thus the series revisited relatively clichéd stories and stereotypes of Australian history, proceeded to debunk and, regretfully, disavow these mythic foundations until the critique of heritage left nothing but the future as the space of (prospective) inheritance. Morris notes that in this 'critical quest',

Criticism's job is to banish the phantom by demonstrating its lack of reality. Thus Braddon's first program revealed that most Australians are not and never have been hardy bush pioneers, that we aren't all white or male, and that Ned Kelly was a criminal ...

The logical conclusion of the adventure is not the capturing of an identity but the projection of a big picture – a vision of a *future* Australia in which 'true' identity may at last be seized. Braddon's picture had familiar features: a pluri-racial, double-gendered, multi-cultural society with Japanese as a second language, the three R's re-imposed in schools, a healthy debate about republicanism, and hi-tech economic outlook ... The quest for identity is a metaphor of a polemic about the present.

(Morris 1988, p. 181)

This model of cultural criticism has a long history but for our purposes we can identify a reference point closer to home – Australia, in the title of Richard White's influential book, has been 'invented' (White 1981). White pursued the proposition that 'Australia' was an idea that was made – geographically, politically, culturally – rather than essential. It was a proposition which was widely misunderstood. One critic of the book took White to be a vacuous nihilist (White 1997, p. 15). Elsewhere White's insights were first truncated and then adopted as a means of breaking the shackles perceived as holding Australia back from a multicultural, republican and postcolonial future. To achieve this end, the nation and the outdated essences of heritage on which it relied were to be unmasked, denaturalised and denied their mystical power. In general this mode of criticism has few of the virtues of empirical historical scholarship (it is actually possible to write or make film about some people who understood themselves as bush pioneers), an extremely poor sense of the historiography of popular historical imagination (by whom, how and to what effects was history seen as male and white territory?), no grasp of the affective dimension of history (why might I feel that Ned Kelly was much more than a criminal?) and no self-reflexive sense of what is at stake in cultural criticism (how is it possible to engage in gestural demystification and with what results?).

When conjoined with the Bicentenary this model of cultural criticism produced some very peculiar results (Bennett *et al.* 1992; Carter 1994). The multiplication and inclusion of historical identities (or perhaps more accurately back-projected identity politics) demanded by this state-sponsored affair and the truncated model of cultural criticism obsessed with demythologising, became both hypercritical of 'the past' and locked in a nostalgic embrace with a past which, sadly for them, never was – hence the resort to the future. The past seemed a fearful place for two reasons. The criticism-riddled 'invented-ness' of the national past meant, in this framework, that heritage could not offer any ground from which to speak. And, to make matters worse, the Aboriginal boycott kept the focus on the Bicentenary's historical 'big lie' (not 200 but 40,000 years) and the evasion of the question of the meaning of those 200 years when 'White Australia has a Black History'. Heritage, in other words, could not carry the burden of the past in the present during the Bicentenary. In some senses then, the Liberal Party was right, if for the wrong reasons, to claim that: 'Even people's confidence in their nation's past came under attack as the [critics] attacked Australia's heritage.' This cleverly reverses the logic of 1988 as it articulates the mismatch between a comfort of heritage and fear of the future. For the Liberal Party (and others) heritage was something to be reclaimed from the cultural critics who found it damaged and wanting, and from an Aboriginal boycott that found it broken and irreparable. They wanted to renovate and reinstall an older unitary heritage which was precisely that excluded by the pluralism of 1988 – a proud race-portrait both antiquated and radically minoritarian in its rigorous exclusions. The model of cultural criticism which informed much of 1988, on the other hand, could find no viable heritage model and hence projected a race portrait of multicultural happy families on fast forward, ghosted nevertheless by the spectre of Trugannini.

'Race' portrait (2): 1991–1997 – from the dead to the stolen

> To the Aborigines who are proud of their heritage it is indeed a day of mourning; we mourn the death of the many thousands of Aborigines who were brutally murdered; we mourn the loss of our land and the rape of our women by the white invaders.
>
> (An Aboriginal Petition to the King 1937)

The Aboriginal boycott of 1988 was not an absence but a massive presence in national culture. Like the gesture of delegates to the Reconciliation Convention turning their backs on Howard, the boycott was a 'labour of the negative' (Taussig 1999), a strategy of refusal which generated new conditions of possibility. It was and remains an extraordinarily productive cultural and political intervention. Not only did the boycott radically undermine the authority of the Bicentenary to represent all Australians, but it placed unresolved questions around colonialism at the very centre of attempts to articulate the nation. In a moment I will discuss the explicitly political reverberations of this new centrality for Aboriginality in relation to the so-called 'Battle for History' and One Nation. However I want to begin by pursuing the hypothesis that an Aboriginal boycott of a heritage celebration (1988) contributed significantly to Aboriginality and heritage becoming newly foundational for cultural institutions in Australia. Of course, if this has occurred, it could not have happened without the long history of Aboriginal organising and the post-1988 work of Aboriginal people and their supporters in myriad organisations and forms. Nevertheless, I do want to suggest that the decade of the 1990s saw Aboriginality and heritage assume animating and transformative roles in unexpected places. In asserting this I am not referring to *Aboriginal heritage*, which I understand as being those institutions, practices and representations which can be said to belong to Aboriginal people in definite and relatively autonomous ways relating to Aboriginal nationhood. Rather I'm adapting Marcia Langton's conception of Aboriginality as referring to an intercultural zone (Langton 1993, p. 31). *Heritage and Aboriginality* then refers to those spaces constituted by 'Aboriginal people and non-Aboriginal people who engage in ... dialogue' about the intercultural zones of (differentially and unequally) shared heritage.

The 1991 Royal Commission into Aboriginal Deaths in Custody was charged with inquiring into the deaths in custody of 99 Aboriginal and Torres Strait Islander men and women between 1 January 1980 and 30 April 1989. Its final report runs to eleven volumes and contains sweeping recommendations encompassing police and custodian practices, health, drug use, education, post-mortem practices, self-determination, reconciliation and much else besides. Yet on page seven of the National Report Overview is a section headed 'The Importance of History' in which Commissioner Elliot Johnston draws the readers' attention to the 'legacies of the history of two centuries of European domination of Aboriginal people' and goes on:

> I include in this report a chapter on that history. I make no apology for doing so. I do so not because the chapter adds to what is known but because what is known is known to historians and Aboriginal people; it is little known to non-Aboriginal people and it is a principal thesis of this report that it must become more known.
>
> (Royal Commission 1991, p. 7)

The proposition is that a significant question of public policy bearing on a range of governmental institutions cannot be comprehended without public culture 'knowing' a history which has been forgotten or repressed.

That the Royal Commissioners felt 'history' to be of such central importance is, I think, remarkable enough, despite the fact that historicist understandings of public policy questions (or the historicist role of precedent in judicial proceedings) are not uncommon. Nevertheless, the passion with which the Royal Commission argues its historical case is strikingly similar to the judgments of Justices Deane and Gaudron delivered in the Mabo case a year later:

> We have used language and expressed conclusions which some may think to be unusually emotive for a judgment in a court ... [T]he reason which has led us to describe, and express conclusions about, the dispossession of the Australian Aborigines in unrestrained language is that the full facts of the dispossession are of critical importance to the assessment of the legitimacy of the propositions that the continent was unoccupied for legal purposes and that the unqualified legal and beneficial ownership of all the lands of the continent were vested in the Crown.
>
> (Bartlett 1993, p. 42)

These comments not only reinforce the 'importance of history' but add a second element which is new in relation to the status of Aboriginality and heritage within public culture. It is not just that 'a distortion in the history of Australia' (Council 1993, p. 7) has been corrected. A 'new' history is required, a new history which is not only a different history in relation to Aboriginal people but also different in relation to non-Aboriginal people. In Mabo this is implicit in the question of whether 'the continent was unoccupied for legal purposes'. In the Deaths in Custody Royal Commission Report, the problem is posed more explicitly:

> There is the other side of the coin, the effects of history upon the non-Aboriginal people. ... [F]or a complex of reasons the non-Aboriginal population has, in the mass, been nurtured on active and passive ideas of racial superiority in relation to Aboriginal people ... which sits well with the policies of domination and control that have been applied.
>
> (Royal Commission 1991, pp. 9–10)

In other words it is not just a question of 'adding' a black component to Australian history but of Aboriginal history transforming the category of Australian history.

However for Aboriginality to assume a new and distinctive role in public culture required a shift from history to heritage. In other words, telling a new historical story is one thing and a significant gain at the level of representation. But putting a new historical understanding into effect, making it play a role in governance, shifts the matter to the terrain of what I'm calling heritage. It was almost there in the Royal Commission but the emphasis was not so much on the past in the present as on the 'legacy of history [explaining] the over-representation of Aboriginal people in custody' (Royal Commission 1991, p. 11). It was almost there too in Mabo, in which the High Court found that although the Crown gained radical title over the territory 'it did not become the beneficial owner of the land, which remained in the possession of the indigenous people [and] that the Crown extinguished native title in a piecemeal fashion over many years as the wave of settlement washed over the continent, but native title survived on the Murray Islands' (Reynolds 1996). The emphasis on the piecemeal extinguishment of native title effectively meant that native title survived on the Murray Islands as an historical anachronism or because of the incompleteness of colonisation. This logic enabled a judge in a subsequent native title claim to assert that 'the tide of history' had washed away the rights to land of the Yorta Yorta people in south-eastern Australia – that is, to valorise only one side of history in the present (Alford 1999). The decisive steps necessary to install Aboriginality and heritage at the centre of public culture came in the Wik case and *Bringing Them Home*.

In the judgment in the Wik case, brought down in December 1996, the High Court extended the Mabo ruling by holding that native title rights could co-exist (subject to certain important restrictions) with rights held under a pastoral lease. The Court found that the inheritance of two different kinds of legal rights –

native title rights and rights in relation to land under Crown law, each with different historical legitimation – continued to co-exist in the here-and-now. Finally *Bringing Them Home*, the Human Rights and Equal Opportunity Commission report into the history and consequences of the removal of Aboriginal children from their families, made fully explicit a new governmental sense of heritage. Even as they wrote the report Ronald Wilson and Mick Dodson were, I think, responding to pre-emptive attacks which had already circulated. Subsequently these attacks have attempted to both undermine the historical veracity of the Report (*Quadrant* was prominent in these efforts and they continued in 2000 with John Herron, the Minister for Aboriginal Affairs, denying the existence of a stolen generation) and to place the events, policies and responsibilities around the stolen generations firmly in a past radically disconnected from the present; this second disposition underpins the Prime Minister's refusal to offer an apology. Somehow Wilson and Dodson seem to have already heard these protestations when they wrote:

> The actions of the past resonate in the present and will continue to do so in the future. … In no sense has the Inquiry been 'raking over the past' for its own sake. The truth is that the past is very much with us today, in the continuing devastation of the lives of Indigenous Australians. That devastation cannot be addressed unless the whole community listens with an open heart and mind to the stories of what has happened in the past and, having listened and understood, commits itself to reconciliation.
>
> (*Bringing Them Home* 1997, p. 3)

This is the new and distinctive configuration of heritage and Aboriginality which will challenge Australian cultural institutions for many years to come. After the 'silence' is broken, after the Other side is acknowledged, after historical memory and 'the consequences' are admitted, after the double-ness of colonialism's impact on black and white is recognised, comes the moment when Aboriginality becomes part of heritage, a material and potent component of history in the present. A transformed notion of heritage decisively underpins not only reconciliation but all attempts to fashion just relationships between Aboriginal and non-Aboriginal peoples in at least two ways. First the inheritance of colonisation, for both indigenous and non-indigenous people, is refigured. The 'old' Australian heritage is simply no longer tenable. Second, this 'new' Australian heritage is placed at the centre of national governance, potentially affecting notions of territory and cultural identity, political representation and authority at the most basic levels.

There is every reason to expect that these processes are ongoing. This expectation has been reinforced, as I've been completing this essay, by Corroboree 2000, the march across the Harbour Bridge and the conference which was the culmination of ten years of work by the Council for Aboriginal Reconciliation. None of these issues have been fully worked through in public culture; questions of reparation, reconciliation and a treaty remain unresolved. Paul Patton has noted that Mabo (and my argument would add the decision in Wik, the Royal Commission and *Bringing Them Home*) 'draws attention to the differences of cultural historical situation which separates indigenous and non-indigenous citizens' (Patton 1997, p. 88). These cultural historical differences reside, for both Patton and Henry Reynolds, in a 'recognition' which is unfinished: '[because] Aboriginal law is not fully recognised as a body of law grounded in the sovereign authority of Aboriginal peoples the issue of sovereignty will remain with us for some time to come' (Reynolds 1996). A similar, although far from welcoming, assessment has been made by Geoffrey Blainey who objected to the decision in Mabo because it posed a threat to 'the sovereignty and unity of the Australian people' (cited in Patton 1997, p. 84). Blainey is both right and wrong. He is right because this constellation of reports and judgments actually destabilises two of the central underpinnings of the nation: the 'historicity of a territory and the territorialisation of a history' (Poulantzas 1980, p. 114). However, it does not necessarily follow, as Richard Mulgan asserts, 'That the undermining of non-Aboriginal legitimacy is a potent obstacle to reconciliation' (Mulgan 1998, p. 185). In fact only some versions of 'non-Aboriginal legitimacy' are undermined by the cultural transformations I've discussed here. Equally the new status of Aboriginality and heritage actually creates the conditions of possibility for thinking and constructing different kinds of nationhood based on different models of sovereignty and collectivity. The beginnings of such processes are already evident in regional land-management agreements, in AFL football, in some ventures in Aboriginal tourism, in music and elsewhere. But these are not cultural and political configurations waiting to be discovered, they are 'reconstructive practices towards nationhood' (Curthoys and Muecke 1993, p. 190). Before turning to these questions in the final section of the chapter, I want to examine some of the impediments to beginning this process in another 'race portrait' – a new assertion of whiteness.

'Race' portrait 3: 1992–1998 – future directions to one nation

> One regime values permanence and accumulation, the other transience and turn-over. One fears invasion, the other metaphorically solicits it. Threatened by the 'foreign', the 'primitive' and by 'ghosts', imperialist discourse tends towards closure: it paranoically defends the borders it creates. A touristic space must be liberal, and open: the foreign and the primitive are commodified and promoted, ghosts are special-effects: the only 'barrier' officially admitted is strictly economic.
>
> (Morris 1998, p. 182)

After the boycott of 1988, Aboriginal organisations and their supporters continued the long march of 'pragmatic and dogmatic gradualism' (Watson 1993) through governmental, judicial and cultural institutions. By contrast, and in response to the heritage conundrums posed by the Bicentenary, a very different ideological and rhetorical battle took place in the sphere of formal national politics. In February of 1992 (the year in which the Mabo judgment was delivered) the then Prime Minister, Paul Keating, was alleged to have 'handled' or touched the Queen in a manner which breached archaic protocols in relation to the body of the monarch. This provoked a minor outcry in the UK. In response John Hewson, leader of the Opposition, attempted to use this incident to mark Keating's disrespect for Australia's cultural and political heritage and to articulate this disdain with support for an Australian republic. The Prime Minister struck back: 'The Opposition', Keating claimed, 'were relics of the past, "xenophobes" who remained British to their bootstraps despite that nation's decision not to help Australia defend itself against the Japanese advance in 1942' (Brawley 1997). This was not the first time that Keating had mobilised historical rhetorics as Prime Minister, and his heritage speech at Redfern is perhaps the greatest historical speech given by an Australian Prime Minister. For an array of reasons including his personal predilections, the importance of social memory in the political culture of the NSW Right and the skills and inclinations of his staff (particularly those of Don Watson, one of his speech writers), Keating had 'a readiness uncommon in recent prime ministers to take note of recent trends in historiography and to use them in the service of promoting a particular myth of nationalism' (Bolton 1994, p. 149). More broadly, he had remarkable talents in mobilising history in the service of his 'big picture' politics.

Keating was more than happy to engage in a 'battle of history' (as it's been called) in heritage disputation about Menzies and Whitlam, White Australia, Kokoda and Singapore, republics and monarchies, Asia, immigration, modernity and so on. But by the end of his period as Prime Minister he had lost this battle, not in relation to these specific issues but on the key heritage terrain identified by Howard in the expression 'black armband history', and elaborated by One Nation in terms of Aboriginal privilege. The gigantic differences between Keating and Howard in style and political persona often obscured the fact that they both depended significantly on occupying particular heritage positions. As Meaghan Morris argues:

> Howard's triumph ... was to provide a historical framework that made this new, future-oriented and violently divisive rhetoric seem to be a way of *returning* to a more secure and socially cohesive past ... when so many rural and working-class people were economically ravaged *and* feeling culturally despised ... his aura of drabness and littleness gave Howard a formidable power to be *historically* 'shifty'.
>
> (Morris 1998, p. 222)

At least as early as 1988, in shaping the *Future Directions* document, Howard was laying claim to his 'antiquarian' version of heritage. But it was not until he articulated his objections to a 'black armband' view of history that Howard proudly hung his own race-portrait:

> This black armband view of our past reflects the belief that most Australian history since 1788 has been little more than a disgraceful story of imperialism, exploitation, racism, sexism and other forms of discrimination.
>
> I take a different view. I believe that the balance sheet of our history is one of heroic achievement and that we have achieved much more as a nation of which we can be proud than of which we should be ashamed.
>
> (Howard 1996)

This is a classic example of the divisive logic at the heart of Howard's historically shifty vision of both politics and heritage, either heroic or disgraceful, certainly not both and other things besides.

The continuities between this kind of heritage rhetoric and that adopted by the freight train that was One Nation during 1996–98 have been widely discussed (Birch 1997; Gray and Winter 1997). Here I want to examine the efforts of one cultural critic to think historically about the use of heritage within formal politics. Just before the 1998 Queensland election Janet McCalman, a celebrated Melbourne historian, wrote about One Nation on the op-ed page of the *Age* under the title, 'Two nations rise to threaten a peaceful land' (McCalman 1998a). McCalman's sermon (I don't say this disrespectfully; it's just an attribution of style) began with a description of the last day of teaching a course in Australian history at the University of Melbourne. The 'moment of truth' in the classroom came when an American student, after enumerating some of the lessons grasped during the semester, said, 'But you have a good country here. It's safe and peaceful. It's a very good place to live. You are very lucky.' McCalman concurs with the judgement and then writes: 'This makes the rise of One Nation ... all the more heartbreaking ... One Nation ... wants to create two nations, one of insiders and another of outsiders. *And yet this is to fly in the face of our history*' (my emphasis). While it might not be defensible, this is a clear and definite position. The new party is historically aberrant. One Nation is either not *in* Australian history (perhaps it travelled from the US on one of the neo-conservative rafts which have provided flotsam for some right-wing Australian beach scavengers since the 1970s) or it is not *of* Australian history and hence is unsustainable in the historical conditions of Australia.

A fortnight later in another column piece, this time analysing the results of the Queensland election, McCalman wrote about the work of two scholars who had conducted detailed qualitative studies of the electoral base of One Nation (McCalman 1998b). The lesson to be learned from this work was that 'the poor', 'the dispossessed', 'the unemployed', 'the working poor' and 'the truly forgotten people' are not Hanson supporters. On the contrary, One Nation drew its support from, in McCalman's words, 'the classic Australian whingers – aggrieved souls who imagine they are forgotten because they have not done quite as well as they had hoped'. Yet, after taking considerable succour from the fact that nearly three-quarters of Queensland voters did not vote One Nation, she argued that in 'One Nation's heartland of the Atherton Tablelands and in the sugar-growing country that was built on indentured labour … racism has deep historical roots' (McCalman 1998b).

Herein lies the problem. For McCalman, One Nation is an historical aberration yet One Nation's supporters live in regions where racism is deeply historical. This is a contradictory yet illuminating position. McCalman's 'safe and peaceful' present (much like Howard's 'relaxed and comfortable' Australia) cannot admit a heritage which is rooted in colonial racism (along with many other 'traditions' more palatable to contemporary cultural critics). This contrasts sharply with the way Justice Brennan grounded his judgment in Mabo: 'the dispossession of Aboriginal people underwrote the development of the nation' (Bartlett 1993, p. 50) – and which, as I've suggested, goes some way toward developing a different idiom for heritage. Paradoxically, McCalman's pluralist and inclusive heritage (very bicentennial) simply cannot admit One Nation as a product of actual historical processes. Thus the only heritage mechanism for understanding One Nation is as an anachronism, a cultural formation belonging to another time. This was precisely the strategy used in the *Bulletin* front page image of Hanson tucking into a plate of pie and chips with a beer on standby and the same tactic used when *Sixty Minutes* sought to position Hanson in the 1950s. Even more damning for urban political elites is the fact that One Nation is an autochthonous anachronism belonging to those places (like the Atherton Tablelands or certain whingeing suburbs) that should have no role or status in defining Australia or Australian heritage in a globalised world. In other words, both One Nation and McCalman (along with many other critics) share a common understanding of the role of heritage – to unite and underpin a singular nation polity. For One Nation the problem is with 'minority' attempts to threaten this unity of past and place by foreigners, Aboriginal people and metropolitan citizens of the globe. For many critics, One Nation is a 'minority' attempt by ideologues, whingers and outdated yokels to undermine the 'good country' which history has delivered. Back and forth in simple inversions. Is it possible to think of a model of heritage which does not rely on a solid unitary nor, its flip side, the disreputable minority?

Vernacular heritage perhaps?

My argument thus far has been that discourses around 1988, Aboriginality and One Nation index some of the tensions that have recently bedevilled national heritage. These very ordinary crises in the efficacy and legitimacy of representation are a conundrum for a pluralist national heritage. 1988's inclusiveness set a benchmark. On the one hand the admission of everybody's stories left older notions of heritage substantially (if nostalgically) intact while, at the same time, it produced such diverse and incoherent heritage gestures that their meaning and significance seemed ineffective. On the other hand the Aboriginal boycott of 1988 exposed both the positivity of 1988 and the absolute limits of its pluralism; Aboriginal heritage simply would not be one more positive addition to an affirming story of Australian civilisation. The elaboration of Aboriginality and heritage in various governmental institutions since 1988 has made it clear that white Australian heritage has depended on the exclusion of Aboriginality. It is not a case of just adding some black stories but, I believe, of exploring how those exclusions claimed the space of heritage which now remains to be reinvented on the ruins of that project. One Nation, Hanson's fellow-travellers and some cultural critics have taken a different route, preferring to stake out true heritage as guaranteed by history's gifts to those seated at the table: the rest are mere servants, beggars or rubbishers. Together these heritage discourses seem to open up the question of a post-pluralist heritage. Is it possible to think about the deployment of history in relation to citizenship and governance in ways which might avoid some of the limitations exemplified in the mundane crisis of heritage? I want to suggest that thinking about heritage in this vernacular offers some real utility.

For a long time it has been recognised that one of the central problems of history as a general category has been its claim to universality. Rather than history being an aggregation of all the routes from events in the past to events in the present, universal history has been understood as a grid on which any of those events might be traced (Mink 1987). So, for example, histories of nations, while particular in their timing, pace and leading players, are usually thought of as histories of development and achievement or of that destiny remaining to be accomplished. For this reason specific or micro-histories tend to suffer one of two fates at the hand of history-in-general. Either they are incorporated into the grid of a larger historical narrative – Ballarat as contributing to Australian history – or they are absences, mere traces, like so many other gold towns. This does not mean that the micro-histories disappear, only that most have no place in grand historical narratives. When it comes to heritage, that is, the use of historical understanding in citizenly and governmental registers, these processes are usually even more exclusionary because heritage, and particularly national heritage, is necessarily more formal and often codified. A national register of historic houses, for instance, contains only those houses which possess heritage as assessed in terms of architectural taxonomy or broad historical significance. The idea of such a register including all houses possessing heritage significance – your heritage significance and mine and the next person's – makes no sense because the role of democratic heritage is to exemplify by selection those objects and narratives which can represent a general collective historical understanding. Nevertheless specific or micro-heritages can be enduring and significant and it's these kinds of understandings that I want to identify as vernacular heritage. Vernacular heritage can describe those understandings of heritage which are marginal to, or silenced by, the authority of 'official' heritage; vernacularity might reside in language or idiom; shared but particular historical experience, say of displacement (Read 1996) or political affiliation or suppressed cultural or sexual identities and rituals, say the pre-respectable Mardi Gras. I'm not wanting to give the vernacular a nativist gloss. Vernacular heritage is not necessarily geographically specific; it could include a quirky local museum and equally the rituals of remembering shared by a dispersed immigrant community.

Ranajit Guha has provided a stimulating discussion of vernacular histories in the context of postcolonial India (Guha 1992). He argues that vernacularity exists (and existed) in 'accents, idioms and imaginaries' foreign to the lexicon of post-enlightenment reason and, in this sense, is 'unspeakable' in the language and rationality of colonisation. This does not mean, however, that vernacular pasts disappear, only that once they are articulated in relation to history they must 'speak' the grammar of power; in his particular argument, they must find a place in a terrain mapped by nationalist historiography. Guha argues that vernacular histories have taken two forms in India, each of which preserves the force of the Latin root of vernacular: verna meaning 'home-born slave'. There is the discourse of the happy slave – Indian history as the story of England's work in which the slave speaks his master's voice, parroting the place which colonising history has reserved for his story. There is also the idiomatic story of the slave which, though in her master's language, is not in her master's voice. This second story is not an authentic or nativist voice, but it is a historical document to the extent that it preserves traces of the violence that enables the story to be told in the language of domination. So, the transposition which enables speech in the master's language still resonates with the memory of slavery. How does this understanding of vernacular heritage as a 'third term' between formal history and 'unspeakable' micro-histories help illuminate the notion of vernacular heritage in Australia? First, it is important to recognise that the term is not evaluative; that is, vernacular histories are not necessarily good or bad, accurate or inaccurate. Second, while vernacular histories are not authentically subaltern, they do preserve elements of experience which have been marginalised or excluded from general historical discourse. Third, vernacular histories exist in tension with official history; they are not reducible to elements of a historical narrative but seem to have a capacity to disrupt or reorganise historical understanding.

This sense of history may sound esoteric, however it seems less so if we return to the questions of Aboriginality and heritage which we have already discussed. The Royal Commission, the judicial proceedings and *Bringing Them Home* were all governmental instances in which Aboriginal and non-Aboriginal people produced spaces in which otherness (including vernacular histories) and difference were recognised. The practical import of this recognition necessitated translation which, as Patton reminds us, Derrida describes as 'an always possible but always imperfect compromise between two idioms' (cited in Patton 1997, p. 95). In other words, royal commissions and courts had to recognise and acknowledge the particularity and partiality of their idiom in order to listen to another idiom being translated for them, a dialogue which was then, paradoxically, 'returned' in another form (Frow 1998). Thus Aboriginality and heritage actually includes and extends Noel Pearson's understanding of native title itself as a concept which belongs to the space between two bodies of law and by means of which one recognises the other under certain conditions: 'Native title is therefore a space between two systems, where there is recognition' (Pearson 1996). Metaphorically these encounters produced new cultural spaces which I've described as spaces of Aboriginality and heritage – reports, rulings, commentary, organisations and agreements – which exist between indigenous and non-indigenous people but belong exclusively to neither. It is in this sense that this new space of Aboriginality and heritage is vernacular.

Conversely, 1988 and One Nation can be seen as examples of heritage discourse which failed to take up the virtues of vernacular heritage. 1988 depended on an irredeemably white and narrowly national history, yet it simultaneously critiqued and mourned such heritage and indulged in gestural pluralism by celebrating heritage as an inclusive patchwork. In contrast we might think of another bicentennial example. On 25 January 1988, after marching through Sydney, Aboriginal people and their supporters gathered at Kurnell to perform vernacular ceremonies at a place where Cook had come ashore. This articulation of vernacular heritage as a shared commitment to reconciliation in place has since been elaborated across the country as indigenous and non-indigenous people have come together to hold meetings, share stories, produce inscriptions and make commitments to a future they share (Read 2000). Some of the building blocks which made One Nation came from the kind of vernacular heritage given voice in Les Murray's poetry, heard when loggers take on conservationists and celebrated in the primitive socialism of the National Party. However One Nation transformed this 'raw' material. First, Hanson was adept at fuelling a sense of the vernacular as besieged and damaged (as many people's lives had literally been damaged by a decade of economic reforms). Second, One Nation generalised these reactions in the form of a political program which called for national defence against a host of enemies. In this second move the vernacularity of its roots were undone. But there are other models. The Stockman's Hall of Fame in Longreach, like much pioneering history before it has, in large part, been concerned to articulate a vernacular heritage as locally and historically significant which, in this case, doesn't necessarily evoke a return of the Australian legend (Trotter 1992; Thomas 1996). Similarly, Landcare organisations throughout the country and ventures like the Bookmark Biosphere Reserve in the South Australian Mallee are seeking to articulate a vernacular heritage and a culture of sustainable land and water use practices.

Learning from these examples might involve being far more circumspect about when and how we speak of national heritage as singular and unified. There are some moments when it is important to invoke national heritage, for example, to prohibit the export of cultural property. But generally, rather than thinking in terms of heritage and civilisation, race or nation, rather than stitching many plural historical experiences into one national heritage comforter, we could be content with a more disaggregated sense of heritage. To think of vernacular heritage means to understand the embeddedness of the past in the present as various and shifting. Most of us do not spend most of our time expressing or enacting national heritage. On the contrary, our everyday senses of heritage are inherently vernacular – different but shared idioms connect us with friends and workmates, neighbours and family, correspondents and acquaintances and strangers. To understand heritage as vernacular recognises diversity as a practice which defines our cultural lives. It also holds out the virtue of thinking about heritage as articulating different temporalities, idioms and feelings in a space of translation and exchange. Vernacular heritage may also be an effective antidote to the paranoid and defensive hollowness of 'the story of our people ... for all our people ... broadly constituting a scale of heroic and unique achievement against the odds' (Howard cited in Birch 1997, p. 9).

📖 Guide to further reading

This essay has taken an idiosyncratic route through particular questions which conjoin heritage and cultural institutions. This approach is indebted to Meaghan Morris (1988), a book which overflows with innovative provocations as to how to rethink history (and heritage) in popular culture, and to Tony Bennett's distinctive and original configuration of cultural history, *Culture: A Reformer's Science* (Sydney: Allen & Unwin, 1998).

The best introduction to heritage in Australia is provided by Graeme Davison (2000). The historiographic logic of Graeme Davison *et al.* (eds) (1998) also offers many resources on these questions. Studies of particular aspects of Australian heritage can be found in Tony Bennett, *The Birth of the Museum: History, Theory, Politics* (London: Routledge, 1995); Tim Bonyhady, 'The stuff of heritage' in Tim Bonyhady and Tom Griffiths (eds) *Prehistory to Politics: John Mulvaney, the Humanities and the Public Intellectual* (Melbourne: Melbourne University Press, 1996); Peter Cochrane, *Simpson and his Donkey: The Making of a Legend* (Melbourne: Melbourne University Press, 1992); essays by Cochrane, David Carter and Ken Taylor in David Headon, Joy Hooton and Donald Horne (eds) *The Abundant Culture. Meaning and Significance in Everyday Australia* (Sydney: Allen & Unwin, 1994); Graeme Davison and Chris McConville (eds) *The Heritage Handbook* (Sydney: Allen & Unwin, 1991); Tom Griffiths, *Hunters and Collectors: The Antiquarian Imagination in Australia* (Cambridge: Cambridge University Press, 1996); Chris Healy, *From the Ruins of Colonialism: History as Social Memory* (Cambridge: Cambridge University Press, 1997); Ken Inglis, *Sacred Places. War Memorials in the Australian Landscape* (Melbourne: Melbourne University Press,

1998); and John Rickard and Peter Spearritt (eds) *Packaging the Past: Public Histories* (special issue of *Australian Historical Studies* 24, 96, April 1991). The work of David Lowenthal, *The Past is a Foreign Country* (Cambridge: Cambridge University Press, 1985) and *The Heritage Crusade and the Spoils of History* (London: Viking, 1996) has been influential in how heritage is understood today. Of less influence but enduring importance are Patrick Wright, *On Living in an Old Country* (London: Verso, 1985) and Raphael Samuel, *Theatres of Memory: Vol. 1 The Past and Present in Contemporary Culture* (London: Verso, 1994).

The field of Aboriginal studies is huge, while efforts to consider the central cultural significance of Aboriginality in Australia are only beginning. Marcia Langton (1993) and Stephen Muecke, *Textual Spaces: Aboriginality and Cultural Studies* (Sydney: University of New South Wales Press, 1992) are of major significance. Other important books include Bain Attwood (ed.) *In the Age of Mabo: History, Aborigines and Australia* (Sydney: Allen & Unwin, 1996); Jeremy Beckett (ed.) *Past and Present: The Construction of Aboriginality* (Canberra: Aboriginal Studies Press for the Australian Institute of Aboriginal Studies, 1988); and Eric Michaels, 'For a cultural future: Francis Jupurrurla makes TV at Yuendumu' (*Art & Text*, 1989). As this chapter was going to press an important essay on the stolen generation appeared: Robert Manne, *In Denial: The Stolen Generation and the Right* (Melbourne: Schwartz Publishing, 2001).

References

Alford, K. (1999) 'White-washing away native title rights: the Yorta Yorta land claim', *Arena* 13, pp. 67–83.

Anderson, Benedict (1991) *Imagined Communities: Reflections on the Origin and Spread of Nationalism* (Revised Edition), London: Verso.

Bartlett, R. (1993) *The Mabo Decision, and the full text of the Decision in Mabo and Others v State of Queensland*, Sydney: Butterworths.

Bennett, Tony *et al.* (eds) (1992) *Celebrating the Nation. A Critical Study of Australia's Bicentenary*, Sydney: Allen & Unwin.

Birch, Tony (1997) '"Black armbands and white veils": John Howard's moral amnesia', *Melbourne Historical Journal* 25, pp. 8–16.

Bolton, Geoffrey (1994) 'Beating up Keating: British media and the republic' in D. Grant and G. Seal (eds) *Australia in the World: Perceptions and Possibilities*, Perth: Black Swan Press.

Brawley, Sean (1997) '"A comfortable and relaxed past": John Howard and the "battle of history"', *Electronic Journal of Australian and New Zealand History* www.jcu.edu.au/aff/history/article/brawley.htm

Bringing Them Home: Report of the National Inquiry into the Separation of Aboriginal and Torres Strait Islander Children from their Families (1997) Canberra: Commonwealth of Australia.

Burchell, David (1987) 'The Bicentennial dilemma', *Australian Society* 6, pp. 22–4.

Carter, David (1994) 'Future pasts' in D. Headon *et al.* (eds) *The Abundant Culture. Meaning and Significance in Everyday Australia*, Sydney: Allen & Unwin, pp. 3–15.

Cochrane, Peter and David Goodman (1988) 'The great Australian journey: cultural logic and nationalism in the postmodern era' in Janson and Macintyre (eds), pp. 21–44.

Council for Aboriginal Reconciliation (1993) *Making Things Right: Reconciliation after the High Court's Decision on Native Title*, Canberra: Council for Aboriginal Reconciliation.

Curthoys, Ann and Stephen Muecke (1993) 'Australia for example' in W. Hudson and D. Carter (eds) *The Republicanism Debate*, Sydney: New South Wales University Press, pp. 177–200.

Davison, Graeme (2000) *The Uses and Abuse of Australian History*, Sydney: Allen & Unwin.

Davison, Graeme *et al.* (eds) (1998) *The Oxford Companion to Australian History*, Melbourne: Oxford University Press.

Frow, John (1998) 'The politics of stolen time', *Australian Humanities Review* www.lib.latrobe.edu.au/AHR/archive/Issue-February-1998/frow1.html

Goodman, David (1992) 'Postscript 1991 – explicating openness' in Tony Bennett *et al.* (eds), pp. 191–8.

Gray, G. and C. Winter (eds) (1997) *The Resurgence of Racism*, Clayton, Vic.: Monash Publications in History 24.

Guha, Ranajit (1992) 'The authority of vernacular pasts', *Meanjin* 51, 2, pp. 299–302.

Hewison, Robert (1987) *The Heritage Industry: Britain in a Climate of Decline*, London: Methuen.

Hope, R. (1974) *Report on the National Estate*, Canberra: AGPS.

Howard, John (1988) *Future Directions*, Canberra: Liberal Party of Australia.

— (1996) Sir Robert Menzies Lecture, 18 November 1996, reported in *The Australian*, 19 November.

Janson, Susan and Stuart Macintyre (eds) (1988) *Making the Bicentenary*, a special issue of *Australian Historical Studies* 23, 91.

Langton, Marcia (1993) *Well, I Heard it on the Radio and I Saw it on the Television … An Essay for the Australian Film Commission on the Politics and Aesthetics of Filmmaking by and about Aboriginal People and Things*, Sydney: Australian Film Commission.

McCalman, Janet (1998a) 'Two nations arise to threaten a peaceful land', *Age* 10 June.

— (1998b) 'In the heartland of the poor, One Nation still fails to appeal', *Age* 24 June.

Mink, L. (1987) *Historical Understanding*, Ithaca, NY: Cornell University Press.

Morris, Meaghan (1988) 'Panorama: the live, the dead and the living' in Paul Foss (ed.) *Islands in the Stream: Myths of Place in Australian Culture*, Sydney: Pluto Press, pp. 160–87.

— (1998) *Too Soon Too Late. History in Popular Culture*, Bloomington: Indiana University Press.

Morris, Meaghan and Iain McCalman (1998) 'Public culture' in *Knowing Ourselves and Others: The Humanities into the 21st Century, Vol. 3 Reflective Essays*, Canberra: Department of Employment Education, Training and Youth Affairs, pp. 1–20.

Mulgan, R. (1998) 'Citizenship and legitimacy in post-colonial Australia' in N. Peterson and W. Sanders (eds) *Citizenship and Indigenous Australians. Changing Conceptions and Possibilities*, Cambridge: Cambridge University Press, pp. 179–95.

Murphy, John (1988) 'Conscripting the past: The Bicentenary and everyday life' in Janson and Macintyre (eds), pp. 45–54.

Murray, Les (1982) *The Vernacular Republic: Poems 1961–81*, Sydney: Angus & Robertson.

Patton, Paul (1997) 'Justice and difference: the Mabo Case' in P. Patton and D. Austin-Broos (eds) *Transformations in Australian Society*, University of Sydney: Research Institute for Humanities and Social Sciences, pp. 83–98.

Pearson, Noel (1996) 'The concept of native title at common law', *Australian Humanities Review* www.lib.latrobe.edu.au/AHR/archive/Issue-March-1997/pearson.html

Poulantzas, Nicos (1980) *State, Power and Socialism*, London: Verso.

Read, Peter (1996) *Returning to Nothing: The Meaning of Lost Places*, Cambridge: Cambridge University Press.

— (2000) *Belonging. Australians, Place and Aboriginal Ownership*, Cambridge: Cambridge University Press.

Reynolds, Henry (1996) 'After Mabo, what about Aboriginal sovereignty?', *Australian Humanities Review* 1, April www.lib.latrobe.edu.au/AHR/archive/Issue-April-1996/Reynolds.html

Royal Commission into Aboriginal Deaths in Custody 1991, National Report Overview and Recommendations (Commissioner Elliott Johnston), Canberra: AGPS.

Taussig, Michael (1999) *Defacement: Public Secrecy and the Labor of the Negative*, Stanford University Press.

Thomas, Julian (1996) 'Heroic and democratic histories: pioneering as a historical concept', *The UTS Review* 2, 1, pp. 58–71.

Thomas, Nicholas (1999) *Possessions: Indigenous Art, Colonial Culture*, New York: Thames & Hudson.

Trotter, Robin (1992) 'Pioneering the past; a study of the Stockman's Hall of Fame' in Tony Bennett *et al.* (eds), pp. 160–74.

Watson, Don (1993) 'Birth of a post-modern nation', *Weekend Australian* 24–25 July, p. 21.

White, Richard (1981) *Inventing Australia: Images and Identities 1688–1980*, Sydney: Allen & Unwin.

— (1997) 'Inventing Australia revisited' in W. Hudson and G. Bolton (eds), *Creating Australia. Changing Australian History*, Sydney: Allen & Unwin, pp. 12–22.

Chapter 14

Indigenous Presences and National Narratives in Australasian Museums

Nicholas Thomas

It has become something of an axiom in discussions of the collection of Indigenous peoples' artifacts that the abstraction of things from ritual activities or everyday uses for sale in the tribal art market, and for storage or display in private collectors' cabinets and public museums, is an operation of *decontextualisation*. And in a sense it surely is: the space of the specimen is often not a mere vacancy or absence, but a non-space of a singular and radical kind. The unnatural isolation of the displayed object appears to be especially poignant now, given that mainstream audiences have become increasingly aware of the singular values that Indigenous objects once had within the fabric of sociality, and still retain from an Indigenous perspective: these are not simply tools or art works, but – to use the Maori word – *taonga* or inalienable possessions. That understanding is part of a broader reimagining of the histories of Australasian white settler societies. I have picked that awkward and dated geographic label to remind us that in the last quarter of the nineteenth century, when magazines such as the *Australasian Sketcher* made the term current, both countries were highly conscious of the singular character of their antipodean coloniality, as, in a different way, we are today. National histories are re-presented with the best of intentions, which means that Indigenous presences are to be acknowledged. It is the awkward character of that acknowledgement, the ways in which it has worked and not worked, that I explore in this essay, through discussion of two recent exhibitions in national institutions.

Let me begin by going back to decontextualisation. The grievous abstraction of Indigenous things from Indigenous lives is not an operation that Western institutions have performed exclusively upon the artifacts of non-western or tribal peoples. Rather, it mirrors what is understood as the key attribute of the modern art museum: that is, the displacement of painting and sculpture from religious and aristocratic situations into a space in which things seem defined by an absolute functionlessness, by a similar evacuation of private significance, exchange value, use and context. Certainly, modernists and contemporary artists may produce particularly for the museum, but our galleries include many works ranging from religious icons to far more recent pieces of so-called craft or decorative art that were made with churches or dining tables rather than display cases in mind. One of my starting points is that this familiar and obvious point – that things in museums are decontextualised – is a bad assumption to begin with, if we are concerned with the meanings and politics of museums and exhibitions. My purpose is not to deny that Indigenous artifacts were removed from community uses, and too often stolen; I am not questioning the desirability of repatriating material or otherwise restoring the rights of the groups from whom things were taken. The point is rather that exhibited things are not 'decontextualised', but contextualised in special and powerful ways. Equally importantly, these 'contexts' are not simply social or institutional relations that are external to objects and exhibits: context is projected and defined, to some degree, by content.

Perhaps I can make this clearer by drawing attention to another sort of apparent 'decontextualisation' that's very familiar. We often see racks of disembodied clothes and footless shoes, together with many other objects isolated from their functions, in department stores and other shops. Although there are some analogies between the presentation of these commodities and the exhibition of museum specimens, the objects don't seem strangely isolated, because we know that they're being displayed for sale. At other levels, they are there to make class and subcultural distinctions visible in material form; and they could be seen, ideally, to empower consumers by enabling them to imagine themselves variously in the terms suggested by fashionable clothes, books, health foods or exercise equipment. Arrays of things in the market may thus be abstracted from their most obvious and specific uses, but in fact they do all kinds of things; perhaps most importantly, they teach us not only to desire specific objects, but to invest our efforts of self-definition in that desire.

By the same token, museum objects may be removed from their primary intended uses – the mask floats headlessly, the jug is sadly without wine – but they are nevertheless making themselves useful, busily and perhaps in too many ways. The context is quite different to that of the market, but also similar to it in the sense that objects have specific meanings, but also more general and implicit effects, in teaching habits of viewing and registers of aesthetic and historical recognition. Exhibitions may present particular bodies of artwork, convey information about fields of natural history or specific arguments concerning history and nationhood; their pedagogy may be disguised as entertainment or aesthetic stimulation. But they also convey attitudes toward art, heritage and technology, ethics of self-refinement, and perceptions of citizenship. With respect to the last, I am not suggesting that either art galleries or museums of natural history have generally been directly concerned with civics education in a narrow sense, but it is obvious that many institutions present the natural environment, histories of military experience and artistic traditions alike, from a specifically national point of view, encouraging viewers to imagine themselves as Australians or New Zealanders, at once intimately and collectively connected with a natural and cultural heritage. The museum proffers both particular memories, and a habit of memory that is nationalised; just as it suggests that artworks do not cohere merely as the products of individual artists, local milieux or aesthetic movements, but also, and in more powerful and embracing terms, in national canons. In suggesting that galleries and museums convey habits of collective and national consciousness, I am only restating a point that has become familiar: these institutions, like schools, health services and censuses, are very much part of the business of government that interested Foucault in his later work.

To appreciate a connection between an individual's aesthetic responses and the efforts of a dispersed modern bureaucracy to socialise a population is not however to suggest that the museum should now be understood as an instrument of surveillance or discipline in any strong or repressive sense. Museums may make vigorous efforts to define their audiences and present them with certain understandings of history and culture, but their aspirations are often more powerful than their accomplishments. Confusion and contention may be endemic features in public representations of nationality, but there is perhaps a special reason why the rhetoric of many exhibitions is not grasped, or not accepted, by their audiences. Artifacts and artworks are objects that can be ordered and captioned and presented in ways that suggest a story, but their material characteristics, and the objectified intelligence that they carry, may undermine or conflict with whatever larger narrative is implied or expressed.

Let me illustrate this briefly through reference to an exhibition that took place in Sydney in 1941, and that at the same time gets me back to the theme I have drifted away from, that of the relation between Indigenous presences and national narratives in the settler societies of Australia and New Zealand. I mentioned earlier that I wanted to draw attention to the fundamental similarity between the cultural logic of colonisation in the two countries, which sometimes simply excluded Indigenous people, or denigrated them, yet also frequently celebrated Indigenous folklore and art. And I argued that Indigenous reference provided the means for Australians or New Zealanders – writers, composers, artists and designers – to fashion their own distinctive national cultures that would not simply be impoverished and displaced versions of British tradition. As Margaret Preston put it, with characteristic urgency, 'The attention of Australian people must be drawn to the fact that [Aboriginal art] is great art and the foundation of a national culture for this country' (Preston 1941, p. 46). Affirmation and appropriation thus went hand in hand.

Early in 1941, staff at the Australian Museum began to prepare an exhibition of Aboriginal art, together with material that demonstrated its potential as a stimulus for modern china, fabric, architecture and design; the enthusiasm of arts and crafts practitioners to provide work meant that the show expanded rapidly, with the result that it ended up taking place at the David Jones auditorium, rather than in the more limited space available at the museum (Figures 1, 2). (It is tempting to talk further about the hybrid gallery-department store space, especially because there has been a long tradition of displaying pieces of tribal art in the middle of the fashion departments in that particular store; nothing complements a Perri Cutten suit quite so well, it seems, as a Sepik mask.) One might have anticipated that the anthropology curator, Frederick McCarthy, who otherwise wrote extensively on Aboriginal art and archaeology, might have been using the designers' interests as a vehicle for the promotion of the Indigenous forms in their own right. Though the Aboriginal work itself only constituted one section of the exhibition, museum staff went to considerable lengths to obtain photographs of rock paintings and engravings, and loans of 'weapons, utensils, sacred objects and ornaments' from collections in Melbourne and Adelaide as well as around Sydney. In the event, however, the claims McCarthy made for Aboriginal art in a press release, and in an article in the museum's magazine, were not only modest but broadly consistent with a primitivist settler-nationalism that saw Aborigines providing the new nation with a singular prehistory and a set of distinctive

Figure 1 Some exhibits in the 1941 Australian Museum exhibition, 'Australian Aboriginal Art and its Applications' (Australian Museum)

Figure 2 Exhibition view of 'Australian Aboriginal Art and its Applications' (Australian Museum)

motifs, that would have a future, not in new expressions of Indigenous culture, but in craft produced by white settlers for white settlers. As he wrote:

> It is not contended that aboriginal art equals the abstract and imaginative qualities, or the richness of design, of the art of many other primitive peoples, nor that it approaches the magnificence of the art of the classical civilizations, but it may be claimed that the variety and simplicity of the wide range of motifs and equally numerous techniques ... give it a character sufficiently distinctive to identify it with the people, and for this reason it may be said to represent a definite phase of art in Australia. Adapted with intelligence and taste, aboriginal art can make a unique contribution to modern Australian craft work ... In addition, the myths and legends, daily life and art motifs, form an inspiration that may give rise to a national decorative element in Australian architecture.
>
> (McCarthy 1941, pp. 355–6)

Given the hesitancy of this assessment of Aboriginal art, it is striking that the critics of the day were ambivalent about the white 'applications', rather than their Indigenous sources. One reviewer was circumspect, noting that while the barks showed 'the aboriginal to be a sensitive artist with a true feeling for design' the paintings 'should be compared with the crude decoration they have inspired on the glassware on view nearby' (*Sydney Morning Herald*, 12 August 1941). Another was much more categorical:

> Best exhibits by far were the aboriginal bark-paintings ... The aboriginal stuff
> was swell, but all the modern application wasn't. (Glaring examples of the
> unswell were of the china and glass, and that *gay* little frieze. All horrible
> beyond belief ...).
>
> *(Australia: National Journal,* 1 September 1941)

And this in a magazine, Ure Smith's *National Journal*, that had featured these
'applications' a good deal in its own pages. Paradoxically, then, in this case, the
effort to assimilate Indigenous culture to a distinctively national school of design
had underlined the incommensurability of Indigenous and settler forms, and
hardly sustained the idea that a transition from one to the other, from an aboriginal prehistory to a settler future, represented any kind of cultural progress. In
this case, content could be seen to have contradicted context, or at least to have
unsettled both the particular agenda of the exhibition and the larger idea of
national cultural development that it manifested.

Of course, this understanding of national history, from indigenous prehistory
through pioneer accomplishment to the expansiveness of antipodean modernity, is
no longer unashamedly embraced, either officially or in public perceptions, in
Aotearoa New Zealand and Australia. I do not want to go into the similarities and
contrasts between Indigenous experience and debates about race relations in the
two countries, and am merely concerned with the point that a history of Indigenous activism, together with shifts in the dominant settler population's attitudes,
have prompted governments to take the project of redressing dispossession and
discrimination more seriously; over the same period, museums have become
theatres for the renegotiation of the national histories that they showcase.

The Voices exhibition at the Museum of New Zealand, which was opened
about the beginning of 1993, has perhaps been the most unsuccessful of recent
attempts to display an inclusive and democratic account of national history in
a major public institution. Voices, so named for its emphasis on sound and
recorded commentary, is of some importance because it was presented as a
kind of trial for approaches to the museum's new harbourside building –
planned to open in 1998 – which, quite appropriately, was to be organised
around the understanding of the country as a bicultural nation that has been
officially adopted in fits and starts over the last decade. The exhibition followed
from much consultation and was certainly well-intentioned. It not only emphasised the Maori presence (Figure 3), but also incorporated a good deal of
environmental history, and foregrounded women's experiences of events that
had conventionally been seen almost exclusively from a male perspective.
Unfortunately this was done in too heavy-handed a way, and one journalist – a
woman, as it happens – observed rather archly that you could leave the exhibition with the sense that men had played no part at all in World War II (McLeod
1994). Reports in the media suggested that many older Pakeha visitors were put
out by what they saw as the belittling of the accomplishments of pioneers, who

Figure 3 'Voices' exhibition, Te Papa/Museum of New Zealand, 1996
(Collection of the Museum of New Zealand Te Papa Tongarewa)

were charged with wholesale deforestation. What was remarkable, though, was that the show appeared to offend absolutely everybody, in the sense that Maori were equally dissatisfied.

The artist and art historian Brett Graham wrote that he'd looked forward eagerly to the exhibition, but found the mock bush lifeless and petrified, and other sections 'strangely spiritless' (Graham 1993, p. 13). He was struck by the fact that the story of Polynesian canoe voyaging and colonisation – which retains fascination for audiences remote from the Pacific – was 'relegated to a tiny corner' when 'the most dominant and perhaps least successful feature ... was a mock galley of a sailing ship, celebrating European arrival' (p. 14; Figure 4). This was a point that had occurred to me, when I first walked through the exhibit: if curators had really wanted to challenge the 'master narrative that has provided our historical perspective up to the present', as one had expressed the aims, sawing up a lot of timber to create an awkward immobile replica of one of Cook's ships seemed a curious way to go about it – though it is perhaps inadvertently interesting, because this is the kind of thing that cargo cult followers in Melanesia are always supposed to have done. Maybe we have more affinities with our Pacific neighbours than we generally imagine.

Figure 4 'Voices' exhibition, Te Papa/Museum of New Zealand, 1996
(Collection of the Museum of New Zealand Te Papa Tongarewa)

I suggested earlier that artifacts sometimes overwhelmed the narratives that curators attempted to frame them with, and perhaps this is what occurred here: it was too easy to pass over the texts that aimed to engender ambivalence about early discovery and settlement, and simply be overwhelmed by the monumental size of the ship that seemed to diminish all the indigenous pieces that came before it. It could also be suggested that the installation failed on technical grounds, in the sense that the plurality of voices produced a cacophony. Brett Graham had written that 'the best speakers on the marae choose their words ... wisely, economically. Here the voices seemed to scream in competition until I felt uncomfortable, claustrophobic' (1993, p. 14). The value of inclusive plurality, in other words, could be seen to contradict the values of the Indigenous tradition that the curators sought to include.

Though the curatorial group was divided evenly between Maori and Pakeha, as between men and women, it is possible also that Maori preferences concerning the presentation of *taonga* were overlooked. Many conversations have suggested to me that a relatively conventional mode of museum presentation, which remains the approach in other sections of the Museum of New Zealand, and in other institutions in the country, in which artifacts are isolated on walls or pedestals and spot-lit, in fact seems wholly appropriate to many Maori, because the presence and power of their *atua* and *tupuna* or ancestors, together with the *mana* of sacred heirlooms, are emphasised. Placing these things 'in context' by associating them with everyday traditional subsistence activities, by surrounding them with images and words, distracts the viewer from the sheer power of the things themselves, and in that sense may paradoxically effect a more invidious decontextualisation than the artifact's isolation in the space of the specimen.

I do not want to speculate further about, or speak for, Maori responses, and instead comment upon what seems to me to have been the most significant underlying flaw of Voices. This is that the values rather than the form of the national narrative were altered; adjustments that seemed to be required by the idea of bicultural nationhood were made, but a certain kind of history remained intact. That history began in a particular natural setting; it had an indigenous opening chapter that was followed by white discovery, settlement and twentieth century experience, which was marked particularly by the great wars. This is the basic story that virtually all of us, I imagine, had at school. Altering the customary assessments of these moments – such that Cook *et al.* are disparaged rather than celebrated – does not so much empower Maori as deprive anybody and everybody of the opportunity to engage with the complexities of eighteenth-century exploration, of the promises and the risks of enlightenment on the beaches, of the uncertainty around 'discoveries' that were regarded as morally problematic at the time.

More importantly, it fails to identify or articulate an autonomous Indigenous history in which nature, prehistory and Cook would not, self-evidently, have defined the chapters. By gesturing toward the incorporation of a Maori perspective within a national history, the exhibition forestalled the possibility that incompatible histories might be presented in tension. The laudable idea that everybody should be included seemed to presuppose, in this case, the terms on which people and stories might be included. The point is not that people have different versions of histories, like bosses' and workers' accounts of a strike: some might have histories that do not belong to a birth-and-development of the nation model. A Maori counterpoint to a Pakeha history might take the form of an exhibit with no chronological sequence at all, that instead presented ancestors who embodied both past and future in principle, as they both commemorated and anticipated a plethora of more particular accomplishments and transactions. I am not putting this forward as a utopian projection of how a genuinely postcolonial exhibit might look, at some point in the future, but rather suggesting that this is one way in which Maori and others can *already* respond to exhibits that may otherwise appear to be conventionally ethnological. Almost inadvertently, that old museology empowered the objects that it encased, and created scope for Indigenous people to empower themselves by reclaiming the objects – mainly in a symbolic and political sense rather than through physical reappropriation – which led to the objects being re-empowered in turn. Most visitors to museums in Aotearoa New Zealand are impressed not only by the aesthetic dynamism of the Maori pieces they encounter, but also by the Maori *mana* that dynamism seems to exemplify. In this case, surely, the content of museums has helped shape their context.

If this is so, the appropriate course of action must be to validate these Indigenous perceptions of Indigenous objects. This must mean curatorial control and the continuing liaison with indigenous communities that I imagine most in the museum world would now support in principle. The Voices exhibition looks more and more like an extension of the social or popular history strategy from the less privileged groups within white society into the domain of settler–Indigenous relations; the strategy comes to pieces in that context because it is not a question of differing perspectives or retelling a history from below, as I already noted, but a more fundamental matter of acknowledging profound cultural differences that extend to constructions of history itself. But if I have argued that these differences can be better addressed by exhibitions that foreground the intelligence of Indigenous artifacts themselves – and the kinds of historical imagining those artifacts suggest – that can surely only be a partial solution. It would be partial because Indigenous cultures are not, of course, wholly autonomous of the national narratives that white settlers lurch between celebrating and lamenting. How can museums and exhibitions mark this interplay, and the conflict of colonisation, without according Indigenous people a marginal role within an inevitably larger national history, without, in effect, assimilating them?

This brings me to the National Gallery of Australia. The rehang of the Australian galleries there, unveiled in June 1994, was generally commended and not much debated. The only public critique of which I am aware was contained within an otherwise mainly positive review by Humphrey McQueen, whose objections focused upon the inclusion of mid-nineteenth century Aboriginal artifacts in the rooms containing paintings of the same period (Figure 5). According to McQueen:

> The meanings of those Aboriginal pieces are ... being expropriated as surely as was the country of the peoples who made them. The juxtaposition of cane baskets with marble busts has the opposite effect of the one intended. Instead of highlighting Aboriginal creativity, the display is an inversion of Batman's offer of beads and blankets in exchange for the Port Phillip district. In the NGA's context, the artefacts are not even tokens, but trinkets.
>
> (McQueen 1994, p. 25)

Much as I respect Humphrey McQueen as a cultural historian, I don't find this assessment of these galleries persuasive. His argument is really that a naive effort to affirm Aboriginal creativity led curators to place baskets with paintings as though they exhibited artistic qualities of the same order; yet this strategy, he suggests, can only obscure the meanings of the Aboriginal pieces, and most

Figure 5 The Australian galleries, National Gallery of Australia, 1997
(National Gallery of Australia)

particularly the fact that they are not artworks in any European sense. He goes on to stress that 'to say that the products of 19th-century Aboriginal communities were not Art is not to devalue their design qualities, but rather to appreciate how different those cultures were from industrial capitalism'.

This strikes me as more valid as a critique of an earlier exhibition of global masterpieces that occupied the large gallery immediately off the NGA's entrance which included the famous Lake Sentani double figure and the Gallery's paintings by Rubens and Tiepolo. The approach here was similar to that of the Sainsbury Centre at the University of East Anglia, where Jacob Epstein and Francis Bacon rub shoulders with dazzling inlaid shields from the Solomon Islands, and many other African, Oceanic and native American pieces. All of these works are put forward as works of fine art, and the old evolutionist ranking of cultures is neutralised on a relativist level plain. Most curatorial strategies of course entail both gain and loss, and it is perhaps important to see this affirmation of the products of non-European cultures as retaining some value, especially when 'the Western canon' understood in exclusive terms, retains eloquent proponents. But the drawbacks of this relativism are perhaps more conspicuous. It insists on a general equivalence of value while obscuring the particular ground from which various aesthetic expressions emerge. It removes an invidious principle of linear progress but treats cultures as so many discrete systems, rather than as milieux that have become mutually entangled through exchange and colonisation. Hence the overall form of this exhibit conveys no sense of any specific relation between the people of Lake Sentani and those of Europe, even though this particular piece is said to have been submerged in a lake to avoid destruction at the hands of missionaries, and though, like a number of other Oceanic pieces, it has been widely reproduced, as much because it was once in the collection of a well-known modernist artist as for its own interest. If facts of this kind, together with the power of the carving itself, make up an uneasy amalgam of meaning, they have no significance in the context of its juxtaposition with Tiepolo or Rubens. Even if we go into the histories of each of these pieces, the gaps are extreme, and we are left simply with a set of powerful yet disconnected works of art.

I find the effect of the Australian galleries to be very different. This is not because the works are more aesthetically proximate. In some ways they are less so: whereas the double Lake Sentani figure can immediately be categorised as a piece of sculpture broadly comparable to Western figurations of the human body, the pieces in the case in the centre of the room seem absolutely non-representational; their intricate and powerful patterns can be regarded as the decorated surfaces of utilitarian objects, that strike us immediately as being fundamentally different from the canvases decorated by von Guerard, Chevalier and others, on the surrounding walls. Surely it would be difficult to find human products more categorically different than these fighting shields and baskets from eastern Australia, and the Antipodean expressions of the tradition of romantic landscape painting. Yet in another sense these works are close. We could even say that they are locked together, in a sense in which the Tiepolo and the west Papuan carving are not.

And this is because of a fact that most visitors to those Australian galleries will be conscious of. Von Guerard and others were documenting a process of colonisation, and the fact that the accomplishments of pioneers were closely linked with the marginalisation of Aboriginal people is sometimes made explicit in their works, that, in a general sense, image the same ground as the artifacts emerge from. Aboriginal and colonial-settler societies were certainly becoming entangled, but it would not be true to say that Europeans and Aborigines shared a history in any meaningful sense. I am not really concerned with the curators' intentions, but I take this exhibition not to fail in 'highlighting Aboriginal creativity', but to succeed in underlining an incommensurable difference between the aesthetic practices of colonisers and colonised that marks wider differences between ways of life, relations to place and perceptions of history in this period. One body of work depicts the land; the other reflects subsistence practice intimately connected with country, and tribal conflict that may have been occasioned by dispute over it, or may have had quite different causes: how can we know? I am suggesting, then, certainly, that the juxtaposition of these pieces allows viewers to engage with the distinctive creativities of the various producers, but more immediately and powerfully compels them to reflect upon the paradox of their difference and their connection.

The implication surely goes beyond any notion that there might be 'two sides' to the story of the settlement of Australia – a narrative of resistance that would balance the narrative of accomplishment. The latter is charted out by the galleries' progression from Cook voyage artists through Glover and Duterreau through to the Heidelberg school and beyond, but there is no sense that Aboriginal experience either simply precedes, or parallels this, in some negative version of the pastoral myth. What we have, rather, are simply a number of implements. Several are intricately patterned, and one, one of the so-called fighting shields, bears a dynamic zigzag. Because of my interest in the optical vigour and complexity of many Pacific art forms, I am inclined to assume that this visual energy complemented, and was taken to exemplify, the energy of the bearer; the fighter's physical prowess, in other words, was augmented by aesthetic brilliance manifest in these kinds of artifacts, and surely in body paint.

The fact that this must be speculation, and that the viewer does not know whether the geometric patterns are actually iconographic and meaningful as well as merely optically compelling, marks the decontextualisation that McQueen referred to, yet I would see this abstraction from place and practice as being painfully evident (and in some sense unavoidable for all viewers, rather than apparent only to a sophisticated minority peculiarly mindful of the politics of curatorial presentation). It's worth stressing that this exhibition is one in which the choice of an art historian or even a cultural historian, rather than simply a connoisseur, is conspicuous: Duterreau's effort to image a grand reconciliation between the Tasmanian Aborigines and the colonial state in the person of George Augustus Robinson is nothing to write home about, as a painting, but is rightly included as an attempt to grapple with the issue of national narrative and Indigenous presence that we all know is with us still. In this context, it is the very decontextualisation of the so-called artifacts that speaks loudest.

The implication is not only that Indigenous ways of life in south-eastern Australia were radically disrupted. It is that no smooth assimilation of this history within national narrative is possible. We are left with a sense that there are other histories and other practices, perhaps in a condition of enduring estrangement, rather than on the point of some happy cultural and political synthesis. In some larger sense, the gallery may aim to image such a synthesis, or at least may aspire to value white and Indigenous Australian art equally, and present the stories of both. That is the sort of thing we expect such institutions to do; but in this case the array of content seems in the end to resist any unitary narrative, and if this is so, it is only true and appropriate to the disorderly and contradictory character of history and art history in a cross-cultural, settler-colonial situation.

Note

An earlier version of this chapter was written for the 1995 'Museums Australia' conference and was previously published in *Humanities Research*, Winter 1997; it is used here with permission. The treatments of Indigenous presence in Te Papa and the National Gallery of Australia today (2001) are more and less successful respectively than the projects described here.

📖 Guide to further reading

I discuss some of the issues reviewed here at greater length in Thomas, *Possessions: Indigenous Art/Colonial Culture* (London: Thames & Hudson, 1999). See, for related discussions, Chris Healy, *From the Ruins of Colonialism: History as Social Memory* (Cambridge: Cambridge University Press, 1997), Donna McAlear, 'First Peoples, museums and citizenship' in Tony Bennett, Robin Trotter and Donna McAlear (eds) *Museums and Citizenship: A Resource Book* (special issue of *Memoirs of the Queensland Museum* 1996, vol. 39, 1, pp. 79–114), and D. McIntyre and K. Wehrer (eds) *National Museums, Negotiating Histories* (Canberra: National Museum of Australia, 2001).

References

Graham, Brett (1993) 'An infinity of voices', *Midwest* 3.

McCarthy, F.D. (1941) 'Australian Aboriginal art and its application', *Australian Museum Magazine*, 1 September.

McLeod, Rosemary (1994) 'The mighty MONZ: artless at heart?' *North and South*, October, pp. 70–80.

McQueen, Humphrey (1994) 'Capital outlook for home-grown art', *Weekend Australian*, 18 June.

Preston, Margaret (1941) 'Aboriginal art', *Art in Australia*, 1 June.

Chapter 15

Indigenous Media and Policy Making in Australia

Helen Molnar

Introduction

> Culture becomes the 'property' which proves the existence of a group – it marks
> the group's existence in a concrete way and, as well, provides it with a sense
> of worthiness, resources, Indigenous recognition and self-esteem.
>
> (Fitzgerald 1991, pp. 202–3)

This chapter explores the cultural and political reasons underlying the growth
of Aboriginal and Torres Strait Islander media in Australia over the last
25 years. It also discusses the role that federal government departments and
agencies have played in this development, namely the Aboriginal and Torres
Strait Islander Commission (ATSIC), the Department of Communication,
Information Technology and the Arts (DCITA), the Department of Education,
Training and Youth Affairs (DETYA), the Australian Broadcasting Authority
(ABA), the Australian Broadcasting Corporation (ABC) and the Special Broad-
casting Service (SBS).

Anglo-Saxon Australia and 'the other'

Appropriate Indigenous communications policies, which recognise the uniqueness of Indigenous culture and languages, are yet to be implemented in

313

Australia. Some policies, such as ATSIC's broadcasting policy, have developed considerably over the last decade and do refer to the importance of Indigenous culture. However, unlike Canada or New Zealand, there is no acknowledgement of the significance of Indigenous languages and culture in the 1992 Broadcasting Services Act. This lack of recognition has been an ongoing problem for Indigenous media development.

In 1996 there were 386,000 Aborigines and Torres Strait Islanders out of a total Australian population of just over 18 million. This number is considered approximate because it is difficult to make an accurate assessment in remote areas. Aborigines and Islanders live in urban and rural areas, and in remote Australia they form a significant part of the population. Indigenous communities are very diverse and have distinct language and cultural differences. Pan-Indigenous approaches are therefore inappropriate as they fail to take this diversity into account.

In 1989 the federal government announced its National Agenda for a Multi-cultural Australia. This agenda acknowledged that Australian society had changed markedly since World War II and now included people of many different backgrounds. The agenda also stated that increasing recognition was being given to the special status and place of Aborigines and Torres Strait Islanders in Australian life. The ideal underlying a multicultural society is a 'fair go for all'. This assumes that there is equality and sharing between cultures, with each culture being able to retain its own identity 'by regulating the amount of interaction it has with other cultures' (Budby 1984, p. 7). In reality, however, some cultures are more equal than others.

Aborigines and Islanders in particular are disadvantaged by multiculturalism. They have been largely excluded from Australia's history and dominant Anglo-Saxon society, and the numerous ethnic groups tend to be seen by government as more powerful economically and politically (see Hodge and Mishra 1991, p. 26). As a result, much of the debate about multiculturalism has focused on the need to foster the languages and cultures of newly arrived migrant groups, for example, Greeks, Italians, Turks, Vietnamese, but Indigenous languages and culture have not been accorded the same respect. This is an historic problem, which started with European contact in 1788.

When the English colonised Australia, they dismissed Indigenous culture as prehistoric and simple, and Aborigines and Islanders as childlike and not human. On the basis of the cultural and physical differences they perceived, Europeans subsequently defined Aboriginal and Islander culture in opposition to Anglo-Saxon culture, categorising it as 'alien' or 'the other'. It is this 'otherness' that still sets Aborigines and Islanders apart from multicultural Australia. This has also resulted in a major problem for Aborigines and Islanders because non-Indigenous Australians have defined Indigenous identity. Australian history gave 'semiotic control' to the European colonisers, so the image of Aborigines and Islanders is not theirs. They have instead been a 'semiotic pawn on a chess board controlled by the white signmaker' and can only move within certain prescribed areas (Goldie 1988, p. 60). One consequence of this is that the dominant European constructed representation of Aborigines and Islanders in Australian history, literature and media has focused on their apparent hopelessness in comparison to the non-Indigenous population. At the same time there has been hardly any discussion about the strength and endurance of Indigenous culture and its diversity and richness.

The combined effect of these assumptions has resulted in the widespread belief that Indigenous culture is 'worthless' and dying, because it supposedly does not equip Aborigines and Islanders for life in a Western industrialised society. Non-Indigenous Australians have further reinforced this view by consigning Aborigines and Islanders to the past as safe pieces in museums that can be viewed from a distance, so that they do not 'interfere with the processes by which national identity was being constructed' (Hodge and Mishra 1991, p. 25). The portrayal of Indigenous Australians as relics has in turn led to dehumanisation and the assumption that Indigenous culture is static and no longer capable of change or innovation. As a result, 'all that is left for us is a decision to make reference to it or not' (Underwood 1981, p. 62).

While the 1967 Referendum established the right of Aborigines and Islanders to be citizens in their own country, it did not redress the more serious problems regarding their place in Australian society, nor the need to respect their culture and history. Consequently Aboriginal and Islander children are still made aware of their identity in non-Indigenous society from an early age with terms such as 'black', 'boong', 'blackfella' and 'dirty black' (Keen 1988, p. 6).

Since the 1970s, aided by the Whitlam government's commitment to self-determination and the cessation of previous assimilationist policies, Aborigines and Islanders have sought to control more of their own affairs so that they are not always in the position of being 'objects' of governments and welfare agencies. A crucial part of this control is a new sense of Indigenous identity. This chapter argues that the media can play a major role in this process by promoting Aboriginal and Islander culture and languages.

Culture, language and identity and the media

TV is like an invasion. We have had grog, guns and diseases, but we have been really fortunate people outside the major communities have had no communication like radio or TV. Language and culture have been protected by neglect. Now they are not going to be. They need protection because TV will be going into those communities 24 hours a day in a foreign language – English.

(Glynn quoted in Ginsburg 1991, p. 97)

Indigenous Australians have used oral transmission to pass on their culture through the generations. But European colonisers dismissed oral culture because it was not written down, and viewed it reductively so that its full scope and complexity was misunderstood. As a result, they were unable to see that 'even in the harshest environments, Aboriginal people had a great heritage of songs, stories, dances, dramatic performances, ground drawings, body paintings and objects' (Berndt and Berndt 1985, p. 48).

These misleading assumptions about Indigenous culture were again obvious in 1984 in a major review of Aboriginal and Islander broadcasting, *Out of the Silent Land*, published by the Department of Aboriginal Affairs (DAA). The central premise in the report was that prior to the electronic media, Aborigines and Islanders had few means of communication. As indicated above, this was not the case. Moreover, remote Australia was far from silent and has been described as a 'land abuzz with information, with news travelling rapidly through the use of smoke signals and message sticks for distant transmissions' (Michaels 1986, p. 2).

Another misleading assumption, noted earlier, is that Indigenous culture is dying out. Yet, as Sykes and Sykes argue, Aboriginal and Islander culture is very resilient, especially as it has survived over 200 years of continuous oppression (Sykes and Sykes 1986, p. 1). The campaign for land rights, and the considerable developments in Aboriginal and Islander broadcasting, art, music, literature and theatre over the last three decades, further indicate this resilience and the strength of contemporary Indigenous culture.

However, the dismissal of Indigenous beliefs and lifestyles has meant that Aborigines and Islanders 'have been told that we are worthless, that our culture is invalid, that formal education is not for us. We have no ownership, no true recognition of our culture, our history, or ourselves with the mainstream system', (Woods 1990, p. 4). A meeting of educators in Darwin in 1990 discussed the sociocultural issues affecting Aborigines and Islanders today. One of the resolutions stated that there was:

> The strong and urgent need for Aboriginal and Islander culture in all its forms, including Aboriginal languages, to survive, to be maintained as a viable and distinctive element in the multicultural web of Australian society, and to develop further.
>
> (Ingram 1990, p. 5)

Language is at the heart of culture. It is a form of cultural expression, and every group in society should have the right to express themselves in a way that is appropriate to their culture and lifestyle. Aborigines and Islanders have largely been denied this right because English is the language of our government, institutions, education system – and the media. When Aborigines and Islanders use standard English, they are speaking and writing from 'within the invading culture', using words that are not neutral, but which are skewed because they belong to a particular cultural context (O'Donoghue 1992, p. 57).

Aborigines argue that the government has placed their languages and culture 'at the bottom of their list of priorities' (ALA 1989, p. 14). They also say that the government has taken a primarily 'welfarist' approach to their languages and does not understand that they are central to their future *(Land Rights News* 1987, p. 13). This is despite the fact that governments have come to realise that they could communicate far more effectively with Aborigines and Islanders if they were allowed to speak in their own languages through interpreters (Black 1983, p. 10).

At the time of colonisation there were an estimated 250 to 300 Aboriginal and Islander languages with as many as 600 to 700 dialects. By 2000 only about 100 of these remained, and some are under severe threat. But the wider Australian public is unaware that there is a diversity of Aboriginal and Islander languages, and that these languages record a history, worldview and culture that it would be a national tragedy to lose (Fesl 1985, p. 30).

Prior to the 1970s, when the policies of assimilation were in force, Aborigines and Islanders had been under extreme pressure to adopt non-Indigenous values, lifestyles and language. So much so that Aboriginal and Islander culture, history and languages became stigmatised. As a result of this stigma many parents 'regarded their Aboriginal language as not useful and unworthy of passing down to future generations' (Fesl 1985, 29). They also did this to spare their children 'the torment and trauma they had experienced', so that when they died the languages died with them (Fesl 1985, p. 29). This denigration of Aboriginal and Islander languages has had the effect of discouraging younger Aborigines and Islanders from learning their languages. They have witnessed the dependence of their elders on the European social security system, and the way non-Indigenous Australians run their communities and see their elders as 'powerless'. This 'discourages them from taking their parents as models or continuing to speak the traditional languages' (Shopen *et al.* 1987, p. 144). In addition to this, for many years Aboriginal and Islander children were forcibly removed from their families and placed within non-Indigenous institutions where they were punished for speaking their languages (see HREOC 1997). Aboriginal children were also not encouraged to speak in their own languages at school until the 1970s (Black 1983, p. 10).

Today Aboriginal and Islander children attend schools in which English is taught as the dominant language, and study non-Indigenous history and literature. Bilingual schools have been set up in Aboriginal communities, but Indigenous language education suffers from ad hoc planning and poor funding (Black 1983; Fesl 1985; ALA 1989; Shopen *et al.* 1987). In urban areas, Aborigines and Islanders have had to learn English to survive. Consequently there is now a generation of young urban Indigenous people who can no longer speak in language.

Along with school, the media (radio, TV, videos, music, cinema) are significant sources of information and entertainment for Aboriginal and Islander children. During her three-year study of Aboriginal languages, Annette Schmidt found that the media were the 'major instigator in the promotion of English as the most viable and prestigious code', and that they failed 'to recognise Aboriginal languages as viable codes of communication' (Schmidt 1990, p. 6). Schmidt argues that the media promote English by 'constantly and subtly supporting glossy Western role models, identities and values which are associated with English' and are 'incongruous with Aboriginal identity and the use of Aboriginal language' (Schmidt 1990, p. 6).

In the 1980s there was a significant resurgence of language awareness and pride among many Aboriginal and Islander groups. Since that time, Indigenous Language Centres have been established in all states and Indigenous Language policy is now part of ATSIC's responsibilities. This revival of interest in language has been closely linked to an increased awareness of Indigenous identity and political and social rights. Kwementyaye Buzzacott explained why this was so important at the Aboriginal Languages Association Conference in 1989:

> If we lose our language, if we lose our culture – and in some parts we've lost our country – we become lost ourselves; our spirit, our feelings become weak and break down. We all have to talk and help each other to keep our language strong.
>
> (Buzzacott in ALA 1989, p. 15)

Reclaiming language has therefore become part of a process in which Indigenous Australians are reversing loss of identity, loss of meaning, and loss of community worth (Schmidt 1990, p. 106).

Indigenous-produced radio and television can play a crucial part in this revival of Indigenous languages and culture. Recommendations from the ALA's 1989 conference *Keeping Language Strong* and Schmidt's report, along with numerous research papers, stress the media's importance for language and cultural maintenance and regeneration, and note the ways in which the electronic media can complement bilingual education programs. The media's ability to produce material cheaply and to transmit information to many people is particularly useful, because the media in this way can help overcome the lack of resources available both for Indigenous language education and for the recording of languages. At the same time, the media can promote language skills informally by producing entertainment, news and music in language.

However, for the electronic media to effectively promote Indigenous culture and languages, they must be controlled by Aborigines or Islanders and programmed by them. A central part of self-determination is the right to shape and control one's own information, as well as the right to receive appropriate information to further one's own developmental goals. This is important for Indigenous Australians as state and federal governments have often used Aboriginal funds to employ non-Aboriginal administrators who in turn determine 'what is best' for Aborigines and Islanders, often without any consultation (see *Land Rights News* 1992, p. 16; Foley 1992). Moreover, some Aborigines and Islanders feel that governments set up projects for them to fail as this further justifies government control. Lippman expands on the reasons for this:

These agencies very often do not accord with the concept of self-determination, since it would take away from their powers. Their multiplicity and the fact that many have their own private agenda outside the influence of Koori communities in itself limits the power of Koori organisations.

(Lippman 1992, p. 1)

The resulting compartmentalisation of Aboriginal and Islander culture among government departments and agencies is viewed by Aborigines and Islanders as serving the interests of bureaucrats rather than theirs. Pat Dodson expressed this strongly when he said:

We don't have the opportunity to stop being Aborigines. We are Aboriginal 24 hours a day; it's not a social issue we can take up and drop. Non-Aboriginal people can take an interest for a while and drop out. The same with governments when it's politically expedient.

(Dodson quoted in Stevens 1987, p. 11)

However, in arguing for Indigenous-controlled broadcasting, it needs to be stressed that this does not absolve the government of its responsibility to properly resource Indigenous television and radio so that there is adequate funding for staff, training, equipment and software.

The mass media and racism

The mainstream media's portrayal of Indigenous people has been another major reason why Aborigines and Torres Strait Islanders have sought out their own media. Media scrutiny is credited with leading to the setting up of the Royal Commission into Aboriginal Deaths in Custody. Along with this, the media have exposed blatant forms of racism, resulting in action being taken to curb the more excessive examples. But the Human Rights and Equal Opportunity Commission's (HREOC) National Inquiry into Racist Violence (NIRV, 1991) found that racism is 'endemic, nationwide and very severe' and that Aborigines and Islanders face racism 'in almost every aspect of their daily lives' (*Land Rights News* 1991, p. 18). The media, as public institutions entrusted to represent all publics, not just one, must consider what their role is in relation to this endemic racism because, as Stuart Hall says, the media is the place where ideas about race are 'articulated, worked on, transformed and elaborated' (Hall 1990, p. 12).

However, in Australia, the only mainstream media organisations which attempt to promote some degree of intercultural understanding are the national public broadcasters, the ABC and SBS.

The overall lack of diverse programming and minority viewpoints in the mainstream media is a concern because the mass media are the 'main means by which most Australian residents receive information about race issues' (HREOC 1991, p. 355). Irene Moss, then Race Discrimination Commissioner, emphasised this when she said 'that the Australian community relies almost solely on the media for their information on Aboriginal issues' (Moss 1991, p. 8). The media could play a significant role 'both in communicating and soliciting the ideas, fears and resentments of racism and in informing and educating Australians about each other' (HREOC 1991, p. 355). But it would appear that they are not doing so. The NIRV examined the media's role in race relations, and found that

> The perpetuation and promotion of negative racial stereotypes, a tendency towards conflictual and sensationalist reporting on race issues and an insensitivity towards, and often ignorance of, minority cultures can all contribute to creating a social climate which is tolerant of racist violence.
>
> (HREOC 1999, p. 356)

This view of the media was reinforced by Aborigines during the NIRV, when they described the media as one of the major tools of their oppression 'because the media are the ones that create all the negative thoughts in people's heads out there' (Moss 1991, p. 5; see also Meadows 1988; Meadows with Oldham 1990).

There are instances of overt racism in the media, but it is more accurate to say that the Australian media suffer from unthinking and instinctive racism, or what Hall refers to as inferential racism. This is more widespread and insidious. Hall describes inferential racism as:

> Those apparently naturalised representations of events and situations relating to race, whether 'factual' or 'fictional', which have racist premises and propositions inscribed in them as a set of unquestioned assumptions. These enable racist statements to be formulated without ever bringing into awareness the racist predicates on which the statements are grounded.
>
> (Hall 1990, p. 13)

Inferential racism happens despite the fact that Aborigines and Islanders have many supporters in the mainstream media and is the result of how news is defined and produced. Western news is based on the premise of 'news of exception', therefore bad news is good news, and good news is no news. Consequently, major news themes are disorder, conflict, violence and law and order, with the focus being on any perceived ruptures or threats to the dominant Anglo-Saxon society (Bennett 1983, p. 8). So for example, a land rights story is often reduced to a dispute between 'black and white', rather than being put in the broader context of Indigenous history and culture.

Aborigines and Islanders have been portrayed negatively in the mainstream media since the first newspaper was sold in Australia (WAAMA 1990, p. 5). As recently as 30 years ago, the widely read national journal, *The Bulletin,* had a masthead, which read 'Australia for the White Man'. Even today Aborigines and Islanders are rarely present in the mainstream media, and are therefore largely invisible. The media, in this way, continue to reflect what Professor W.E.H.

Stanner referred to in 1968 as 'a conspiracy of silence about the Aboriginal role in our history' (quoted in Reynolds 1983, p. 14).

When Aborigines and Islanders do appear in the media it is usually as one of the following media perpetuated stereotypes: victim of poverty or alcoholism, criminal, welfare recipient (therefore assumed to be lazy), radical spokesperson or activist (threat to the public), a failure (unable to deal with Western lifestyles and values), as a mob or group of people (depending on the context, seen as either 'hopeless' or 'threatening'), and finally, the nomad, the media's preferred view of Aborigines. The mainstream media's approval of this last category has meant that they present traditional Aborigines in remote areas as the 'real' Aborigines. Urban Aborigines, and Aborigines of mixed heritage, are disadvantaged because of this and can be depicted as 'half-castes' and 'agitators' cashing in on their black heritage.

As well as these stereotypes, there are two themes running through the news media's coverage of Aborigines and Islanders. The first depicts Aborigines and Islanders as a monolithic group, devoid of cultural diversity, while the second perpetuates the belief that Aborigines and Islanders would be better off assimilating to a non-Indigenous lifestyle and values. Their powerlessness is further reinforced by the camera, which frames them as 'objects', robbing them of their individuality and humanity, and by news conventions, which authorise the journalist or non-Indigenous expert to speak on their behalf while they remain voiceless. This continues to be one of the major themes running through Australian history, literature and the media, that the 'other' cannot represent themselves, they must instead be 'represented by others who know more about them than they know about themselves' (Hodge and Mishra 1991, p. 27).

The lack of Indigenous perspectives to counter these media images means that media myths about Indigenous history, lifestyle and values are not challenged. The fundamental problem is that media images of and messages about Aborigines and Islanders, as indicated above, 'are constructed within the dominant Anglo-European cultural framework for consumption principally by those who share this framework' (Jennett 1983, p. 28). A journalist giving evidence to the Royal Commission into Aboriginal Deaths in Custody expanded on this:

> Racial stereotyping and racism in the media is institutional, not individual. That is, it results from news values, editorial policies, from routines of news gathering that are not in themselves racist or consciously prejudicial. It results from the fact that most news stories are already written before an individual journalist is assigned to them, even before the event takes place. A story featuring Aboriginals is simply more likely to be covered, or more likely to survive sub-editorial revision or spiking, if it fits existing definitions of the situation.
>
> (quoted in Eggerking and Plater 1992, p. 2)

This is not to say that the mainstream media cannot make changes – they can, but only at the margins. It is very difficult to see them committing more space and time to understanding Indigenous issues because Indigenous Australians are not regarded as a commercially attractive demographic. Even the ABC and SBS are not immune from these concerns, and their budget restrictions do not augur well for funding for niche or special interest programming.

What does become clear, however, is the importance of Indigenous Australians producing their own media to disseminate information to their communities. Two recommendations of the *Royal Commission into Aboriginal Deaths in Custody* (1991) address this:

> That, Aboriginal media organisations should receive adequate funding, where necessary, in recognition of the importance of their function; and
>
> That, in view of the fact that many Aboriginal people throughout Australia express disappointment in the portrayal of Aboriginal people by the media, the media industry and media unions should encourage formal and informal contact with Aboriginal organisations, including Aboriginal media organisations where available. The purpose of such contact should be creation of a better under-standing, on all sides, of issues relating to media treatment of Aboriginal affairs.
>
> (vol. 4 1991, p. 59)

Since the 1970s Aborigines and Islanders have responded to the concerns detailed above by increasingly developing their own radio, television and film.

Indigenous media development in Australia

In the mid-1970s there were a small number of Indigenous radio, film, video and print practitioners. Now, in 2000, the Indigenous media sectors – radio, print, film, video and television – are very much established and Indigenous multi-media and online services are developing. In recognition of the importance of the Indigenous media sector, in 1993 ATSIC provided funding for the National Indigenous Media Association of Australia (NIMAA) secretariat which is located in Brisbane. NIMAA now represents all Indigenous media sectors.

Aborigines and Torres Strait Islanders have embraced the use of electronic forms of media, in some instances more quickly than non-Indigenous Australians have. They have used the power and prominence of the electronic media to counter negative images of Indigenous people in the mainstream media. Radio, television and community video can do this by 'authorising' Indigenous languages and culture in the same way they do Anglo-Saxon culture. By airing Aboriginal and Islander cultural material, the media make Indigenous culture and issues part of the public agenda and signal their importance.

At the same time, Aboriginal and Islander electronic media content signifies that Indigenous culture, far from being dead, is alive and relevant to our times. How this is achieved is illustrated in the following description of one of the leading video makers at Yuendumu, Francis Jupurrurla Kelly:

> Jupurrurla, in his Bob Marley T-shirt and Adidas runners, armed with his video portapak, resists identification as a savage updating some archaic technology to produce curiosities of a primitive tradition for the jaded modern gaze. Jupurrurla is indisputably a sophisticated cultural broker who employs video-tape and modern technology to express and resolve political, theological and aesthetic contradictions that arise in uniquely contemporary circumstances.
>
> (Michaels 1987a, p. 26)

The media can be used not just to reclaim culture, but also to bring about cultural regeneration which embraces the future. This is vital, as it is impossible for Aborigines and Islanders to return to precolonial life. The effects of genocide, cultural suppression and the impact of the modern world have all had an ineradicable impact on Indigenous culture and lifestyles. Consequently Indigenous 'resistance is not seen as trying simply to defend an existent cultural identity' but is instead the forging of a new culture built upon 'signs of the past' which rejects the models sought to be imposed (Fry and Willis 1989, p. 160). Aborigines and Islanders are thus using the electronic media to create new cultural forms and new methods of distribution. In doing so, they are re-establishing communications networks between Indigenous communities, networks that have been disrupted due to colonisation. One example of this is the Tanami Network in Central Australia. In 1991 four Indigenous communities in the Tanami Desert established a compressed videoconferencing network using satellite technology. The Tanami Network links Yuendumu, Kintore, Lajamanu and Willowra with Alice Springs, Darwin, Sydney and the rest of the world. The network is owned by the communities and funded by the government departments and other user groups who buy time on it.

The network's uses currently include family and ceremonial contacts between Aboriginal communities; family contacts with Indigenous people in custody; videoconferencing as a means of consultation and representation to plan service delivery arrangements; the delivery of secondary and tertiary courses to Aboriginal students including videoconferencing links; telemedicine applications of videoconferencing in the context of remote health services; and recruitment and promotional interviews for government and private sector agencies; and videoconference auctions of Aboriginal art and other items within Australia and off-shore (Toyne 1997).

As a result of the success of the network, there are now plans for an Outback Digital Network, linking more than 60 remote Indigenous communities in Western Australia, the Northern Territory and Queensland. The aim of the extended network is to provide videoconferencing, e-mail, fax and telephony.

A feasibility study is currently underway with funding from the federal government's Regional Telecommunications Infrastructure Fund (RTIF).

Indigenous radio

The most extensive and well-known Indigenous media sector is community radio. The first Aboriginal public radio (now referred to as community radio) program went to air on 5UV in Adelaide in 1972. By the 1980s, Indigenous broadcasters were producing programs on non-Indigenous community stations in every Australian state and territory. During this period Indigenous broadcasters also began to broadcast weekly on the ABC and SBS.

There are now 96 licensed community Indigenous stations in Australia, with 80 of these in remote communities. The others are in metropolitan and regional areas. There are also a number of the aspirant groups broadcasting on non-Indigenous community radio. Interestingly, in the 1990s some Aboriginal community stations have become important vehicles for reconciliation, so much so that non-Indigenous Australians have asked to be volunteers at these stations.

The growth of Indigenous community radio has been very important because 'access' to non-Indigenous community radio stations is always conditional. In a number of instances, Indigenous people have not been treated well at some non-Indigenous-run community stations (Molnar 1993). In practice, there is a significant difference between 'access' – where one assumes a client status – and *control*. Indigenous control of the media means that

> Aboriginal broadcasting can only be developed by Aborigines themselves, on their own terms; it must come from the grassroots and develop upwards, not be 'created' by some government agency at the top and then imposed.
>
> (Macumba quoted in Noble and Elsegood 1984, p. 64)

In addition to the network of Aboriginal stations, there are two other Indigenous radio networks. The National Indigenous Radio Service (NIRS) was established in 1996 and it aims to provide a continuous stream of quality Indigenous programming via satellite to Indigenous radio stations throughout Australia. The other Indigenous radio network is The Aboriginal Program Exchange (TAPE). TAPE began operating in 1985 and distributes programs weekly on audio cassette tape to all Indigenous radio stations and Indigenous media associations broadcasting on non-Indigenous community radio stations. TAPE compiles the material from programs sent in by Indigenous radio stations and broadcasting groups.

Government policy

The ATSIC 1997–98 Program Policy and Guideline Statements say that the goal of Aboriginal and Torres Strait Islander broadcasting (radio, television and video production) is to secure the empowerment of Aboriginal and Islander peoples through:

- control of their own broadcasting and communications services,
- access to other broadcasting and communications services, and
- production of their own linguistically and culturally relevant programmes, in recognition of their status as Indigenous Australians (ATSIC 1997, p. 122).

Since the establishment of ATSIC in 1990, it has played an important role in the development of Indigenous broadcasting, in particular radio. Given the public service nature of Indigenous broadcasting, it is doubtful that the sector would be as significant as it is today without this funding assistance. However, the recognition of the link between Indigenous culture and the media has not happened overnight, and is still not widely appreciated.

For most of the past 25 years, Indigenous communications policy has followed behind Indigenous media development. During the 1970s and 1980s, Aborigines and Torres Strait Islanders had to fight to get themselves onto the federal government's media policy agenda.

The underlying problem facing Aborigines and Torres Strait Islanders is that most Indigenous media are dependent on government funds. Only some of the larger Indigenous media associations can generate a reasonable level of revenue, but this amount is not enough to allow them to operate independently of government. Aboriginal and Islander media associations therefore require clear guidelines and assurances from government about the level and type of funding they can receive. To date, however, this has not happened. There are a number of reasons for this, namely:

- The number of federal government departments and agencies involved in Indigenous media policy and funding, each with their own departmental agenda;
- The difficulty Indigenous Australians have had convincing government departments and agencies of the uniqueness of their culture and the link between culture and the media;
- The tendency of some government officials to dismiss Indigenous broadcasting as 'just community broadcasting', rather than recognising that it provides a first level of service to Indigenous communities;
- Related to this, a view held by some government officials that Aborigines and Torres Strait Islanders are happy to 'volunteer' their services for the good of their communities, thus neglecting the need for proper resources for training and salaries; and
- Government provision of technology without additional resources to make this operational.

The main government departments and agencies involved with Indigenous broadcasting are DCITA, ATSIC, DETYA and the ABA. DCITA is responsible for all broadcasting and communications policies in Australia, with the exception of Indigenous Broadcasting, which is ATSIC's responsibility. When devising its Indigenous Broadcasting policy, ATSIC has to take into account the broader policy framework established by DCITA. ATSIC also directly funds a number of Indigenous media associations, providing money for wages and capital costs, and training. DETYA provides training programs, mostly on a short-term basis. The ABA is the regulatory body and it allocates licences. Unfortunately, these government departments and agencies rarely work together in a coordinated way. In the early phases of the Broadcasting for Remote Aborigines Community Scheme (BRACS) project, for example, when training was urgently needed, the departments involved did not invite the Department of Education, Employment and Training (now DETYA) to the planning discussions. As a result, BRACS training was delayed. This lack of coordination also means that there is no holistic approach to Indigenous broadcasting. Consequently, when DEET did deliver training it was in the context of other DEET projects and did not take into account the training requirements of the BRACS operators.

The first attempts to formulate an Indigenous media policy were made in the 1970s by the Department of Aboriginal Affairs (DAA). But broadcasting sat very uneasily in DAA, and its apparent lack of interest in this area meant that Indigenous media growth in the 1980s happened in a piecemeal way (Michaels 1986, p. 95). Currently, Broadcasting and Languages form one department within ATSIC, the successor to DAA, and to date this department has managed to avoid any budgetary cutbacks. However, the 35 ATSIC regional councils that distribute the broadcasting funds are not all committed to Indigenous media development. For some years, a number of BRACS operators have received little or none of their operational costs because the councils have preferred to allocate these funds to projects they see as more important. In fairness to the regional councils, their overall budgets are limited and the needs great. However, it does need to be said that the link between Indigenous broadcasting and culture, and the fact that Indigenous media can offer a first level of service by disseminating relevant information on a range of areas such as health, education, the environment and small business advice, is not widely recognised by government departments or within ATSIC. The lack of an holistic approach, referred to earlier, also means that there is no mechanism for encouraging the whole-of-government commitment necessary to disseminate information for Indigenous communities through Indigenous media. Such a commitment would have the additional benefit of providing extra funding for the Indigenous media.

In 1983 to 1984, in response to the Aboriginal and Islander concerns about the impact of the soon to be launched domestic satellite, DAA set up a Task Force, chaired by Eric Willmot from DAA, to report on existing and potential Aboriginal and Islander media needs. *Out of the Silent Land* was the first comprehensive study of Aboriginal and Islander broadcasting completed in Australia, and its recommendations have influenced Indigenous media policy for over a decade. The report, however, has some critical flaws that need to be touched on briefly (see Michaels 1986, pp. 114–17; Michaels 1987b, pp. 16–17). The first and most serious was the lack of extensive consultation with remote Aborigines and Islanders about their communication needs. The Task Force instead relied on information from organisations it considered to be representative of all Indigenous remote community needs. One of these was the ABC. Secondly, the Task Force failed to recognise that Aborigines wanted access to the satellite in their own right, and recommended that the ABC be the major source of Indigenous programming and training. This is a role that the ABC did not want, and it was completely contrary to Aboriginal and Islander arguments for Indigenous control of content and transmission. Thirdly, the Task Force adopted a technological solution without consideration of the necessary infrastructure to support it. In adopting this solution, the Task Force failed to recognise the complexity of communications and cultural needs in these communities.

Willmot's primary concern was that Indigenous Australians living in remote areas should have the means of producing community radio and television. To this end, DAA was given the task of administering a new broadcasting scheme to serve Aborigines and Islanders in remote areas – BRACS. Wilmot, however, did not give sufficient attention to the needs of Indigenous Australians living in urban and regional areas:

> Urban and rural blacks have always been able to receive electronic media. In a general sense they have not been isolated. But culturally, they have been just as isolated as those in remote areas. What little is seen and heard of Aboriginals in mainstream media is usually produced by whites, and often misrepresents Aboriginality.
>
> (Powis 1985, p. 31)

DAA believed that urban and rural Aborigines and Islanders would be better served by gaining access to non-Indigenous-run community radio, and if possible, the mainstream media. This view was based on DAA's assumption that Aborigines and Islanders in urban and rural areas needed to live within the dominant framework of a non-Indigenous society. The Willmot Task Force had recommended this division of Indigenous media, but the Task Force had worked on the false premise that Aborigines and Islanders in towns and cities had sufficient access and encouragement to be involved with non-Indigenous community radio and the mainstream media (Powis 1985, p. 30). In coming to this conclusion, the Task Force also reinforced a stereotype represented in the mainstream media – that Aborigines and Islanders living in remote areas are the 'real' Indigenous people and have the most to lose in terms of language and culture.

As a result of the Willmot recommendations, DAA funded remote and regional Indigenous media, rather than urban and rural Indigenous media associations.

ATSIC has continued this policy, with a few exceptions. This is further illustrated in a 1992 interim report published by ATSIC in which the Commission said that it had directed funding towards rural and remote areas of Australia, with the result that, per capita, Aborigines and Islanders in the Northern Territory received 46 times the amount of funding that those in NSW receive. However, the largest Indigenous population lives in New South Wales, and Indigenous broadcasters in urban and rural areas in this state have received very little funding.

In spite of the emphasis on funding remote initiatives, the results of this funding have not always been effective. The first phase of the BRACS project was marred by problems. DAA's view of BRACS was limited, as it saw the scheme as a technological answer that could be neatly packaged and given to 80 remote Aboriginal and Islander communities, often with no consultation. The radio and video production equipment was delivered, and in a number of instances lay unused because the community had not been resourced to use it. ATSIC attempted to redress the problems with the first phase by funding the BRACS Revitalisation Scheme (BRS). It differed from phase one as the equipment was of a much better quality and training was part of the package. However, there is still a critical flaw – namely, in a number of communities there has not been enough consultation between the community and the ATSIC Regional Councils about the potential of BRACS. Thus some community councils have not integrated BRACS into the daily activities of the community, and a number of ATSIC Regional Councils, as noted earlier, still do not pass on the full operational funding required to operate BRACS.

The next major policy development occurred in 1997, when ATSIC commissioned another major review – *Digital Dreaming*. The review examined each sector of the Indigenous media and explored the potential for Indigenous media and communications to offer a first level of service. It also argued that the Indigenous media could be a major source of employment for Aborigines and Islanders if they received adequate funding. The review team identified a number of key issues:

- that in view of the unique service Indigenous media offer their audiences, the federal government consider Indigenous media funding as an investment in Indigenous services and information dissemination;
- that federal government departments are encouraged to work with Indigenous media outlets to improve their service delivery to Indigenous people, particularly those living in rural and remote areas;
- that ATSIC works with all Indigenous media sectors to plan five-year funding and development strategies, so that sustained rather than ad hoc policies can be implemented;
- that ATSIC, DETYA and DCITA adopt a coordinated approach to policies, training and funding for the Indigenous media sector; and
- that in view of the convergence of content production, delivery systems, and service providers, ATSIC should develop integrated strategies for making the best use of this technological environment.

The 500-page report made 131 recommendations, and ATSIC has accepted all of these and prioritised them for implementation. At the time of writing, it is not clear how this implementation will proceed.

Some of the key recommendations made in *Digital Dreaming* were subsequently endorsed by the Productivity Commission in its final report on Australian broadcasting in April 2000. The submissions made to the inquiry by ATSIC and NIMAA (National Indigenous Media Association of Australia) stressed the need for centralising the management and organisation of Indigenous media through a statutory body, tentatively called Indigenous Communications Australia (ICA). The *Digital Dreaming* review identified this entity as an Indigenous Media Authority. ATSIC and NIMAA also proposed a National Indigenous Broadcasting Service (NIBS) involving radio and television, and administered by ICA.

In its response, the Productivity Commission acknowledged that broadcasting is important for Indigenous communities because it provides 'a primary level of service in remote areas and in local languages' (2000, p. 3). It noted that Indigenous broadcasting was also an important source of news and information for Indigenous people, and a vehicle for better communications between Aborigines and Islanders and other Australians. Significantly, the Commission stated that the objectives and management of Indigenous media are 'very different from those of community broadcasters' (2000, p. 28). This was clear in its recommendations relating to Indigenous media:

> Recommendation 6.6: The ABA, in consultation with the broadcasting industry and the public, should develop a series of templates for licence areas with different characteristics, setting out the number of national, community and Indigenous services for which spectrum should be reserved (2000, p. 34).
>
> Recommendation 8.6: Spectrum should be reserved for Indigenous broadcasters to provide a primary service for Indigenous communities, where appropriate (2000, p. 37).

The Productivity Commission also recommended that the government 'examine the need for, and feasibility of, establishing an Indigenous broadcasting service' (2000, p. 37). In April 2000, ATSIC called for tenders for this feasibility study.

The Productivity Commission's acknowledgment of the 'unique role' of Indigenous media in Australia is vastly different from the view held by some government officials that Indigenous broadcasting is 'just community broadcasting' and marginal at best. The outcomes of the NIBS feasibility study are not known at this stage. However, for the NIBS and ICA to become a reality, DCITA will have to rethink its position on Indigenous broadcasting. To date, its funding involvement has been minimal and it has resisted arguments that Indigenous community broadcasting is different to non-Indigenous community broadcasting. In part this is because it does not want to take on the responsibility for funding the Indigenous media sector. DCITA funds the ABC and SBS, and *Digital Dreaming* recommended that it also fund ICA as the third national broadcaster. ATSIC's broadcast budget is not sufficient for the current number of broadcasters, let alone the establishment of ICA and the NIBS. Given the enormous growth in Indigenous broadcasting, it would be a timely recognition of its significance if the federal government provided funding for this sector under the same funding umbrella as the other two national public broadcasters. This would give ATSIC more flexibility to fund special projects and to work with other government departments to improve their interaction with the Indigenous media.

Conclusion

Over the last 25 years, Aborigines and Torres Strait Islanders have set up their own media (radio, video, television and online services), often with little government support. Policy for the most part has followed behind Indigenous initiatives. So much so that it was only in the 1990s, with the development of ATSIC's broadcasting policy, that the critical link between Indigenous culture, politics and the ability of the Indigenous media to offer a first level of service was addressed. However, the recognition of the uniqueness of Indigenous broadcasting is not appreciated by all sections of ATSIC, or by other government departments working in this area. As such, the Productivity Commission recommendations are a major step forward – but key issues such as resources for staff, training and equipment will have to be addressed if the Indigenous media sectors are to develop further. ATSIC, DCITA and DETYA will need to be involved in this process as equal partners. Most significantly, these departments and related agencies will need to acknowledge that services designed to 'address the needs of the majority of Anglo-Australians' will fail to cater for the needs of many Indigenous Australians because:

> Cultural and language differences, remoteness, unique histories and particular emotional needs mean that equality in the provision of services to Indigenous people will frequently require distinctive approaches ... The objective of specialist services is to ensure equity of access and to overcome the discrimination which clients would otherwise experience if required to have their needs met by mainstream services.
>
> (HREOC 1997, p. 321)

This recognition is still some way off.

⌨ Websites

Some of the most interesting material on Indigenous media, history, culture and politics can now be sourced through the internet. Valuable sites are www.nimaa.org.au – this site provides details on the work of the National Indigenous Media Association of Australia as well as links to member sites. The Australian Institute for Aboriginal and Torres Strait Islander Studies has a wealth of resources on Indigenous culture, history and languages and some material on the media. Its site is www.aiatsis.gov.au. The Aboriginal and Torres Strait Islander Commission and the Australian Broadcasting Corporation also have sites with links to a range of resources – www.atsic.gov.au and www.abc.net.au/message/links.htm. The national Indigenous newspaper the *Koori Mail* can be found at www.koorimail.com and for those interested in following up Indigenous multi-media developments, www.indiginet.com is a good site.

References

Aboriginal Languages Association (1989) *Keeping Language Strong*, Alice Springs: Institute for Aboriginal Development.

ATSIC (1997) *Program statements for the Social and Cultural Division for 1998/99*, Canberra: ATSIC.

— (1998) *Digital Dreaming: A National Review of Indigenous Media and Communications*, Canberra: ATSIC.

Australian Broadcasting Tribunal (1992) *Inquiry to Review Radio and Television Program Standards Relating to Discriminatory Broadcasts*, Background Paper No. 2, North Sydney: ABT.

Bell, Philip (1991) *Multicultural Australia in the Media*, A Report to the Office of Multicultural Affairs, Sydney: Corporate Impacts Pty. Ltd.

Bennett, Lance (1983) *News The Politics of Illusion*, New York: Longman.

Berndt, Catherine and Ronald M. Berndt (1985) *Aborigines in Australian Society*, Clayton, Vic.: Pitman Publishing.

Black, Paul (1983) *Aboriginal Languages of the Northern Territory*, School of Australian Linguistics, Darwin Community College.

Bostock, Lester (1993) *From the Dark Side (Portrayal of Aboriginal Images)*, Sydney: ABA.

— (1997) *The Great Perspective*, second edition, Sydney: SBS.

Budby, J.R. (1984) 'Aborigines in multilingual Australia', *Aboriginal Child at School* 12, 3, pp. 3–12.

Department of Aboriginal Affairs (1984) *Out of the Silent Land*, Report of the Task Force on Aboriginal and Islander Broadcasting and Communications, August, Canberra.

Eggerking, Kitty and Diana Plater (eds) (1992) *Signposts: A Guide For Journalists*, Sydney: Australian Centre for Independent Journalism, UTS.

Fesl, Eve (1985) 'Saving Aboriginal languages', *Education News* 18, 9, April, pp. 28–30.

Fitzgerald, Thomas K. (1991) 'Media and changing metaphors of ethnicity and identity', *Media, Culture and Society* 13, pp. 193–214.

Foley, Gary (1992) 'For Aboriginal sovereignty' in Eggerking and Plater (eds), pp. 65–7.

Fry, Tony and Anne-Marie Willis (1989) 'Aboriginal art: symptom or success?', *Art in America* 77, 7, pp. 108–17, 160, 163.

Ginsburg, Faye (1991) 'Indigenous media: Faustian contract or global village?', *Cultural Anthropology* 6, 1, pp. 92–112.

Goldie, Terry (1991) 'Signifier resignified: Aborigines in Australian literature' in Anna Rutherford (ed.) *Aboriginal Culture Today*, Sydney: Kangaroo Press.

Goodall, H., A. Jabubowicz, J. Martin, L. Randall and K. Seneiratne (1990) *Racism, Cultural Pluralism and the Media*, a report for the Office of Multicultural Affairs, Canberra: Office of the Prime Minister.

Hall, Stuart (1990) 'Racist ideologies and the media' in Manuel Alvarado and John O. Thompson (eds) *The Media Reader*, London: BFI Publishing, pp. 7–23.

Hodge, Bob and Vijay Mishra (1991) *Dark Side of the Dream*, Sydney: Allen & Unwin.

Human Rights and Equal Opportunity Commission (1991) *Racist Violence, Report of the National Inquiry into Racist Violence in Australia*, Canberra: AGPS.

— (1997) *Bringing Them Home, Report of the National Inquiry into the Separation of Aboriginal and Torres Strait Islander Children from Their Families*, Sydney: Sterling Press Pty Ltd.

Ingram, John (1990) 'Tertiary education for all: the challenge from Aboriginal Australia', a paper presented at the Education For All Conference, 14–19 October, Darwin.

Jennett, Christine (1983) 'White media rituals about Aborigines', *Media Information Australia* 30, pp. 28–37, 55.

Keen, Ian (ed.) (1988) *Being Black: Aboriginal Cultures in 'Settled' Australia*, Canberra: Aboriginal Studies Press.

Land Rights News (1987) 'Languages policy hijacked', 2, 4, p. 13.

— (1991) 'Racism found everywhere', 2, 22, p. 18.

— (1992) '1993 – for the World's Indigenous People', 2, 25, p. 16.

Lippman, Lorna (1992) 'Self-determination', newsletter, Victorian Chapter of AIATSIS, July.

Meadows, Michael (1988) 'Getting the right message across: inadequacies in existing codes make imperative the development of a code of conduct for Australian journalists reporting on race', *Australian Journalism Review* 10, pp. 140–53.

Meadows, Michael with Cheyenne Oldham (1991) 'Racism and the dominant ideology: Aborigines, television news and the bicentenary', *Media Information Australia* 60, pp. 30–40.

Michaels, Eric (1986) *Aboriginal Invention of Television Central Australia 1982–1985*, Canberra: Australian Institute of Aboriginal Studies.

— (1987a) *For A Cultural Future: Francis Jupurrurla Makes TV at Yuendumu*, Melbourne: Arts and Criticism Monograph Series, Artspace.

— (1987b) 'Aboriginal Air Rights Resuscitated', *Broadcast*, July, pp. 16–17.

Molnar, Helen (1993) 'The Democratisation of Communications Technology in Australia and the South Pacific: Media Participation by Indigenous Peoples, 1970–1992', unpublished PhD thesis, Department of Politics, Monash University, Melbourne.

Molnar, Helen and Michael Meadows (2001) *Songlines to Satellites: Indigenous Communication in Australia, the South Pacific and Canada*, Sydney: Pluto Press.

Moss, Irene (1991) 'Media response on Aboriginal and ethnic issues', paper presented to the Reporting Cultural Diversity Seminar, 14 June, Australian Centre for Independent Journalism, Sydney.

Noble, Grant and Phillip Elsegood (1984) 'Anticipating Aussat with trepidation', *Media Information Australia* 34, pp. 63–74.

O'Donoghue, Lois (1992) 'Creating authentic Australia(s) for 2001: an Aboriginal perspective' in Eggerking and Plater (eds), pp. 60–4.

Powis, Tina (1985) 'Black radio signals ward against whitewash', *New Journalist*, December, pp. 30–2.

Productivity Commission (2000) *Broadcasting: Inquiry Report*, Report Number 11, 3 March, Canberra: Ausinfo.

Reynolds, Henry (1983) *The Other Side of the Frontier*, Ringwood, Vic.: Penguin.

Royal Commission into Aboriginal Deaths in Custody (1991) Vol. 4 Canberra: AGPS.

Royal Commission into Aboriginal Deaths in Custody: Regional Report of Inquiry into Underlying Issues in Western Australia (1991) vol. 2, Canberra: AGPS.

Schmidt, Annette (1990) *The Loss of Australia's Aboriginal Language Heritage*, Canberra: The Institute Report Series, Aboriginal Studies Press.

Shopen, Tim, Nicolas Reid, Glenda Shopen and David Wilkins (1987) 'Ensuring the survival of Aboriginal and Torres Strait Islander languages into the 21st Century' (paper presented to the Friends of Bilingual Education Conference, ANU), *Australian Review of Applied Linguistics* 10, 1, pp. 143–57.

Stevens, John (1987) 'Crossroads for people trying to feel their way', *Age Saturday Extra* 31 October, pp. 1, 5.

Sykes, Roberta B. and Russell B. Sykes (1986) 'Technological change and Black Australian culture – threat or challenge?' Paper No. 5, speeches from the Symposium – The Law and the Future: The Impact of Scientific and Technological Change, March, Commission for the Future, Melbourne, pp. 1–5.

Tanami Network (1997) 'Submission for an Outback Digital Network', presented to the RTIF, Yuendumu, August.

Toyne, Peter (1997) 'Outback Digital Network Submission for Networking the Nation', Darwin.

Turner, Neil (1998) 'BRACS Report' (unpublished) for ATSIC, Canberra.

Underwood, Robert A. (1981) 'Role of mass media in small Pacific societies: the Case of Guam', *Pacific Islands Communication Journal* 10, 3, pp. 60–72.

Western Australian Aboriginal Media Association (1990) *YARNING with the Media*, Perth.

Woods, Davina (1990) 'The background to and some concerns about the national Aboriginal and Torres Strait Islander education policy', paper presented at the Education For All Conference, 14–19 October, Darwin.

Chapter 16

Regions, Regionalism and Cultural Development

Robin Trotter

Regionalism, culture and tourism

There are increasing claims in socio-economic and cultural discourses that the local is being subsumed within a new global culture and that local identities, as historically and culturally constructed, are giving way to a more 'globalised' citizenry. More ambiguous and complex arguments assert that regionalism offers a counterbalance to globalisation. How local, regional, national and international relationships are being worked out in 'the regions' themselves is the underlying theme of this chapter. Intersecting this is another set of issues that centre on community, citizenship and national identity. All of these issues materialise around, and are relevant to, tourism: hence the value of analysing this matrix of relationships through a series of case studies of regional tourism in Queensland. These studies will show that, to a greater or lesser degree, tourism and the images it constructs and generates have been used to shape or transform the identities of the regions in question.

Regionalism: reaction or innovation?

In discussing regionalism, the critical frameworks of analysis are notions of culture and place. If we take seriously the anthropological definition of culture (Williams 1983), then cultural analysis involves looking at how people share their lives and how they interact with their environments: in short, it involves understanding the relationship people construct between 'space, place and environment' (Harvey 1996, p. 44). 'Social constructions of space and time are not wrought out of thin air', Harvey argues, but out of the experiences of 'material survival', the 'objective facts' to which individuals and institutions respond, the processes of social reproduction, and the 'cultural, metaphorical and intellectual skill' that humans accrue (211–12).

In understanding how regions emerge as constructions of time and place it is useful to first define the term 'regionalism' and then to review some of the historical movements that maintain, even exacerbate, tensions between regional and urban cultures. Defining regionalism is problematic because, as George Kimple points out, regions do not 'exist in reality, [they] cannot be directly perceived, have no constant characteristics or clear boundaries' (Kimble 1951; cited in Gilbert 1960, p. 158). Despite these definitional problems, regionalism has a relevance and currency, especially in cultural debates. Terry Smith has defined regionalism as 'a description of a particular set of conditions of cultural creativity, potentiality and obligation, in which valuing occurs primarily (but not exclusively) with reference to place' (Smith 1999–2000, p. 3). It is also 'a set of facts of circumstance, or choice' and it is about self-definition – 'self-definition by contra-definition, comparison, differentiation by degrees to other identities' (3). Regionalism is not only defined by geography (Carter 1994, p. 7; Hoffie 1994, p. 12): it is also a state of mind (Ravenswood, 1994, p. 4). Nor is it a 'singular position'. As Kate Ravenswood argues, regionalism 'is a series of positions and strategies, adopted at best as a means of empowerment, and at worst as an excuse' (Ravenswood 1995, p. 4). Ravenswood argues against a simplistic core/periphery model that regards regionalism as a single position opposed to the power of monolithic centres:

> There are no two regional areas alike. There are economic differences, policy differences and locally inscribed political differences. They may have differing internal structures and they probably have to cater to different audiences. (5)

That regions are relative becomes evident when we consider attempts at definition. For example, within the context of the global system, Sydney may aspire to the designation of a 'global city' alongside London, Tokyo, and New York. Yet Sydney also forms part of the Australian 'triangle' of Canberra, Sydney and Melbourne that defines all areas outside these centres as regional. In this discursive mapping, Queensland, Western Australia, South Australia, Tasmania and the Northern Territory are all allocated regional positions. Yet the capitals of these 'regional' states are the centres of their own regions. Despite the obvious relativity of regions, there are officially designated regions based on political and administrative jurisdictions (local, state and federal), statistical regions delineated by the Australian Bureau of Statistics (ABS) and, increasingly powerful, tourist regions drawn up by state tourism departments. Less clearly defined are physiographic, biogeographic and economic regions.

Clearly, there are problems with defining regions. Morever, the strategies for constructing regions can also be exclusionary; for example, Aboriginal 'regions' or areas of tribal responsibility – either in traditional or historical terms[1] – are invisible in these regional constructs. The notion of a region as 'fixed' does not accommodate the possibility of new regions, those that disappear, or those that might be ephemeral, and militates against the possibility of overlapping or contradictory regions.

To accommodate the vagueness and uncertainty associated with defining a 'region', a definition that takes culture as its base, rather than physical or economic features, is appropriate to this current discussion. Michael Bogle provides us with such a definition: 'Loosely defined, regionalism is the adoption of goals that bene-fit, support or reinforce regional values' (Bogle 1988, p. 74). Bogle asserts that regionalism is a vehicle for enhancing access, empowering the local, restoring 'a sense of community' and encouraging a holistic approach to art and culture (80).

But what is the relationship between regionalism and globalisation? In the 1980s the slogan 'think globally, act locally' was popularised as a response to accelerated urbanisation, economic globalisation and the digital convergence revolution. These changes have generated new relationships between economy, state and society so that 'internal regionalisation' has become a 'systematic attribute of the informational/global economy' (Castells 1999, vol. 1 p. 102; see also vol. II pp. 243–308). Concurrent with these national and international relations, new linkages are being forged between the local and the global – sometimes called 'glocalisation' – where local governments look to global 'terms of reference' in establishing policy and practices (Borja and Castells 1997, p. 214; see also Robertson 1991 and 1995). Whilst globalisation is seen by some as a threat to local culture, especially where Americanisation or Europeanisation is perceived as the outcome of globalising tendencies, there is also a contradictory heterogenising effect that sees existing cultural forms reinforced alongside the generation of new hybrid forms. This argument asserts that 'local governments acquire a revitalised political role through the structural crisis of areas of author-ity and power that is affecting nation states in the new global system' (Borja and Castells 1997, p. 5). Responses of localities or regions to globalisation differ from those of the nation; moreover responses between regions also differ.

Globalisation therefore provides challenges for regionalism that have the potential to undermine the recently developed regional 'turn' and to reorient relationships of regions away from national and historical centres to new global centres as regionalism starts to serve different interests.

Regionalism in Australia

The history of regionalism in Australia reveals radical shifts in perceptions. Regionalism has 'evolved through three stages: from problem to policy to problematic, from a negative lack through a positive advantage to a puzzling uncertainty' (Smith 1999–2000, p. 3). Since the colonial period, decentralisation has been seen as a 'problem'. Early responses to the 'problem' saw the formation of Decentralisation Leagues in the 1880s. The 1920s saw regional development programs initiated as a response to regional issues. Finally, in the 1970s the Whitlam Government took up the issue of regional development as a federal government responsibility and established it as a policy area. One outcome of this – the most sustained and substantial – was the commitment of federal funding to develop the twin cities of Albury-Wodonga as a model decentralised regional city. After the dismissal of the Whitlam Government, and during the recessionary period of the late 1970s and early eighties, regionalism was largely ignored by government. Only in the last two decades has it again re-emerged as a problematic associated with the new global system (Aplin, Foster and McKernan 1987, p. 180).

Whilst regionalism has represented an intermittent concern for federal governments, this is not the case for Queensland. Here regionalism has long been close to the heart of government because of the colony's, and later state's, history of development. Early settlement saw a consolidation of the economically and politically strong regional centres of Rockhampton, Townsville and Cairns. These regional cities have also experienced a history of international exchange of commodities and people, in contrast to the more parochial experiences of most regional cities in other Australian states. Throughout the history of Queensland the impetus to growth has maintained competitive pressure on the capital, located in the south-eastern corner of the state. Exacerbating this competitive thrust has been a strong perception by the northern cities that the state's capital, Brisbane, and the south-east region were aligned more with southern centres of power than their northern outposts (Doran 1981). The Queensland political scene has long been a battleground between agrarian interests representing the regions and urban-based interests (Fitzgerald 1984). Queensland, therefore, represents an especially clear case of the tensions revolving around cultural identity that emerge between regional areas and the provincial and metropolitan centres of social, political, economic and cultural power.

Regionalism and culture

It is conventional wisdom that cultural innovation and cultural expression occur in the cities. According to Stuart Hall, cities are:

> The places where human creativity flourished; from them came the world's greatest art, the fundamental advances in human thought, the great technological breakthroughs that created new industries and even entire new modes of production ... places that developed the solutions – technological, organisation, legal, social.
>
> (Hall 1995, p. 275)

In contrast, Nigel Calder has asserted that capital cities are more concerned with the past and that 'the great changes typically occur on the periphery' (quoted in Timms and Christie 1988).

The federal government, like state and local governments, is now engaged in responding to demands for government involvement in culture at a regional level. This might appear as something of a knee-jerk reaction to the Hanson phenomenon or the more recent 1999 defeat of the Kennett Government in Victoria by a 'regional revolt'. However, direct federal intervention into cultural funding was re-initiated in the mid-1990s. This included funding of the touring programs Playing Australia and Visions Australia, support for festivals and the establishment (as an initiative of the 1996 budget) of the Regional Arts Fund. Also acting as a funding base for the development of regional programs and as a lobby group is Regional Arts Australia (RAA) – a creation of the Arts Council of Australia (a federation of independent local arts organisations). But, as 'regionalists' have argued, regional cultural development involves more than looking to 'the bush' for inspiration or 'taking art to the country'; it is about cultural development *in* the regions and taking that regional culture *to* the cities.

In Queensland, the major mechanism of government for funding regional cultural development is the Regional Arts Development Fund (RADF). Established in 1990, the RADF is structured and administered as a partnership between the state's Arts Department, the relevant local government body and the local community. The birth of the RADF can be located generally in the interest in cultural development and cultural planning that came to the fore in the late 1980s and early 1990s. This paralleled work by the Australia Council and the Federal Office of Local Government which culminated in the launch of a Local Government Cultural Development Strategy in 1992. The Local Government Association of Queensland (LGAQ) took up the challenge and, at its annual conference in 1995, adopted a policy acknowledging that local governments have a role in cultural development. This role was to include 'planning and policy development, facilitation, advocacy, promotion and provision of services and facilities' (Queensland Local Government Cultural Development Strategy).

The RADF's origins can also be more specifically tied to the 1989 Arts policy of the Queensland Australian Labor Party. That document promised the establishment of a regional arts development fund to the value of $5 million with proceeds of interest to be disbursed through a new funding program. This fund was to facilitate the growth of professional and amateur arts activity at the local level, to redress the lack of cultural development in regional and rural centres and to ensure rapid and balanced arts development throughout Queensland (Australian Labor Party 1989, p. ix). The RADF also provides opportunities for local government authorities to bring funds into their respective regions.

In addition to government programs there are a number of arts organisations with a mandate to serve regional Queensland. These promote arts and/or cultural pursuits, act as lobbyists, provide professional training and development, and liaise between community and government. These organisations may be regionally based (such as Arts West, which serves the Central West region, or Arts Nexus, which acts as a service organisation across cultural sectoral groups in Far North Qld); arts or sector-based (such as Museums Australia (Qld) and the Regional Galleries Association of Queensland); or broadly service-based (Flying Arts is an example of an organisation that takes artists, teachers and exhibitions to regional venues). The extent and vitality of these organisations reflect the strength of regional culture as well as the need for such services and support in a large state with a dispersed population.

Regionalism and cultural tourism

In what ways do art and culture connect into regionalism and tourism? To explain the connections here, we turn back to the 1980s when a cultural industries model emerged. This linked arts and culture to an economic interest and, at the same time, shifted attention from creativity and the production of art and culture to its dissemination (UNESCO 1982; World Commission on Culture and Development 1995; del Corral 1995). The model recognises the value and volume of cultural activity that takes place outside the arena of public subsidised forms of culture – popular culture, youth culture and commercial film, radio and television – and broadens out the concept of culture from a narrow and elitist 'arts model' to one that incorporates the leisure, entertainment and tourism sectors. Increasingly governments (state and local), arts and cultural organisations, and the cultural sector in general have engaged with these moves to develop a new 'language' and new practices. On the agendas of these bodies are value chains and business plans which refer to industry models, value adding and cultural consumption. Tourism, in particular the newly constructed category of 'cultural tourism', is proffered as the appropriate means of ensuring that arts and cultural activities are sustainable. A cultural industries model not only has impact on the production and consumption of culture but intersects with new notions of personal and community identities. The tourism industry exemplifies this approach:

> Australia is increasingly being recognised as an exciting, unique, diverse and sophisticated tourist destination which has much to interest visitors beyond its world-renowned natural attractions. Australia has a wide range of cultural assets including museums, art galleries, historic and indigenous sites, performing arts and live concerts designed to enrich, educate and entertain visitors.
>
> (Foo and Rossetto 1998, p. 1)

The potential of tourism to provide and build arts audiences has also been recognised by the Australia Council.[2] Since the mid-1990s the Council has embarked on an extensive effort to promote the marketing of the arts and development of audiences with a range of research programs to survey regional Australia and the diversity of arts products that mark and celebrate regional differences (Australia Council 1998). A principal strategy for increasing audiences and attracting tourists is to encourage an enthusiastic local audience. An example of the ways in which one canny arts organisation is linking local and tourist interests is revealed in the Kuranda Arts Cooperative League's marketing plan:

> The way to the heart of a tourist is through the locals. Tourists want to experience the 'real thing'. By appearing to be only for the locals, you can increase your general appeal ... Travellers love the sense of discovery. The Kuranda Arts Cooperative marketing approach is a brave, bold attempt to tap into the psychology of tourists who feel inundated with brash 'souvenir' overkill.
>
> (Australia Council 1998, p. 125)

Heritage – as tangible objects and intangible values – is also a significant marker of local, regional and national identity. Heritage tourism takes as one of its 'principles' the belief that 'each heritage place or area has its own significance, value and requirements for conservation' (Australian Heritage Commission and Tourism Council Australia 1999, p. 10). The economic motive to heritage is stressed in Gene Dayton's study of Queensland heritage. He argues that a heritage-led economic recovery is being developed in the regional areas of the state, but more specifically in those regions with declining populations and economic downturn: 'in regions where economic/population growth is strong "heritage" is of little interest to the commercial sector. In regions with declining or stagnant economic/population conditions "heritage" often plays (or tries to play) a major economic role in the local community' (Dayton 1997, p. 143).

In the process of cultural and spatial differentiation associated with the cultural industries, tourism – in particular cultural tourism and its sub-category heritage tourism – has become a key player, with local government, community institutions and organisations and private interests all involved in constructing, marking and marketing diversity and difference at local, regional and state levels. Within the tourism industry culture has multiple roles. It is 'a resource, a product, an experience and an outcome' (Craik 1997, p. 113). However, in industry usage and rhetoric, culture is taken as a given, especially in 'cultural tourism', which is defined as a form of tourism that 'involves excursions into other cultures and places to learn about their people, lifestyle, heritage and arts in an informed way' (Craik 1995, p. 6).

The Grand Tour of the late nineteenth century provided tourists with visual experiences such as the sights of Europe or the exotic spectacle of the pyramids; modern tourism turns more on providing different cultural experiences such as engaging with the culture and lifestyles of 'others' or participating in adventure activities. The tourism industries, as well as those individuals, organisations and local government bodies anxious to gain a share of the tourist dollar, are all complicit in identifying (and constructing) culturally and geographically unique and distinctive sites as destinations for experiential activities. In this context, the local and regional differences that emerge out of distinct histories and social developments are the raw materials from which more elaborate forms of difference are articulated. The fetishisation of difference that drives consumption in contemporary capitalism (Williamson 1978) not only acts to ensure the variety and volume of attractions for the tourism industry but is also taken up in response to such centralising and homogenising pressures as nationalism and globalisation. This then feeds into the reconstruction of identities (personal, local, state and national).

The case studies

The construction (and reconstruction) of regional cultural differences are explored in what follows – a study of cultural tourism in Queensland. This involves a broad-brush view of the state's major regions – North and Far North Queensland, Central Western Queensland, and the South-East region – that looks at how transformative pressures on land and resources, and development of policies and practices at state and local level, are impacting on these regions. As broad acre pastoralism (the traditional economic base of the state) makes way for new and emerging economic activities (modernised agricultural activities, tourism, education, services and biotechnology) so the relationships between hinterlands and their urban centres come under pressure. At the same time, new relationships are formed between the local, the nation and the world. These forces of change have transformative effects on economic, political and social spheres and, more importantly for this study, on the cultural realm. Within this environment, cultures (Indigenous and non-indigenous) are being challenged, questioned, and mobilised under fresh mandates.

The case studies, taken from the major regions, provide more detailed analyses of specific responses to these pressures. And, given the connections already established between culture and tourism, this study of how regional identity is taken up and reproduced or reconstructed in tourism rhetoric will show the impact of tourism on regional imaging. Moreover, attention to culture as an 'outcome' of tourism implicates tourism as a force for, and mechanism of, cultural change (Mathieson and Wall 1982; Nash 1989; Crick 1991). Each of the regions has responded differently – adopting different strategies (or going on without one) because of their specific relations to the metropolitan city, the nation and the world, their different histories and the particular structures of their respective regions.

Far North and North Queensland

The following study of two cities – Cairns and Townsville – located in the Far North and North Queensland respectively, reveals different socio-cultural responses to tourism, responses that reflect regional differences shaped by economic and historical events specific to each. Cairns and Townsville provide interesting and contrasting responses to tourism and the construction of cultural 'identities'.

Cairns is the tourist centre of Far North Queensland and a major tourist attraction for Queensland. The 'tropicality' of Cairns is summed up in the City Council logo that depicts sun, sea and palm trees. Cairns also embraces tourism, seemingly without reservation or ambivalence. Cairns is truly a tourist mecca. It is also a tourist frontier – a frontier to the tourist attractions of reef, rainforest and 'the rock' (Uluru) and the front door to the Tablelands and Outback. The cityscape of Cairns pulsates with tourist activity – tour shops, dive shops, souvenir shops, food shops, shell shops, trendy boutiques and art galleries. Although modernisation and an accompanying shift into mass tourism have been rapid affairs – starting in the late 1970s and early 1980s – Cairns looks back to a long history as a tourist destination. In 1907 noted author and naturalist E.J. Banfield, in a tourists' guide to the North Queensland Coast, described Cairns as 'the show place of North Queensland'. So numerous were tourists that no one would 'find himself an object of interest here' (quoted in Historical Society of Cairns 1988).

Nearly one hundred years later the natural beauties still attract tourists but, with the tourism industry and governments' promotional activities focusing on international tourists – especially the Japanese and Asian markets and American and European backpackers – the tourist mix is different and the attractions more diverse. Today Cairns is the entry point for tourists heading north to Cape Tribulation, south to the Gold Coast and beyond, east (to the Great Barrier Reef), and west to the Outback or Uluru. Tourist images for Cairns focus on these natural attributes and on showcasing Indigenous culture, in particular the Tjapukai Aboriginal dance theatre and Aboriginal Cultural Park.

Cairns' cultural resources have been developed not only for local residents but also to attract international tourist audiences. Whilst there is, to date, no branch of the state museum, a regional gallery was opened in 1995. This is one of the most recent additions to the state's listing of regional galleries and also the largest one. The gallery policy is to showcase international works as well as those of artists and craftspeople of Far North Queensland. More long standing has been a large cohort of commercial galleries with much of the artwork depicting the North's natural heritage – its rainforests and reef or, increasingly, indigenous artworks. Their target markets are well-heeled international tourists, with galleries increasingly using the internet as a worldwide marketing strategy.

Despite the tourist bonanza that Cairns and its hinterland has experienced in the last two decades some probing reveals there are ambivalent attitudes to tourists and the tourism industry. During interviews with tourism and cultural organisations one commentator referred to 'tourists pushing locals out' and stated that development was proceeding at a high cost to locals in terms of quality of life, living space, traffic, shopping facilities and sheer numbers of people. Comments from letters in the local media also illustrate a level of community resentment and suggest that a critical level of irritation between hosts and guests may have been reached in the Far North. Over-crowding, over-commercialisation and inequities associated with the distribution of tourism profits are some of the irritants. One writer in the *Cairns Post* complains: 'If we persist in becoming even more of a tourist destination, we should multiply our focal points, not suffocate them with people. It is not only tour buses "polluting" Kuranda, it is thousands of people with their drink cans, chip wrappers, chewing gum and shuffling feet' (M.F., Edge Hill, 4.6.1993).

On the other hand there is a demand for more tourists from other quarters with the establishment of two major tourist facilities – a city casino and a skyrail from Cairns to Kuranda. Both these projects, however, were the subject of protracted campaigns of protest from local Aboriginal groups, conservationists, environmentalists and heritage interests (see Holden and Duffin 1998).

There have been numerous government responses to the tourism 'problem'. In 1991 the state government commissioned a report on development issues facing the Cairns region. The impacts associated with tourism were identified as rapid development and growing numbers of national and international tourists. These developments had forced changes in the social structure and cultural heritage of both Indigenous and traditional rustic communities. There was a growing disparity between older residents and migrant populations with respect to incomes and lifestyles. But tourism was also seen by some as offering new employment opportunities that would slow the drift of young people out of the area, and as a means of reducing the isolation of the region by introducing cheaper and improved travel to other parts of the country and to Asia. The tourism strategy released in 1994 aimed to develop tourism sustainably, and to broaden its reliance on nature tourism to include cultural tourism (especially the Indigenous product).

Since the implementation of the strategy, Cairns has seen the relocation and expansion of the successful Tjapukai cultural product, an increase in training for Indigenous people, completion of the Skyrail, and redevelopment of the Cairns airport to cater for increasing international air traffic. The Cairns City Council Corporate Plan for 2000–2005 designates the city 'as a truly international city' with a population comprised of 'long term residents and domestic and international visitors' (Cairns City Council 2000, pp. 7, 10).

In policy, as well as government and industry rhetoric, Cairns is represented as a city committed to tourism. Nevertheless, occasional expressions of resentment to tourism emerge around various issues: levels of overseas investment (too much, too little, or too concentrated), overcrowding, increasing crime rates, race relations and racial conflict. Tourism also shapes the regional relationships that Cairns negotiates. Cairns competes with Brisbane as an entry point, especially for Japanese tourists, and this competitiveness exacerbates a long history of strained relations. Attesting to the multiple identities of the Cairns region, the draft Corporate Plan focuses on two regional relationships that position Cairns as 'the centre' of two different regions: 'The City of Cairns has a role to act as a regional centre within both Far North Queensland and the Asian Pacific region' (Cairns City Council 2000, p. 14).

Townsville, although not a mecca for tourism like Cairns is, nevertheless, a tourist city. It is the jumping-off point for Magnetic Island immediately off the coast, and for the Barrier Reef islands of Hinchinbrook, Bedarra, Dunk and Orpheus. Northward lies Mission Beach resort and a variety of rainforest or beach tourist destinations. Townsville is also a door to the west – to Charters Towers and beyond. This wealth of natural attractions has sustained a long history of tourism in the Townsville region. Despite this history and an over-supply of tourist assets, there is a more ambivalent attitude to tourism than is evident in Cairns. On one hand the media in Townsville frequently carry complaints that the tourists are not coming, or at least not coming in the numbers that are required to provide the cream on the region's bread and jam. Part of this discontent is associated with the fact that Cairns, only 300 kilometres to the north, is inundated with both domestic and international tourists. There is evidence of a push to further develop the Townsville region's tourism with an active local tourism organisation. Discussions in the course of fieldwork with a wide range of people involved in cultural policy administration, museums and heritage organisations, as well as tourism, revealed concerns about Townsville 'becoming like Cairns'. In contrast, others articulated the view that tourism provided a resource the city should exploit to greater advantage. It was acknowledged that Townsville had not developed as rapidly as other major destinations in North Queensland. As the director of the Townsville Art Gallery suggested, a different 'type' of tourist visits Townsville compared to those who visit Cairns. Townsville is cheaper – not so 'glitzy'. The tourist here is more likely to be looking for an opportunity to 'get away from the rat race'. The gallery, he believed, drew approximately 40 per cent of its visitors from overseas or inter-state and 60 per cent from Townsville or its immediate environs.

Townsville is also the administrative centre of North Queensland; a centre for commercial activities; the northern base for the armed services; and an academic and scientific research centre with James Cook University, the Australian Institute of Marine Studies and the Great Barrier Reef Marine Park Authority – all industries and sectors that require a highly educated labour force. This, and the multi-functionality of Townsville, tempers its tourist image. Moreover, in the economic structure of the region tourism is a relatively minor sector with public administration and defence, wholesale and retail trade, manufacturing, transport and communications, finance and construction categories representing almost 75 per cent of the workforce (Hornby 1993, pp. 40–5).

Townsville also sees itself as a 'cultural' city with a regional gallery and two major museums – the Museum of Tropical Queensland (a branch of the Queensland Museum and a social history community museum) – as well as numerous special interest and local museums. Art historian and curator Ross Searle, in his history of art in North Queensland, notes that Townsville established an Art Society before a Royal Queensland Art Society was founded in Brisbane (Searle 1991). Besides the regional gallery, the city also supports an arts space, Umbrella Studios, but according to arts writer Peter Anderson, the commercial gallery sector has been slow to develop (1996, p. 24). The decline over the last decade of the city centre and the growth of suburbia, he suggests, have been contributing factors in stifling a sense of community and inhibiting the development of a modern arts infrastructure. Nevertheless, Townsville does demonstrate a commitment to heritage, the development of cultural facilities and a proactive approach to community cultural development (Hornby 1993).

Cairns has traditionally represented itself and been represented as epitomising the tropics. In its literature and art, the imagery is typically luxurious, languid, sensual and exotic. There is a strong sense of cosmopolitanism that is partly a legacy of history, and partly a consequence of tourism and the pattern of tourism flows and levels of foreign, particularly Japanese, investment. Townsville, on the other hand, is more sub-tropical in climate and could be said to take itself more seriously, with its historical aspirations to take the role of commercial and cultural leadership of the northern part of the state. It aspires to a form of tourism that accommodates the region's social and cultural history as well as its contemporary needs.

Fitzroy and the Central West[3]

Patterns of land usage and economic restructuring are changing the way Central Queenslanders perceive themselves and the ways outsiders see them. New ventures in tourism (attractions, trails, heritage, farm stays etc.) are part and parcel of the transformation of the region (Holmes 1988). As broad acre pastoralism makes way for new economic activities, so the relationships between hinterlands and the region's nucleus mutate, as do those relationships between the local, the nation and the world. Rockhampton, as the administrative centre for Central Queensland (covering Fitzroy and Central West regions), articulates and identifies strongly with its western or 'Outback' areas, seemingly more so than do the far northern cities. So it is to the Central West region that this study now turns as exemplar of a Central Queensland 'culture'.

The whole of the Central Queensland area, with its traditionally strong reliance on rural exports, is vulnerable to economic downturns as well as natural disasters of 'droughts and flooding rains'. Pastoral industries in the west have experienced momentous changes over this period with fluctuations between adversity and prosperity. During bad times the very existence of these industries has seemed threatened; there has been a demise of the traditional way of life on the stations and employment of both domestic and station workers has declined dramatically (Moffat 1987, 1989). Pastoral holdings have undergone substantial change and many of the central west towns that previously existed to service the needs of outback people have declined. Rural infrastructures have shrunk with closures of many small businesses, banks and the government services that provide the lifelines for rural areas. The reduction of services has been accompanied by further loss of jobs in rural areas. As John Holmes has argued, a new balance is being established between market and non-market resource values with changes in patterns of land tenure, ownership and property rights. There is, he suggests, a growing 'ascendancy' of amenity over commodity and non-market over market values in particular regions (Holmes 1995).

In the climate of economic uncertainty which prevailed during the mid-1970s the proposal for an outback heritage centre and tourist complex promised that such a tourist facility would help overcome the recurrent cycles of boom and bust characteristic of rural economies. Lobbyists from Longreach, the administrative centre of the Central West, claimed it would form the basis of a tourism industry for the region that would stimulate the local economy and generate improved services and educational facilities for residents (*Longreach Leader*, 13 November 1981). In 1988 the Australian Stockman's Hall of Fame was opened at Longreach, and by 1994 half a million visitors had passed through the Centre (*Stockman's Hall of Fame Newsletter*, September 1994, p. 1).

In discussing the Central West as a region, it needs to be stressed that this region also encompasses smaller sub-regions as well as other types of 'region'. A 'region' that is purely a product of tourism marketing is found in the Central West – the Matilda Highway. As the promotional material states, the Matilda Highway is a 'travel experience rather than the name of a main road'. It has no separate identity and its origins lie not in the planning of a road transport system but in the conception of a marketing project to popularise and sell towns, scenic regions, historical sites and areas as an extended 'region'. It is a route that has been 'constructed' by marketing strategists, local and state tourist bodies, and community organisations. The Matilda highway starts at Cunnamulla near the border of Queensland and New South Wales and takes in various highway routes – the Mitchell, Landsborough, and Barklay Highways and the Burke and Karumba development roads. All are incorporated into the Matilda Highway system. According to the *Queensland Motoring Holiday Guide*, the Matilda Highway is 'A remarkable journey though Queensland's outback from Cunnamulla to Karumba in the Gulf of Carpentaria' (Matthews 1992, p. 3). Sights the visitor will experience include opal fields, sheep stations, cattle properties, rodeos, historic sites, museums, towns, bush hotels and national parks. Wildlife, open spaces and 'interesting outback characters'.

Unlike the descriptions of lush tropical and biologically diverse coastal regions or of the dramatic landscapes of the Northern Territory typical of tourism literature, attempts to represent Queensland outback landscapes are problematised by the image of a vast, empty land – an image which frustrates elaboration and rich description as the following extract from the above publication reveals:

> Most of Queensland's outback consists of flat plains and you will experience a wonderful sense of freedom on these wide, open spaces. Beneath the land lies the vast Great Artesian Basin and its subterranean hot water supply, which provides a lifeline for people and stock through its 2000 or so bores. Further north, there are the rolling hills of the Cloncurry-Mount Isa region, and then the vast rivers, floodplains and wetlands that lead to the Gulf of Carpentaria.
>
> (Matthews 1992, p. 3)

The opening of the Australian Stockman's Hall of Fame at Longreach as a museum/heritage complex has provided the impetus for other tourist projects in the region. The Matilda Highway connects Longreach with, and helps to construct, a tourist region identified as Outback Queensland. Although it is sustained by marketing, this is nevertheless a region – one that crosses geophysical and administrative boundaries.

The Hall of Fame, although it identifies itself as a 'national' institution, has become an ideological core for 'Outback Queensland'. Disparate and far flung tourist attractions that represent a range of 'pasts' and different 'histories' are linked physically by the Matilda Highway and iconically through the notion of 'Outback Queensland'. Operating within the overarching discursive framework of the pioneer legend, these sites draw on and expand those meanings articulated in the Hall of Fame. Even oppositional perspectives are accommodated, as can be seen at the Australian Workers' Heritage Centre at Barcaldine, a town approximately 100 kilometres east of Longreach. This Centre was promoted as a commemoration of the Shearers' Strike of 1891 and the 'birth' of the Australian Labor Party. At the same time the facility was expected to make a contribution to cultural tourism as a key feature in a heritage trail for visitors to Western Queensland, to provide employment and to revitalise the town. Although there were a number of themes articulated in the early rhetoric of the Centre, centrality was given to its connections with labour and the Labor party, as well as to the making of 'history' and the State's political institutions. Today the Centre's involvement in the tourist region at once subsumes and incorporates the earlier alignment in the service of another interest – the Outback regional values that the Matilda Highway constructs and confirms – values that link back to the Stockman's Hall of Fame.

Thus, at Barcaldine, and at more recent tourist developments appearing along the Matilda Highway, regional, political and social differences are being obscured by the overriding hegemony of the Hall of Fame. The Hall acts as the central repository for, and disseminator of, the idea of the Outback as a region and also articulates a core set of values (pioneering) and core interests (economic recovery). In just over a decade the Hall of Fame has grown from a solitary and isolated destination into the ideological centre of a tourist region marked and marketed by the Matilda Highway. What were once individual places, communities and local cultures are subordinated to a marketing strategy and to structures that impinge on, and draw in, the activities of local organisations and individuals.

Ipswich and a model regional arts museum

Ipswich is a city adjoining the state capital, Brisbane. The Canadian/USA analogy of 'sleeping next to an elephant' might be applied to Ipswich and, similarly, Ipswich is endeavouring to maintain its regional identity separate from the metropolis. Ipswich has also undergone change through amalgamation of the former city with the surrounding shire to create an enlarged Ipswich region. As a city whose economy, up until the mid 1970s, was based on manufacturing, mining and heavy industry, Ipswich has in recent decades suffered the vicissitudes associated with a shift to a service and information economy. In the process of economic restructuring, and as a satellite city of Brisbane, Ipswich was becoming a high unemployment, high social services region. Exacerbating the demographic shifts and the economic crisis was the loss of the city's major department store that had, for 120 years, represented for Ipswich residents 'the focal point of the city ... a meeting place and retreat' (Denoon 1997, p. 135).

Economic restructuring of Ipswich has seen a turn to the service and information sectors and industries. Building on the presence of a Royal Australian Air Force base (the largest in Australia and the largest employer in the region), the Ipswich City Council has also encouraged the University of Queensland to open an Ipswich campus. The Council is also proud to have been the first Australian local government authority to establish a community-based internet service provider – Global Info Link (GIL). As a result of these moves, Ipswich is now experiencing population growth and increased cultural diversity. The city also has the highest per capita personal computer usage of any region in Australia (Global Arts Link, p. 7). This development places Ipswich in a favourable position to participate in the global flows of information and knowledge as a 'local management node' (Borja and Castells 1996, p. 17).

A Corporate Plan (1997–2000) was developed as a framework for reshaping Ipswich as a 'key regional centre of South East Queensland' (Ipswich City Council 1997, p. 12). The object was to ensure social, environmental, economic, land use and infrastructure developments to residents, and to put in place strategies to attract tourism and investment to the region (15). The branding and image around which the city and its region were to be restructured was that of the 'Smart City'. To meet these objectives, to revitalise the central business district, and to provide a regional icon, it was proposed to transform the old Town Hall into a modern regional art gallery. After extensive consultation with numerous community and professional groups and individuals, Global Arts Link (GAL) was opened in 1999 and describes itself as:

> A new type of visual arts museum created for and enriched by the Ipswich community ... Global Arts Link blurs the boundaries between the visual arts, social history and popular culture. We have chosen to use new technologies like multimedia to tell stories, interpret art and engage visitors.
>
> (www.gal.org.au)

GAL is innovative in its approach to culture and art. It expands on the traditional domain of the art gallery to incorporate social history and popular culture. Using the technologies and linkages of GIL, the new facility has incorporated extensive IT services into its exhibitions with multi-media presentations, computer terminals, and electronic databases and programs. Promotional material claims: 'GAL's ability to infuse technology wisely into all aspects of its operations will determine its success' (GAL, p. 9). Underpinning the development of GAL is a commitment to reform the museum by embracing the 'new museology' that accords people, not objects, the highest priority. The new gallery's literature and its staff make frequent references to humanistic values, to museums as instruments of social change, and to the responsibility of museums to ensure equal access and participation. These are not merely rhetorical iterations; they are principles that have informed the planning and community consultation processes that preceded the opening of GAL and they have been informing principles in developing audiences for the facility. Long before the gallery opened, GAL set about building audiences with the simple, but long established, tradition of the morning tea. At these popular gatherings local personalities addressed a range of topics and historical themes. These functions encouraged people to collectively remember the city, its workplaces and work experiences, its social life and experiences of war, depression, sports, commemoration and celebration (Denoon 1997; also Quinn 1998). The morning teas also replicated some of the socialising experiences that had been associated with the department store destroyed by fire. So, it is not surprising that the Mayor of Ipswich describes GAL as the 'cultural heart of the community':

> In a community the size of ours Global Arts Link seems to form in some ways the cultural heart of the community, and especially because of its historic content and building. I refer to Global Arts Link as the community's living room, a place where people can come together in an atmosphere of mutual understanding, celebration, cultural achievement, with provocative questions that can be raised in a safe haven. Global Arts Link is accessible to the broadest segment of the community.
>
> (GAL, p. 9)

This 'cultural heart' also serves other purposes: attracting tourists; building linkages between business, government and cultural sectors; and reaching new audiences and markets. The new facility will, gallery staff claim, build the capacity of Ipswich residents in technology and computer use 'in everyday life': it will connect them to the community, to the nation and to the world. Through GAL, the Ipswich region looks beyond its immediate metropolitan centre to focus on the global village and the global market. Nevertheless at the same time Ipswich positions itself as a destination for day tourists from Brisbane.

In constructing its region as part of the global village and global markets rather than as a satellite of Brisbane – its political and economic centre – Ipswich is responding to the emerging importance of extra-regional relationships. It is positioning the city within the 'mosaic of global innovation' through a series of cultural and economic linkages (Gordon 1994; Castells 1999). Ipswich also operates within national and state frameworks and exists in uneasy neighbour-hood-relations with Brisbane. These relationships between regions and centres and regions and the global, are, however, tenuous and fluctuating. GAL, despite its global outreach, also turns to Brisbane for an extension of its audiences.

Conclusion

None of the regional identities discussed above has been 'wrought out of thin air'. Each has been formed out of specific historical, cultural, and socio-economic factors at work in the respective regions – whether these relate to geographic spaces or, in the case of the Matilda Highway, a space defined by a marketing strategy.

Global Arts Link in Ipswich demonstrates the potential role of culture and cultural tourism in shaping the future of regions. Planners of the GAL experience have drawn on the rhetoric and practices of the cultural industries and have integrated this cultural product into a broader cultural and economic strategy for the Ipswich region, with tourism a new strategic development.

Economic restructuring also drives the tourist-led economic revitalisation of the Matilda Highway development. But here the theme draws on the pioneering legend and reconstructs rural towns as custodians of that legend. At the same time, industry and community efforts are directed at enticing interstate and international tourists into Queensland's remote arid regions to experience a traditional 'outback experience' that is, ironically, brand new.

In contrast, both Cairns and Townsville have had long, and intimate, associations with tourism. Contemporary tourism is, however, taking new bearings and addressing new markets. As a consequence, both these regional cities are remaking their images and in this process are forging global linkages. These new regional connections are already impacting on 'sense of place' and nationhood as global consumers and tourists link into the new cultural markets and tourist flows that Far North Queensland seeks to exploit.

From the above case studies we might formulate some conclusions about regionalism with the most important being that regional cultures are not necessarily a mirror of the metropolis and of urbanised cultures; they do have their own values and distinctivenesses. One of the impacts of globalisation, as has already been pointed out, is the mobilisation of these differences. Tourism too draws on, and encourages, differences between rural regions and urban centres as an incentive to travel. Whilst cities are increasingly marketing themselves as destinations in their own right regions are increasingly attempting to sell themselves as 'escapes' for city people.

As regions and regional destinations market themselves to broader audiences and develop interstate and global linkages that bypass capital cities, regional identities are increasingly severed and dislocated from state and national frames of reference. At the same time, city cultures are increasingly attempting to align themselves with international flows (of capital and tourists) and drawing less and less on the regions for cultural identity. In these transformative processes tourism has become a key player in local or regional identity formation.

Notes

1 Traditional relationships to land are based on ties to the land that pre-date 1788, whereas 'historical' relationships to land arise where people have been removed from traditional lands and relocated in different areas during 'historical' times.
2 The work of the Australia Council Research Unit in developing quantitative data on international visitors and their visiting patterns to museums and galleries during the 1980s and early 1990s was instrumental in establishing the ground for subsequent efforts in audience development.
3 This section draws on the doctoral thesis of the writer, 'Touring the Past: A Study of the Relationship between Museums, Heritage and Tourism in Queensland', Griffith University, 1996.

📖 Guide to further reading

The literature relating to the areas of regionalism and globalisation is extensive but tends to focus on international aspects. Regionalism and globalisation tend to be two sides of the same debate. See Castells (1999), and Borja and Castells (1997). Other books of interest are Harvey (1996) which gives an insightful discussion of the relationship between space, place and identity; also Anthony D. King (ed.) *Culture, Globalisation and the World System* (Houndsmills: Macmillan, 1991) and Mike Featherstone (ed.) *Global Modernities* (London: Sage, 1995). *The World Commission on Culture and Development* (1995) brought together global, cultural and developmental issues and this has been updated by UNESCO (2000).

Peter Timms and Robyn Christie (1988) ignited an Australian debate around regionalism and culture. This has been picked up in the journal *Periphery* in issues in 1994 (no. 19), 1995 (no. 23), and the double issue in 1999/2000 (nos. 40–41).

Whilst regionalism and globalisation issues are often drawn together, tourism – especially cultural tourism – is a more discrete area of study, especially in respect to theoretical discussion of the issues. Two key seminal texts on tourism are Dean MacCannell's *The Tourist: A New Theory of the Leisure Class* (London: Macmillan, 1976) and Valene L. Smith's edited collection *Hosts and Guests: The Anthropology of Tourism* (Second Edition, Philadelphia: University of Pennsylvania Press, first published in 1977 and reprinted in 1989). Other useful texts are Chris Rojek and John Urry's (eds), *Touring Cultures: Transformations of Travel and Theory* (London and New York: Routledge, 1997) and Urry, *The Tourist Gaze: Leisure and Travel in Contemporary Societies* (London: Sage, 1990).

More recently an Australian perspective on tourism has emerged as Australia is increasingly seen as a prime tourist destination. Whilst the depth and variety of writing on tourism in Australia is increasing, writers who have established the field and who also address cultural tourism include Colin M. Hall, who has a number of books in the area; of special interest here would be Hall and Simon McArthur (eds) *Heritage Management in New Zealand and Australia: Visitor Management, Interpretation, and Marketing* (Oxford: Oxford University Press, 1993). Jennifer Craik's *Resorting to Tourism: Cultural Policies for Tourist Development* (Sydney: Allen & Unwin, 1991) is about tourism policy but also has a Queensland focus. A seminal study of cultural tourism in Australia is the report of Peter Brokensha and Hans Guldberg, *Cultural Tourism in Australia: A Report on Cultural Tourism*, commissioned by DASET (Canberra: AGPS, 1992). The Australian Heritage Commission's *Tourism for the Future: A Selected Bibliography on Ecotourism and Cultural Tourism* (Canberra: Australian Heritage Commission Bibliography Series No. 13, AGPS, 1994) is also a useful resource.

The journal *Annals of Tourism Research* is essential reading for contemporary debates around tourism at both a theoretical and an applied level.

References

Anderson, Peter (1996) 'Impressions of Townsville', *Periphery* 29, November, pp. 24–5.

Aplin, G., S.G. Foster and M. McKernan (1987) *Australians: A Historial Dictionary*, Sydney: Fairfax, Syme & Weldon.

Australia Council (1998) *Miles Ahead. Arts Marketing that Works in Regional Australia*, Sydney: Australia Council.

Australian Heritage Commission and Tourism Council Australia (1999) *Draft Heritage Tourism Guidelines. A Discussion Paper*, Canberra: Australian Heritage Commission and Tourism Council.

Australian Labor Party (Queensland Branch) (1989) *Reaching a New Audience*, Brisbane: ALP.

Bogle, Michael (1988) 'The heart of the heart of the country: the argument for regionalism in collecting policies' in Peter Timms and Robyn Christie (eds).

Borja, Jordi and Manuel Castells (1997) *Local and Global. The Management of Cities in the Information Age*, London: Earthscan Publications.

Cairns City Council (2000) *Corporate Plan 2000–2005*, Cairns: Cairns City Council www.cityofcairns.qld.gov.au/council/corporate_plan.html

Carter, Paul (1994) 'Virtually a paradise', *Periphery* 19, May, p. 7.

Castells, Manuel (1999) *The Information Age: Economy, Society and Culture,* Vol. I *The Rise of the Network Society* (first published 1996), Vol. II *The Power of Identity* (first published 1997), London: Blackwell.

Craik, Jennifer (1995) 'Is cultural tourism viable?', *Smarts* 2, May, pp. 6–7.

— (1997) 'The culture of tourism' in Chris Rojek and John Urry (eds) *Touring Cultures. Transformations of Travel and Theory*, London and New York: Routledge.

Crick, Michael (1991) 'Tourists, locals and anthropologists: Quizzical reflections on "otherness" in tourist encounters and in tourism research', *Australian Cultural History* 10, pp. 6–18.

Dayton, G. (1997) '"Heritage" as representation of regional culture: an exploratory study from Queensland' in W. Mules and H. Miller (eds) *Mapping Regional Cultures*, Rockhampton: Rural Social and Economic Research Centre, Central Queensland University.

del Corral, Milagros (1995) 'UNESCO's approach to cultural industries in the information society', *Proceedings, UNESCO Asia-Pacific Culture Forum*, Seoul, November/ December.

Denoon, Louise (1997) 'The development of Global Arts Link, Ipswich', *Culture and Policy* 8, 2, pp. 135–8.

Doran, Christine (1981) *Separatism in Townsville, 1884–1894: 'We Should Govern Ourselves'*, Studies in North Queensland History No. 4, Townsville: History Department, James Cook University of North Queensland.

Fitzgerald, Ross (1984) *From 1915 to the Early 1980s: A History of Queensland*, Brisbane: University of Queensland Press.

— (1982) *From the Dreaming to 1915: A History of Queensland*, St Lucia: University of Queensland Press.

Foo, Lee Mai and Alison Rossetto (eds) (1998) *Cultural Tourism in Australia. Characteristics and Motivations*, Canberra: Bureau of Tourism Research, Occasional Paper No. 27.

Geertz, Clifford (1973) 'Thick description: towards an interpretive theory of culture' in C. Geertz (ed.) *Interpretation of Cultures*, New York: Basic Books, pp. 319–35.

Gilbert, E.W. (1960) 'The idea of the region', *Geography* 45, pp. 157–75.

Global Arts Link, n.d. *Global Arts Link Ipswich. A New Model Visual Arts Museum for Australia*, Ipswich: Ipswich Arts Foundation.

Gordon, Richard (1994) *Internationalization, Multinationalization, Globalization: Constructing World Economies and New Spatial Divisions of Labour*, Santa Cruz: University of California Centre for the Study of Global Transformations, Working Paper No. 94.

Hall, Peter (1995) 'The roots of urban innovation: culture, technology and urban order' in Commonwealth of Australia/OECD, *Cities and the New Global Economy*, Conference Proceedings, vol. 1, Canberra: AGPS, pp. 275–93.

Hall, Stuart (1995) 'New cultures for old' in Doreen Massey and Pat Jess (eds) *A Place in the World? Places, Culture and Globalisation*, Oxford: Oxford University Press.

Harvey, David (1996) *Justice, Nature and the Geography of Difference*, Oxford: Blackwell.

Historical Society of Cairns (1988) *Bulletin* 332.

Hoffie, Pat (1994) 'Looking forward/looking back on regionalism', *Periphery* 19, May, p. 12.

Holden, Annie and Rhonda Duffin (1998) *Negotiating Aboriginal Interests in Tourism Projects: The Djabugay People, the Tjapukai Dance Theatre and the SkyRail Project,*

Brisbane: Griffith University, Centre for Australian Public Sector Management.

Holmes, John (1988) 'Remote settlements' in R.L. Heathcote (ed.) *The Australian Experience*, Melbourne: Longman Cheshire.

— (1995) Paper presented to Australian Frontiers Conference, Longreach, April.

Hornby, Frank (1993) *The Townsville Region: A Social Atlas* (3rd edition), Townsville: Townsville City Council.

Ipswich City Council (1997) *Corporate Plan 1997-2000*, Ipswich: Ipswich City.

Kimble, George H.T. (1951) 'The inadequacy of the regional concept' in L. Dudley Stamp and S.W. Woolridge (eds), *London Essays in Geography*, London: London School of Economics and Political Science, pp. 15–74.

Lawson, Ronald (1980) 'Towards demythologizing the "Australian Legend": Turner's frontier thesis and the Australian experience', *Journal of Social History* 13, 4, Summer, pp. 577–8.

Local Government Association of Queensland Inc. (1994) *Revealing the Heart of our Communities. The Queensland Local Government Cultural Development Strategy*, Brisbane: Local Government Association of Queensland, Queensland Department of Housing Local Government and Planning, Arts Queensland, and the Australia Council for the Arts.

Mathieson, Alistair and Geoffrey Wall (1982) *Tourism. Economic, Physical and Social Impacts*, London and New York: Longman.

Matthews, Anne (1992) *Queensland Motoring Holiday Guide. The Matilda Highway*, Brisbane: Queensland Tourist & Travel Corporation.

McQueen, Humphrey (1979) 'Queensland: a state of mind', *Meanjin* 38, 1, April, pp. 41–51.

Mitchell, Patricia OAM (1998) 'Keynote address', First National Regional Arts Conference, Mount Gambier, October.

Moffat, Angela G.I. (1987) *The Longreach Story: A History of Longreach and Shire*, Milton: Jacaranda Press.

— (1989) *A History of the Graziers' Association of Central and Northern Queensland 1889–1989*, Bowen Hills: Boolarong Publications.

Nash, Dennis (1989) 'Tourism as a form of imperialism' in V.L. Smith (ed.) *Hosts and Guest: The Anthology of Tourism*, Philadelphia: University of Pennsylvania Press, pp. 37–52.

Quinn, Elizabeth (1998) 'Bread and Circuses? The Role of Cultural Industry Policies in Urban Regeneration', unpublished MA thesis, Griffith University, Queensland.

Ravenswood, Kate (1995) 'Regional oligarchies and the structuring of regionalism', *Periphery* 23, May, pp. 3–5.

Robertson, Roland (1991) 'Social theory, cultural relativity and the problem of globality', in A. D. King (ed.) *Culture, Globalisation and the World System*, Houndsmills: Macmillan.

— (1995) 'Globalisation: time-space and homogeneity-heterogenity' in Mike Featherstone *et al.* (eds) *Global Modernities*, London: Sage.

Searle, Ross (1991) *Artist in the Tropics. 200 Years of Art in North Queensland*, Townsville: Perc Tucker Gallery.

Smith, Terry (1999–2000) 'Between regionality and regionalism: middle ground or limboland?', *Periphery* 40–41.

State Parliamentary Labor Party (1989) *Reaching a New Audience: Arts Policy Priorities of a Goss Government*, Brisbane: ALP.

Timms, Peter and Robyn Christie (eds) (1988) *Cultivating the Country, Living with the Arts in Regional Australia*, South Melbourne: Oxford University Press.

UNESCO (1982) *Cultural Industries: A Challenge for the Future*, Paris: UNESCO.

— (2000) *Culture, Trade and Globalisation. Questions and Answers,* Division of Creativity, Cultural Industries and Copyright Sector for Culture, UNESCO, 14 April, www.pch.gc.ca/network-reseau/eng.htm.

Ward, Russel (1966) *The Australian Legend,* Melbourne.

Williams, Raymond (1983) *Keywords,* Oxford: Fontana Press.

Williamson, Judith (1978) *Decoding Advertisements: Ideology and Meaning in Advertising,* London: Marion Boyars.

World Commission on Culture and Development (1995) 'Rethinking cultural policies' in *Our Creative Diversity: Report of the World Commission on Culture and Development,* Paris, pp. 231–53.

Index